At the Barriers

At the Barriers

On the Poetry of Thom Gunn

Edited by
JOSHUA WEINER

The University of Chicago Press
Chicago and London

Joshua Weiner is associate professor of English at the University of Maryland and the author of two books of poems, *The World's Room* (2001) and *From the Book of Giants* (2006), both published in the Phoenix Poets series by the University of Chicago Press.

The University of Chicago Press, Chicago 60637
The University of Chicago Press, Ltd., London

Printed in the United States of America

18 17 16 15 14 13 12 11 10 09   1 2 3 4 5

ISBN-13: 978-0-226-89043-2 (cloth)
ISBN-10: 0-226-89043-0 (cloth)
ISBN-13: 978-0-226-89044-9 (paper)
ISBN-10: 0-226-89044-9 (paper)

Library of Congress Cataloging-in-Publication Data

At the barriers : on the poetry of Thom Gunn / edited by Joshua Weiner.
p. cm.
Includes bibliographical references and index.
ISBN-13: 978-0-226-89043-2 (cloth : alk. paper)
ISBN-13: 978-0-226-89044-9 (pbk. : alk. paper)
ISBN-10: 0-226-89043-0 (cloth : alk. paper)
ISBN-10: 0-226-89044-9 (pbk. : alk. paper) 1. Gunn, Thom—Criticism and interpretation. I. Weiner, Joshua.
PR6013.U65Z55 2009
821'.914—dc22

2009004284

∞ The paper used in this publication meets the minimum requirements of the American National Standard for Information Sciences—Permanence of Paper for Printed Library Materials, ANSI Z39.48-1992.

This Book Is Dedicated to Thom Gunn

IN MEMORIAM

(1929–2004)

and

To His Readers

EVERLASTING

CONTENTS

ACKNOWLEDGMENTS

The contributors wish to thank the Hornbake Library at the University of Maryland, College Park, and the Bancroft Library at the University of California, Berkeley, for access to their holdings of Thom Gunn's manuscripts; the Graduate Research Board and the Department of English at the University of Maryland, for material support; Thom's brother Ander, for the use of his photograph of Thom for this volume's cover; and Mike Kitay, for permission to print excerpts from unpublished writings and the several published poems, in their entireties, in this volume.

August Kleinzahler's essay, "The Plain Style and the City," originally appeared in *The Threepenny Review* (1995). Thanks to Wendy Lesser for permission to reprint. And, with August Kleinzahler's permission, the volume editor has made minor corrections and added some explanatory notes that did not appear in the original publication.

Thom Gunn's "Two Versions of 'Meat'" and an earlier version of Joshua Weiner's "Gunn's 'Meat': Notations on Craft" originally appeared in *AGNI* (1992). Thanks to William Pierce for permission to reprint.

Yvor Winters's "The Castle of Thorns" is reprinted from *Collected Poems* (Swallow, 1952) by permission of Ohio University Press.

Thanks to Liz Countryman and Lindsay Bernal, who assisted with diligence, concentration, and a genuine enthusiasm for the subject of this book. Thanks also to Laura Leichum for her hawkeye and good sense in reading the copyedited manuscript and page proofs. The anonymous readers for the Press who evaluated the manuscript were forthright and helpful through their criticism, and the book improved because of it. To Randolph Petilos, my editor at University of Chicago Press, and the first person who wanted to read this book, thanks and gratitude times two; he encouraged it from its inception and proved a keen guide through what, for me, were new waters. Large thanks, as well, to the contributors to this volume, who knew how to hurry-up-and-wait with little complaint, much graciousness, and a welcome degree of wit; their company in this endeavor has been much of its reward. My wife, Sarah Blake, and my sons, Eli and Gus, deserve more than thanks for putting up with my distraction and disappearance during the writing and editing of this book. Love beyond measure is hardly enough. "His countering pull, his own devoted arm."

ABBREVIATIONS

BC	*Boss Cupid*
BL	Bancroft Library
CP	*Collected Poems*
FT	*Fighting Terms*
HL	Hornbake Library
OP	*The Occasions of Poetry*
SL	*Shelf-Life*
SM	*The Sense of Movement*
TMNS	*The Man with Night Sweats*

Introduction

JOSHUA WEINER

> and anyone who chooses may come in past the barriers
>
> —Thom Gunn, "At the Barriers"[1]

The barriers are real: physical, psychological, aesthetic, social; and they combine in the space where personal and political life find dramatic expression. In the poem from which the epigraph and title of this book are taken, the literal barriers (set up by the police) mark off Dore Alley in the South of Market district of San Francisco, the site of an annual gay celebration and part of a larger fair along Folsom Street, in the city where Thom Gunn made his home for more than forty years. Gunn calls the poem a "Whitmanesque celebration" of plurality, one that takes pride in the homosexual majority at the fair but which is open to everyone: "mixed couples too, all are welcome, / for it is an open place, once you have found the way in, like the field / where the poet and lover are active, an Arcady of tarmac." The fair, in other words, is an imagined open space made real in a world too often closed to men and women attracted to others of the same sex; it is a carnival inversion of the structures in place in the larger society, a new figure in which "the barriers at each end," writes Gunn, "are both inclusive and exclusive."[2]

If Gunn's vision of the fair is a Romantic one, it is by no means sentimental, for he sees there, too,

> complication and conflict, humans cannot get by without them,
> black boots on the black street making a show, a play,
> a play of strength, a show of power put on to be disarmed
> through the lingering dénouement of an improvised masque

in which aggressiveness reveals its true force as love,
its body as love at play.

(Gunn is alluding here to Ben Jonson's masque, a kind of court entertainment, which, in Jonson's text, carries the note, "as performed *at the barriers*," a place for athletic contests, such as tilting.)

"I suspect it doesn't really come off," Gunn, with characteristic deprecation, writes of the poem; yet he thought enough of it to include it in his *Collected Poems* (1994), and it stands at the very least as a significant gloss on Gunn's flexible feeling for open and closed form; inclusiveness of imagination and exclusiveness of discerning judgment; the life of instinct and the life of intellect; attraction to embodiments of physical power and the duplicity of meaningful play within expressions of power; originality developing forcefully from derivation. Ben Jonson joins Walt Whitman to Robert Duncan "at the barriers," a place where mutual attraction and contest are performed.

For Gunn, as for all of us, barriers are sometimes desired—they help us make distinctions; yet for Gunn, too, the imperative is always to stay *at* them, where they are set up, so as to leap past them to another place; until, like the figure of the biblical David in the last phrase of the last poem in Gunn's last book, one makes "the final leap."[3]

Gunn said in an interview that he didn't have a "poetics," a theory of poetry, but that one could probably assemble such a theory for him based on his practice, though it would be full of inconsistencies and, though he doesn't say it, would in that way resemble many of the poetic theories out there.[4]

In "Transients and Residents," however—a poem that has received scant attention—one comes across lines clearly stating some of Gunn's principles as a poet, less suggestive of his mastery of language and form, and more indicative of something like an imaginative process expressing a sense of social feeling:

Starting outside,
You save yourself some time while working in:
Thus by the seen, the unseen is implied.
I like loud music, bars, and boisterous men.
You may from this conclude I like the things
That help me if not lose then leave behind,
What else, the self.

I trust the seedling wings,
Yet taking off on them I leave to find.

I find what? In letters that I send
I imitate unconsciously the style
Of recipients: mimicking each friend,
I answer expectations, and meanwhile
Can analyze, or drawl a page of wit,
And range, depending on the friend addressed,
From literary to barely literate.
I manage my mere voice on postcards best.

Part of the excitement and unique appeal of this poetry is in how Gunn combines a kind of Augustan discursiveness—conversational metrical lines with alternating end-rhymes—and a Romantic searching, captured above in the imagistic fusion of *seedling wings:* what he would become he would find in imaginative flight. Yet the gesture itself is not allowed to stand; the poet turns on it skeptically—the self he seeks to leave in order to discover new possibilities of being becomes a kind of cipher for assuming each identity he meets, until the singular voice of the postcard note arrives, as *mere voice,* however much his. A matter (though no simple matter) of technique and theme, such designs affect us, yet it is somehow the whole human cloth in Gunn's poems that a reader accepts with gratitude: the voice is humane, direct, candid, unselfconscious, personal, *and,* apparently, objective. The human scale of response is precisely appropriate to the occasion of the poem, as Gunn liked to call it. A reader trusts him not to exaggerate beyond the facts, yet to explore the subject beneath them.

Image, emblem, symbol, figure, allegory, archetype, trope. However you want to name the verbal patterns enacting the phenomena of mind involving nature, of self remaining permeable, inquisitive, receptive, Gunn's poems always impress by locating the idea inside each experience of the body, and of bringing to formal life the seemingly physical sensation animating any idea about experience. Outside revealing inside, inside containing outside. As does Allen Ginsberg, as does Whitman, and William Blake before them, Gunn rejects the convenient dualisms in order to leave the self behind, that categorical identity, and grow new leaves, branching in directions unanticipated. Thus, correspondences, new "structures of rime," new perceptions of deeper patterns in the culture and in the mind, as his friend Robert Duncan insisted on, point the way.

A critical biography of Thom Gunn has yet to be written, though the facts have been rehearsed any number of times (most recently and cogently by Clive Wilmer, for the *Oxford Dictionary of National Biography*). Because the essays in this volume emphasize different aspects of the life, I only wish to observe that the one sentence most often quoted is the characterization Gunn, in an autobiographical essay, makes of himself: "My life consists on continuities—between America and England, between free verse and metre, between vision and everyday consciousness."[5] That continuity, that he most memorably reformulates later in his elegy on Duncan—that "you add to, you don't cancel what you do"—flies as one of Gunn's standards, inherited from Duncan but no less now his own.

Since Gunn's death, his whole body of work has been gaining the status of legend; what one finds in it, if one attends to the whole, is a poet of ceaselessly developing sensibility. From striking the pose of a kind of ironic, heroic adventurer embodied in tough, brainy, metrical, and cross-rhymed stanzas, Gunn grew to absorb the American moderns as a consequence of his move in 1954 to California, where he studied at Stanford under Yvor Winters, and where he later learned from Duncan how to fuse the Romantic and the modern.

What this quick summation fails to capture, however, is the accomplishment of Gunn's body of work *as* a body of work: how it creates the image of a self-critical process that leads to new shoots of creative production. It is not a question of formal revolution—Gunn never broke his style, which, even in his free verse, remains more "closed" in its referentiality than open. As August Kleinzahler notes in the essay in this volume, "There's not an aleatory bone in his body." No, there isn't. However difficult the move from accentual-syllabics to syllabics to free verse was for Gunn in the early 1960s, the new rhythms brought an alteration deeper than technique as they led to new perceptions of relation, of relatedness; his growing feeling of connection with others; his attempt to emerge deliberately from the chrysalis of what he names, in his 1963 notebooks, "The Lonely Man" and "The Man of Energy," and "to find an adequate embodiment of the man who helps, really an extension of the other[s]."

A few years later, Gunn would lay out the process of his "Self-Education" in his notebook:[6]

1 Nobody watches him, not even himself.

2 He imitates, to be like others.

3 He endows himself with an identity, to be unlike others.
4 He seeks purposes.
5 He seeks to lose identity, to join everyone.

Out from isolation, he adopts imitation, self-endowment, searching, losing, joining. ("You must do the best you can," he writes in his notebook, "there is no fixed self.") These notebook entries only highlight what is nakedly evident in the work: a process of growth that has become an emblem of self-knowledge reminiscent of John Keats's—only it's as if Keats had lived happily to the age of seventy-five.

At the time of Gunn's death in 2004, there was no book-length study of his work. One could find chapters about his poetry in larger studies: *The Survival of Poetry* (1970), edited by Martin Dodsworth; Alan Bold's binocular *Thom Gunn and Ted Hughes* (1976); Merle Brown's *Double Lyric* (1980); Neil Powell's *Carpenters of Light* (1980); and Blake Morrison's study of *The Movement* (1980). Shorter essays popped up here and there, notably in two birthday celebrations, one in *PN Review* (1989) on the occasion of Gunn's sixtieth, and the other in *Agenda* (1999), on his seventieth. These pieces include short general appreciations and short, pointed treatments of particular poems, themes, or formal elements. There is an important essay by Gregory Woods in the *Agenda* issue, on the subject of Gunn's homosexuality, that extends the view of Woods's study, *Articulate Flesh* (1987). The issue also contains one of my favorite essays, by August Kleinzahler, on Gunn's plain style, which is reprinted here, with the hope of making it more widely available.

One can find some of the most interesting recent thinking about Gunn in Paul Giles's *Virtual Americas* (2000), a study of "the transatlantic imaginary" that counterintuitively situates Gunn and Sylvia Plath side by side, in a kind of geographical chiasmus of expatriate transplanting. Giles reads Gunn's various poses in his poems as unnatural, by which he means they involve high degrees of stylization; this is an important insight into how Gunn's transparent style offers a verbal strategy for contradiction and self-parody. No one else has approached this topic of duplicity, which speaks to Gunn's use of language, form, and modes of self-presentation, with such insight. Finally, the only full-length monograph to appear in any language (to my knowledge) is in Italian, Stefania Michelucci's *La Maschera, il Corpo e l'Anima* (2006).[7]

There seemed to be room, therefore, for another kind of book about Gunn, in English, that pushed our understanding and critical appreciation further. I couldn't write it myself; I didn't know enough. The subject of Gunn's poetry is rich, nuanced, complex; it involves layered allusions and intertextuality; and it draws from history, mythology, and contemporary culture. But I did know others, and *of* others, who shared my love for this poet's work. I would enlist them and try to assemble the book I most wanted to read, written by those I most wanted to hear from.

At the Barriers: On the Poetry of Thom Gunn brings the early Gunn further into focus with essays by Eavan Boland, Neil Powell, and Alfred Corn. Boland gives us a young Irishwoman's unique account of first encounters; Powell analyzes with panache the variety of early poses Gunn strikes, inflected by his homosexuality; and Corn, I believe for the first time, connects the homosexuality to Gunn's growing commitment to existentialism during the 1950s. Not unrelated to the Corn essay, David Gewanter enlarges the issue of sexuality by tracing it to mortality in a meditation on how Gunn figures the human body throughout his work.

Keith Tuma takes a distinctively broad view by looking at Gunn's identity as an Anglo-American poet through the lens of British and American modernism; August Kleinzahler extends the discussion specifically in relation to Gunn's style, but also by turning our attention to poems by Charles Baudelaire, who remained an influence on Gunn throughout his life, and long after the grip of French existentialism had loosened.

Tom Sleigh picks up those abject strains in Baudelaire to consider Gunn's countercultural transvaluations; John Peck interprets the countercultural forces in Gunn's work and its stylistic development by tracing them through a depth-psychology reading that unearths Gunn's reach into the major conflicts of the 1960s and beyond. Clive Wilmer's essay on Gunn, Shakespeare, and the Elizabethans shows how Gunn's dramatic power and shape-making integrity reach back to his favorite poet.

Paul Muldoon and Wendy Lesser write incisively about two underrecognized poems of central interest to Gunn's body of work: Muldoon on "Considering the Snail," from the second, experimental section of *My Sad Captains* (1961), which vividly indicates Gunn's growing feel for unpredictable rhythms, his own "deliberate progress"—sexual, social, formal—as poet and person; and Lesser on the elegy, "Duncan," that opens Gunn's last book, *Boss Cupid* (2000), which enacts the tension of that very same progress. Gunn considered this poem his best.[8]

Robert Pinsky's deft and illuminating portrait of Gunn "inside and outside," "at the barriers," captures the essential "all-of-the-above" paradox of Gunn's shrewd genius.

All these writers knew Thom personally to some capacity, and their criticism to different degrees takes on memoirist qualities. The book is thereby a historical document in its own right: its claim on readers is not only the subject of Thom Gunn's poetry but the light it casts on the culture of poetry he worked in and its portrayal of the problems and opportunities that his poetry suggests to working writers in the early twenty-first century.

I happen to know most of these writers myself; some of them I came to know through Thom—through conversation and recommendations, and sometimes from a book Thom would put into my hands. Now those of us who knew him—as an intimate friend or more incidentally—aim to put this book in the hands of Thom Gunn's readers. This includes Brian Teare, whom I found through luck or serendipity in my search for a poet who could lay bare how Gunn's work signified in a post-Stonewall gay culture. Although there have been a few other "queer studies" readings of Gunn (most notably by Robert Martin and Gregory Woods), Teare explores Gunn's poetic process as a gay man during a period of great turbulence and transition by simultaneously narrating the progress of his, Brian's, own complex reading, as a young gay poet, of Gunn's work. I think it is a first.

Finally, a note on my own contributions. "Misanthropos" is a poem I've always instinctively understood to be central to Gunn's body of work, but not one I've ever felt to have grasped fully—in spite of, or maybe even because of, the available criticism about it. It's not a poem that has been very well served by a previous generation of critics. Here, I read the poem as an existential and self-reflective drama about the discovery of new rhythms for poetry, in addition to being a narrative about the aftermath of global war.

Concerning "Two Versions of 'Meat'": I reprint it here for two reasons. The first is substantial: because of where we sit historically, some presume that progress in the art of poetry involves a re-visioning from the more formal to the less formal, along the line of a literary historical cliché. But Gunn's poem "Meat" moved from the *less* to the *more* formal (his sense of continuity was always a two-way conduit); and the two versions of "Meat" exist now side by side as an exemplary case of how form and rhetoric convey different qualities of experience, instinct, and intellect. I wish to preserve the case.

The second reason is sentimental: when I asked Thom, in 1992, for permission to reprint the free verse "Meat" to accompany a short essay on the two versions for *AGNI*, he responded that he was "thrilled to my tits" that someone had taken up the subject. I like to think that he'd be thrilled again by the reappearance of the two versions that suggest so much of his experiential range and technical flexibility; and that he'd take some private pleasure, too, in the cross-circuited complementary attentions gathered here in an admittedly, and I hope adequately, weird wide net of a book.

PART ONE

In England

All That You Praise I Take: A Glimpse of the Young Thom Gunn

EAVAN BOLAND

One evening, when I was a student at Trinity College in Dublin, I went to an outdoor poetry reading. It was a close, sunny evening in May. The occasion was Shakespeare's quatercentenary. A manicured patch of ground, called the Fellows' Garden, was the place. Derek Mahon was the reader. He was a student there, as I was. He began with poems by Thom Gunn and then read some of his own.

I knew of Mahon by name. But Gunn I had never heard of—neither his name nor his poems. I listened and listened. It all sounded strange to me—those blunt and thumping stanzas about cold roads and dance halls. And yet something about it was also familiar, startling, and thrilling. I was surprised, engaged, and lost.

My reaction was hardly surprising. This was a new world. I was familiar with W. B. Yeats but knew little enough of contemporary British or American poetry. Books came slowly into Dublin. It was still an insular literary city, absorbed by the recent history of its own Literary Revival. English and American poets were not yet visible. And, in any case, I was a foggy, out-of-touch teenager. If I had known more I might have been more aware of the irony of the arc that British poetry was describing right in front of me: from the imperial stance of an Elizabethan master to the tentative disaffection of this postimperial maverick.

I might also have been aware—although only with hindsight—that this Northern Irish poet, reading Gunn's work in the late sunshine, would himself become a defining voice in the disruptions that the poetry of the next decade would bring to Ireland. I might even have reflected that Mahon and I fulfilled our roles as auditor and audience by standing on the solid ground of colony, in a college intended for the Anglo-Irish, its smooth granite constructed to shelter an entirely different set of misfits.

My intention here is to sketch something of the young Thom Gunn as he first appeared to me: as a poet from a different world whom I tried to apprehend and, at first, only partially understood. This is a description of an inexact process. I don't offer this piece as a scholarly or complete view of his first book, but rather as a snapshot—I will look only at a couple of poems from *Fighting Terms*—of how younger poets first understand older ones.

Why write about Gunn this way? Because his first book, *Fighting Terms,* has a Janus face that I think is unique to first books in the 1950s. Metrically, it makes a continuum with British poetry and looks to the past. But tonally it looks to a wide, improvised horizon, a future where irony and sexual dissidence would become a lens into a new poetic persona and a different configuration of modernism. Formally, the book fits easily on a bookshelf beside George Barker or Dylan Thomas. Tonally, it is restless, seeking out the wider future of the decade, especially in the United States. No wonder then that in those years, and with those first poems, Gunn could seem so available and exciting to the American poet Philip Levine. "Fifty years ago," Levine writes:

> I picked up a copy of *Poetry* in a library in Tallahassee, Florida, and discovered nine poems leading off the issue by Thom Gunn, a name I'd never heard before. With their charged conversational voice full of anger and mockery in tightly controlled stanzas, the poems were like nothing I'd ever read. In the contributors' column I discovered he was English, though nothing in the writing seemed foreign to me except, perhaps, the technical wizardry. These poems—which I later reread in his book *Fighting Terms*—had a peculiar power to simply carve the moment of their discovery into my consciousness.[1]

The poet I heard Derek Mahon read then was musically familiar. But his voice and tone seemed strange—challenging and subversive of what went before. It would take me time to translate this apparent contradiction into an understanding of *Fighting Terms.* The truth is, if I had tools or capacities to make Gunn legible at all, they were not critical ones. They were, in fact, the hand-to-mouth fractions of experience and intuition with which I eagerly read his early poems.

I was born in Ireland, but I spent six years in England as a child. They were, as it happens, the years of the composition and publication of

Fighting Terms: from 1950 to 1956. It was the memory of those years that produced the first shock of recognition in the Fellows' Garden in Trinity. I also spent three years in New York beginning at the age of twelve. Something of that molten vernacular might have been at the back of my mind that evening in Trinity.

But if the thought of disruptive outsiders eluded me then, it doesn't now. For that is exactly what the young Gunn was. *Fighting Terms* was brought out by Fantasy Press in England in 1954. Gunn was twenty-five at the time, and the book was published in the United States four years later. In fact, it was the later, Hawk's Well Press edition, with its dark blue and black cover, that Mahon was reading from that evening.

The book contains twenty-three poems. Their subject matters range across a combative terrain of love, sexuality, and self-identification. They are often formal, often rhymed. But the tone is more abrasive. And the music—metered and insistent—is definitely heavy metal.

The poems are compelling. The voice is already recognizable. It is easy to see the tones of the later Gunn in these first tryouts of the younger one. Nevertheless, it would miss something about the marvel and surprise of *Fighting Terms* not to recognize how unexpected it was as a first book. The questions have to be asked: Where did it come from? How in an England just emerging from war and sacrifice did this abrasive voice get rooted and nourished? How in a society where Georgianism had rooted and perished, and modernism had not rooted but was dominant, did this poet find himself? The answers may be complex. But the questions are necessary. To get back to those texts you have to go to context. And the context begins on a foggy island.

To start with, there is simple history: By 1950, England was out of dreams. The ration book had replaced rhetoric. The language of war, sacrifice, and empire was exhausted. The state was uppermost; the nation had dwindled away in the realities of hardship and recovery. It may be unfair to accuse the young Gunn, as he was often accused at that time, of offering only the "machismo of the welfare state." Nevertheless the phrase points to a moment of disillusion—a step down from the grandiosity of war and shared intent. This was an island with little to offer its poets: neither Tennyson's glory nor Wilfred Owen's purpose.

I knew something of Gunn's hinterland, but without knowing it was his. I had, as I wrote earlier, spent six years of my childhood in England, in the grit and yellow fogs of London, eating the postwar food against my will: rabbit and marrow and chocolate pudding and the bowls of dripping carefully laid out for snacks at my school. Sausage rolls were sixpence. A mug of tea could be paid for with the oddly ornate threepenny bit. Everything seemed gray.

Later I would understand that the social aftermath was only a surface for Gunn—that, in fact, it could hardly be more for any British contemporary poet at that moment. Under the shimmer of event and counter-event, of political shifts and new politics, an intense struggle was being waged for the soul of British poetry. The once-gritty modernism of T. S. Eliot had become merely oracular in "Four Quartets." The bardic voices of George Barker and Dylan Thomas filled the 1940s with a resistant and romantic music.

Above all—and this was a crucial formative influence on Gunn—with the removal of W. H. Auden to the United States at the start of the Second World War, something ominous had happened: the public poem had failed in Britain. Auden, who had swept through the 1930s staring down from his poems on that decade of nightmares "as the hawk sees it or the helmeted airman," was gone. What was left?

"Lofty in the Palais de Danse" is one answer. It is the seventh poem in *Fighting Terms*. To an American reader, the second part of the poem's title may be slightly mysterious. To someone from Ireland or Britain—anyone who witnessed the 1950s or 60s there—it is all too plain a reference. Those noisy, smoky, bleak dance halls filled with bad music and hopeless encounters, with faux French names, were littered through small towns and big cities alike. Sexual repression and postwar disillusion defined the interiors, a thrown-together ugliness the exteriors. And it is here that the voice in the poem situates itself, right in the middle of the bravura and loneliness of one of these encounters:

> You are not random picked. I tell you, you
> Are much like one I knew before, that died.
> Shall we sit down, and drink and munch a while
> —I want to see if you will really do:
> If not we'll get it over now outside.
> Wary I wait for one unusual smile.[2]

Here is Gunn's early sophistication with enjambment and meter. The poem also displays his powerful capacity, even so early, to put an abrasive vernacular behind a musical pentameter and to make the stanzas pause and then pounce. The poem is voiced in the melodies and staccato rhetoric of a disillusioned speaker. This is postwar, de-mobbed Britain. The speaker is a young man. He is outside a dance hall. And he is remembering a woman he once loved who died. At the same time he is comparing her to the casual pickup he finds there.

> I never felt this restiveness with her:
> I lay calm wanting nothing but what I had.
> And now I stand each night outside the Mills
> For girls, then shift them to the cinema
> Or dance hall . . . Like the world, I've gone to bad.
> A deadly world: for, once I like, it kills.
>
> The same with everything: the only posting
> I ever liked, was short. And so in me
> I kill the easy things that others like
> To teach them that no liking can be lasting:
> All that you praise I take, what modesty
> What gentleness, you ruin while you speak.

This is signature Gunn. The blunt, drumming iambics, the slant rhymes and the heat-seeking voice—these would all become part of his methodology. Less visible but just as important is the skilled use of two voices here—one assertive and one reflective.

> And partly that I couldn't if I would
> Be bed-content with likenesses so dumb.
> Passed in the street, they seem identical
> To her original, yet understood
> Exhaustively as soon as slept with, some
> Lack this, some that, and none like her at all.

"Lofty in the Palais de Danse" is a flagship poem in *Fighting Terms*. It provides one of the locales where Gunn, as a young poet, can make his poetic manifesto plain. Voice-driven and abrasive, resistant to any accommodation with romantic nuance, this displaced speaker is central to his purpose. The sounds and claims of the voice are central. They suggest the desolation of the present moment. They sketch, even if in a slighting way, some of the immediate past: the de-mobbed state, the recent encounter with death, the distrust of the body.

There is certainly a concealed and charged narrative in "Lofty in the Palais de Danse." Nevertheless, it would be a mistake—and one too often made in looking at postwar British poetry—to confuse background and foreground. The desolate towns and hard-hit cities of England are only bit players in *Fighting Terms.* Far more important is an unseen permission for swashbuckling, for costume drama and posturing, that Gunn had learned elsewhere. If England was grim realism, the poems in *Fighting Terms* are often the very opposite. They are colorful theatricals on a rainy afternoon—an implied critique of what the climate invited.

In many ways, however, the poems of *Fighting Terms* are also a veiled inventory of loss. Certainly, the public elegy is missing; the private restiveness is uppermost. It would be decades before Gunn reinvented public grief in *The Man with Night Sweats.* What emerges from *Fighting Terms* is a new note—a private intensity of voice made more convincing because it lacks the reinforcement of a sanctioned public poem.

The abrasions of *Fighting Terms* then can be seen as occasions for self-invention rather than social comment. But they are something else as well. It is common to cite the influence of F. R. Leavis on Gunn and therefore on *Fighting Terms.* Certainly, Leavis was a profoundly influential teacher at Cambridge in the years when Gunn was there. But the poems in this book struggle free of influence and nationhood in subtle ways. They are studies in tonal resistance. And if, in poems like "Lofty in the Palais de Danse," Gunn looks back to the struggles of a recent past, the poems are also plainly pointing toward the new arrangements of voice and cadence in the postlyrical poem.

It may seem odd in this regard to compare a British lyric poet of the time with a New York experimentalist, and yet Gunn and Frank O'Hara share certain characteristics as poets: both constructed their poetic personas from marginal and unsanctioned elements; both built their tone out of transgressions; and both were deeply interested in inauthenticity, which is the byproduct of a structured society.

The poem that clarifies this is "Carnal Knowledge." It is the poem Derek Mahon read first that late spring evening. It is, in fact, the first poem in *Fighting Terms*—a superb heraldry of sexual dissent, a prophecy of the new era that would be issued where private sexuality would become the basis of a newer, reinvigorated political poem.

In "Carnal Knowledge" the 1940s are still there: George Barker and Dylan Thomas are ghostly presences; Auden, a less ghostly one. The blunt cadences, pushed against the conversational tone, produce a powerful, hypnotic melody of attack and recall. The poem is wonderful to hear. The seventeenth-century mentorship of song and irreverence reappears and is absorbed into this exuberant statement. It all makes for a heady and unexpected mix:

Carnal Knowledge

Even in bed I pose: desire may grow
More circumstantial and less circumspect
Each night, but an acute girl would suspect
My thoughts might not be, like my body, bare.
I wonder if you know, or, knowing, care?
You know I know you know I know you know.

I am not what I seem, believe me, so
For the magnanimous pagan I pretend
Substitute a forked creature as your friend.
When darkness lies without a roll or stir
Flaccid, you want a competent poseur
Whose seeming is the only thing to know.

I prod you, you react. Thus to and fro
We turn, to see ourselves perform the same
Comical act inside the tragic game.
Or is it perhaps simpler: could it be
A mere tear-jerker void of honesty
In which there are no motives left to know?

Lie back. Within a minute I will stow
Your greedy mouth, but will not yet to grips.
"There is a space between the breast and lips."
Also a space between the thighs and head,
So great, we might as well not be in bed:
For we learn nothing here we did not know.

Thom Gunn left England after the publication of *Fighting Terms*. He put behind him the gray towns and dark horizons, the island weather and sexual claustrophobia. I have often wondered what he missed, what he lost. But the truth is, like Odysseus, he traveled well.

Fighting Terms is the book of an outsider, a dissenter. He brought that wayward gift for being an island maverick and added it to the culture of the West Coast. He made a wonderful, unusual arc between rootedness and experiment, between being the outsider and someone who has insider access. Few poets in our time have been as deeply nourished by tradition and as lovingly open to change.

I understood *Fighting Terms* better when he published *The Man with Night Sweats.* The project of that book, published in 1992, has a magical imaginative symmetry with his early work, with those first blunt, hammering stanzas. In poem after poem in *The Man with Night Sweats,* Gunn returns to the iconic images of these early poems—to the soldiers, the lovers, the emblems of male strength—and to the bravado of voice and gesture. But this time he rewrites them as images of suffering, of bodily weakness, of the ravages of disease, and the cost of sexual pleasure. The beautiful coherence of the later book is in the act of imaginative rescue, cast in mythic reversal: from strength to weakness, from glory to humiliation. It is a fine and fitting reversal for the poet who loved strength and celebrated action—and would not have been possible without these early poems.

Young Gunn: Coming Out Fighting

NEIL POWELL

1

During the London Blitz of 1941, Thom Gunn, who was a twelve-year-old pupil at University College School, was evacuated from the capital and—as he explains in "My Life Up to Now," the memoir he contributed to Jack Hagstrom and George Bixby's bibliography of his work—"sent for a year or so to a boarding school in Hampshire."[1] This unnamed school was a famously progressive one called Bedales; and among Gunn's near-contemporaries there was a radical publisher's son, the future painter Michael Wishart. It's in Wishart's evocative if chronologically fuzzy autobiography, *High Diver,* rather than in Gunn's tactful memoir, that we catch our most revealing glimpse of the emerging adolescent poet: "Thom had a quicker wit than all the other boys. He was beautiful in a frail, dark way. Mindless fellows . . . mistook Thom's delicacy of form and thought for weakness, which developed his toughness."[2]

Delicacy of thought (and, in a sense different from Wishart's, of form) wrapped up in protective toughness: this isn't a bad description of Gunn's early poetry. His readers were quick to notice the juxtaposition, often with a degree of puzzled surprise, which suggests that they hadn't fully understood its origin; for among the delightfully regenerative aspects of homosexuality is the way in which the gay man's images of himself and his desired other may change places, overlap, or elide. Perhaps he'll put on his leather disguise, look in the mirror, and think: "I could go for him." Does that sound familiar? It should: "In goggles, donned impersonality, / In gleaming jackets trophied with the dust, / They strap in doubt . . ."[3] The key imagery of Gunn's first three collections repeatedly alludes to the homosexual iconography of the 1950s, and its power is immeasurably increased by being strapped into tight verse forms. The biker would become an especially potent symbol for him: the combined erotic charge of man, machine, and leather, with auxiliaries such as the tattoos of "Black Jackets" (and their important subtext of painful ritual), is inextricably linked to a pursuit of freedom that is both sexual and existential. If there's an answer to the question implicit in the last line of "On the Move"—"Nearer to *what*?"—it's the one supplied by an even better-known coded gay lyric, "Somewhere," which ends *West Side Story:* "There's a place for us . . ."

But before the biker, in Gunn's formative erotic imagination, there was the soldier: back in London from his Hampshire exile, he found himself "eyeing the well-fed and good-looking G.I.'s who were on every street, with an appreciation I didn't completely understand."[4] I can't imagine it took him long to work it out. Once he'd left school, however, two years' National Service in the army showed him that military life might actually consist of "boredom, drudgery, and endurance,"[5] a discovery shared with many of his contemporaries: he remembered a fellow student, newly arrived with him at Trinity College, Cambridge, answering his name at a roll-call with the words "Here, Sergeant."[6] That was in 1951, the year he wrote "The Soldier," an extraordinary poem that, because it predates his preoccupation with poses and masks, has a sensuous openness we won't meet again in his work for a decade or so. These are the first two stanzas:

> Yours is the brightness in orchards of bullets
> Before day.
> Shake the wet bough and the drops will tumble
> Quiet and grey.
> And lying in sterile mud,
> Hear them hiss in your blood.
>
> Feel how a pine-needle presses the palm:
> Without piercing:
> But when the drops in sanctified calm
> Will be blessing
> Feel them tatter the skin
> You will have your bright medals then.[7]

This is surprisingly intimate from the outset, with its close-up images of wet boughs and pine needles; the tone of its physicality is closer to love poem than to war poem. Or so we might suppose, until we remember that there is indeed a war poetry very like this: Wilfred Owen's. Then, several aspects of "The Soldier" click into place: there's the use of approximate assonance ("bullets" / "tumble") and half-rhyme ("piercing" / "blessing") where the scheme demands rhymes; then, in the third stanza, "fumbling" / "tumbling" recalls an identical rhyme and a famous phrase, "An ecstasy of fumbling," from Owen's "Dulce et Decorum Est"; finally, a half-rhymed couplet—"You'll make fine eating then, / Flesh gone, and the worm in"—returns us to the opening orchard image. In borrowing from Owen, Gunn surely glimpses the kinship of their shared sexuality.

Gunn's readiness to borrow was hugely beneficial to him as a young poet: "I was at my usual game of stealing what could be of use to me"[8] was how he self-disparagingly described the greedy assimilation of influences in *The Sense of Movement,* but the process had already begun at Cambridge. There, he developed "a rather crude theory of what I called 'pose,' based partly on the dramatics of John Donne, somewhat perhaps on W. B. Yeats's theory of masks, and most strongly on the behaviour of Stendhal's heroes";[9] other sources included Shakespeare and Jean-Paul Sartre. Gunn continues in *My Cambridge:* "The theory of pose was this: everyone plays a part, whether he knows it or not, so he might as well deliberately design a part, or a series of parts, for himself."[10] It seems a simple enough idea, but it brilliantly solved three distinct, though clearly related, problems: it enabled Gunn to combine disparate literary influences (such as Donne, Yeats, and Stendhal) into the coherent literary style of his early collections; it supplied a philosophical template in which Sartrean existentialism and Yeatsian masks both played their part; and it provided a neat way of juggling with sexual identity at a time when homosexuality was illegal and enthusiastically prosecuted.[11]

So the Trojan War soldier who appears in "The Wound," the poem that opens *Fighting Terms* in its revised editions (and in Gunn's *Collected Poems*), is nothing like the Owenesque figure in "The Soldier": he is, indeed, so much a creature of pose and mask that it's hard to tell quite what's going on in the poem. It's "about someone recuperating from a mysterious wound," according to Gunn, introducing a reading in 1984: "perhaps in a state of fever, he dreams he takes part in the Trojan War and, after becoming several other participants, one after another, he dreams he is Achilles, the Greek warrior."[12] Elsewhere, Gunn explains, more ambiguously, that the speaker is "at one time Achilles, the real soldier in a real war, and at another time the self who dreamt he was Achilles."[13] Such glosses—apart from confirming that "The Wound," like so much of *Fighting Terms,* is concerned with the divided self, inner and outer, man and mask—don't notably solve the poem's main puzzle (and perhaps aren't meant to do so). What is the wound? We need, as often with young Gunn, to follow a literary signpost:

> And while my belt hung up, sword in the sheath,
> Thersites shambled in and breathlessly
> Cackled about my friend Patroclus' death.[14]

This signpost isn't to *The Iliad,* but to a text far more central to Gunn's imagination: Shakespeare's *Troilus and Cressida.* These are the crucial lines:

> ACHILLES: I see my reputation is at stake:
> My fame is shrewdly gor'd.
> PATROCLUS: O then beware:
> Those wounds heal ill that men do give themselves.[15]

Achilles, at this point in the play, is suffering from something very like existential *mauvaise foi:* he sulks in his tent, refusing to fight, and is upstaged by lumpish Ajax. Ulysses tauntingly suggests that this is because Achilles is in love with Hector's sister Polyxena, while Patroclus (closer to home and to the truth) acknowledges the force of a different rumor: "They think my little stomach to the war / And your great love to me restrains you thus."[16] And indeed it's the death of Patroclus that will spur Achilles on to kill Hector, anti-heroically accompanied by that ancient gang of Hell's Angels, the Myrmidons. Meanwhile, Achilles' psychological wound—and that, surely, is the sense of Gunn's "The huge wound in my head. . . ."—is an injury that afflicts both his public reputation and his self-esteem, resulting from a dislocation between inner and outer man that prevents either from functioning properly; that its personal context should be the most solidly realized gay relationship in Shakespeare is clearly to Gunn's purpose, too. For he had experienced something like the wound, and more importantly its healing: in the summer vacation of 1952, hitchhiking through France, he "experienced a revelation of physical and spiritual freedom that I still refer to in my thoughts as the Revelation."[17] This gave him the energy to undertake a rigorous "apprenticeship in poetry," the confidence to formulate his theory of "pose," and thus the means of bringing his own divided self into workable harmony. Perhaps that is why "The Wound," which owes so much to this process, remained Gunn's favorite poem in *Fighting Terms,*[18] while his roadside revelation explains the rapturous empathy with Saul becoming Paul in a wonderful slightly later poem, "In Santa Maria del Popolo."[19]

In *Fighting Terms,* the soldier isn't necessarily a divided self nor is the divided self necessarily a soldier. The National Serviceman who gives his name to "Lofty in the Palais de Danse" is an altogether simpler creature whose lumpen demotic explains Gunn's preference at this time for classical or literary contexts:

> You praise my strength. The muscle on my arm.
> Yes. Now the other. Yes, about the same.
> I've got another muscle you can feel.
> Dare say you knew. Only expected harm
> Falls from a khaki man.[20]

I dare say we knew too, but in retrospect we can see that these lines aren't just ludicrously crass: they are also wrongly gendered. In other words, while "I've got another muscle you can feel" is a terrible and improbable chat-up line for a 1950s boy to try on a 1950s girl, it becomes far more probable (if not much less terrible) if spoken between two gay men. A parallel problem afflicts the infuriatingly flawed "Carnal Knowledge," a poem that doesn't quite work in either its 1954 or its 1962 version: Gunn was fully aware of this and in his *Collected Poems* narrowly decided to restore the 1954 text and with it not only the riddling, alternating refrain ("You know I know you know I know you know" and its obverse) but also calamitous Loftyisms such as "Cackle you hen, and answer when I crow."[21] In "My Life Up to Now," he mildly rebukes readers who, "aware that I am homosexual," infer "that the thing 'known' is that the speaker would prefer to be in bed with a man"; this, he says, "would be a serious misplacement of emphasis," and so a "reader knowing nothing about the author has a much better chance of understanding" the poem.[22] To which the only answer is: yes and no. The general point is the constant, unanswerable reproach to the literary biographer: knowing nothing about an author gives life back to the poem, which is where it should be, rather than to the poet, and the fact that we know relatively little about the greatest writer in the English language, Shakespeare, actually allows us more space to read and interpret his plays. Nevertheless, the specific point is perhaps a shade disingenuous. This author, as early as *Fighting Terms,* is recognizably a gay man, and the poem is addressed to a woman; and a reader in possession of these two facts isn't going to be led astray by them:

Abandon me to stammering, and go;
If you have tears, prepare to cry elsewhere—
I know of no emotion we can share.
Your intellectual protests are a bore
And even now I pose, so now go, for
I know you know.[23]

The poem's universality—its recognition that encounters between heterosexuals can end like this too—isn't compromised by our biographical knowledge here, while gay readers will ruefully acknowledge the authenticity of a scene that was played out in so many of our younger lives.

Meanwhile, the balanced Apollonian and Dionysian facets of the divided self are everywhere in *Fighting Terms*. They are there, for instance, in "The Beach Head," in the choice between heroic action ("Shall I be John a Gaunt . . . ?") and introspective cunning ("Or shall I wait and calculate my chances . . . ?");[24] in "Lerici," where the contrast between "submissive" Shelley and "masterful" Byron is spiced by a string of words with Shakespearian sexual connotations (such as "expense," "thriftless," and "spend");[25] in the role-reversing "Tamer and Hawk," with its allusive nod to Thomas Wyatt's "They flee from me . . ."; and in that other homage to Renaissance England, "A Mirror for Poets," where "Wheels, racks, and fires" and "the glamour of pain" are juxtaposed with "Arcadia, a fruitful permanent land."[26] In "Looking Glass" the self is divided between a derelict present and an edenic past, so that the looking glass, another mirror for poets, unexpectedly reflects not through space but through time. The feeling of dislocation is more unsettlingly extreme in "The Secret Sharer": this alludes to Joseph Conrad's identically titled story, in which a young sea captain, in command of a ship for the first time, hides his double—a stowaway wanted for murder—in his cabin and experiences the recurring sensation of watching *himself*, sleeping, whispering, finally escaping to freedom; when elsewhere on the ship, the captain has a constant sense of his "other self" within the cabin. Gunn's poem transposes the idea to an urban landscape; like Conrad's captain simultaneously inside and outside his cabin, he imagines himself in a snowy street, looking up at his own window, calling his own name:

The curtains were lit, through glass were lit by doubt.
And there was I, within the room alone.
In the empty wind I stood and shouted on:
But O, what if the strange head should peer out?

Suspended taut between two equal fears
I was like to be torn apart by their strong pull:
What, I asked, if I never hear my call?
And what if it reaches my insensitive ears?[27]

In the final stanza, the perspective alters: we're with the other Gunn, comfortably in bed, unaware of his alter ego on the street. This is what happens when the two selves, like those of psychologically wounded Achilles, become fatally disconnected.

2

All the same, we've come a long way from Achilles. "The Secret Sharer" is a gentler sort of poem that has shed most of its armor, and its tone places it among an interesting cluster of dream-and-waking poems. In "Without a Counterpart," for instance, the speaker wakes, terrified and apparently alone, to imagine a vast bleak landscape that anticipates the desolate, emptied world of "Misanthropos":

Last night I woke in fright: you were not there.
I seemed to face across a deep sad plain
Hedged at one end, a hillock in the centre.
And I was chained, to wait and starve alone,
And could not think what I was waiting for.[28]

This is the first of several ominous dream-landscapes in Gunn; but its sinister details—"Two reed-lined ponds," "a long volcano," "prickly turf"—gradually resolve into the eyes, nose, and stubble of his lover's face. The poem's weakness is an overexplanatory last stanza (by which time we shouldn't need to be told of that "bad hole in the ground," "It was your mouth, and all the rest your face"), but its strengths are ample compensation: the sense of waking nightmare is entirely convincing (as Theseus has it, in *A Midsummer Night's Dream*, "Or in the night, imagining some fear / How easy is a bush supposed a bear?");[29] the images don't quite collapse into the absurdity they perilously skirt; and the poem has a directness that makes some of the other poems in *Fighting Terms* look contrived. Its sexuality must have been clear to attentive readers from its first appearance in 1954 (interestingly, it seems not to have appeared in any periodical before being collected there).

"Without a Counterpart" *does* in fact have a counterpart: or, rather, two. The less significant one is "Ralph's Dream," part of an abandoned sequence to have been called "The Furies," published in the *London Magazine* in January 1955. This describes Ralph's elaborate nightmare, in which he first confronts a grotesque monster and then finds himself trapped in a mysterious room. His partner Marie, sleeping soundly beside him, moves in and out of the dream rather as the male partner does in "Without a Counterpart": at one point, she seems to elide with the vanquished monster ("It seemed at once a body he had used"), while later, in the room where his belt is hung up like Achilles', he realizes he is

> waiting not for Marie, instead
> For someone whom he could not give a name,
> Waiting for someone in this fendered room—
> The name was smuggled off by gangs of shame
> For his own comfort, rich dupe waiting whom?[30]

It seems reasonable to assume that the nameless other is unnameable because male; the clotted diction and wobbly syntax, incidentally, are pretty typical of the piece. Much more successful is "Light Sleeping," written in 1953 and eventually collected in *The Missed Beat*. Here, the situation is almost identical to that in "Without a Counterpart": two men are in bed together; one wakes to a nightmare vision; but, in this poem, the other is awake and observes everything. The insomniac's sense that night is shifting and unstable is perfectly evoked in the opening stanza:

> John could not sleep, though swaddled from the cold;
> He heard the hours pass, sea on the shore,
> And lay in power of light, which rolled, unrolled,
> Working, a white hypnosis on the floor,
> Towards the other side, the moving breath.

Suddenly his friend, who had until this point been "easy in the bed," sits bolt upright and, staring out at the moon, starts to speak in a strangely rapt, hypnotic style:

> "Inside the moon I see a hell of love.
>
> "There love is all, and no one is alone.
> The song of passion deafens, so no choice
> Of individual word can hold its own

Against the rule of that anonymous noise.
And wait, I see more clearly: craters, canals

"Are smothered by two giant forms of mist
So that no features of the land remain.
Two humming clouds of moisture intertwist
Agreed so well, they cannot change to rain
And serve to clean the solid ground beneath.

"Singing there fell, locked in each other's arms,
Cursed with content, pair by possessive pair:
Committed centuries to lie in calms
They stayed to rot into that used-up air
No wind can shift, it is so thick, so thick."

The ringing voice stopped but, as if one must
Finish in moral, stumbled on and said:
"In that still fog all energy is lost."
The moonlight slunk on, darkness touched his head.
He fell back, then he turned upon the pillow.[31]

G. S. Fraser, who included the poem in his anthology *Poetry Now* (1956), acutely remarked five years later that the word "content" here "carries a strong anti-feeling," while the word "calms" "instead of suggesting 'calm after storm' recalls the rotting, glistering sea on which the ship lay becalmed in 'The Ancient Mariner.'"[32] I'm sure Fraser is right—that echo of Coleridge will remind us that English Romantic poetry is second only to English Renaissance poetry in its formative influence on Gunn—but I think he misses the allusion that informs the entire poem, the echo of a great Elizabethan sonnet, on which Gunn wrote in some detail[33] and which clearly haunted him for many years:

With how sad steps, O moon, thou climb'st the skies;
　How silently, and with how wan a face.
　What, may it be that even in heav'nly place
That busy archer his sharp arrows tries?
Sure, if that long-with-love-acquainted eyes
　Can judge of love, thou feel'st a lover's case;
　I read it in thy looks; thy languished grace
To me, that feel the like, thy state descries.

Then even of fellowship, O moon, tell me,
Is constant love deemed there but want of wit?
Are beauties there as proud as here they be?
Do they above love to be loved, and yet
Those lovers scorn whom that love doth possess?
Do they call virtue there ungratefulness?[34]

Philip Sidney addresses the moon directly and asks it a number of increasingly urgent questions, whereas Gunn's speaker meditates upon the moon, but the tone is unmistakably similar: so much so that the Gunn poem, which seems a little strained at first glance, reads much more naturally after the Sidney. And of course it then becomes clear that "Light Sleeping" is picking up key ideas from *Astrophel and Stella* and recasting them in still more obsessive form: where Sidney is tentative in assigning a reason for the moon's "sad steps," Gunn decisively sees "a hell of love"; Sidney's anguished question—"Do they above love to be loved, and yet / Those lovers scorn whom that love doth possess?"—is answered by Gunn's vision of lovers "locked in each other's arms, / Cursed with content, pair by possessive pair." For Sidney, the questioning form admits the slender possibility of a world in which love doesn't inescapably lead to unhappiness; for Gunn, love is by definition hellish, because it is possessive, and the vision of the moon offers only confirmation, not consolation. Yet that vision *is* mitigated by what at first appears to be the poem's awkward construction: the monologue is framed by the observing consciousness of wakeful, "appalled" John, whose view of the matter is very different from his friend's. Fraser guesses that "the two men may be different aspects of the poet's one personality," which correctly identifies this as yet another poem about the divided self but makes a solidly realized scene sound oddly disembodied: he couldn't easily say, in 1961, that "Light Sleeping" is also quite obviously about two male lovers in bed.

3

By the time "Light Sleeping" appeared in *New World Writing* in April 1955, Gunn was himself in the New World: he had arrived early in September 1954, "spending my twenty-fifth birthday in mid-Atlantic and landing in New York during a hurricane."[35] With blessed serendipity, his route to join his American partner Mike Kitay took him to a creative writing fellowship at Stanford, where he studied with Yvor Winters—of whom, when he applied for it, he'd barely heard. Winters, with his interests in the poetry of the English Renaissance and twentieth-century America, his combination of critical rigor and personal kindness, might have been specifically invented to be Gunn's mentor at this time. And then there was California. Christopher Isherwood once said that, for him in the 1930s, "Berlin meant Boys."[36] For Gunn, California in the 1950s meant San Francisco and gay bars; James Dean, Marlon Brando, Elvis Presley; icons, bikes, and rock 'n' roll. That—along with a heady mix of Winters, Sartre, and Yeats—is the raw material of *The Sense of Movement.*

That "On the Move" is a sort of love poem, as well as a sort of self-love poem, now seems almost too obvious to mention. The reader of *Fighting Terms,* who already knows that Gunn can be in two places at once within a single poem, will be untroubled by the pronominal shifts between "one," which obviously includes the author, and "they," which less obviously does: "one" becomes "they" with the "donned impersonality" that is assumed when "One joins the movement in a valueless world,"[37] so we shouldn't doubt that Gunn pictures himself among the bikers. Or, to put it differently: "one" is the poet who "got a motorcycle which I rode for about one month"; "they" are the sexually ambiguous Marlon Brando and his friends in *The Wild One;* and part of the poem's purpose is to superimpose the two. The success of "On the Move," Gunn's best-known poem if not necessarily his best, has much to do with the fact that a reader might enjoy and understand it as a brilliant combination of social observation and philosophical discourse, without bothering about its erotic force. But the sexual energy is there from the start, prefigured by the "gust of birds / That spurts across the field," confirmed in the noise that "Bulges to thunder held by calf and thigh," and reaching its climax (which seems the right word) in the opening lines of the final stanza:

> A minute holds them, who have come to go:
> The self-defined, astride the created will
> They burst away. . . .

Gunn's chosen instrument here, as in "Lerici," is the Shakespearean sexual pun: we might pass innocently over "come" and "go," if it were not for "will" in the following line.[38] The word was a favorite one of Gunn's, and we can readily see why: it has Sartrian and Yeatsian as well as darker twentieth-century connotations (as in Leni Riefenstahl's *Triumph of the Will*) and, beyond these, the Elizabethan senses of "sexual desire" and "penis," of which the motorbike—the "created will"—is a symbolic extension. There is, of course, much more to "On the Move" than this: not least, the way in which human uncertainty and imperfection are contrasted with the "direct instinct" of birds and saints who "complete their purposes," a counterbalance that notably extends the poem's range.

The surprising scope of "On the Move" is one reason (and the more supple versification is another) why it seems so much more effective than either "The Unsettled Motorcyclist's Vision of His Death" or "Black Jackets." I suspect that the first of these really begins with Gunn's inability to resist a pun, in this case the twin meanings of "unsettled" ("uncertain" and "unseated"): but the poem lacks his characteristic sense of doubleness—"But I am being what I please"[39] suggests a relatively uncomplicated self—and its view of the relationship between man and nature is simplistic in comparison with "On the Move." "Black Jackets" is more interestingly edgy. It's set in a San Francisco leather bar, and its stance of benign voyeurism is shared with the roughly contemporaneous "Market at Turk" and "Modes of Pleasure," as well as with several much later poems: "Bally *Power Play*," for instance, or "San Francisco Streets." Its focus is a "red-haired boy who drove a van" on weekdays and "Wore cycle boots and jacket here / To suit the Sunday hangout he was in,"[40] although we're not told whether he actually owns a bike (people who drink in gay leather bars often don't). Gunn's interest is in the boy's half-fledged quality, midway between innocence and experience, and partaking of both: on the sleeve of his jacket, "Remote exertion had lined, scratched, and burned / Insignia," yet that awkward "Remote" seems to include both detachment and reverence, distancing him from the "heroic fall or climb" or perhaps even suggesting that the jacket is second-hand, its scuffs and its identity not his own. Meanwhile, the other drinkers are "Concocting selves for their impervious kit"—reforging identities from "donned impersonality"—as the reflections from their black jackets send across the dimly lit bar the "sudden and anonymous hints of light," which no doubt invite sudden and anonymous sexual encounters. At the end of the poem, the red-haired boy is still apart from them, recollecting "his initiation":

> And one especially of the rites.
> For on his shoulders they had put tattoos:
> The group's name on the left, The Knights,
> And on the right the slogan Born To Lose.

The poem, which seems to have been moving toward important points both on its philosophical level (to do with identity and belonging) and in terms of quasi-erotic ritual, is fudged by its final couplet: the group's name and artless slogan steer it away from any further details of the "initiation" and safely close it down.

Where "Black Jackets" begins in the silence between records on a jukebox, "Elvis Presley" opens with the record itself:

> Two minutes long it pitches through some bar:
> Unreeling from a corner box, the sigh
> Of this one, in his gangling finery
> And crawling sideburns, wielding a guitar.[41]

For many young writers of my generation, that was the most explosive opening to a poem we'd ever read; I can't be alone in remembering exactly when and where I read it. (One afternoon in the summer term of 1962, when I was fourteen and had just decided to write poetry, I picked up A. Alvarez's recently published Penguin anthology *The New Poetry* in the local bookshop, took it back to school, opened it at random. . . .) What I hadn't realized until then was that you could write a formal and thoughtful poem about rock music. All the same, Gunn begins by hedging his bets: "this one," "gangling finery" and "crawling sideburns" all imply disdainful distance. But "wielding a guitar": the guitar becomes a weapon, the "gangling finery" a uniform, and Elvis a surrogate soldier. By the end of the poem—by which point on that first reading my head was in real danger of falling apart—he's become much more besides: "Our idiosyncrasy and our likeness," exactly like the bikers of "On the Move," who "turns revolt into a style" and for whom "the pose held is a stance" that "may be posture for combat." These, we can now see plainly, are the fighting terms of Gunn's erotic discourse; but this wasn't always so easy to see or, if seen, to express. John Fuller, in a 1962 essay on Gunn, was actually being rather brave (rather than, as he may sound, insufferably arch) when he inquired:

> Combat against what, we ask? What is the real significance of Presley? Or is the poet off on some erotic sidetrack, a piece of disguised butch-ery? One need not multiply examples of ambivalence about the motorcyclists and sadists in some of these poems.[42]

But that, of course, is just what Gunn delightedly invites us to do: it's no accident that, in *The Sense of Movement,* "Elvis Presley" is flanked on one side by "Market at Turk"—that sly syllabic portrait of a street-corner hustler—and on the other by "Lines for a Book."

Although "Lines for a Book" and "The Beaters" are both seriously flawed (the latter is among the relatively few exclusions from Gunn's *Collected Poems*), they are worth defending from the indignant misreadings they once provoked. Kenneth Allott, for example, in his note on Gunn for *The Penguin Book of Contemporary Verse* (1962), cited a remark of Frank Kermode's about "the preoccupation with toughs" before primly adding: "he does not appear to see how strongly this preoccupation rules in *The Sense of Movement,* or how unattractive such pieces as 'Lines for a Book' and 'The Beaters' really are."[43] But the crucial, much-missed point about "Lines for a Book" is that to write yearningly of "the overdogs from Alexander / To those who would not play with Stephen Spender"[44] is not to attack Spender but to sympathize with him, whose "parents kept me from children who were rough"[45] and who wanted to play with the rough boys every bit as much as Gunn did. "The Beaters," though damaged beyond repair by the "swastika-draped bed,"[46] is otherwise an audacious attempt to think rationally about sadomasochistic gay sex. How much Gunn actually enjoyed beating or being beaten is beside the point here, although a biographer would want to know; the poem's significance lies in its imaginative equation of domination and submission, pain and pleasure, balanced opposites of the sort that recur in Gunn's early work. As he wrote in "To Yvor Winters, 1955"—and it's a neat trick to scatter further hints of his own sexuality, from "boxer's vigilance" at the start to "tough in will" at the end, through a tribute to the solidly heterosexual Winters—

> You keep both Rule and Energy in view,
> Much power in each, most in the balanced two:
> Ferocity existing in the fence
> Built by an exercised intelligence.[47]

The poems that focus on soldiers or bikers by definition provide only part of a complex picture. As we can see from the early dream poems and from quieter pieces in *The Sense of Movement* such as "At the Back of the North Wind" or "Before the Carnival," and as we discover more clearly from his later work, there's another Gunn, the man within who is fond of cats and cooking and pot plants (yes, and *pot* plants too). This is the poet who is liberated with such breathtaking candor and freshness of tone in the syllabic second half of *My Sad Captains:* there, the release of iambic pressure brilliantly matches a sense of exhilaration that the reader of poems such as "Waking in a Newly Built House," or "Flying

Above California" or "Light among Redwood" will hardly need to be told is sexual as well as spatial. The gentler self that at first appeared mostly in dreams at last emerges into broad daylight—or, indeed, into the sunlight which gives its title to the final poem in *Moly,* that marvelous book which miraculously combines freedom and iambics in some of Gunn's finest poems. But that, as they say, is another story.

Existentialism and Homosexuality in Gunn's Early Poetry

ALFRED CORN

In the early 1950s, when Thom Gunn began publishing, the reigning ideology among artists who subscribed neither to religion nor communist politics was existentialist philosophy. The thinker most often cited as a model was Jean-Paul Sartre; and then, because of her connection to him, Simone de Beauvoir. Although Albert Camus had at first been associated with existentialism, by the late 1940s he withdrew from its ranks, whether or not this defection was always known to the general public. Existentialism developed on the parallel tracks of philosophy and literature, but its influence extended to the nonverbal arts as well. Some of the abstract expressionist painters espoused the philosophy and came to consider their work as an exploratory action, not defined in advance by a preordained goal. The canvas recorded a series of choices made in the course of facture—pivotal, collaborative, and cumulative brushstrokes whose meaning became final only when the painting was complete. Some jazz musicians described their performances as existential as well: beginning with no format or plan, they improvised as they went along, discovering the overall shape and emotional content of the piece gradually and *in process*. These concrete, aesthetic applications of the new philosophical system may or may not appear sufficiently rigorous to qualify as applied existentialism, but we can see in them a connection to Sartrean axioms such as "Existence precedes essence," or, "man is, before all else, something which propels itself towards a future and is aware that it is doing so . . ."[1]

Thom Gunn had no formal training in philosophy, nor was existentialism taught at Cambridge during his undergraduate years. Nevertheless, it formed a climate of opinion that no intellectual or artist in or outside the academy would have failed to notice. Some of its prestige came from the high regard accorded in that period to French culture in general, a regard based on a century of extraordinary French achievement: Baudelaire, symbolism, and surrealism in poetry; Flaubert, Proust, and Gide in fiction; and Degas, Monet, Gauguin, Matisse, and Picasso in painting. In his autobiographical writings, Gunn speaks of an ecstatic, life-changing experience he calls "the Revelation," which occurred to him during a trip to France when he was an undergraduate: "And one day, hitch-hiking along a road in France, I experienced a revelation of physical and spiritual freedom that I still refer to in my thoughts as the Revelation. It was like the elimination of some enormous but undefined problem that had been across my way and prevented me from moving forward. But now I suddenly found I had the energy for almost anything."[2] That "the Revelation" took place in France does not seem accidental. In any case, the same essay goes on to describe Gunn's development of an aesthetic that drew on, among other sources, France and Sartrean existentialism. He speaks of

> a crude theory of what I called "pose," based partly on the dramatics of John Donne, somewhat perhaps on Yeats's theory of the masks, and most strongly on the behaviour of Stendhal's heroes. I was to find support for it from other sources, notably from some of Shakespeare's characters, like the Bastard in *King John* and Coriolanus, and later from Sartre. It was, as you can see, literary in character, but its principal source was the Revelation on the road in France, with its intimations of unbounded energy. The theory of pose was this: everyone plays a part, whether he knows it or not, so he might as well deliberately design a part, or a series of parts, for himself.[3]

The "theory of poses," with its connection to dramatic literature matches statements made by Sartre in the lecture cited above. For example: "Moreover, as Gide has very well said, a sentiment which is play-acting and one which is vital are two things that are hardly distinguishable one from another." Sartre's reputation seems, half a century on, to be based mainly on his authorship of plays, including *No Exit, Flies, Dirty Hands,* and *Kean.* This last play, which enjoyed a successful London revival in the 2007 season, has as its protagonist the celebrated nineteenth-century Shakespearean actor. Kean not only cites Shakespeare's "All the world's a stage" speech but he puts it into action, adopting several personae (or "poses") during the course of the performance, thereby establishing a connection to existentialist philosophy: the actor (and by extension all humanity) has no essential identity in advance of assuming a role and putting it into play.

In the "Cambridge in the Fifties" essay, Gunn also mentions meeting a fellow undergraduate named Tony White: "It was he who first got me to read Sartre's plays and Camus's novels." Gunn then reports receiving a 1954 New Year's card from White, inscribed with wishes for "panache, logique, espagnolisme, l'imprévu, singularité . . . from one Étranger to another."[4] And in "My Life Up to Now," Gunn characterizes his early beginnings as a poet in the following terms: "Suddenly everything started to feed my imagination. Writing poetry became the act of an existentialist conqueror, excited and aggressive."[5] In this same essay he makes a further (and final) statement about the influence of existentialism: "*The Sense of Movement*, then, was a much more sophisticated book than my first collection, but a much less independent one. There is a lot of Winters in it, a fair amount of Yeats, and a great deal of raw Sartre (strange bedfellows!)."[6]

Autobiographical confirmation that existentialism contributed to Gunn's development as a poet might seem to settle the question once and for all, but the component of Gunn's sexuality needs to be brought in as well. Consider these facts: Before the Sexual Offences Act of 1967, all homosexual acts were illegal in England, though *not in France.* "Cambridge in the Fifties" mentions that John Holmstrom, one of the friends accompanying Gunn on his second trip to Paris, acquired several Jean Genet novels and smuggled them into England. (Genet was at that date banned in the United Kingdom.) In the essay Gunn doesn't say whether he read these novels or not. Nor does he speak of the study *Saint Genet, comédien et martyr* (Saint Genet, Actor and Martyr) that Sartre published in 1952. No English translation of the book appeared before 1963, but of course Gunn could read French, and the book was in any case widely reviewed and discussed when it first came out.

Far from condemning Genet for his homosexual and criminal activity, Sartre's study holds him up as an existential hero, a rugged individualist who ignores Judeo-Christian ethics and finds an outlaw identity for himself not sanctioned by custom or tradition. In this argument, homosexuality is a choice, an act of will that incidentally or purposely establishes the freedom of the chooser. No a priori ethical or religious system contributes to the decision; moreover, one of its effects is to nullify those systems. Like all atheists who came after Dostoyevsky, Sartre had pondered a statement made by the character Ivan in *The Brothers Karamazov:* "If there is no God, all things are lawful." Sartre, too, would locate his own life and aspirations in a metaphysical landscape designated by the famous Nietzsche title *Beyond Good and Evil.* To subscribe to an atheist and postethical moral philosophy doesn't necessarily mean, though, that the philosopher can always find in himself the will to commit crimes demonstrating indifference to the claims of religion or consensus ethics. Sartre, as far as we know, never committed any crimes; in fact, the stance he first adopted was the secular humanist's. Yet he did eventually endorse Stalinism and by extension the political violence and murder it entailed. Meanwhile, it's clear that he considered his views on Genet as respectable, postethical opinion, an opinion that might empower others to will for themselves an existence created and acted out "beyond good and evil."

I'm not arguing that Genet agreed with Sartre's estimate of his own literary aims or moral convictions; or that Sartre was right to regard homosexuality as the first in a series of choices or acts of will that go on to construct the so-called homosexual lifestyle. What does seem plausible to me is that Gunn, hesitant about his sexuality and aware that homosexual encounters were criminal under British law, found in existentialism a philosophical justification for a sexual propensity already active in his psyche. Because he couldn't in most social circumstances make his sexual orientation known, he was forced to "pose" as heterosexual. Making a virtue of necessity, Gunn could view this artificial persona as the springboard to assuming other poses not devised in response to legal or social coercion. His "theory of poses," which emphasized conscious choice in the manufacture of identity, could allow him to be more vivid, more daring, readier to exhibit "panache, logique, espagnolisme, l'imprévu, singularité," in Tony White's words.

Gunn's autobiographical writings give us the portrait of a young man unusually sensitive and rather pliant. If he titled his first book *Fighting Terms,* a book containing poems with aggressive and often soldierly content, we can understand these as part of a program or strategy of "poses," the choice and implementation of an identity not innate in the author. And why not? The whole point of existentialism is freedom from an essence or identity assigned in advance. Apart from the sanctioned murder of warfare, the poems explore other instances of outlawry, such as looting and rape. Though Gunn didn't commit crimes like these, his poems' presentation of them is neutral and nonjudgmental. In a fictive realm beyond good and evil, he adopts many imaginative personae and through them, as for himself, discovers credible experiences and emotions.

Actually, "The Wound" describes the assumption of *several* identities, some at odds with the others. First, the speaker of the characterized monologue or soliloquy tells us he has received a serious head wound (an imagined situation, based on no real incident in Gunn's life). Then he describes, as though they were his own, experiences of several characters involved in both camps of the Trojan War, not excluding Helen. The poem concludes with a passage from Achilles' point of view. Of course, the *Iliad* mentions no head wound that the Greek hero received: Homer's fiction has been further fictionalized. Gunn's narrator devises these words for Achilles: "I was myself: subject to no man's breath: / My own commander was my enemy." This sounds like the radical freedom proposed by existentialism, yet a mask makes the statement, a mask worn by Gunn's wounded persona and, therefore, a double mask. Another way of putting things is that Gunn has imposed a "pose" on the poem's speaker. The narrator posing as Achilles hears of Patroclus's death and, despite his head wound, calls for armor and makes ready to fight. At which point his partially healed head wound opens again.

Without being explicit, this concluding incident smuggles in a homosexual theme by recalling the celebrated love of Achilles and Patroclus. It also suggests that the "wound" is itself a metaphor for homosexuality. We should compare that metaphor to a similar one in W. H. Auden's "Letter to a Wound," the fourth section of part 1 in *The Orators,* a work Gunn must have read, given that he is on record as having admired Auden's early work.[7] Auden's persona writes to his "wound" as to a lover and revisits an incident in which he told a prostitute he had no need of her services because he can avail himself of a "friend." Meanwhile, Gunn's narrator describes his period of convalescence as a time of "joy," during which his imagination could range freely and appropriate experience lived by characters other than himself. Using the metaphor of an unhealable wound for homosexuality is, of course, offensive today, but, at a period when variant sexuality was regarded as a sin, a crime, or an illness, the metaphor wouldn't have seemed unwarranted. Applying it, we can understand the poem as making a connection between poetry, homosexuality, and the "theory of poses." It's helpful here to consider Camus's existential fable about Sisyphus, who, condemned by the gods to push a rounded stone up a hill and watch it roll down again, before repeating the process ad infinitum, decides that freedom is again his if he decides he wills and *chooses* his relentless task. Likewise, Gunn will "choose" his wound, his sexuality, and allow it to fuel the genesis of poems based on poses. *Fighting Terms* is composed almost entirely of persona poems, conceived at varying distances from Gunn's actual personality. "La Prisonnière" is cast in the voice of Proust's Marcel, though further fictionalized. "Carnal Knowledge" opens with the statement "Even in bed I pose . . ." and includes the riddling refrain "You know I know you know I know you know." The oblique connection with homosexuality in poems like "The

Wound," "La Prisonnière," and "Carnal Knowledge" would probably have been lost on most of Gunn's early readers. That the poems drew on existentialist philosophy and literature most likely escaped notice, as well. But in the light of Gunn's autobiographical writings and the poems that came later on, we're able to understand relevant subtexts and draw useful inferences from them.

It's not enough simply to accept the comment Gunn made about his second book, *The Sense of Movement,* to the effect that it contained a "great deal of raw Sartre." Confirmation needs to be found in the poems themselves. Actually, we can begin with the epigraph from Pierre Corneille's *Cinna* that opens the volume: "Je le suis, je veux l'être" ("I am that, I choose to be that"). This is spoken by Emperor Augustus in the third scene of act 5, immediately after he pronounces one of Corneille's most famous lines: "Je suis maître de moi comme de l'univers" ("I am the master of myself just as I am of the whole world"). Application of these sentiments or convictions to the life of a twentieth-century citizen in a democratic country is dubious. Yet we can see the aptness if we understand it as an exaltation of the will, a seconding of existentialist concepts. Furthermore, if we substitute "homosexual" for the first "le," the intention becomes even clearer: "I am homosexual, I want to be that." Like Camus's Sisyphus, Gunn decides to affirm his situation rather than lament it, no matter what private or social or legal disadvantages were involved. If he wills and *chooses* his sexuality, he transforms an innate psychic propensity into an expression of freedom. One reason it's important to reflect on Gunn's privileging of the human will is that, in the English poetic tradition, the faculty of willing is generally devalued, regarded as a poor second to unconscious, unpremeditated feeling and action. By contrast, in French tradition *la volonté* is held in high esteem, partly because it is connected to the conscious faculty of reason and partly because it attests to firmness of character, which enables the human agent to surmount difficulty and suffering in the interest of achieving a goal. It is a virtue associated with ancient Rome, and therefore important in the Latin civilizations that developed in former Roman provinces. We've noticed that Gunn singles out several Roman characters in Shakespeare as his models, and Corneille's Augustus qualifies as yet one more. In some ways, Sartrean existentialism is merely a more intense development of a central theme in French culture, the culture that produced Louis XIV, Napoleon, Gide, de Gaulle, and Genet. These are personalities constructed on the heroic scale, who take stock, decide who they want to be, and then do whatever it takes to achieve that goal.

Turning to the poems in *The Sense of Movement*, we find many recurrences of the theme of will: in "The Nature of an Action," "My cause lay in the will, that opens straight / Upon an act for the most desperate"; in "The Unsettled Motorcyclist's Vision of His Death," "My human will cannot submit / To nature, though brought out of it"; in "Lines for a Book," "To be insensitive, to steel the will"; in "Market at Turk," "with bootstraps and Marine belt, / reminders of the will"; in "Julian the Apostate," "Then strains to lift his bones erect, and fling / To the pure will of exclamation mark"; in "To Yvor Winters, 1955," "and fewer still / Control with the deliberate human will"; from the same poem, "And, as you do, persistent, tough in will, / Raise from the excellent the better still."

Throughout the volume, will is associated with toughness, with hardness, with assertive self-definition, with combativeness, with satisfying sexual encounters, with the development of a personal and a literary style. The volume's first poem, "On the Move," touches on most of these themes and connects them to existentialist concepts. It's difficult fifty years on to recapture the surprise or discomfort that greeted the emblematic heroes of this poem. The disproportion between young men who rode motorcycles and traditional heroes such as Achilles or Napoleon is striking. It's unlikely that many poetry readers of the 1950s would have bothered to see the film *The Wild One* (1953), directed by Laslo Benedek and starring Marlon Brando at his most magnetic. It depicts the life of rebellious American motorcyclists, giving a more or less accurate picture of what had been going on in California during the decade before the film appeared. Gunn couldn't have seen it in England, where the film was banned, but quite clearly got to know it once he had moved to California. It launched a vogue for black leather jackets that has never since entirely been abandoned, and one of Gunn's author photographs from this period shows him wearing just such a jacket. And how are his heroes described?

> On motorcycles, up the road, they come:
> Small, black, as flies hanging in the heat, the Boys,
> Until the distance throws them forth, their hum
> Bulges to thunder held by calf and thigh.

Farther on:

> Much that is natural, to the will must yield.
> Men manufacture both machine and soul,

And use what they imperfectly control
To dare a future from the taken routes.

And:

One joins the movement in a valueless word,
Choosing it, till, both hurler and the hurled,
One moves as well, always toward, toward.

And again:

A minute holds them, who have come to go:
The self-defined, astride the created will
They burst away . . .

The poem's conclusion must be understood as a pause, not an end:

At worst, one is in motion; and at best,
Reaching no absolute, in which to rest,
One is always nearer by not keeping still.

In fact, this is followed by more than two dozen poems, including those cited above as concerned with the theme of will. At this point in the discussion, there's probably no need to dwell too insistently on the Sartrean character of "On the Move." Yet it may be clarifying to pause a moment on the term *Geworfenheit* (thrownness), used by Martin Heidegger to describe the human condition of being "thrown" by birth into a life situation that is undergone instead of being chosen. The human task is then to alter or transform given conditions by choice until we arrive at an existence compatible with our deepest identity. Heideggerian philosophy is one of the sources of Sartre's existentialism. In the passage above, Gunn describes motorcycle and rider as "hurler and hurled," a centaurlike fusion of man and machine where both entities control forward motion through a terrain, though neither does so entirely. When Gunn says that the riders are "astride the created will," he attributes an existential agency to the machine, and we can't fail to see a sexual suggestion as well. The ancient sexual content implicit in the figure of the rider and his mount has here been adapted for a riding machine.

There is more. In Elizabethan English, "will" could refer to the penis, and any reader who knows this fact assumes that Gunn, a close student of Shakespeare, also knew it given that Shakespeare made several bawdy puns on his nickname "Will." That double meaning helps explain the emphasis throughout this volume on hardness and the implementation of desire (in Gunn's life and poetry, homosexual desire). Yet in an interview[8] Gunn said he was not aware of the double meaning until the early 1960s. Even so, he acknowledges the connection: "Obviously there [is] a sexual connotation to it, like in my first two books *Fighting Terms* and [*The*] *Sense of Movement,* but I didn't know this until the '60s." So then Gunn did come to see the "sexual connotation" in his use of the word while still denying that he intended it. How to resolve the paradox? Perhaps the double sense of the word "will" *was* in fact mentioned in Gunn's undergraduate courses, and then he forgot or repressed that knowledge while composing his early poems. A second possibility is that his recourse to the word in contexts involving sex reflects psychological symbols and archetypes intrinsic to human psychology in the Western tradition. These archetypes originated that double meaning for the Elizabethans, allowing it as well to operate unconsciously for others with no special knowledge of sixteenth-century English diction. I think I can let the case rest here without taking shelter under the embattled critic's favorite loophole, the Intentional Fallacy.

Incidental to the writing of Gunn's poems of the late 1950s and into the 1960s was a paradigm shift in what we might regard as the iconic representation of the male homosexual, a shift that began in America. An earlier model was the Aesthetic ideal pioneered by Walter Pater and Oscar Wilde, where a sensitive and artistic older man became the pedagogue and sexual partner of a beautiful boy. Both figures were soft, mild-mannered, and refined in speech, or, according to some judges, "effeminate." But this paradigm began to be supplanted in America and then in Europe when models such as Genet's fictional characters and actors such as Marlon Brando and James Dean came to be perceived as more potent and compelling than the older homosexual archetype. The new paradigm involved two grown men of roughly the same age, affecting working-class clothing like blue jeans, boots, and denim or leather jackets. They used rough, substandard diction and profanity, even if they had been brought up in middle-class environments. Instead of being soft-limbed, they lifted weights to increase muscle mass, and they did not try to be clean-shaven or even especially clean. By the end of the 1960s, they grew mustaches and beards. Any sign associated with masculine gender was accentuated, and working-class occupations and pastimes were valorized more than the middle-class equivalents. We see all of this prefigured in the poem "Market at Turk" cited above, where a male prostitute is described along with his alluring garb, a figure similar to the protagonist of John Rechy's *City of Night,* which was published a few years later.

Gunn, a product of the middle class and a gilt-edged university education, participated in this shift partly as an act of will, the application of his "theory of poses" and existential approaches to identity. We may say its manifestations in the poems of *The Sense of Movement* don't extend beyond subject matter; the diction and the approach to poetic form belong to an older, elevated tradition. But in subsequent books, Gunn begins moving toward informal diction, less exacting meter, and a preference for daily experience as opposed to literary allusion. I believe it's also true that his use of existentialism began to recede in importance for him, in part because Sartre's prestige began to decline around 1960. Meanwhile, the liberalizing of societal attitudes, as epitomized in the decriminalization of homosexuality, meant that it was no longer necessary to devise elaborate philosophical justifications for what more and more came to be viewed as a natural and nonpathological behavioral variant. Gunn remained an atheist as an existentialist must, but he was confronted with fewer and fewer instances where a choice could alter the entire direction of his life. He had forged the main outlines of his identity earlier on. The hard, muscled cuirass of the Roman centurion already existed, embodied in the form of his first books, a suit of armor that could be hung on a wall more for contemplation than for actual use. He could become more Californian, more pacific, more hedonist—at least until the AIDS epidemic of the 1980s arrived and drove him back to the stark contrast between life and death, Being and Nothingness.

Gunn, Shakespeare, and the Elizabethans

CLIVE WILMER

1

When Thom Gunn's mother committed suicide in 1943, he went to live with a pair of unmarried aunts. Charlotte Gunn had had six sisters, and these two ran a farm at Snodland in Kent. They had taken it over from their father, Alexander Thomson, whom Gunn's brother Ander remembers stuffing his boots with straw to keep out the cold. On weekdays, Gunn lodged in London at the home of a friend of his mother's so that he could carry on at the distinguished independent day-school he had been attending. Both school and lodging were in Hampstead, the most affluent and cultured of London suburbs, to which Snodland must have provided a marked contrast. Extremely run-down today, it was never well-off and was then half-agricultural and half-industrial: the town's main business was a cement works, which tended to coat the landscape in white dust. The aunts lived in a fairly ordinary nineteenth-century house, but the farm buildings were Elizabethan, and there was something about their way of life that must have reminded Gunn of an earlier time: an era of outlaws and pirates. The aunts were radical women with unconventional views. One of them had, in that most prim of eras, borne a child fathered by a passing soldier. For an upper-middle-class boy from a comfortable suburban background, a life in such a place must have included some feeling of adventure, and adventure is something Gunn's poetry is usually in quest of.

The Snodland farm perhaps helps to explain "At the Back of the North Wind,"[1] a beautiful but enigmatic poem that draws on a book of the same name by George MacDonald, a Victorian writer whose romances Gunn had enjoyed as a boy. But there is something in his weekly alternation between a formal and sophisticated modern life and this older pattern of living that points to the character of Gunn's imaginative world. He is rightly thought of as a poet of modern cities, but it was not for their rational order that he loved them: it was rather for their openness to the transient and unpredictable. And his poetry does have a rural dimension, too; it often celebrates a sort of pastoral utopia that is, on the one hand, Californian—much of *Moly,* for instance, and several poems from "The Geysers"[2]—and, on the other, timeless and placeless: indebted, I would guess, to his childhood reading, to the novels of MacDonald and E. Nesbit, and to Nathaniel Hawthorne's retellings of classical myths.[3] He liked artistic formality, but he liked his forms to contain, and indeed express, anarchic passions. I am trying to suggest not that life in rural Kent was anarchic but that it might have opened a youthful imagination to the timeless and unexpected, to the perennial patterns of human experience and its intermittent chaos. Gunn was living in Snodland when David Lean's film of *Great Expectations* was shot on nearby Romney Marsh. When the crew departed, a gibbet got left on the skyline, an image that haunted him long afterward and fed his imagination. That gibbet need not have been Victorian; it could have belonged to any time but the present. It could have belonged, as the farm buildings did, to Elizabethan Kent.

2

In an interview from 1992, Gunn touches on the relation of sophisticated tradition to pre-civilized imaginings:

> I've noticed recently I've been particularly attracted by various things in visual art or in poetry that I explain to myself as being a mixture of the extremely sophisticated and the primitive. I was just pointing out . . . some lines from Spenser's "Epithalamion." They're the ones about who is it "which at my window peeps." It is the moon, who "walks about high heaven all night." It's a wonderfully sophisticated and ornate kind of poetry, and suddenly this tremendously physical, almost anthropomorphic image of the moon walking around the sky. It's so magnificent! . . . I think that sometimes when my poetry comes off—anybody's poetry comes off—it's making use of two strengths at once: a very conscious arranging strength, keeping things in schematic form, but also the stuff you can call primitive or unconscious.[4]

Gunn's first book, *Fighting Terms* (1954), is full of such encounters—of the sophisticated with the primitive, of the skillfully ordered with the anarchic, of the tender with the violent. In "Looking Glass," there is the first of Gunn's many street people, "damp-booted, unemployed,"[5] imagining the order of a garden. In "The Wound,"[6] the modern conscript, compelled to serve against his will, is transformed by dream into the heroic Achilles, similarly devoid of loyalties, but also split apart by volcanic passions: "I was myself: subject to no man's breath: / My own commander was my enemy." The speaker's tenderness in "Tamer and Hawk"[7] declares itself through enslavement and predation. In "The Beach Head,"[8] the speaker courts a desired lover in the language of a military raid. But perhaps most revealing in the light of Gunn's comment about Edmund Spenser is "A Mirror for Poets,"[9] which evokes the classic era of our literature, an age whose most sophisticated, learned, and morally earnest poet, Ben Jonson, had his thumb "branded for manslaughter." There are no gibbets in the poem, but "Wheels, racks and fires / In every writer's mouth."

Jonson's age, of course, is Shakespeare's age, and Spenser's, as well. No period of English history is more packed with national icons and symbols, yet its energy seems to derive from something more elemental, even anarchic. It was, from early on, the world in which Gunn's imagination found its home. Everyone seems to agree that, in August Kleinzahler's words, "Gunn is an Elizabethan poet in modern dress."[10] For Michael Schmidt, "His English roots are deep in the sixteenth and seventeenth centuries," and the Elizabethan influence is apparent "even . . . in his . . . free-verse poems."[11] This influence is never academic: in Gunn's hands the inherited forms and conventions seem utterly natural and breathe with his own modernity. The "Street Song" from *Moly,* for instance, the spiel of a Californian dope-peddler, deliberately imitates Elizabethan song. In writing it, Gunn drew on a wonderful song of John Dowland's, "Fine knacks for Ladies,"[12] to which he had been introduced by Yvor Winters, who wrote about it with insight and contagious enthusiasm. Dowland's persona is also a peddler, another semi-anarchic character, who, beggar though he be, understands the nature of true love:[13]

> Fine knacks for ladies, cheap, choice, brave and new!
>   Good pennyworths! but money cannot move.
> I keep a fair but for the fair to view;
>   A beggar may be liberal of love.
> Though all my wares be trash, the heart is true.

As Winters points out, "The poem is not a street song; it is a poem on love and on the art of poetry and on a relationship between the two, and it is one of the most deeply serious and deeply moving short poems in the Elizabethan period—the peddler is purely metaphorical."[14] This is undoubtedly true, and no one who has heard the recording of the song by the great counter-tenor Alfred Deller or explored the poem's verbal ambiguities could doubt that it is a profoundly sophisticated work of art. But this is not to say that the peddler is unimportant. He calls himself a "beggar," and we are surely meant at some level to take that seriously—as Gunn undoubtedly would have done, given his lifelong interest in what he called "the life of the street."[15] A beggar, we realize, can understand the nature of true love, because he has nothing material to gain or lose by it. The rich man's generosity, by contrast, is often a means of gaining yet more power:

> Great gifts are guiles and look for gifts again;
>   My trifles come as treasures from my mind.
> It is a precious jewel to be plain . . .

It is here that the value of poetry comes in. In this most contrived of verbal arts, the speaker forgoes the power of language to deceive. Like Cordelia in *King Lear,* the truest lover is the plainest spoken, and Dowland's song would not be out of place in a Shakespeare play. It seems reasonable to assume that, just as the peddler is something more than a metaphor, the song has its origin in the street cries of Dowland's London. The same can be said for other songs of the period. Gunn also admired Thomas Campion, whose "Cherry Ripe"[16] is similarly based on the street cry, as are the songs of Autolycus, the singing peddler in *The Winter's Tale.* Autolycus is a rogue and a bit of an anarchist; Gunn's Midday Mick, we feel, would have something to say to him. Both men lay out their wares with unshakeable assurance, Mick calling out the names of his drugs—"Clara Green, Acapulco Gold, / Panama Red"—as Autolycus sings, like Dowland's beggar, of *his* fine knacks for ladies:[17]

> Golden quoifs and stomachers
> For my lads to give their dears:
> Pins and poking-sticks of steel,
> What maids lack from head to heel:
> Come buy of me, come! come buy! come buy!
> Buy, lads, or else your lasses cry.
> Come buy!

These songs—Shakespeare's and Dowland's and Campion's—thrive on the two combined strengths Gunn found in Spenser: "a very conscious arranging strength" together with "the primitive or unconscious."

True to that model, "Street Song" functions at a sophisticated level. From the outset the persona is both a drug-dealer "too young to grow a beard" and the Hermes of the epigraph to *Moly:* "in the likeness of a young man, the down just showing on his face."[18] Hermes is the messenger of the gods who travels through the universe from Olympus to the Underworld and back. The dealer has likewise visited other worlds:

> Call it heaven, call it hell,
> Join me and see the world I sell.
>
> Join me, and I will take you there,
> Your head will cut out from your hair
> Into whichever self you choose.[19]

Quite as much as Dowland's peddler, then, this is a tradesman who deals in the immaterial—not love in this case, but vision. But he is also quite literally a dealer and a Californian street boy, circa 1970. Students, in my experience, often read this poem moralistically, but it is neither a warning against drug-taking nor an apologia for it. Like all Gunn's poems, "Street Song," undoubtedly moral, is far from moralistic, part of its morality residing in its refusal to make judgments. In any event, such disputes only serve to confirm one's sense of the poem as dealing with the realities of contemporary life as much as with the timeless world of the gods. Its modernity is underpinned with Elizabethan resonance. There is the convention of the street song sung by a "sturdy vagabond." There is the meeting-place between order and anarchy. There is the rough-edged balladic meter, recalling such songs as Feste's in *Twelfth Night* or the Fool's in *Lear.* There is also something Shakespearean in the character: a young man poised between adolescence and maturity, "too young to grow a beard" yet active in the dangerous adult world: like Adonis in *Venus and Adonis,* like the young men Rosalind and Viola play at being, like the street-boys in Gunn's "Nasturtium"[20] or his very Elizabethan "San Francisco Streets"[21] from *The Passages of Joy:*

> Fuzz is still on the peach,
>   Peach on the stem.

Your looks looked after you.
    Look after them.

That Gunn's Elizabethan roots, as Schmidt remarked, are as apparent in his free verse as in these songs can be seen in another poem from *The Passages of Joy,* "Sweet Things,"[22] as also in an earlier one, "An Amorous Debate"[23] from *Jack Straw's Castle.* The latter is a complex literary joke, packed with literary reminiscence. Its rambling free-verse manner owes something to Edward Dorn's mock-epic *Gunslinger,* whose Wild West protagonist is also a knight-errant from medieval romance. Gunn's modern lovers similarly recall the world of the Renaissance love poet with his logic-chopping metaphysical bent. The opening lines—

Birds whistled, all
Nature was doing something while
Leather Kid and Fleshly
lay on a bank and
gleamingly discoursed

—hint at the setting of John Donne's "The Extasie": in both poems a swelling bank does service for a bed, which appears to be a part of the convention.[24] And the ending, where the lovers melt "one into the other . . . the way the Saône / joins the Rhône at Lyon," seems to draw on a poem of the early French Renaissance by Maurice Scève (1501?–ca. 1563), one of those poems in which an erotic analogy is used, as in much of Donne, to evoke divine union:

    N'apperçoy tu de l'Occident le Rhosne
Se destourner et vers Midy courir,
Pour seulement se conjoindre à sa Saone
Jusqu'à leur Mer, ou tous deux vont mourir?[25]

The speakers of Donne's amorous discourse and others like it—Andrew Marvell's "To His Coy Mistress," for example—are preternaturally articulate young men who will use every trick in the philosophical book to persuade their ladies how right it would be to sleep with them. As my description suggests, there is often a note of parody or irony in such poems. Gunn takes this further by turning discourse into dialogue. It is a "debate" in which the woman, Fleshly, has more to say than the man, Leather Kid, though he, as we soon discover, needs no persuading. Like

Dowland's peddler, he favors the plain style: "Let's fuck" is his response to Fleshly's ornate overture. As things turn out, however, his body is less committed than his mind: his passion is for himself, and, despite the masculine armor ("the obduracy of leather") and the "hard cock," he is very far from being a manly man. He is perhaps, like Shakespeare's many narcissists, "sick of self-love."[26] As with Adonis, Bassanio, and the young man of the Sonnets, there is something sexually ambiguous about him—and in this he resembles Gunn's pubescent street-boys. The leather armor looks back to the bikers of "On the Move"[27] and "Black Jackets,"[28] to say nothing of more metaphorical kinds: the "resilient chilly / hardness" of the speaker in "Touch,"[29] for example.

The model for Gunn's use of dialogue is probably Shakespeare's *Venus and Adonis*. There, too, Venus reclines on a "primrose bank" and urges Adonis to "Bid me discourse." She does so "gleamingly": "Love is a spirit all compact of fire, / Not gross to sink, but light, and will aspire."[30] But Venus is nothing like so ideal a lover as her discourse suggests. As with Gunn's lovers, it is she who is the sexual aggressor—the Goddess of Love, no less—while the object of her attraction is one of Shakespeare's many young men who, addicted to masculine pursuits—war or, in this case, hunting—are wary of the bedroom. Leather Kid is not exactly wary, but the passionate embrace that, unlike Adonis, he happily submits to, concludes with him sucking at "the nearest flesh to / his mouth which turned out / to be his own arm." It is here that Adonis *is* comparable. Venus, conscious of having all the qualities a red-blooded male could desire, identifies Adonis's aversion with self-love:

> Is thine own heart to thine own face affected?
> Can thy right hand seize love upon thy left?
> Then woo thyself, be of thyself rejected;
> Steal thine own freedom, and complain on theft.
>   Narcissus so himself himself forsook,
>   And died to kiss his shadow in the brook.

Adonis's self-love is captured here in the striking figure of epizeuxis—"himself himself"—the verbal equivalent of mirror-gazing. His narcissism, like Leather Kid's, seems to foreshadow homosexual desire and may be related to Gunn's obsession with doubles, most notably in "The Allegory of the Wolf Boy."[31]

The importance of *Venus and Adonis* to this discussion, however, lies most of all in the language of sexual desire. Sexual activity is characteristically play, desire is "hot courage" (l. 276), sexual indulgence is expressed in images of feeding, sexual advances in terms of war, conquest, looting, hunting, falconry, even murder—most strikingly, Venus "murders with a kiss" (l. 54). These are tropes that recur throughout Gunn's poetry, from the martial lovers of *Fighting Terms* to the cannibal Jeffrey Dahmer in "Troubadour,"[32] Gunn's last tribute to Elizabethan song.

The relevance of Elizabethan poetry to "An Amorous Debate" is clear from the first line. "Sweet Things" is nothing like as literary or self-conscious and much more simply rooted in modernity, though we may want to compare the "sweet things" of the title with the "honey secrets" (l. 16) offered by Venus to Adonis. It draws a humorous moral analogy between "mongoloid Don" with his self-indulgent love of candy and ice cream and the poet's lust for "a scrubbed cowboy." The poem is typical of the loose-limbed, streetwise free verse Gunn uses in *The Passages of Joy* to explore his urban cameos. The rhythms are conversational, the tone casual; line-endings in the manner of William Carlos Williams or Robert Creeley engender a sense of hesitancy, the search for meaning enacted in their hovering. As the significance of his narrative dawns on the lustful speaker, we get these lines:

> Boldly "How about now?" I say
> knowing the answer. My boy
> I could eat you whole. In the long pause
> I gaze at him up and down and
> from his blue sneakers back to the redawning
> one-sided smile. We know our charm.
> We know delay makes pleasure great.
> In our eyes, on our tongues,
> we savor the approaching delight
> of things we know yet are fresh always.
> Sweet things. Sweet things.

Crucial to the casually sinuous flow of this passage is the emergence into it of two brief sentences: "We know our charm. / We know delay makes pleasure great"—sentences as firmly set in iambic tetrameter as any line from Elizabethan poetry. It is not, of course, simply a matter of meter, but of a certain tone that is reinforced by the meter. A similar quality can be found in some lines from a song Gunn greatly admired, "Now winter nights enlarge" by Thomas Campion:[33]

This time doth well dispense
With lovers' long discourse.
Much speech hath some defence
Though beauty no remorse.

Campion's tone has the same anonymity as Gunn's,[34] the same tendency to reach away from the personal toward the general. In "Sweet Things," the "I" is precisely at this point replaced by "we," and the statements quoted are, like Campion's, truisms, but truisms (as the context reminds us) grounded in personal feeling and personal experience. The lines irresistibly call the songbooks to mind and link this transitory twentieth-century moment to the ancient traditions of love poetry, including those drawn on by Campion or by Shakespeare.[35]

What we see in both these poems, in their different ways, is how the informal manner of a distinctively modern and American kind of poem can be deepened and enriched by reference to the golden age of English poetry. The gain is the more remarkable since it brings such resonance to a body of writing that is candid about the subculture from which its author speaks. In the case of "An Amorous Debate" it is a matter of specific reminiscences. In "Sweet Things," perhaps more profoundly, it is the eruption of a certain tone embodied in particular rhythmic and formal devices. In either case, the allusion is effortless. Such effortlessness was due to profound knowledge: a knowledge not scholarly or encyclopaedic, but the product of a lifetime's engagement with specific poems read over and over again.

To take a third example, "Touch," mentioned above, is a free-verse poem about long-term lovers falling asleep and, in unconsciousness, rediscovering their closeness. Loose-limbed in structure though it is, it demands comparison with Donne's "The Good-Morrow," in which a pair of lovers wake, symbolically, to a new depth of union: "And now good morrow to our waking soules."[36] In "Touch," moreover, there is a striking use of what, when we read Donne, we think of as metaphysical imagery. Donne's poem, in his characteristic way, makes use of alchemy and voyages to the New World, much as elsewhere he refers to "[t]he New Philosophy."[37] By the end of "Touch," Gunn's lovers have sunk into "an old / big place" that "seeps / from our touch in / continuous creation."[38] That is to say, they continuously create it in their living. At the same time, "continuous creation" is one of the modern theories of the universe: what is sometimes called the Steady State theory, now superseded, I am told, by the Big Bang. If this were simply the substitution of self-consciously modern categories for sixteenth- or seventeenth-century ones, it would not be of much significance. (Some of the weaker poems in *The Sense of Movement* can be faulted for doing precisely that.) But in "Touch," Gunn created a poem that, modern in every aspect, is profoundly aware of the past. Hence the substitution of night for Donne's morning, of sleeping for his waking, and so on. Hence, even more important, where Donne gathers his thought into repeated complex stanzas, Gunn writes a poem of process, the thought groping through halting syntax and reaching out over awkward, indeed precipitous, enjambments:

> Meanwhile and slowly
> I feel a is it
> my own warmth surfacing or
> the ferment of your whole
> body . . .

This, too, is "continuous creation."

3

During his first Cambridge long vacation, Gunn read the whole of Shakespeare. "[D]oing that, [his supervisor] Helena Shire later remarked, adds a cubit to anybody's stature."[39] The quotation occurs in "Cambridge in the Fifties," one of three autobiographical essays Gunn wrote in the 1970s. It is striking how often the name Shakespeare occurs in them—as often, it seems, as the names of friends and relatives. In some sense, of course, as Gunn knew, a loved poet is always one's companion. "When I read (let's say) George Herbert," he once said, "I really do think of him as being some contemporary of mine."[40] Like many of us, Gunn first read Shakespeare as a schoolboy and reread him every year for the rest of his life. That is to say, he knew Shakespeare in his full inwardness longer, and possibly better, than he knew his closest friends. That is the nature of the literary life and not unique to Gunn. Nevertheless, he seems to have felt it more continuously and consistently than anyone I have known. "Donne and Shakespeare," he wrote, "spoke living language to me, and it was one I tried to turn to my own uses."[41] We should not be surprised, therefore, to find Shakespeare's language and versification organic to Gunn's use of modern English.

Gunn's sense of the vitality of Shakespeare was enhanced for him by an accidental circumstance of his undergraduate years. Student theater at

Cambridge is often ambitious, and those who do well in it often go on to theatrical careers. In Gunn's three years at the university, it produced some of the giants of late-twentieth-century British theater. It was presided over by George Rylands, one of the last alumni of the Bloomsbury Group, who both lectured at the university and directed plays professionally. His association with John Gielgud, notably in directing the latter's *Hamlet,* is legendary. Still more important was the presence among Gunn's contemporaries of Peter Hall and John Barton, both to be major figures in Shakespearean production. Performances of Shakespeare plays, both in the theater and on summer evenings in the college gardens, were among the enchantments of his happy Cambridge years. The star actor of that time was his close friend, Tony White, with whom he shared an enthusiasm for French literature. White played several major parts (in Gunn's phrase) "as romantic-existentialist characters,"[42] existentialism then being the intellectual fashion of contemporary Paris. Through his friendship with White, Gunn socialized with the dramatic fraternity and among them met Mike Kitay, his lifelong partner. No actor himself and, despite his love of dressing up, not histrionic in temperament, Gunn brought several theatrical notions over into his poetry: the notion, for instance, that to create an identity we adopt a pose—Achilles or the leather-jacketed biker. Shakespeare's plays themselves, moreover, are imbued with the suspicion that our lives are inseparable from ephemeral roles and "one man in his time plays many parts."[43] In the essay "Cambridge in the Fifties" Gunn relates his theory of the pose to "some of Shakespeare's characters, like the Bastard in *King John* and Coriolanus,"[44] and it is clear that White's dramatic performances fueled this sense of real life as a drama. His friends' Shakespeare productions gave compelling body to the very books he was reading with most excitement. There was moreover the opinion of his teachers—notably F. R. Leavis with his insistence on "realization" in literature—that books, as Gunn's mother had taught him in boyhood, were "not just a commentary on life but a part of its continuing activity."[45] That sense of continuity remained for him the determining value of poetry. It is impossible to imagine his account of a young man's sexual experiences without the example of Donne, or his response to the tragedy of AIDS without Ben Jonson. Overwhelmingly, though, the model is Shakespeare.

It is a paradox central to Gunn's poetry that, while he was often thematically concerned with the creation of identity—with the choice of self that is touched on in "Street Song"—he had no interest in creating a personal style or, to recall a cliché of the 1960s, in "finding his own voice."

Both Colin Falck and August Kleinzahler have related this anonymous manner to his love of the Elizabethans. In 1976, responding to the publication of *Jack Straw's Castle,* Falck made an astounding claim:

> Gunn has been accused of lacking poetic personality . . . but are we really so sure what poetic personality means, or why it matters?—what Shakespeare's poetic personality was . . . and whether the work we admire "him" for was good because of it, in spite of it, or quite independently of it? . . . The poet who has given us the lines of most near-to-Shakespearian power in twentieth-century English or American verse could well be Thom Gunn in "The Wound."[46]

As Falck goes on to imply, this is not a matter of nostalgia or pastiche. "The Wound" is from *Fighting Terms* (1954), and the predominant manner of that book—as of, to some extent, *The Sense of Movement* (1957)—was anti-Romantic in its distancing. Falck refers to "Gunn's speciality of using ceremonious forms in an insolently ill-made way and with a flat modern content." I am not sure he was being quite so self-consciously Movement-ish as that sort of language suggests, but it is almost true to say, as Falck does, that "'The Wound' is the great exception in Gunn's early verse, the only poem where he commits himself straight out to poetic intensity." I would want to add a few others, "Incident on a Journey" and "Tamer and Hawk," in particular, but it is certainly the case that "The Wound" goes all out for the heroic manner and achieves it, despite the fact that the Achilles figure at its center is shadowed by—to quote from another of the poems—"A clumsy brute in uniform":[47] the bored, unheroic, modern National Serviceman that Sergeant Gunn had recently been. That figure, from whose dreams the noble language springs, guarantees that at some level this poem remains a modern one. The method of the poem is modern, too. The complex metaphor of the wound in the head may recall a Donne conceit or an extended metaphor in a Shakespeare soliloquy, but it has also been filtered through the poetry of Yeats, which Gunn had only recently discovered. It is really a Yeatsian image, unanchored and allowed a kind of symbolist associativeness.

The key to the poem, however, is in Shakespeare, who provides not only its heroic language and postures but its Yeatsian "mythology," the body of narrative expectation the poem is free to allude to. It takes its account of the Trojan War not from Homer but from *Troilus and Cressida,* a play whose importance for Gunn is underscored by the epigraph to the first part of *My Sad Captains* (1961), which comes from a speech by Troilus:

"The will is infinite and the execution confined, the desire is boundless and the act a slave to limit."[48]

Those lines occur in act 3, scene 2: an amorous debate between Cressida and Troilus. Equipped with the Petrarchan rhetoric of a Romeo, Troilus is surprised to discover—like Gunn's Fleshly—that Cressida does not need very much persuasion. As the words "will" and "desire" suggest, the ideally philosophical and the bluntly sexual (near-relatives, perhaps, of the sophisticated and the primitive) are constantly colliding in this play. In the scene in question, Troilus reflects on the nature of romantic love, much as Romeo does, but with the difference that his use of "will" includes its cruder meanings, libidinous or genital; and for the acts that follow from those meanings, the lady Cressida is readier than he is. As Troilus makes his lengthy vows of truth, she twice interrupts with "Will you walk in, my lord?"—which is only a milder version of "Let's fuck." At the same time, the words "will," "execution," "desire," and "act"—or "deed," to give a frequent synonym—bear further significances, both political and military, in the play. *Troilus and Cressida* is about a war in which sex and ideas of honor are at issue.

Almost uniquely among poets of our era, Gunn is preoccupied with masculine honor and personal courage, and the capacity for risk, much celebrated in his poems, is intimately bound up with desire. These, surely, are the issues he brings over from *Troilus* into "The Wound." As Falck suggests, the first thing that reminds us of Shakespeare in the poem is its rhetorical power. Despite a touch of Yeatsian obscurity, the symbolism is reasonably clear: the wound is the self-division in the consciousness of the speaker, a soldier who "fought in turn / On both sides" of what turns out to be the Trojan War. His diffused identity is stabilized by rest, in suspended action and in dream, so that midway through the poem he can proclaim, glorying in existential freedom: "I was myself: subject to no man's breath: / My own commander was my enemy." That newly firm self occupies Achilles' tent, but when the news comes of Patroclus's death, he is thrown back into conflict. He leaps into action—

> But, when I thought, rage at his noble pain
> Flew to my head, and turning I could feel
> My wound break open wide.

Somewhere between dream and action and "between the thought and felt,"[49] he is hurled back into passive suffering. Readers aware of Gunn's homosexuality and the double life he had to live in that repressive era, will wonder if the conflicts are not between actual and desired selves, between the self he was and the self he had to appear to be, between a masculine self and a self whose gender is strangely undefined, though the poem says nothing directly to validate such interpretations.

It is here that the Shakespearean context proves illuminating. Achilles in *Troilus and Cressida,* it will be recalled, is refusing to participate in the war and devotes his languorously vacant days to play with his friend Patroclus. It is in the presence of Patroclus that Ulysses strikes a blow at Achilles' pride. He reminds him how a heroic reputation, if not renewed in action, can evaporate; he taunts him, moreover, with the news that the Greeks have adopted Ajax rather than himself as their champion to meet Hector in single combat. When Ulysses leaves, Patroclus turns to Achilles:

PATROCLUS: To this effect, Achilles, have I mov'd you.
A woman impudent and mannish grown
Is not more loath'd than an effeminate man
In time of action. I stand condemn'd for this:
They think my little stomach to the war
And your great love to me restrains you thus.
Sweet, rouse yourself; and the weak wanton Cupid
Shall from your neck unloose his amorous fold,
And, like a dew-drop from the lion's mane,
Be shook to air.
ACHILLES: Shall Ajax fight with Hector?
PATROCLUS: Ay, and perhaps receive much honour by him.
ACHILLES: I see my reputation is at stake:
My fame is shrewdly gor'd.
PATROCLUS: O, then, beware:
Those wounds heal ill that men do give themselves.
Omission to do what is necessary
Seals a commission to a blank of danger;
And danger, like an ague, subtly taints
Even then when we sit idly in the sun.
ACHILLES: Go call Thersites hither, sweet Patroclus:
I'll send the fool to Ajax and desire him
To invite the Trojan lords after the combat
To see us here unarm'd: I have a woman's longing,
An appetite that I am sick withal,
To see great Hector in his weeds of peace,

> To talk with him and to behold his visage,
> Even to my full of view.[50]

I can think of nothing that better demonstrates the intimacy of Gunn's identification with Shakespeare. It is not that he takes on Shakespeare's matter wholesale. On the contrary, the meaning of Achilles' wound in *Troilus* is quite different from that of Gunn's persona, and, fine as Shakespeare's conceit is here, it is not elaborate, while the development of Gunn's creates the substance of his poem. It is rather that Gunn picks up hints from Shakespeare that he elaborates in his own way, though the way is somehow congruent with their source. Patroclus, for example, has often been called Achilles' catamite. Though *The Iliad* gives little justification for such a view, Shakespeare is clearly conscious of it, allowing Thersites to refer to Patroclus as Achilles' "masculine whore."[51] The passage I have quoted is dense with homosexual feeling. Achilles' inactivity, says Patroclus, seems loathsomely "effeminate," and he lays the blame on their relationship: the other generals think "your great love to me restrains you thus." He then goes on to speak of the power over Achilles of "wanton Cupid." The editor of the Arden edition, Kenneth Palmer, is confident about the meaning of this sentence. Ulysses has just taxed Achilles with trying to win the hand of a Trojan princess: "Patroclus," Palmer insists, "is pleading that Polyxena should be abandoned: he is not referring to himself, nor to Achilles' affection for him."[52] No doubt there is good reason for this reading, but it must be admitted that the sense is at least ambiguous, with Cupid following so swiftly on Patroclus's use of the endearment "Sweet." And further homoerotic resonances follow as by contagion: Achilles, for instance, has "a woman's longing" for "the Trojan lords . . . / To see us here unarm'd."

But there is a deep complexity lodged in all of this, one that is not only fundamental to our understanding of homosexuality but at the heart, I would argue, of Western civilization. What is it to be effeminate? Why are the endearments expressed by Achilles and Patroclus so feminine in feeling? Why are Achilles' inactivity and his longing to meet his enemies seen as woman-like behavior? Homer's world, one would have thought, is almost exclusively masculine, and Achilles exemplifies the masculine ideal of the warrior. One can see that to depart from that ideal might be thought effeminate, yet it is also true that such behavior seems a consequence of the masculine culture: brothers-in-arms become attached to one another. It is also the case—in the classical world the Renaissance looked to, as well as in Renaissance Europe itself—that all-consuming sexual passion in men was considered effeminate, even when that passion was heterosexual. Sensitivity to such a charge is implicit, for instance, in the poems of Catullus. So we arrive at a paradoxical situation in which men, at their most masculine—whether as soldiers or as passionate lovers—are thought of as effeminate. In that context, the address of Shakespeare's sonnets to a young man, though it has a striking precedent in the poems of Michelangelo, is of peculiar interest, the love-sonnet having been a medium, by and large, for the expression of obsessive heterosexual desire. Reviewing *The Passages of Joy,* Donald Davie, a critic normally sympathetic to Gunn, complained that the overt homosexuality of the later work entailed "the sacrifice . . . of any profound resonances" from earlier periods of English poetry.[53] This might be thought a puzzling remark, and Gunn responded to it trenchantly:[54]

> I don't see that at all, and I don't quite understand how it operates in his mind, as if the subject matter were so *modern* that there can be no influence from any poet earlier than (I think he says) Whitman. Well there *is* Marlowe! There are others who one knows were homosexual. There are also most of Shakespeare's sonnets. We don't know what Shakespeare's primary sexual preferences were, but he does rather more than take up the subject. So it's not without precedents.

In the early 1950s, gay men were almost universally imagined as effeminate in manner.[55] There is much here, it is true, about effeminacy, but the context otherwise could hardly be more masculine, and it was always the masculine that excited Gunn—sexually, socially, and in his use of language. Sexual ambiguity is at issue in the Achilles scenes from *Troilus,* a play in which the stereotypical behavior of both sexes is problematized, as it is rather less disturbingly in, say, *As You Like It* and *Twelfth Night.* We are less likely to notice it in the mature tragedies, yet a non-effeminate masculinity nonetheless touched with homoerotic feeling seems to have been present for Gunn in other plays, most compellingly in *Coriolanus.* Gunn's list of Tony White's "romantic-existentialist" performances begins with his Aufidius,[56] and the relationship between Aufidius and Coriolanus was still exemplary for him in a 1992 interview. Talking of the relationship in his poems between violence and tenderness, he quoted from "The Missing,"[57] with its lament for "'the gay community' (a phrase I always thought was bullshit, until the thing was vanishing)":

> I did not just feel ease, though comfortable:
> Aggressive as in some ideal of sport,

With ceaseless movement thrilling through the whole,
Their push kept me as firm as their support.

And he commented:

> If you use the idea of sport, you think of the violence of the push, yes, but there's an ambiguity: an embrace can be a wrestler's embrace or it can be an embrace of love. . . . [I]f you look at it at any one moment, if it's frozen, it could be either, and maybe the two figures swaying in that embrace are not even quite sure which it is. Like Aufidius and Coriolanus: they embrace, they're enemies. They embrace in admiration at one point. . . . It could turn, at any moment, from the one to the other, I suppose.[58]

The bond between the two warriors has many resonances. There is, for instance, as in "The Wound," a sense of the soldier whose loyalty is to honor and emotion rather than to nation or any other conception of community. Coriolanus *seems* the noble Roman hero, but when the chips are down it is his own honor that concerns him, which makes it possible, where Aufidius is concerned, for respectful enmity to be reconfigured as admiring friendship. Still more important is the reversion to enmity at the end:

AUFIDIUS: Ay, Martius, Caius Martius! Dost thou think
I'll grace thee with that robbery, thy stol'n name
Coriolanus, in Corioles?
You lords and heads o' th' state, perfidiously
He has betray'd your business, and given up,
For certain drops of salt, your city Rome,
I say "your city," to his wife and mother;
Breaking his oath and resolution, like
A twist of rotten silk, never admitting
Counsel o' th' war: but at his nurse's tears
He whin'd and roar'd away your victory,
That pages blush'd at him and men of heart
Look'd wondering each at others.
CORIOLANUS: Hear'st thou, Mars?
AUFIDIUS: Name not the god, thou boy of tears![59]

As a soldier, Aufidius is a devotee of Mars, whose name is at the root of Martius, his rival's "surname" (i.e., the Roman *nomen*, the name of the *gens* or tribe, inherited through the father). Coriolanus has betrayed the male line and the masculine deity. So the tough soldier's contempt for "the boy of tears" is contempt for a man who has given in to his mother. The subject of Gunn's own mother, his loyalty to her memory and her role in his poetry, is something I have dealt with elsewhere, but, for the present purpose, it should be kept in mind that he broadly accepted the myth of the gay male as mother's boy.[60] In "Rites of Passage," that Freudian version of Shakespeare's Ovid, he names his Muse:

> I stamp upon the earth
> A message to my mother.
> And then I lower my horns.

If that is first of all a message to Mother Earth, it also refers to his lifelong communication with the buried woman who governed his life.[61] Volumnia in *Coriolanus* accuses her son, in attacking his native country, of treading "on thy mother's womb / That brought thee to this world."[62]

It is in Gunn's first three books that allusions to Shakespeare and variations on his themes are at their most specific. "Carnal Knowledge" includes fashionably Eliotesque "quotations" from *Othello, Lear,* and *Julius Caesar.* [63] Though the reference to John a Gaunt in "The Beach Head" has nothing to do with his role in *Richard II,* the dramatic pose of the poem recalls the cocky and "self-fashioned" Shakespearean loner,[64] the Bastard in *King John,* say, or, more negatively, Edmund in *King Lear,* who also stands behind "A Village Edmund," a ludicrous piece of self-parody, which after the first edition of *Fighting Terms* disappeared from the canon.[65]

I have already discussed "The Wound," and I shall shortly be looking at "Tamer and Hawk," with its very Shakespearean metaphor from falconry.[66] That poem shares a strategy with "During an Absence,"[67] which builds an elaborate conceit out of *Romeo and Juliet.* But, as in "The Wound," it is Shakespeare's Greek and Roman plays that seem the most obsessive of his sources. Brutus, Mark Antony, and Coriolanus occur in "A Plan of Self-Subjection," "Vox Humana," "Claus von Stauffenberg," and "My Sad Captains."[68] The sexually ambiguous figure of Alexander the Great falls into the same penumbra as these other classical heroes, also cropping up in "Lines for a Book" and "From an Asian Tent."[69] In "A Plan of Self-Subjection," Gunn draws several of them together:

> As Alexander or Mark Antony
> Or Coriolanus, whom I most admire,
> I mask self-flattery.

And yet however much I may aspire
I stay myself—no perfect king or lover
Or stoic. Even this becomes unreal.
Each tainted with the other
Becomes diseased, both self and self's ideal.

Shakespeare and the classical heroes associated with him become, for Gunn, the poet, much as they had for the actor Tony White, paradigms for a certain way of life: masculine, courageous, resilient, without self-regard or self-pity, with even a touch of asceticism. The further characteristic one now assumes, unstated in those more inhibited times, is homosexual desire—a secret desire for the hardness that in moral and aesthetic terms is openly admired.

It is not difficult to imagine how exciting it must have been for a gay man coming to maturity in the 1950s to discover that the greatest poet in our language may sometimes have written out of homosexual feelings. For one thing, the contempt for "fags" and "queers" in that now-distant era was all but universal, and a young man with Gunn's sense of dignity, who had learnt through his mother's suicide the value of self-containment, must have rejoiced at the thought that a figure so universally honored might have felt much the same as he did. Among the "few with historical / names" he summons along with his friends in "My Sad Captains," Shakespeare must have been prominent. The sense of belonging to a secret fraternity of honor must have been enhanced by what now seems the extraordinary silence of that time on sexual matters in general, but especially where Shakespeare was concerned. When I interviewed Gunn for *The Paris Review* in 1992, I asked him about his insistent use of the word "will" in his early poems and Shakespeare's persistent, obsessive play on the word's sexual meanings, notably in the sonnets. He replied:

> I didn't find out till years later that when Shakespeare uses the word *will* it means the penis. I don't think we had adequately footnoted editions of the sonnets in those days, because I read through all the footnotes in my edition . . .
>
> INTERVIEWER: But do you think it's significant none the less?
>
> GUNN: Yes, I do. So I was getting it unconsciously. But I don't think I found out until my thirties. I was astonished when I did![70]

Once he had come out as gay in the 1970s, Gunn defended his silence on the matter of his sexuality by referring to the oppressions of the law, but he very much regretted those silences. This is understandable, but what he regretted as a gay man we need not regret as his readers. His participation in the conspiracy of silence, however unwilling, produced some of his finest discoveries. Two of the poems mentioned above, "During an Absence" and "Tamer and Hawk," might be said to gain from a mismatch between overtly heterosexual vehicle and covertly homosexual tenor. In the best analogies, it should be stressed, the incomparable element is as valuable as that which is compared. "During an Absence" uses the comparison with Shakespeare's play to *contrast* the speaker's love and Romeo's; "Tamer and Hawk," written when Gunn was an undergraduate but among his very finest performances, develops a metaphor from the sport of falconry, a range of imagery that inevitably calls Shakespeare to mind.[71] It will be useful to cite a few examples. The sport provides powerful metaphors for sexual predation in both *Venus and Adonis* and *The Rape of Lucrece.* But it is images of taming and of wildness that bear most on "Tamer and Hawk." In *The Taming of the Shrew,* for instance, Petruchio outlines a plan to bring his wife to heel; he will tame her much as falconers tame hawks—deprive her of food and sleep until she needs him.[72]

> Thus have I politicly begun my reign,
> And 'tis my hope to end successfully.
> My falcon now is sharp and passing empty,
> And till she stoop she must not be full-gorg'd,
> For then she never looks upon her lure.
> Another way I have to man my haggard,
> To make her come and know her keeper's call,
> That is, to watch her, as we watch these kites
> That bate and beat and will not be obedient.
> She ate no meat today, nor none shall eat;
> Last night she slept not, nor tonight she shall not. . . .
> He that knows better how to tame a shrew,
> Now let him speak: 'tis charity to show.

The untamed bird, the "haggard," provides Shakespeare with many images. It belongs to the world of amorous discourse, a metaphor for the proud woman resistant to male charms. Beatrice in *Much Ado about Nothing,* for example, is not exactly a shrew, but the sharpness of her wit holds men at bay. As Hero says,

[S]he is too disdainful.
I know her spirits are as coy and wild
As haggards of the rock.[73]

Most memorable of all is Othello, persuading himself that his wife, who appears so true, is actually "wild":

If I do prove her haggard,
Though that her jesses were my dear heart-strings,
I'd whistle her off and let her down the wind
To prey at fortune.[74]

In all these cases, the problematic woman is conceived of as a falcon difficult or impossible to tame. The falcon's prey only comes into it in the last example, where "To prey at fortune" means to fend for oneself. In Gunn's poem, the terms are utterly different:

I thought I was so tough,
But gentled at your hands,
Cannot be quick enough
To fly for you and show
That when I go I go
At your commands.

. . . .

You but half-civilize,
Taming me in this way.
Through having only eyes
For you I fear to lose,
I lose to keep, and choose
Tamer as prey.

In Shakespeare it is the addressee—in his case, a woman—who is compared to the bird; in Gunn it is the male speaker—the equivalent of Petruchio or Othello. And the tamer instead—Petruchio or Othello or, by implication, Benedick—is given the role of the addressee, in effect the poet's heartless Muse. I doubt if many readers in 1954 realized that this was a poem of gay love, but most of us, I suspect, sensed something irregular in it. The irregularity would have focused itself in the poem's sadomasochistic implications. The lyrical beauty of the versification—has any modern poet ever sounded so like an Elizabethan songwriter without actually writing mere pastiche?—is expressive of tenderness and close bonding. Yet the poem speaks of predation, and any faithful paraphrase would draw attention to cruelty, power, and violence. It belongs to the sensibility Gunn associates with *Coriolanus:* "an embrace can be a wrestler's embrace or . . . an embrace of love." This surely reveals the secret of Gunn's capacity to occupy Elizabethan modes without a hint of academic exercise. It is as if he takes a cue from Shakespeare—from *Coriolanus,* from *Troilus,* from *Venus and Adonis*—and develops it in a language and form, which, naturally modern, has roots in Elizabethan manners and modes. But where Shakespeare's conventions assume a "straight" society, Gunn adapts them to specifically gay themes. Not that he thought of his work as "gay poetry." He rejoiced in the successes of Gay Liberation, but resisted the poetry of identity politics. As he wrote of Robert Duncan:

> [H]omosexuality is as central to Duncan's poetry, to its origins and its realization, as it is to Marlowe's or Whitman's, whose work can hardly be discussed comprehensively without taking account of it. Yet, as I have implied, he is no more than they *merely* a Gay Poet, sexuality being only an important part of his whole subject-matter.[75]

To take this argument further, no one could ever claim Shakespeare as a writer defined by a specific sexuality, though sexual ambiguity, I would argue, is near the heart of his work. Indeed, a case could be made for saying that Shakespeare's ambiguity is the very thing that makes him so universal. Gunn learned infinite things from Shakespeare—as most good English poets have—but this one seems to have been his own discovery.

4

The more one reads Thom Gunn's last book, *Boss Cupid* (2000), the clearer it is that he knew his work was over. This book, which begins with the *ars poetica* "Duncan," is the only one of his books to end, as Prospero ends *The Tempest,* with a farewell salutation to his audience: "A brief bow following on the final leap."[76] Moreover, *Boss Cupid* includes a number of poems—"To Cupid" and "A Wood Near Athens" notably—that are plainly intended to be read as summations. The latter poem is most visibly indebted to Dante, Pound, and Pound's versions of Cavalcanti, but its title quotes the setting of *A Midsummer Night's Dream,* and the movement of the verse is in the Shakespearean spirit. Like several other poems in *Boss Cupid*—"Abishag," quoted above, for instance—these summations are written in blank verse, not a form one associates with Gunn, but outstandingly Shakespeare's form and used by Gunn in the spirit of the master.

When his own mastery became a matter of reflex—as is often the case with poets in old age—Gunn came to be less dependent on his sources, though of course they continued to inform his work as deeply as they ever had. A final case in point would be a poem from the early 1980s: "Falstaff," the first in the sequence "Transients and Residents."[77] The relevance of Shakespeare's fat rogue to this candid and lively portrait of an old friend is at first sight fairly marginal. Falstaff does not wear a burnoose, though one can imagine him in something similar, and one takes it that so flowing a garment would sit well on his massive gut. There is also the sense of a life of revelry with little in the way of responsibilities and a gang of street boys to follow him around. All that is reasonably clear, but perhaps there is more. We learn that Gunn's "Old friend" is in decline, suffering from cancer and, with age, losing his magnetism: not discarded by Prince Hal exactly, but discarded nonetheless, pushed aside by the processes of life. And we may read that interpretation back into *Henry IV*, part 2, first because Falstaff is more than a character: the old anarchist is a life-force, and his dismissal stands in part for Hal's maturation—his recognition of the need for order and his growth away from the phase for which, in imagination, Falstaff stands. Behind that suggestion is a further one: that the bond between Falstaff and Hal, as much competitive as affectionate, and based on the complex relations of father and son, is like a relationship between male lovers. This is, of course, not to say that that is what Shakespeare was trying to represent—though it might conceivably be so—but that, as Jorge Luis Borges put it, "each writer creates his precursors," and that the genuinely innovative poem, in Eliot's understanding of tradition, changes the "ideal order" of "the existing monuments."[78] The effect of Shakespeare on Gunn was so profound that, once Gunn's readers have noticed it, their reading of Shakespeare will be modified and, in the process, substantially enriched.

PART TWO

Across the Water

Thom Gunn: The Plain Style and the City

AUGUST KLEINZAHLER

It's closing on fourteen years now that I went to see Thom Gunn give a talk on Basil Bunting's long poem *Briggflatts*.[1] It was at an art space just south of Market on a little street called Natoma.[2] I found it incongruous not only that Thom Gunn would be speaking about Bunting but that either one of them should be given time at this particular venue, which usually devoted itself to Language poets who actually had some currency at the time, or the sort of stuff that sounds like Gertrude Stein on quaaludes, stretched out like taffy to great lengths.

I went, naturally, to hear what Gunn had to say about the poem. Bunting and *Briggflatts* were the poet and poem that had meant the most to me. But I was also there to make sure Bunting wasn't patronized by an establishment figure, an Oxbridge and Faber man who enjoyed prestige and a cushy university appointment while Bunting lived in council housing or in comparably meager circumstances, his work largely ignored.

I needn't have worried. Gunn's talk was of the first order. His reading of the poem was close, appreciative, and smart. The critical voice was modest. Gunn resisted the broad claims that usually attend the reexamination of neglected figures, particularly those identified with the avant-garde. He located the poem in a tradition, pointed out its virtues, explained what the poet was up to, and, in general, recommended reading it in very strong, if understated, terms. I was deeply impressed. I wrote to Bunting about the talk. He replied, in essence, *go figure*, but was probably pleased. Bunting would have been hard-pressed to say anything appreciative about a *Sothron*, an Englishman from the south, who couldn't hear his northern music and would *maul* the poem in reading it aloud.

The reason I mention this episode, apart from disclosing my own, highly localized silliness, is that my attitude was symptomatic of a larger condition, a condition that has to do with canons. Bunting belonged to the avant-garde, or had at least allowed himself to be taken up by the American *outsiders* like Robert Creeley, Allen Ginsberg, et al. Gunn did not. It might be noted here in passing that Bunting thought Charles Olson was a charlatan, could make neither heads nor tails of Robert Duncan, who adored Bunting's work, had no interest whatsoever in the Beats, though he was personally fond of Ginsberg, and certainly didn't cotton to Ashbery and O'Hara. No, his allegiances were to an older outsider tradition: Pound, Eliot, Williams, Zukofsky, MacDiarmid, David Jones, Lorine Niedecker. He allowed himself to be taken up by the younger Americans and enjoyed their company for the most part, but had little interest in their work. He was a tough, canny old survivor, and he got lucrative, easy work on this side of the Atlantic.

Canons are insidious things, and no one more than Thom Gunn in his critical writings has tried harder to subvert and extend them, at least official canons. And none of the canons is more religiously strict than the *outsider* or *avant-garde* tradition. Which can generate strange results in strange places: I remember as a student in British Columbia, where I studied with Bunting, the head of the creative writing department told his classes that Bunting was a fond old man full of tales (read: *no talent*) and a "creation of the Black Mountain School, no more." Ah, life in the provinces . . .

I certainly wanted to have another look at Gunn's work after that talk. I had a vague notion of his poetry from anthologies, poems that, quite frankly, struck me as rather fussy and elevated in tone. And terribly formal, which is not at all a welcome posture among those of my generation who cut their teeth on W. C. Williams and Donald Allen's anthology, *New American Poetry* (1960).

A collected poems is a revealing document, nothing at all like a selected, which takes the reader from showpiece to showpiece, with empty space between. It can be fatally revealing, especially if the poet has repeated himself for thirty-five years, which is more often the case than not, or if the mannerisms have hardened over time and glisten, like amber, in the sunlight forty years hence. Bunting wrote, bleakly, in the preface to his own *Collected*: "A man who collects his poems screws together the boards of his coffin. Those outside will have all the fun, but he is entitled to his last confession."

Gunn's sources will seem remote to the contemporary reader of poetry, I think, especially the younger reader. However the Weltschmerz of postwar Britain may have diffused into literary culture, certain tendencies are clearly evident in the early poetry of Gunn and in the work of his older contemporaries, like Philip Larkin, who were grouped together, however artificially, as poets of the Movement. If there was one writer the younger poets were trying *not* to sound like it was Dylan Thomas, first and foremost. Reaction had set in against his overheated rhetoric and what one commentator called his "Id-Romanticism," likewise the New Apocalypse poets who published in *Poetry London* in the 1940s. The younger poets were aiming for a poetry that was tough, lean, smart, and up-to-date. The inclination was strongly nativist, which for Gunn meant the Elizabethans and the ballads, and, out of the ballads, Thomas Hardy. Of the older living poets, Gunn was strongly attracted to Auden, for his wit (in the old sense of the word), mastery of forms, and the fact that he was accessible and of his time.

It's bracing to read F. R. Leavis for the first time after some twenty years of post-structuralist fluff, pirouetting, and contempt for the text. Whether one agrees with him or not, the seriousness and muscular intelligence of his arguments are palpable in the syntax. Gunn attended Leavis's lectures at Cambridge in the early '50s. Leavis argued for a poetry of the waking world, for the movement of modern speech. He liked clear edges, the exercising of intelligence and will. His thrust was away from Romanticism, especially from Romanticism's influence on Victorian and Pre-Raphaelite poetry. What he seems to have detested most was the cloudy, languid dream-world of poetry. And what he championed was a poetry of passionate intellectual interest, bare and subtle, responsive to the age in which it was written, and expressed in the idiom and the rhythms of that age. Sounds modernist, doesn't it? Well, yes and no. In any case, when Gunn's first book came out in 1954, poems he'd written as an undergraduate, the voice and forms were decidedly traditional and the attitudes and subject matter very *now*, for then.

The popular line on Gunn's poetry, trotted out as recently as this past summer by A. Alvarez, in a review of Gunn's *Collected Poems* in the *New Yorker*, is that his first book, *Fighting Terms*, and his next, *The Sense of Movement*, established him as the young lion among poets of his generation; that he came unglued, rather lost, after his move to the States, and with his 1971 collection, *Moly*, had utterly gone down the tubes.[3] Here is Edward Lucie-Smith from the 1970 Penguin collection *British Poetry since 1945*:

> Around 1960, it sometimes seemed as if all the poetry being written in England was being produced by a triple-headed creature called the "Larkin-Hughes-Gunn." Of this triumvirate it is Gunn whose reputation has worn

> least well. The youngest of the Movement poets, he established himself with his first volume, *Fighting Terms,* which appeared in 1954. A mixture of the literary and the violent, this appealed both to restless youth and academic middle-age. . . . Afterwards Gunn went to America.[4]

Kenneth McLeish, in another Penguin compendium, *Companion to the Arts in the Twentieth Century* (1986), writes:

> On present showing, Gunn is living proof of that sad cliché that first thoughts are always the best. . . . His collection *Fighting Terms* was one of the best poetry-books of its time: a combination of urgent style and that sparky, intellectual involvement with "issues" . . . . Gunn became a professor at Berkeley. He continued to publish . . . [but] only *My Sad Captains* (1961) contains anything to match . . . or remotely to rival his own spectacular early work.[5]

Fighting Terms is an extraordinarily accomplished, smart, and precocious performance by a university student. I can't believe that such a performance would even be conceivable today by one so young. Gunn was twenty-two when he entered university, having done his National Service and also having worked briefly in Paris. There is one fine example of his early style in the book, "The Wound," seamless in execution and convincing all the way through, but the poetry in the book is top-of-the-line juvenilia, interesting only with respect to the later work. In truth, very few actually read the book at the time (it was published in an edition of only three hundred copies), but it established his reputation, a reputation amplified and consolidated by *The Sense of Movement,* published by Faber in 1957. Gunn was now famous in England, but three years before he had moved to California, where he would, allegedly, begin his long decline, undone by sunshine, LSD, queer sex, and free verse.

The Sense of Movement is a broad advance but still a very long way from the accomplishment of his mature work. In this second book, Gunn is still awfully young, self-consciously smart, and tough. Young men can't help it. It's biological, like preening one's feathers. If you take a young man in his twenties who can throw a ball hard and far, he will find any excuse to throw that ball as hard and as fast as he can. He will throw it all the time if possible and talk about throwing it when he isn't. He will steer the conversation around to throwing the ball. He is on this earth to throw that ball.

If you have a young man who is unusually well-read and bright, and who has great fluency in the medium, well, he's going to show you just how smart he is and how well he can write. He will take it out on the track and show you how fast he can go from zero to sixty. Gunn would have been at Stanford when most of these poems were written, and studying with Yvor Winters. Winters, like Leavis, was another brilliant, forceful personality. Those types of individuals can be poison for young writers, but Gunn, as he would throughout his career, would take what he could use and move on. Part of his talent, or good fortune, from early on was to make good decisions, often tough ones. (Any poem, for instance, involves a series of hard decisions, sometimes rather daunting ones.)

Winters, like Leavis, very much believed in intellectual rigor in poetry, and moral penetration as well. Like Leavis, he was utterly serious about literature; it was the most important thing in the world. You get that from the writings of both men. Gunn would continue to pursue his interest in the Elizabethans and their successors, most significantly Ben Jonson and Fulke Greville. But he would at this point also be introduced to W. C. Williams and read, with more understanding and depth, Stevens, Pound, and other Americans.

The writing in *The Sense of Movement* is measurably crisper and more assured, also less rhetorical. Gunn starts out as a literary writer and remains so throughout his career, but the world in Gunn's first few books feels at a remove from the poetry. Later on, his reading and the world would come to inform one another with great effect, but not quite yet. What does begin to show clearly in the poetry is Gunn's fascination with the city as subject matter and his use of what is called the "plain style."

Gunn came to Baudelaire early, before Cambridge, and stayed with him. In an interview with Jim Powell in his collection of essays, *Shelf-Life,* Gunn mentions three poems of Baudelaire's that especially intrigued him, all poems from "Tableaux parisiens" in *Les fleurs du mal.* One is "Le cygne":[6]

> Le vieux Paris n'est plus (la forme d'une ville
> Change plus vite, hélas! que le coeur d'une mortel);
>
> Je ne vois qu'en esprit tout ce camp de baraques,
> Ces tas de chapiteaux ébauchés at de fûts,
> Les herbes, les gros blocs verdis par l'eau des flaques
> Et, brillant aux carreaux, le bric-à-brac confus.

Là s'étalait jadis une ménagerie;
Là je vis, un matin, à l'heure où sous les cieux
Froids et clair le Travail s'éveille, où la voirie
Pousse un sombre ouragan dans l'air silencieux,

Un cygne qui s'était évadé de sa cage,
Et, de ses pieds palmés frottant le pavé sec,
Sur le sol raboteux tranait son blanc plumage.
Près d'un ruisseau sans eau la bête ouvrant le bec

Baignait nerveusement ses ailes dans la poudre. . . .

The Paris of old is there no more—a city's shape
changes, alas, more swiftly than the human heart—

only in the mind's eye can I see those makeshift booths,
those piles of rough-hewn capitals and pillars,
the weeds, the massive blocks of stone stained green by puddles,
a jumble of bric-a-brac glittering in shopfronts.

A menagerie used to sprawl there,
where one morning at the hour when beneath the chill clear sky
Toil stirs from sleep, when the streetcleaners
fill the silent air with their miserable uproar,
I saw a swan who just escaped from his cage,
and was scraping the parched roadway with his webbed feet
as he went trailing his white wings on the rough ground.
Beside a dried-up gutter the poor creature, with gaping beak,
was frantically bathing his wings in the dust. . . .

Another is "Les petites vieilles":

Dans les plis sineaux des vieilles capitales,
Où tout, même l'horreur, tourne aux enchantements,
Je guette, obéissant à mes humeurs fatales,
Des êtres singuliers, décrépits et charmants.

Ces monstres disloqués furent jadis des femmes,
Éponine ou Läis! Monstres brisés, bossus

Ou tordus, aimons-les! Ce sont encore des âmes
Sous des jupons troués et sous de froids tissus

Ils rampent, flagellés par les bises iniques,
Frémissant au fracas roulant des omnibus,
Et serrant sur leur flanc, ainsi que des reliques,
Un petit sac brodé de fleurs ou de rébus. . . .

In the twisting folds of old capital cities,
where everything, even horror, turns to magic.
Obeying my irresistible impulses I spy
on odd, decrepit, charming creatures.

Let us love these disjointed freaks who were once women—
heroines, courtesans—broken down monsters, humped or distorted,
for they are still human souls.
Under their tattered skirts and flimsy garments

they crawl along, whipped by the malignant winds,
trembling at the din of buses thundering past,
clutching against their ribs, like holy relics,
their tiny handbags embroidered with flowers or puzzling
patterns. . . .

It would be difficult to overstate what Gunn drew from this sensibility about cities. This from his poem "In Praise of Cities" (from *The Sense of Movement*):

1

Indifferent to the indifference that conceived her,
Grown buxom in disorder now, she accepts
—Like dirt, strangers, or moss upon her churches—
Your tribute to the wharf of circumstance,
Rejected sidestreet, formal monument . . .
And, irresistible, the thoroughfare.

You welcome in her what remains to you;
And what is strange and what is incomplete
Compels a passion without understanding,
For all you cannot be.

2

Only at dawn
You might escape, she sleeps then for an hour:
Watch where she hardly breathes, spread out and cool,
Her pavements desolate in the dim dry air.

3

You stay. Yet she is occupied, apart.
Out of a mist the river turns to see
Whether you follow still. You stay. At evening
Your blood gains pace even as her blood does.

And from the last section:

4

She presses you with her hard ornaments,
Arcades, late movie shows, the piled lit windows
Of surplus stores. Here she is loveliest;
Extreme, material, and the work of man.

It is worth noting in passing that Gunn here is working in blank verse. He will not abandon rhyme, but he is beginning to stretch out at this point as well as find his subject matter. The city will become his central motif, character, and event being played out on its street-corners, in its rooms, bars, bathhouses, stairwells, taxis. There is also evidence in the 1957 book that Gunn is beginning, here and there, to relax toward his material, to drop the lofty, distanced tone and actually nose around a bit. He's getting interested, and the poetry is beginning to get interesting.

The plain style is what it sounds to be: unembellished, lucid; in diction and movement the way people speak. It doesn't call attention to itself but serves the material of the poem. Among the ancients, Horace, in his epistle to Florus, advises the poet "to master the rhythms and measures of a genuine life." Among sixteenth- and early-seventeenth-century writers, the term *plain style* distinguishes itself from the ornamental figures of the Petrarchan Style. Ben Jonson is probably its chief exemplar. Gunn likes no poet better.

The plain style, however, is not to be confused with the colloquial. And Gunn does not sound especially "plain" to the American reader. The diction is plain, the argument and exposition are clear, trim, and direct, but the tone is oddly formal to most American readers. Gunn's poems certainly don't sound the way Americans speak, for instance. He *is* English, after all, even after forty years in the United States. But he is not trying for the cadences of speech. Meter and rhyme notwithstanding, the *voice* feels alien; the *I* of the poetry carries almost no tangible personality. This can be upsetting to American readers acclimated to the dramatic personalities of recent poetry, Lowell, Berryman, Sexton, Ginsberg, et al. Even in Larkin, the poet who perhaps Gunn most resembles stylistically, there is a strong persona, no matter how stunted or obnoxious. This is by design in Gunn's poetry. The *I* in his poems is the disinterested *I* of the Elizabethans, and, going further back, the *I* of the ballads, and out of the ballads the *I* in Hardy's poetry. (Consider the *I* in *Briggflatts*, an "autobiography.") The *I* in Lowell or Ginsberg, say, is no less willed, and in no regard is it the *I* you'd encounter in conversation with them. But the American reader is accustomed to the illusion of familiarity, intimacy, and Gunn doesn't fork over. He tells us in one interview:

> People do have difficulties with my poetry, difficulties in locating the central voice or central personality. But I'm not aiming for central voice and I'm not aiming for central personality. I want to be an Elizabethan poet. I want to write with the same kind of anonymity that you get in the same way somebody like Ben Jonson did. At the same time I want to write in my own century.[7]

This seems to have upset many reviewers, American especially, of Gunn's poetry over the years. They suggest that Gunn is a very cold chap, indeed, an emotional husk of a man. Presumably, they want to know why he isn't coughing up his guts all over the page as is the custom in contemporary American poetry. Which brings us to the next part of the popular line on Gunn's career: after going to hell in America, squandering his poetic gifts, etc., Gunn was rehabilitated by the AIDS crisis and became an important poet once again because he became a *feeling* poet at last.

The truth is that the trajectory of Gunn's career can be easily enough charted and does not at all resemble what the self-perpetuating notions contend. He grows as a poet from book to book until he publishes *Moly* in 1971. You can see it coming from the poems in part 2 of *My Sad Captains*, in 1961, and in *Poems from the 1960s* in the *Collected*, but the advance to the plateau of *Moly* ten years later is startling. I suppose it's reasonable enough when you consider that Gunn was in his mid-thirties when he wrote *Moly*. His skills and intelligence were abundantly in evidence up to that point, but to this reader, at least, he was a very accomplished but not, for the most part, very interesting poet. One can speculate on the personal: he'd been through a bad bout of hepatitis; he'd quit his full-time job at Berkeley; he'd come out more publicly as a gay man; he'd been dropping acid. But plenty of artists pass through personal change, and their work is not better for it. Any number of Gunn's celebrated contemporaries had already fallen off badly and begun turning into cartoons of themselves and would stay cartoons through middle age. The mid-to-late thirties are pivotal years for an artist, for anyone, really. One can stop, consolidate, accrue interest—in effect, adding rooms on like the Winchester Mystery House. Or one can bet the whole pile and spin the wheel.

Whatever was left of Gunn's considerable late-fifties reputation in England, *Moly* finished it off. One reviewer there wrote: "Without exception the *Moly* poems are dead. Their failure is not essentially a feature of tone. They do not *smell*."[8] When he had sent some of these poems to Winters during the '60s, his old mentor wrote back that maybe he should try writing prose. Change has a cost, and from Winters he would have learned, if he didn't know it already, that career means nothing, only one's art and honesty in that art count for anything.

Moly begins dramatically with a poem of change, metamorphosis:

Rites of Passage

Something is taking place.
Horns bud bright in my hair.
My feet are turning hoof.
And Father, see my face
—Skin that was damp and fair
Is barklike and, feel, rough.

The transformation motif continues through the next poem, "Moly," and gains tremendous pitch through the movement within its couplets:

Into what bulk has method disappeared?
Like ham, streaked. I am gross—grey, gross, flap-eared.

The pale-lashed eyes my only human feature.
My teeth tear, tear. I am the snouted creature

That bites through anything, root, wire, or can.
If I was not afraid I'd eat a man.

Oh a man's flesh already is in mine.
Hand and foot poised for risk. Buried in swine.

I root and root, you think that it is greed,
It is, but I seek out a plant I need.

Direct me gods, whose changes are all holy,
To where it flickers deep in grass, the moly.

The mid-to-late 1960s generated a lot of junk in the arts, junk that really started piling up in the '70s. A loose man, given as much permission as he wants, will make a very loose poem. The '60s and '70s were a time of gross self-indulgence. And it should be remembered that most of what we associate with the best of avant-garde poetry in the late '60s was in fact written in the late '50s and early '60s: Ginsberg, Creeley, Olson, Ed Dorn, Frank O'Hara, Gary Snyder. Gunn, on the other hand, flourished: instead of going prolix and slack (listen to the ten-minute guitar riffs and saxophone solos of the era), he relaxed into his mature voice; a transformation had taken place.

His poetry could accommodate a bit of relaxing. He is still preeminently a poet of closure, intelligence, and will. There's not an aleatory bone in his body. He's Handel, not John Cage. Even in the free verse that had become part of his arsenal, the procedures are not all modernist: elliptical, in medias res, collage, fractured syntax—none of that. His free-verse poems have a beginning, a middle, and an end. They develop rationally. The diction remains *plain*, the *argument* direct; the subject matter is usually city life, often squalid, his characters the vulnerable, along the lines of Baudelaire's "Tableaux parisiens." Also the sexual: the city for Gunn, San Francisco, will become a kind of sexual New Jerusalem, a bit seedy around the edges. What has changed most demonstrably is Gunn's relation to his environment. We are no longer dealing so much with allegories or notions of the city or character: the poems are now trained on actual people and places. If formerly it sometimes seemed in the poetry that there was no *there* there, now the *there* there is very real. Winters felt the poetry had turned journalistic; he seems to have most enjoyed intellectual distance and abstraction, presumably so the mind had room to exercise itself. But if the world, in all its variety, has became a terribly interesting place, then one of the soundest artistic strategies is to clearly and honestly document it. Gunn does a great deal more than that, but the poems from *Moly* on take the reader on a fascinating tour of the era.

One of Gunn's recurrent themes is personal abandon. He likes to treat these subjects, to contain them, in rhyme and meter. The result often makes for handsome poetry. Here is the poet, on LSD, looking up at a neon Hamm's beer sign:

> What sky
>   A pearly damp grey covers it
> Almost infringing on the lighted sign
> Above Hamm's Brewery, a huge blond glass
> Filling as its component lights are lit.
> You cannot keep them. Blinking line by line
> They brim beyond the scaffold they replace.
>
> 2
> What is this steady pouring that
>   Oh, wonder.
> The blue line bleeds and on the gold one draws.
> Currents of image widen, braid, and blend
> —Pouring in cascade over me and under—
> To one all-river. Fleet it does not pause,
> The sinewy flux pours without start or end.
>
> What place is this
>   And what is it that broods
> Barely beyond its own creation's course,
> And not abstracted from it, not the Word,
> But overlappings like the wet low clouds
> The rivering images—their unstopped source,
> Its roar unheard from being always heard.

No other writer tries this sort of thing, much less pulls it off.

The level of achievement from *Moly* and certain of the *Poems from the 1960s* on through *The Man with Night Sweats* (1992) is remarkable, not least of all for having been sustained for nearly thirty years. To quote Gunn in fits and starts on the heels of broad pronouncements does little justice to the breadth of the work. It seems he becomes more adventuresome as he grows older and is not afraid to fall on his ass trying out something different. Sometimes the poems are so emotionally bald and direct that they are deeply disturbing. They say what they have to say very *plainly.* Or sometimes Gunn can sound just like Dryden or Rochester cruising South of the Slot.

But we might well look to the words of Fulke Greville, writing of his own work, to best characterize Gunn's poetry from *Moly* on:

> For my own part, I found my creeping genius more fixed upon the images of life, than the images of wit, and therefore chose not to write to them on whose foot the black ox had not already trod, as the proverb is, but to those only, that are weather-beaten in the sea of this world, such as having lost the sight of their gardens and groves, study to sail on a right course among rocks and quicksands.[9]

Thom Gunn and Anglo-American Modernism

KEITH TUMA

In an interview published in 1989, Thom Gunn told Jim Powell that he had read a critical study of his work that described him as an "Anglo-American" poet and decided that this was what he was.[1] And Anglo-American is what Gunn calls himself in the notes to his *Collected Poems* (1994): "In my early books I was an English poet, not yet Anglo-American."[2] As a category for his poetry, "Anglo-American" has the advantage of acknowledging Gunn's ability to bridge English and American expectations about poetic value. If in recent decades it has been the discontinuities between English and American poetry that have most often been important to poets and critics, Gunn's poetry, read across his career, allows us to think about continuities between "the two poetries."[3] Much as Gunn never became a citizen—he is not an "Anglo-American" in that sense—but remained an Englishman living in America, his poetry is never far removed from its origins in England even as it successfully incorporates, as only a few English poets of his generation do, the American modernism of poets such as William Carlos Williams.

Gunn was able to sustain a sizable readership on both sides of the Atlantic, something few poets in recent years have managed, and this fact is arguably a consequence of what I am pointing to here: his ability to modify his practice without giving up its core values. Gunn's visibility as a poet, however, did not mean that he was able altogether to avoid the rhetoric that has sometimes posed American *against* English poetry (English more often than "British," though the terms are still too often confused) in recent decades. Robert Potts quotes Clive Wilmer's remark that "in the U.S. they don't think [Gunn's] quite American, in the UK they don't think he's quite English."[4] That was one consequence of being an Anglo-American poet in Gunn's lifetime, during which English poetry and American poetry drifted apart, or so it is often said. To be an Anglo-American poet in this sense is also to exist *between* English and American poetry, belonging somewhat to both but comfortably to neither. The same poetry that will seem to some American readers too stiffly formal in its idioms and rhythms, even when it is written in free verse, is viewed as experimental and "Americanized" in England because of its prosody or arrangement on the page—or sometimes because of its subject matter. Against these tendencies we should insist that Gunn's work allows us to think beyond familiar ideas about what constitutes English and American practice in poetry.

While Gunn's comments in interviews suggest that he was mildly amused by the differences in the ways that poems have been valued on opposite sides of the Atlantic, Gunn also seems more or less to have accepted the terms that have often been used in comparisons of English and American poetry. He told Powell, for instance, that free verse is "not particularly English": "What people say about me, and it's probably true, is that in many of my poems I write about an American subject matter in an English way, by which they mean metrical and in rhyme—which may be an English way, though it's been used by some Americans. Of course free verse is not particularly English; very few English people have written decent free verse."[5] There is qualification in Gunn's language ("not particularly") but not defiance. American poetry as more receptive to experiment or innovation, English poetry as having resisted much of what is associated with modernism—by now this is an old story, too familiar to rehearse here. Whatever we choose to make of Gunn's example, Gunn himself seems to have had little interest in complicating the familiar story about English and American poetry. Unlike his friend Donald Davie, his prose does not often develop comparisons between English and American writing.[6]

Gunn's poetry includes poems using Basil Bunting's "flexible line" ("Office Hours") and other poems owing something to the poems of William Carlos Williams and Mina Loy, among other modernists. At the same time, Gunn's modernist-influenced poems typically retain qualities of his earliest poems. Gunn's diction, for instance, never honors the particular at the expense of the abstract. His later poems, with a few exceptions such as "Talbot Road," refer to American settings, and to his experience and the experience of friends and acquaintances in the United States, but Gunn's concerns—what one used to call "themes"—do not change much across his career. The character studies offered in his later poems explore the nature of desire and trust, and the value of spontaneity and discipline, as these relate to self and community, but none of these are new concerns in his poetry. The later poetry will seem to many American readers more humane and less "literary" as Gunn moves away from the existentialism of Jean-Paul Sartre and character types taken from literature or film (from werewolf to biker) and turns his attention to a more intimate rendering of character. But finally there is not all that much that distinguishes "La Prisonnière" in Gunn's first book from the songs for Jeffrey Dahmer in his last, not much difference between these early and late poems about what one can only call all-consuming desire. "La Prisonnière" borrows its tropes from Gothic literature, opening with "Now I will shut you in a box / With massive sides and a lid that locks."[7] "I thought that you were gone, / But you are here and will remain with me,"[8] the opening of the third stanza of Gunn's first Dahmer song, is close to this, apart from the savage irony the facts of the Dahmer story offer the poem.

But I am getting ahead of myself and need to say more about Gunn's move from England to the United States. Gunn came to the United States after his first book, *Fighting Terms* (1954), had been published in the United Kingdom and already with a reputation as an emerging poet. By today's standards, *Fighting Terms* was widely reviewed in the United Kingdom; there were ten reviews of its first edition. Gunn had also had his poems included in G. S. Fraser and Ian Fletcher's anthology *Springtime* (1953) and read his work for John Lehmann's influential BBC radio program *New Soundings,* which is reported to have had as many as ten thousand listeners. And this was only the beginning of Gunn's success. His reputation in the United Kingdom grew considerably during his first years living in the States. By 1962, when Faber and Faber's *Selected Poems by Thom Gunn and Ted Hughes* was published—thanks to classroom adoptions it continued to sell well for years—Gunn was one of the most recognized names among the English poets of his generation.

This was the period when the Movement, the group of poets he came to be associated with, was in the news.[9] Like Philip Larkin, whose poetry and opinions have come to represent the Movement for many readers, Gunn liked to say that his poetry had little to do with the Movement, which Gunn seems to have thought of as a publicity campaign. Remarks like these are par for the course when it comes to poets and movements, but there is truth in them, too. Andrew Motion's biography of Larkin suggests how little interest Larkin had in Gunn's poetry and public image as a poet; he grouped Gunn with Ted Hughes as romantics in leather jackets and mocked them.[10] For his part, Gunn had small use for the cult of Larkin: "The trouble is the English are hung up on Larkin. Larkin was a poet of minute ambitions who carried them out exquisitely."[11] These squabbles did not prevent the poets involved with the Movement from benefiting from the idea that they belonged to a new tendency in British poetry.

Three anthologies did a lot of the work in establishing the poetic values associated with the Movement at the center of British literary culture. These were D. J. Enright's *Poets of the Fifties* (1955), which did not include Gunn's poetry, and two anthologies that did, Robert Conquest's *New Lines* (1956) and Alfred Alvarez's *The New Poetry* (1962). Alvarez's book included work by most of the Movement poets, even as Alvarez himself was critical of Movement poetry. His introduction's attack on "gentility," with its contrast of poems by Larkin and Hughes, also did much (together with Charles Tomlinson's article "The Middlebrow Muse") to set the terms for criticism of the Movement, but it left Gunn's work alone—except insofar as Gunn was already associated with the Movement thanks to his appearance in Conquest's anthology. Joint publication with Hughes no doubt weakened Gunn's association with the Movement for many readers, though, from the first, Gunn's poems about sex ("Carnal Knowledge") and power ("Tamer and Hawk") must have seemed wild by Movement standards. Nevertheless, thanks to the inertia of literary history and its respect for national boundaries, most literary historians continue to think of Gunn as a Movement poet. At the moment it is difficult (though not impossible, as Andrew Duncan has recently demonstrated)[12] to offer a map of post–World War II British poetry that does not mention Gunn as a member of that influential group, whereas it is a rare history of post–World War II American poetry that mentions him at all.

Most of Gunn's readers know that he came to the United States to study with Yvor Winters at Stanford. Langdon Hammer writes that "Gunn's sense of poetic form as an epistemological tool for dealing with experience comes directly from Winters's teaching and criticism,"[13] which probably offers Winters too much credit, since Gunn's sense of poetic form was already well-developed when he arrived in the United States. Hammer thinks that Winters "modeled critical but engaged responses to modernism that were . . . alternatives to the antimodernism of the new English writing of the 1950s known as the Movement,"[14] which is a more provocative claim for the way it distinguishes Winters's critical but respectful reading of modernism from Larkin's description of the work of Pound, Picasso, and (Charlie) Parker as "irresponsible exploitations of technique in contradiction of human life as we know it."[15] If Hammer is right to say that Winters helped to introduce Gunn to a view of modernism that is more respectful than this, it would be some years after his arrival in the United States before Gunn moved beyond his own version of antimodernism. Gunn liked to say that he had taught himself to write free verse by experimenting with syllabic verse in the back half of *My Sad Captains* (1961), but in my view *Jack Straw's Castle* (1976) is the first book that significantly engages modernist poetry. The sequence "Tom-Dobbin" (the so-called centaur poems in *Moly* [1971]), like the poems in syllabics in the earlier book, might be said to prefigure Gunn's engagement with modernism.

It should be said that the antimodernism of the Movement is not a simple matter, even in Larkin's case, and depending on the critic we are talking about, it can be difficult to distinguish Movement ideas about poetry from Wintersian ideas. Donald Davie, perhaps the leading critic among Movement poets, is nowhere as dismissive of modernism as Larkin and other Movement poets could be, and by the 1960s he was promoting the work of Pound. In the early 1950s, Davie's view of modernism was much as Hammer describes Winters's, critical but respectful. And before the Movement had its name, Davie was arguing that British poets would do well to read Winters. Here he is in 1950, reviewing an anthology that Winters edited:

> The British poet today is so nearly insulated from his American colleagues that he hardly knows the work of such established poets as Stevens, Ransom, Tate, Williams, even Hart Crane. Still less does he know the work of these Western poets. Yet this Western school has already passed, as it were, through one generation, and some of those older poets, notably J. V. Cunningham, Howard Baker and Yvor Winters, are regarded in some quarters as among the most important American poets of the day. It is high time some of this work was made available to the British public. Meanwhile it seems worthwhile to take notice of this American publication, for it presents a shift of direction in American poetry analogous in some ways to certain tentative movements over here.[16]

The "tentative movements" to which Davie refers are of course the newspaper and journal publications and everything else that a few years later would become the Movement. While Davie is right about the neglect of American poetry in Britain at this time, his claim that "in some quarters" of the United States in 1950 Winters, J. V. Cunningham, and Howard Baker were thought to be important American poets is probably best described as a minority opinion. A hostile reader might charge Davie with taking advantage of British neglect of American poetry to create a preferred version of recent American poetry for British consumption, though statements about comparative profile or value among one's contemporaries tend to be performative like this, particularly as made in the context of reviews.

Davie's account of the neglect of American poetry among British poets in 1950 is confirmed by Gunn's autobiographical writing from the 1970s; Gunn admits that he had not seriously read Pound before coming to the United States and had read little or nothing by Williams and Wallace Stevens.[17] Neither Williams nor Stevens were in print in Britain when Gunn left for the States. It would also surprise me to learn that Gunn read much work by contemporary American poets—poets of his own generation—while studying at Cambridge.[18] The insularity of the Movement was a rhetorical football; that does not mean that the "little Englandism" of the group was not real.[19]

With a few important exceptions, including T. S. Eliot and the early poetry of Ezra Pound, the fate of American poetry in Britain, modernist poetry especially, in the years immediately prior to World War II is more or less a version of the fate of Pound's *Active Anthology* (1933), a book largely ignored upon its publication in Britain. John Lehmann's journals, *New Writing* in the late '30s and *New Penguin Writing* in the '40s, seem to have published no American poets.[20] This situation did not change much after the war. In the '50s, thanks to the agency of W. H. Auden, who published an anthology of American poetry, and several poet-critics, including Davie, British readers began to take more interest in American poetry, though it is not until the 1960s that it makes sense to speak of American poetry as influencing British poetry. (There were exceptions going back some decades—the influence of Whitman, Eliot, and Pound on Basil Bunting's poetry, for instance.) If you want to see what an insular poetry looks like, read *Poetry Review* in the 1950s. Meanwhile, American poets, while not always deeply informed about developments in British poetry, tended to be eager to find out what was happening in Britain, or they were until the 1960s, when they began to lose interest in British poetry.

There was no journal with a substantial readership in Britain in the 1950s that was as eclectic or as responsive to a range of practice in poetry, no journal as interested in *both* British and American poetry, as *Poetry* magazine was under the editorship of Henry Rago. New to the United States and in his twenties still, Gunn reviewed for *Poetry* under Rago's editorship, as he also reviewed for the British publications *London*

Review and the *Spectator,* the latter a London weekly that promoted the Movement. Besides Gunn, *Poetry*'s British and Irish correspondents and reviewers during this period included Charles Tomlinson, David Wright, and John Montague, three poets with little in common with one another or with Gunn. Their reviews were published beside notes and reviews by a similarly diverse group of American writers, including Kenneth Burke, William Carlos Williams, Robert Duncan, Kenneth Rexroth, Reed Whittemore, and Carolyn Kizer. Rago's interest in the contemporary British scene allowed Gunn a role with the magazine, but Gunn did not yet have Rago's range of interests. Rago published an attack on Movement poetry by Charles Tomlinson, but he also published Gunn's poems, which he knew from other reviewers were identified with the Movement. He published Hayden Carruth's review of several British anthologies and anthologies of American poets edited by British poets—including the first Movement anthology edited by Robert Conquest, an anthology of so-called "Maverick" poetry, G. S. Fraser's *Poetry Now* (1956), and Auden's anthology of American poetry. Carruth noted that no British poet had recently captured the attention of American readers in the way that Auden and Thomas had a decade earlier but added, "The American reviews have always been open to British poetry, of course, and we have seen a good deal of it, most of it not very impressive."[21] The Movement, he wrote, was a "reaction against the excesses of the 1940s":[22] "[T]he Movement poets have a point. The trouble is that it is a small, negative point. They believe in control, clarity of feeling, austerity of technique, a strict abhorrence of excess. They share their retreat, in other words. But they do not seem to know how to advance."[23] Larkin ("too gay") and Enright ("too lush") did not on the evidence of the poetry included in the anthologies really belong to the Movement, Carruth felt, but he applauded the work of Movement poets John Wain, Kingsley Amis, Davie, and Gunn. Gunn's work, especially, he found to include "a quality and rigor of thought which has been more common in America than in England."[24] If he virtually has Gunn as an American poet already, another American critic writing in *Poetry,* Samuel French Morse, wrote in his review of Gunn's *The Sense of Movement* (1957) that Gunn was "the very best of the younger English poets."[25]

In these same richly diverse issues of *Poetry,* Gunn would have been able to read about recent publications by older modernist poets (e.g., Hugh Kenner on Pound's *Rock-Drill Cantos*). He would have encountered poems by several of the poets who were later to be gathered in Donald Allen's *The New American Poetry* (e.g., Frank O'Hara). The magazine even found room for Frederick Eckman's mostly positive review of Allen Ginsberg's *Howl*, where Eckman calls Ginsberg a "shaggy" poet, shaggy being the opposite of "fleecy" in this amusing version of the raw and the cooked.[26] And there is much more. It is difficult to give Winters too much credit for Gunn's introduction to modernism when *Poetry* was this wide-open.

But whatever Gunn was reading in the magazine, and whatever he was learning about modernism from Winters, it all took some time to settle, apparently, as Gunn's reviewing for *Poetry* demonstrates little interest in modernism and no interest at all in the so-called "New American" poetry then taking shape. Instead, Gunn wrote an admiring review of the first book by the Wintersian poet Edgar Bowers and used the occasion to take passing shots at the English modernist Edith Sitwell and the cult of T. S. Eliot. Familiar, too, is his claim that in "Modern Poetry" the "general method is of an attempt to convey meaning through allusions and fragmentary allusions."[27] By way of contrast, Bowers is praised for "commenting on experience rather than attempting to re-create it." This tendency in Bowers's work "runs counter to much modern critical theory," Gunn writes, thinking of F. R. Leavis, who years earlier had promoted the modernism of Eliot and others: "A critic like Dr. Leavis . . . will often complain of a poem he doesn't like that it 'speaks about' human experience rather than offering a 'creative exploration' (i.e., a re-experiencing) of it." Gunn praises Bowers's use of "abstract language," his "lack of sensationalism" and "control" and suggests that Bowers's poems "yield the author's complete intended meaning" rather than "a kaleidoscope of images that the reader can take to mean what he pleases," which must be what Gunn thought happened with the reading of modernist poetry. Another poet he reviewed beside Bowers he found to be too fond of puns and allusions; Gunn writes sarcastically that "[i]t is rather wonderful that we should have reached a point in history where this should be considered complimentary."[28] Nowhere in these reviews does Gunn have time for modernist poetry.

What Gunn says sounds a lot like the kind of thing one heard at the time from Movement poets, though, again, it is a mistake to think of Movement poets as always sharing critical opinions. John Wain admired William Empson's poetry, for instance, and Empson is sometimes spoken of as an older English poet whose work influenced the Movement. But in *London Magazine* in 1957, Gunn complained that Empson's poems were characterized by "muddled imagery, difficulty of reference, an excessive telescoping of statement, unclearness of tone, and some very odd ways with scansion"[29] and attacked the idea that ambiguity was a virtue in poetry, along with the notion that Empson's work was a "healthier" influence than Dylan Thomas's. "The object of a poem is to say something, and, though this something may be very complicated, it is not said well by the means of irrelevant figures or a style as complicated as the subject matter," Gunn argued, expressing his preference for the plain style.[30]

Gunn's criticism can be harsh in these early reviews. In another *Poetry* review where he takes up the work of several of his compatriots, the poetry of Roy Fuller is made typical of the "tone, evidently, most acceptable to the Fifties—that of the man who has put himself *outside* his subject so that he can comment on it calmly."[31] This is not a problem for Gunn insofar as Fuller's dispassionate tone is preferable to the "meaningless passion" of other poetry, and he thought Fuller's poems were better than others by poets who wanted to "present objets trouvés for our admiration."[32] But Gunn admits that this representative 1950s tone can make for tepid and dull poetry: "These faults, I think, are grave, but they are encouraged by the present fashion for the muted, for the offhand, for understatement—a fashion which seems to have got rid of hysteria without replacing it by a robustness that could abet and be abetted by orderliness."[33] Two years later, Davie's article "Remembering the Movement" argued in similar terms that Movement poetry was burdened by "inert gestures of social adaptiveness" and concessions to a middlebrow public, "not to the insularity which orders baked beans on toast in Pavia and thinks all foreigners are dirty, but to the insularity which has ready its well-documented and conclusive sneer at Colette and Marianne Moore, Jean Cocteau and André Gide and Hart Crane."[34]

In the end it is Davie whose views I find closest to Gunn's at this point, but then, as I say, I do not find it easy to distinguish between Davie and Winters in the early 1950s. The same review by Davie I quote above includes this passage:

> The [Wintersian] group, centred upon the Californian University of Stanford, differs from the poets and critics of the Eastern States in believing that a poem is none the worse for being built around a structure of rational discourse, and that a poet's intelligence can be brought into play as effectively when he follows a rational argument as when he has recourse to a witty metaphor or juxtaposition. These poets are not afraid, when convenient, to distinguish between what a poet says and the way he says it. There is all the more reason, in their view, for supposing that a poet cannot write in a void; and that, other things being equal, he will

> write better poetry if he has philosophical training, and if his philosophical training is rationally sound. They recognize the achievement of French symbolists, and of post-symbolists and experimentalists such as Eliot, Pound, Wallace Stevens, and Hart Crane, but they think that this vein is now worked out and that healthy poetry today must find again a basis in rational philosophy. In general they eschew free verse and write in strict metre and rhyme.[35]

From Carruth's review to Alvarez's introduction, Movement poets and critics took a beating for expressing few positive values as part of their poetic program, for the "reactionary" nature of that program. But their values are clear enough here, outlined as a description of Wintersian values. A preference for traditional form and meter, for syntax that allows for orderly or "logical" exposition, and the idea that poetry should incorporate propositions (Gunn's word in the 1950s was "statements") about the world—most Movement poets share that much at least. Much of this is at odds with ideas of the poem attributed to modernist poets. Stéphane Mallarmé's thesis, for instance, as summarized by Gerald Bruns, is that "a poem is made of words but not of any of the other things we use words to produce: meanings, concepts, propositions about the world, narratives, expressions of feeling, and so on. Poetry is not a form of mediation. It is, to put it plainly, not a species of discourse at all but occupies the hither side of speech where language remains thick."[36] Davie was to argue against related claims about the status of poetry as discourse in his discussion of the "post-symbolist" roots of modernism in *Articulate Energy* (1956).

While Gunn began as an antimodernist aligned with Davie and Winters, he went on to write appreciatively about Williams, Bunting, Loy, and other modernist poets, and also about some of his contemporaries whose work is indebted to modernist poetry—Robert Duncan and Gary Snyder, for example. His first important essay on a modernist poet comes in 1965, an essay on Williams for *Encounter.* This was several years after the appearance of the anthologies edited by Alvarez and Donald Allen. In that essay, as in all of his essays on or remarks about modernist poets, Gunn carefully limits what he wants to take from modernism. For example, his praise for Basil Bunting's *Briggflatts* in an essay dating from 1982 has a lot to do with that poem's tempered version of Poundian technique as it is enabled by Bunting's Wordsworthian values. Similarly, when Jim Powell reminds him that *Briggflatts* is written in free verse, Gunn responds that it is a "tightly disciplined free verse, it keeps moving into something very much like meter."[37] In the 1965 essay on Williams, written to persuade the English to read Williams, Gunn contrasts "Imagism, where . . . meaning is to be found in the impulse that causes the poem to be written rather than in the words themselves" with a poetry of "general statement, where the poet explicitly *tells* us what values the images have for him,"[38] concentrating on moments in the work where the American modernist is the latter sort of poet.

In describing Robert Duncan's "marriage of Modernist and Romantic possibilities," Gunn argues that "[b]oth Duncan and Bunting avoid the twin vices of trivialization that in their different ways haunt the English and American poetry of our time: the use of anecdotal subject matter as an end in itself and of technical play as an end in itself. (I take it that Hardy and Williams are behind the one, Stein and Auden behind the other.)"[39] These pairings will be thought odd or unusual by readers who believe that Williams and Stein are closer as poets than Williams and Hardy. While for Pound, as for many early-twentieth-century modernist poets, Hardy's poetry had something to offer modernist practice, it is also the case that, in more recent decades, and especially in Britain, Hardy's poetry has belonged to an English tradition that stands apart from modernism as developed by Pound, Williams, Eliot, and others. If, as seems probable, Gunn was aware of this while writing his essay, his pairings should be read as willful, as part of an effort to ignore the arguments that pose an "English line" against modernism.

It is not that Gunn thought that Williams and Hardy have no differences as poets, but rather that he knew there was something to be learned from both. Gunn admired Williams's "clarity of evocation, the sensitivity of movement, and the purity of language in his efforts to realize spontaneity" and the "habitual sympathy, by which he recognizes his own energy in that of the young housewife, the boys at the street corner, the half-wit girl who helps in the house, the sparrow."[40] But Gunn also admired Hardy's "reflective lyric," which he describes as "essentially impersonal, essentially non-confessional" and "concerned with its subject to the extent of excluding the speaker's personality, even when his emotion is the subject of his poem."[41] Both passages work as descriptions of Gunn's poetry, depending on which poem we are talking about and when it was written, "habitual sympathy" more often being a property of the later work, impersonality of the earlier.

Among "the vices of trivialization" that Gunn mentions in his remarks on Duncan is a mode of anecdotalism that fails to interpret what it presents. Gunn's own "anecdotalism" is sometimes Williamsesque, but one should read it with this remark in mind. Probably it is at its best in the character sketches of *The Passages of Joy* (1982), in poems like "Bally *Power Play*." Much in the way that Gunn says Williams recognized "his own energy in that of the young housewife," Gunn identifies with the sexual bravado of the young man playing pinball in "Bally *Power Play*." Gunn understands, in a way that the young man cannot, the little deaths each pinball suffers, raising pinball to the status of five-act tragedy. The poem is about the young man's sexual power, his need to test its limits, about self-control and self-abandonment. These are familiar subjects in Gunn's work—except that in the early poems he would have begun with a figure taken from literature, film, or history rather than this ordinary young man in a bar. Describing him, Gunn is able to reflect on the relationship of mind and body, on the will as it confronts and tries to order the chaos of the senses.

The poem makes the young man iconic, as aloof as a Greek god, as golden. Or this is what the speaker's desire—easily identified with the poet—makes him before the poem returns him to the status of ordinary young man. A face-to-face conversation contrasting with the poem's cinematic opening is narrated in clipped phrases to end the poem. At the poem's center is a long, twisting sentence describing the fate of the pinball, its movement across the verse line full of the sort of tensions Williams liked to create:

> Everybody looks at him playing
> the machine hour after hour,
> but he hardly raises his gold lashes.
> Two fingers move, his hips
> lean in almost perceptibly.
> He seldom takes his eyes
> from the abstract drama of the ball,
> the descent and the reverses
> of its brief fortunes. He is
> the cool source of all that hurry
> and desperate activity, in control,
> legs apart, braced arms apart,
> seeming alive only at the ends.
> His haunches are up against the wood now,
> the hard edge which he presses
> or which presses him
> just where the pelvis begins,

above what in the skeleton
would be no more than a hole.
Bally's drama absorbs him:
amongst the variety and surprise
of the lights, the silver ball,
appears, rolls shyly towards him,
meets a wheel of red plastic,
at once bounces away from it,
frantically dashes from side to side
and up and down, it is
trapped, it is released,
it springs to the top again,
back to where it entered,
but in the end it must disappear
down the hole at the bottom
—and the fifth act is over
leaving behind it only
the continued inane flickering
of coloured light. Between games
he recognizes me, we chat,
he tells me about broken promises
with a comic-rueful smile
at his need for reassurance,
which is as great as anybody's.
He once told me he never starts
to look for the night's partner
until half an hour before closing time.
The rest is foreplay.[42]

This is free verse, one variety of the free verse that Gunn writes. Even so, the presence of three strong stresses in many of the lines offers a "flexible" structure. Like almost all of Gunn's work, the poem nowhere goes in fear of abstractions and interrupts its description only to call the young man "the cool source of all that hurry / and desperate activity." Lines 20 through 32 especially suggest the "sensitivity of movement" and mimetic syntax of the Williams of *Spring and All* (1923). Throughout the poem, the comparisons that frame the significance of details, like the metaphor of the erotic as "game" or "theater," remain in view. Gunn works—harder than Williams—to lift his poem's particulars into discourse.

"Bally *Power Play*" is written in a free verse productively restrained, its pace slowed and concentrated by habits picked up from the writing of metrical verse. It is some distance from the iambic pentameter that sustains the intellection of early poems like Gunn's "Legal Reform" (1957) to Gunn's later poems in free verse with their lines spread out on the page, as with "The Geysers" (1976), but it is hard to say that one mode is more controlled than the other. Indeed, the second passage below might be *more* formal for the *insistence* of its rhyming and repetition:

> Condemned to life, a happier condemnation
> Than I deserved, I serve my sentence full,
> Clasping it to me at each indication
> That this time love is not the paradox
> By which, whatever it contains, my cell
> Contains the absolute, because it locks.[43]

> lighten, diminish
>   in the dream, halfdream
> halfdream, reality
>   of flickering stream
>
> beneath mud
>   branching
>   branching streams run through
>
> through me
>   the mud breathes
>   breathes me too
>
> and bobbing in the womb, all round me Mother
> I am part of all   there is no other
> I extend into
>   her mind   her mountainous knees
> red meadows   salty seas
> birdbone and pulp, unnamed, unborn
>   I live[44]

These verse lines are not as remote from one another as the existential angst in the first passage is from the chemically assisted well-being in the second. Habits persist—an interest in repetition and in syntactical balance and parallelism as they make not only comparison and contrast but also qualification possible. Likewise, the first poem in the title sequence of *Jack Straw's Castle,* also in free verse, begins in folk song and ends in rhyme.

"The Menace" (1982), one of Gunn's more interesting poems in the mode he inherited from American modernists, reveals his fondness for working with paired terms. One can arrange them as if in a list:

guard	father
executioner	angel of death
delivering doctor	judge
cop	castrator[45]

That's how Gary Snyder might have done it. If the relationship of the paired terms can be questioned (it *is* questioned in the poem), there is also chiasmus, which is used to expose divisions in the self, a tension between the need to affirm the self and the darker wish to extinguish it:

> I am, am I,
> the one-who-wants-to-get-me[46]

"I am, am I" owes as much to Arthur Rimbaud's most famous phrase as the poem elsewhere owes to Freud. Chiasmus makes for an eloquence that the paired terms in lists cannot match.

Gunn never was much tempted by the modernist fashion for the long poem. He told me that a famous English contemporary once asked him after he read his poems in Cambridge if he thought his poems were "like toast," a remark that disturbed him, I think, but which surely was meant to refer to the way his poems value closure. They are poems meant, for the most part, to stand alone; even in verse sequences the emphasis is on closure for the individual poem or section. Gunn's taste for the epigram and the epigrammatic, for controlling or extended metaphor, for "chaste" diction, for all that contains meaning—these remain even as Gunn samples from his modernists. Rarely do the poems look to comment directly on historical or contemporary events, on politics or society, though there is a little more of that kind of thing in *Boss Cupid* (2000).

There are poets for whom everything about poetry and the way that poetry is understood to relate to other forms of discourse is fundamentally changed by modernism. Then there are poets for whom modernism represents a series of local innovations in technique that do not require us to rethink assumptions about poetic language, representation, genre, discourse, and so on—in brief, about poetry as an art form. Gunn is closer to the latter group than to the former, which tends also to locate him as an English poet, since this narrative about the difference modernism makes has more subscribers there.

But one surely *does* see modernist technique in many of Gunn's poems from the 1970s forward, as one can also hear the influence of some of his American contemporaries in a more conversational and relaxed idiom. There is, for example, the use of the word "cock," which would be unimaginable without the example of poets such as Allen Ginsberg and Robert Duncan. Probably it is Robert Duncan's poem "The Dance" behind the prose passage out of Gregory Bateson about the meaning of conjunctions in Gunn's "The Menace." But it is pretty rare for Gunn to relax all the way to prose, as he does in that poem.

More often than his contemporaries, Gunn's select modernists inform his later poems. Mina Loy's "Love Songs to Joannes" might be heard behind the cramped, intellectual, but also erotic discourse of "The Plunge," as it isolates pronouns and syncopates their rhyming:

> down a rope of
> bubbles
>
> trapped where you
> chose to come
>   it
> is all there is
>
> the brute thrust of
> entering this all-
> alien like a bitter
> sheath
>   each
> nerve each
> atom of skin
> tightens against it
> to a gliding
> a moving with—
> if flesh could
> become water it[47]

There's probably less Loy than there is Bunting, but Williams is by far the most persistent influence, if we ignore the influence of canonical English poets like Shakespeare and Jonson (for their songs especially), Donne, and Hardy (for his riffs on the ballad). "The Cat and the Wind" has enough Williams in it to be almost derivative. The poet describes leaves blowing across the next yard, as witnessed by the cat:

> her pupils dwindle
> to specks in
> her yellow eyes
> that stare first upward
> and then on every side
> unable to single out
> any one thing
> to pounce on,
> for all together
> as if orchestrated,
> twigs, leaves,
> small pebbles, pause,
> and start and pause
> in their shifting,
> their rubbing
> against each other[48]

This could be Gunn's answer to Williams's famous poem about the cat stepping into the flowerpot.

As an Anglo-American poet, Gunn grafted ideas about poetry taken from Williams and others—from American poetry—onto a practice established in England. But the English past is never too far in the background in Gunn's work—neither English traditions in verse nor allusions to English culture. I say "traditions" because they are many. Consider, for instance, his poem "Mandrakes," with which I'll close, which has traces of the bardic in it, diffused in a quiet, almost quaint poem. Bardic traces are not much found in Gunn's poetry:

> look for us among those
> shy flowers opening
> at night only
>   in the

shadow, in the held breath
under oak trees listen for

rootshuffle or is it wind
      you won't find us, we
got small a long time back
we withdrew like the Picts
into fireside tale and rumour

we were terrible in our time
gaunt plants fertilized
by the leachings of hanged men
    knobby frames shrieking and
stumping around the planet

smaller and bushier now
prudent green men moving
in oakshadow or among reed
guardians of the young snake
                    rearing from the water
                    with the head and curving
                    neck of a small dinosaur

we can outwait you for
ever if we need, lounging
leafy arms linked along
some park's path, damp fallen leaves
covering our itch to move

mouths open to the wind
sigh entering the sough
from the distant branches

like a rumour at your fireside[49]

It occurs to me that "Mandrakes" can be read as an allegory about the fate of the English—or English poetry—in what is, for the English, supposedly a post-imperial age. It can also be read as a poem about secret or hidden forms of desire as these persist, about paganism. The "rootshuffle" and oak trees bespeak an archetypal English symbolism—one might even hear a little of the Ted Hughes of *Gaudete* (1977) in the poem. As for the Picts, who disappeared but not quite (as the poem has it), you will learn more about them from Wikipedia than you will in this poem. This is not a poetry including history in the manner of Pound or Charles Olson. The Picts function in the poem as a figure for what is backgrounded but not forgotten and establish the poem's vectors of reference as English. The mandrake works in the same way; the plant's legendary status in witchcraft and fertility rituals belongs to England rather than America. The poem *is* arranged in the kind of flexible line that we often call free verse and think of as modernist, though it is probably closer to Bunting than to Williams. It is an Anglo-American free verse perhaps, or might be called that. The idea that mandrakes shriek when pulled from the ground is straight out of *Romeo and Juliet*. As an Anglo-American poet, Gunn was easily pulled from the ground of his English past, but he never really abandoned it.

From Ladd's Hill to Land's End (and Back Again): Narrative, Rhythm, and the Transatlantic Occasions of "Misanthropos"

JOSHUA WEINER

1

"In my teens," Thom Gunn said, "I wanted to be a novelist. I read so many Victorian novels that later when I did my undergraduate work I didn't need to read any more to answer the novel questions on the exams. I wanted to be a novelist very much in the Victorian sense: I've always been interested in character."[1] When a child, he loved Dumas and Stevenson, and later, Dickens, Flaubert, Balzac, Stendhal, Dostoyevsky, Hardy, Henry James, Conrad, Proust, Fitzgerald, Melville, Mann, and Isherwood; he was keenly interested in Walker Percy and William Burroughs; his favorite contemporary novelist was Robert Stone; he also liked Don Delillo, Philip Roth, and enjoyed Irvine Welsh's *Trainspotting* and the hard-boiled excesses of Jim Thompson. ("In a Jim Thompson novel," he once said to me, "shooting somebody is just another way of saying good-bye.") A fan of Philip K. Dick, Samuel R. Delaney, and other science fiction writers, Gunn once told me if he could write like Dick, he would!

But Gunn was turned on to poetry by his absorption in Shakespeare, Donne, and other sixteenth- and seventeenth-century poets, as well as Chaucer, whose vital characters and dramatic situations presaged the novel. Though the novel as a social form provided Gunn a rich resource of settings and dramatic tensions, human figures caught in a web of contingencies, and emblematic postures of individual existence, Gunn discovered his vocation as a lyric poet through his encounter with capacious and analytical poets, whose fictive imaginations captured the force of history, philosophy, and religion prior to the emergence of prose fiction.

In his own poetry, Gunn tried to do the same. One finds throughout Gunn's body of work poems that draw from historic, mythic, and novelistic material. "Autumn Chapter in a Novel," "Rastignac at 45," "Lazarus Not Raised," "Phaedra in the Farm House," "Thomas Bewick," "Merlin in the Cave," "Julian the Apostate," "Tom-Dobbin," "To Natty Bumpo," "Faustus Triumphant," "Philomen and Baucis," and "Claus von Stauffenberg"—all are grounded in narrative situation, make use of narrative frames, and contain fictive characters (and there are many others in Gunn's oeuvre). While these poems may don a persona, address a fictional character, borrow a character expressive of a type, or retell an ancient myth, they operate within lyric definitions—by which I mean a poem of concision and concentration. Yet they also highlight a consistent preoccupation running beneath Gunn's body of work: his perception that modern poetry had lost ground to the novel, and his attempt to restore to poetry some of the relevance he valued in the novel and modern drama. Modern poetry in English at mid-century, in Gunn's view, no longer addressed the complexity of social being; it was too self-absorbed, too riddled with bad ideas. One solution, for Gunn, was to reach outside of lyric conventions of self-revelation, to capture human character with the objective analysis of the novel, yet to do so without giving up the formal virtues of lyric intensity. He kept at it his whole career. There is a period within that career, though, when the issue of narrative comes together with another fundamental formal issue for Gunn and for poetry in the latter half of the twentieth century: the attempt to resolve the tension between open and closed poetic form. How Gunn's use of fictive techniques coincided with his attempt to renew poetic form is the story I want to tell.

After Gunn began in 1960 to draft a poem about the survivor of a global war, he realized that because "there was too much exposition for me to cram into a single short poem" he would have to "extend it into a long poem."[2] He thereby worked further against the generic confines of lyric, hoping to extend poetry's original seriousness of purpose, its capacity to address complex social problems and the tension between personal freedom and commitment; "*a complete attitude to experience worked out in detail,* qualified, supported, given imaginative realization" such as he encountered in the "works of Mann, Proust, Conrad, Camus, or Lawrence, or (to take a living novelist who can stand with them) William Golding."[3]

"My hope for poetry," Gunn wrote in 1963, "is that it can once again become a major genre." The ambition he shared with nineteenth- and early-twentieth-century poets was one of comprehensiveness. "Tennyson and Browning," continues Gunn, "wasted much of their lives and talents in a tremendous struggle to write versified novels and bits of plays, in an attempt, in fact, to retrieve the ground securely held by other genres." Gunn realized that to the modernists T. S. Eliot and Ezra Pound, longer poetic forms and discursiveness "would not do." And "what is special about poetry as a genre," Gunn noted, "is its concentration."

> This is the only real characteristic, which distinguishes it from other forms. (The more diffuse a poem is, the more it approaches other forms.) Concentration, even the shortness of the poem, makes for intensity as another characteristic. Even in poets who seem very relaxed, there is an intensity, at all points, which you don't find in other forms. So that you learn, after you have written a short while, that there must be intensity right at the start of a poem, in the impulse that produces it—intensity to the point of obsession. It is exactly that impulse that is the most important part of any poem, the thing that—preserved and extended—makes what life the poem will perhaps eventually have.[4]

Modern poets would address this formal problem by experimenting with new techniques—primarily fragmentation, juxtaposition, and free verse—in order to compete with the comprehensiveness of prose fiction. Gunn, however, held onto an English metrical tradition (as did other poets of his generation), even as he experimented in the 1960s with the loosened rhythms of syllabics. The issue for Gunn was not a formal one, *per se:* he was not, in that sense, a *formalist.* The problem for modern poets was not one of style, structure, or treatment, but rather to draw from their observations a plausible and persuasive interpretation of life. Yvor Winters called it "a technique of comprehension." Yet how could poetry contain and imaginatively integrate as much reality as the other genres?

In his notebook of 1963, one hears Gunn working out this historical assessment, attempting to define the problem for his own art.

> I read the great poets of this century who wrote in English, and I find many qualities in them, but it is from the novelists and dramatists of the 20th century that I really learn, it is they who have modified and adjusted my understanding, perception, & finally actions as Shakespeare, Donne, Jonson, Pope, or even Crabbe have done. The great modern poets have certainly as intense a preoccupation with particulars as any of these [modern] novelists, but they do not seem inclined to learn from them, to derive

> from them any body of ideas [or] put them together in an attitude that one can take seriously. Pound is probably still the most influential poet of our time. His ideas are not only few but ridiculous. . . . Eliot defines a world of Conradian emptiness. . . . [But] Eliot suddenly shifts the terms from psychological-moral to religious-moral and finds an answer in the fixities of dogma. Yeats constructs a set of beliefs which his greatest admirers cannot take seriously, behind which is a nostalgia for feudalism. . . . Stevens goes farther than the others, but finally he takes refuge in a kind of Church, what he calls Imagination. . . . In each of these writers, serious men dedicating themselves to poetry, there is a central lack.

The lack Gunn senses here may have been for a kind of architecture that organizes phenomena into a comprehensive pattern or structure. Gunn continues:

> With say Mann or Conrad, I can say: "Yes, I recognize this type of experience and I can see how he draws from it such conclusions about human nature, or conduct, or the conditions of existence." With the poets, however, all I say is: "Yes, I recognize this type of experience, but how is it connected with Fascism/The Church/magic-feudalism/the Imagination[?]" They make a leap into abstraction that acts as a denial of their particular observations, a leap which few of us want to follow. [And] much of their best work—maybe ultimately their best poems—has no connection with their answers.
>
> In the sixteenth century, Sidney found it necessary to define the genres of poetry, philosophy, and history. He found that poetry did essentially what philosophy and history did, only more effectively. The other genres were not superseded, but poetry fulfilled certain of their functions better than they could. Poetry had, in fact, all of its action & thought as its domain.

To move forward, Gunn thinks, requires finding a way to reconnect with a premodernist conception of poetry's cultural role.

> There is much that a poet can learn from the novel and drama, but there seems little point in attempting to imitate it directly: of *The Ring and the Book* and *The Confidential Clerk* my reaction is, why not do it in prose, since prose works better in these conventions? What he has to learn is that he has inherited a genre onto which it is still possible for the whole of experience to bear: the body of his work should not be a collection of

> phenomena or of beautiful things, but should add up to a comment on existence just as much as the body of a novelist's work. And some of the poets who have emerged in the last 10 years or so do seem prepared to ignore the limitation of subject imposed by the poets of the last 100 years while being willing to learn from them technically—Edgar Bowers in America & Ted Hughes in England, for example.[5]

Poetry "adding up" to a comment on existence; Gunn wanted this for his poetry, yet he realized by the early '60s that to integrate new kinds of experience he would need a "transatlantic movement" of mind. Gunn had previously situated himself within an English tradition of poetry by bringing new subjects to established verse forms; his next step would be to open his work to an American tradition, to nonconformism and more unpredictability.

At this point Gunn was thirty-four. By the date of this notebook entry, he had already published three books—*Fighting Terms* (1954), *The Sense of Movement* (1957), and *My Sad Captains* (1961)—and received considerable critical recognition. He had left England in 1954 to follow his friend and lover, Mike Kitay, to America, and enrolled for postgraduate work at Stanford with Yvor Winters. The publication of *My Sad Captains* showed him at a moment of apparent transition: the first half of the book holds poems in strict iambic meter and cross-rhymed stanzas; the second half is full of syllabics (mostly sevens and nines). The metrical divide in the contents suggests a strong shift in formal feeling but not a metrical conversion. The shift was to a greater inclusiveness of formal practice, an opening at one end of the banquet hall that did not close off the other. For Gunn would continue to write in traditional metrical forms throughout his life, though he eventually dropped syllabics for free verse, convinced that there was no meaningful difference between the two.[6]

The idea of *occasion* for Gunn was a central one, which he introduced in a well-known defense of Ben Jonson against those who would damn Jonson as merely an "occasional" poet who wrote by the elicitation of external event.[7] The notion that sincere and significant poetry is written only by virtue of an originating deep inward impulse is a received Romantic notion that Gunn wished to dismiss. Occasions were not to be understood simply as social; and social occasions were not necessarily separated from deeper impulses in the imagination of a poet. The need to write springs from a combination of social and private feeling. "[A]ll poetry is occasional," he writes, whether "an external event like a birthday or a declaration of war, whether it is an occasion of the imagination. . . . The occasion in all cases—literal or imaginary—is the starting point, only, of a poem, but it should be a starting point to which the poet must in some sense stay true." Gunn then pushes the point that fidelity to occasion is a form of authenticity. "The truer he is to it, the closer he sticks to what for him is its authenticity, the more he will be able to draw from it in the adventures it produces, adventures that consist of the experience of writing."[8]

I have suggested here that one occasion for the longish narrative poem that Gunn eventually titled "Misanthropos"[9] is his ambition to work out in detail "a complete attitude to experience" he found in the modern novel and in poetry before modernism. But Gunn believed that any given poem might combine occasions. The prompting occasions of "Misanthropos" include structural, rhythmical, and philosophical motives, which for Gunn meant addressing a practical question: what is the right way to live?

"It might be remarked," writes Gunn, "that part of the lack in poets is connected with the decline of the longer forms of poem—the epistle, the narrative, the satire, the epic. The lyric has superseded them, and the lyric cannot contain as much—by way of corroboration, 'build'—as the larger poem and the novel. . . . A good sonnet by Shakespeare doesn't contain as *much* as Mann's *Dr. Faustus*—nevertheless it contains the same effort to explore and understand experience, and its very shortness may lead to a stronger interconnection between the exploration and the understanding."[10]

If the lyric had surpassed larger forms of poetry that at one time had "held their own," so to speak, against the novel and drama, then one way to lift contemporary poetry's diminished status would be to press the advantage of lyric intensity beyond its generic limits by using narrative. By conceiving of a narrative sequence composed of interdependent lyric parts, Gunn was actively working against much of the current of modern poetic sequences dominated by *lyrical* structures. These were "a way of making and viewing poetic constructs," writes M. L. Rosenthal, "that concentrates on something other than logical and narrative and thematic limits."[11] Gunn did not try to explore experience through an open lyric sequence (as did Robert Duncan), nor through extensive meditations on culture and history (as did Eliot, Pound, and, later, Charles Olson), nor through a reimagining of historical space (as did W. C. Williams). With "Misanthropos," Gunn worked through an essentially *narrative* enterprise: to show how a character finds an ethical solution to a social problem, a solution that comes from feeling one's way toward acting in the world. The process of discovery may be interior to the self, but the problem is one of social relation.

We thus find Gunn in 1963 in a tense imaginative moment: a British poet of impressive talents attempting to absorb the prosodic experimentation of twentieth-century America while holding onto a premodern allegiance to formal coherence and continuity; a lyric poet who sees narrative fiction and drama as more successful than poetry in exploring modern experience; and yet a poet who wishes to reinvigorate contemporary poetry without any diffusion of form. A poet whose understanding of human will, informed by existential philosopher-novelists such as Jean-Paul Sartre and Albert Camus, is qualified by his perception of historical and psychological contingency. A poet who is attracted to "the Man of Energy," who seeks also a position of poise, of contemplation, of comprehension; whose desire for personal freedom risks terrible isolation; whose desire to connect with others risks submission to their values.

2

"Misanthropos" is a series of seventeen linked poems divided into four sections ("The Last Man," "Memoirs of the World," "Elegy on the Dust," and "The First Man"). It tells the story of a man who has served as a courier in a global war; he has escaped battle, and, having journeyed to a distant part of the world, and, not having encountered any other people, thinks of himself as the sole survivor. Gunn writes that he "conceived the work at times as science fiction and at times as pastoral."[12] The dynamism of the pastoral genre often lies in its inclusion of anti-pastoral elements—the apparent peace and open freedom of living in harmony with the natural world threatened by war, enclosure, and death. In "Misanthropos," pastoralism is an existential condition in which the misanthropic man must create a new world in the ashes of the old. He tries to lose the old world by immersing himself in the particulars of a present natural world outside of history. Yet his consciousness is hateful and painful, keeping him linked to past conflict. Here is the first poem of part one, "The Last Man":

> He avoids the momentous rhythm
> of the sea, one hill suffices him
> who has the entire world to choose from.

He melts through the brown and green silence
inspecting his traps, is lost in dense
thicket, or appears among great stones.

He builds no watch tower. He lives like
the birds, self-contained they hop and peck;
he could conceal himself for a week;

and he learns like them to keep movement
on the undipped wing of the present.
But sometimes when he wakes, with the print

of stone in his side, a relentless
memory of monstrous battle is
keener than counsel of the senses.

He opens, then, a disused channel
to the onset of hatred, until
the final man walks the final hill

without thought or feeling, as before.
If he preserves himself in nature,
it is as a lived caricature

of the race he happens to survive.
He is clothed in dirt. He lacks motive.
He is wholly representative.[13]

Who is "the last man," and what is the occasion for telling his story? Who is avoiding "the momentous rhythm / of the sea" and learning "to keep movement / on the undipped wing of the present"? It is Gunn, the poet—that's one answer—who in this nine-syllable measure avoids the momentous rhythm of iambic pentameter, finding instead improvisational movements and unpredictable rhythms. The pull of blank verse is almost insurmountable, however, as the first tercet indicates. The line may avoid pentameter, yet the poem's first clause enacts a momentous rising rhythm and fulfills the contract of measure:

Hĕ ăvóids | thĕ mŏmént | ŏus rhý | tȟm
òf | thĕ séa, . . .

Well, he does and does not. The poet avoids "the momentous rhythm" *in* the line, but he enacts it in the clause. The clause makes a pentameter of two triple feet and three duple feet (anapest | anapest | iamb | iamb | iamb—the second iamb divided by the line break). But the opening line is rhythmically uncertain: is it rather a trimeter (anapest | anapest | amphibrach), leading to another anapest at the beginning of line two? The rhythm of the syntax expresses disregard for the end-boundary of line one: the unaccented final syllable of line one ("-thm") joins the first syllable of line two ("of") by force of syntax, to make an iamb across the line boundary—an unorthodox move for a traditional prosody, but one supported by the shift in pattern in the clause, from anapest to iamb. The prosodic identity of the poem's opening, then, remains suspended between old and new. After line two, however, the rhythmic pattern breaks apart, and the poet escapes to his hill. "The hill to which the last man has retreated," writes Gunn in an autobiographical essay, "shares characteristics with both Ladd's Hill in North Kent and Land's End in San Francisco"[14]—San Francisco, where Gunn began to tune his ear to the unpredictable rhythms of syllabics and, subsequently, to free verse. The existential condition of "the last man" thus finds embodiment in an existential rhythm that denies any a priori normative pattern: form and meaning are constructed in the moment; they are discovered, free from the expectation of accent and beat.[15]

While the poet can learn to hear such new rhythms, he does not *un*learn the old ones. The last man's "relentless memory" of battle is, in some sense, too, the poet's inheritance of a cultural memory that arrives, in the five poems of part 1, in the figure of an iambic rhythm and end-rhyming or metrically predetermined verse forms: rhyming couplets (poem 2), blank verse (poem 3), terza rima (poem 4); only to return to syllabics (poem 5). The ethical situation of the abject "last man" is the aesthetic situation of the poet himself: desiring some degree of freedom from a cultural inheritance (war, for the last man; a metrical tradition, for the poet) he discovers such freedom illusory. True freedom—or a truer one—may be discovered in a set of complementary binaries: of cultural memory and futurist vision, of traditional and freer measures, of lyric and narrative, of Ladd's Hill and Land's End. And, as the poem reveals, of "last man" and "first man."

I acknowledge that I am in danger here of confusing the poem with its sources—it's a danger to which Gunn himself was particularly sensitive. His concern was that his homosexuality, once it became an avowed fact of his life, could mislead readers intent on interpreting his poems through a biographical lens.[16] But reading through biographical fact is not quite what I'm attempting here. "Misanthropos" works on two immediate levels—the first is that of the purported subject, a story in verse of "the last man"; the second, very close to the first, offers an allegory about making poems. The title of the poem, the name of its protagonist, the nature of his actions—all of these indicate an allegory, or a poem containing elements of allegory: that is, containing constitutive, interdependent features representative of something else. The allegory works through a philosophical problem: how to live in the world, how to live in history. The problem must be dramatized through the narrative: the choices the protagonist makes when confronted by his circumstances, and how he reacts to events; the way Freedom of Will expresses itself, particularly in relation to Fate.

But the problem of how to live in the world, how to live in history, provokes both a metafictive as well as a narrative problem: how does one write a poem responsive to the history and the future of poetry? The first problem, of how to live in the world, is universal; the second, a problem for the artist. How Gunn responds to the exigencies of poetry inflects how he imagines an answer to the existential problem of the last man.

To see how poetry's demands of historical consciousness reflect existential conscience, one need only look at Gunn's vigorous use of traditional form. In reviving the Elizabethan echo form in poem 2, for example, Gunn's end-rhymes dramatize "a man alone receiving the echoes of his fear":[17]

> At last my shout is answered! Are you near,
> Man whom I cannot see but can hear?
>
> Here.
>
> The canyon hides you well, which well defended.
> Sir, tell me, is the long war ended?
>
> Ended.
>
> I passed no human on my trip, a slow one.
> Is it your luck, down there, to know one?
>
> No one.
>
> What have I left, who stood among mankind,
> When the firm base is undermined?
>
> A mind.

Yet, with a vacant landscape as its mirror,
What can it choose, to ease the terror?
Error.

Is there no feeling, then, that I can trust,
In spite of what we have discussed?
Disgust.[18]

The couplets, by returning the projected voice back on itself, reflect the last man's isolation, in which object and image, question and answer, are caught in a kind of feedback loop: the answer to each question is the question repeated as homonym.[19]

From third-person present (poem 1) to first-person present (poem 2) to third-person past (poem 3), Gunn makes explicit the narrative structure of his various lyric forms; in their interdependency, they show contingent (not transcendent) meaning. Gunn first establishes the dramatic situation (poem 1), then shifts to a performance of the protagonist's voice (poem 2), and then shifts again (poem 3) to a point on the narrative timeline prior to that of poem 2:

Earlier, traveling on the roads where grass
Softened the gutters of the marsh bird's nest,
He walked barefoot already, and already
His uniform was peeling from his back.[20]

As he loses the uniform, "sloughed . . . bit by bit"—like an animal its skin—the man becomes "wholly representative," and "without a role," without an individual identity. He begins to fashion a new skin "of mole and rabbit":

His poverty is a sort of uniform.
With a bone needle he pursues himself,
Stitching the patchwork spread across his lap,
A courier after identity, and sees
A pattern grow among the disarray.[21]

To apprehend the pattern, to make meaning in the wilderness of phenomena—this is the function and value of intellect; to respond to absolute solitude is to find oneself, like Adam, in a new (albeit purgatorial) world.[22] As the blank verse of poem 3 moves to the more thickly patterned terza rima of poem 4, the pursuit of self yields to the appearance of moon and Milky Way, "a luminous field that swings across the sky":

> The ancient rhythm almost comforts, slow
> Bright mild recurrence that he might move by,
> Obedient in the act of breath, and lit,
> Mere life, by matter traveling sure and high.
> But this is envy for the inanimate,
> The youth of things. On the dead globe he sees
> Markings as one might on the earth from it,
> Where relics of emergent matter freeze.
> Down here, two more births followed on the first:
> Life, consciousness, like linked catastrophes.
> Their sequence in him cannot be reversed
> Except in death, thus, when the features set.
> Meanwhile, he must live, as he looks, immersed
> In consciousness that plots its own end yet;
> And since the plotter through success would lose
> Knowledge of it, he must without regret
> Accept the inheritance he did not choose,
> As he accepted drafting for that war
> That was not of his choosing. . . .[23]

The narrative sequence of existence—one is born, then grows into consciousness, ages, loses consciousness, and dies—is an inheritance one does not choose, just as consciousness is received without choice. Yet, given consciousness, one is also given a freedom within that life-sequence: to exercise the will, and to make choices. One is "obedient in the act of breath" because one must live by breathing; but having taken the breath, one is free, as a poet, to invent new combinations of linguistic sounds. In prosodic terms, one could say that within the inherited metrical line emerges an individual rhythmic identity; within the determined sequence there persists a significant degree of freedom. The danger, always, in accepting the inheritance—of consciousness, of history, of a metrical tradition—is complacency on the moral, imaginative, or rhythmic levels. The last man accepted his draft into the war, and served, just as he served others before the war (poem 9), abandoning "my whole self time after time"; "I was presence without full being," thus, one kind of inauthentic existence. His acceptance is not heroic, because his inheriting of consciousness does not lead to an act of will.

The existential exemplar of "Misanthropos" is, finally, not a fictional "last man" but rather the historical figure of Anton Schmidt (poem 11). Schmidt, a *Feldwebel* (sergeant) in the German army, risked his life to help members of the Jewish underground in Poland (which happened to include Abba Kovner, the Hebrew poet) by supplying them with forged papers and military trucks. "Most important of all," reports Hannah Arendt in *Eichmann in Jerusalem*, "'he did not do it for money.' This had gone on for five months, from October 1941 to March 1942 when Anton Schmidt was arrested and executed."[24]

He never did mistake for bondage
The military job, the chances,
The limits; he did not submit
To the blackmail of his circumstances.

I see him in the Polish snow,
His muddy wrappings small protection,
Breathing the cold air of his freedom
And treading a distinct direction.[25]

Schmidt's direction of action is individual, not the *uniform* action of the German army; the limits of his position, his identity, his military job, do not bind his will; he acts to help the victims of a murderous systematic anti-Semitism. Rather such limits create opportunities for free choice. The freedom is cold, though, because the consequences of acting in accord with its moral rigors will lead, in Schmidt's case, to his death. Within the *circumstances*, which are fixed, Schmidt takes his *chances*, which are improvised. The rhyme links the oppositions at a subconscious acoustic level.[26] The poem, "Misanthropos," may be a fictional allegory of a philosophical and artistic problem, but its moral center of gravity is located in an actual historical moment. The historical example adds moral weight to the fictive world of "Misanthropos" and its philosophical tensions. But while the potential consequences for Schmidt are final, those for the poet are not. The risk of using Schmidt's example for the poem is to make it portentous; yet the poem's fiction of catastrophic aftermath gains credibility through the incorporation of a historical particular.[27]

Where Anton Schmidt chooses to tread the "distinct direction" of taking right action in morally compromised circumstances, the last man chooses to "keep to the world's bare surface." He

> must perceive, and perceive what is:
>
> for though the hold of perception must
> harden but diminish, like the frost,
>
> yet still there may be something retained
> against the inevitable end.[28]

The ambition, "to perceive what is" requires, perhaps, someone like Anton Schmidt, a man with "unusual eyes / Whose power no orders might determine." Yet if such eyes are unusual, capable of perceiving "what is" with moral clarity, they are not unique—others perceived the moral conditions of "what is," resisting and defying the Nazi program. This is the hope behind Schmidt's exemplary actions: born of autonomous will, they too might be an inheritance. The last man must face the "world's bare surface," but he finds there paths that are "bare within limits" (poem 5):

> The trick
> is to stay free within them.
> The path branches, branches still,
> returning to itself, like
> a discovering system,
> or process made visible.[29]

The "last man" and poet are fused in the act of making a process visible. The discovering system of bare paths through "endless" "green overtaking green" is not *already there* before the last man makes it "by his repeated tread . . . enacting the wish to move." Nor, one could say, is the poet's "discovery system" *already there* in a prosodic tradition; rather he cuts the path himself, syllable by syllable, enacting his wish to move along a verbal path through an endless inarticulate green of phenomenal, instinctual life. Pattern may preexist its apprehension, but meaning is made in the existential moment: it has no a priori status. Gunn fashions syllabics here to make that process visible (audible); yet it remains open and exploratory even as it returns to itself.

The transatlantic occasion, the poem suggests, is one of synthesis;

Gunn's incorporation of more open "American" rhythmic form, a meter loosened from a traditional accentual-syllabics, is part of the aim, in addition to the synthesis of narrative and lyric form, to increase the capacity of lyric. Gunn uses novelistic techniques, temporal breaks (moving to the scenario's back-story), shifting points of view (from one character to another, from third-person omniscient to first person); thus he further opens the discovery system of lyric to include new rhythms and new verbal experiences.

The narrative climax of the poem arrives with a group of other survivors, forty people (men and women), whom he spies while "hidden behind a rock" (poem 15). As one of the men stumbles with fatigue, he leans upon the rock to rest; the last man, moved by an impulse to make contact that "he does not yet understand," steps out from behind the rock, and startles the other, who "jumps back, staggers, calls / Then, losing balance on the pebbles, falls." The last man catches him; in that moment of physical contact, he triggers a reversal in which he is recognized as "the first man," found in a state of primitive isolation. Other people approach as well "and look at me full, / and as they pass they name me." The last-man-become-first-man finds, in contact with these others, his capacity for speech:

> By an act of memory,
> I make the recognition:
> I stretch out the word to him
> from which conversations start,
> naming him, also, by name.[30]

The Adamic role of first-man-as-first-poet, naming the phenomenal world, is shared in the acts of recognition and reciprocal response. Gunn explicitly figures these acts in language:

> The touched arm feels of dust, mixing with dust
> On the hand that touches it.[31]

The crisscrossing links of epanados create a different kind of reflective image than the Elizabethan echo form of poem 2. The language of this final poem is not just turned on itself through repetition of sound; rather it structures, through grammatical analogue, a physical symmetry of belonging.

The dust, into which "all are reduced to one form and one size" is made up of countless minute parts. In "Elegy on the Dust," the last man sees the irony that

> Each colourless hard grain is now distinct,
>   In no way to its neighbor linked,
> Yet from wind's unpremeditated labours
>   It drifts in concord with its neighbors,
> Perfect community in its behaviour.[32]

This figure of community is barren in the satire of the "Elegy"; in the narrative climax of "Misanthropos," however, dust is the mortar of a mortal commonness, the bare fact of death a link between one person and another. The synthesis of last man and first man, of poem as fiction and poem as personal meditation, can be heard in a final rhetorical move, in which poem 17 shifts from the indefinite ("one") to the definite ("he"), and then to the second-person pronoun ("you"), implying "everyone."

> His own flesh, which he hardly feels, feels dust
>   Raised by the war both partly caused
> And partly fought, and yet survived. You must,
>   If you can, pause; and, paused,
>
> Turn out toward others, meeting their look at full,
>   Until you have completely stared
> On all there is to see. Immeasurable,
>   The dust yet to be shared.[33]

When the poet writes "you," whom is he addressing? Does the voice belong to the last man, to Gunn? The imperative voice is the poet's meditative self-reflection; the culmination of the narrative structure takes the form of a more intimate address, a kind of lyric self-centering that emerges from the narrative form. The poet discovers the ethical will; the second-person pronoun announces it as his, and ours. "The dust yet to be shared" may be "immeasurable"; yet the poem comes to know such immeasurability through varieties of measure, of meter. A poem of apparent formal virtuosity, "Misanthropos" pushes form to yield an *ethos about form* that is more importantly one beyond form. "The poem," writes Gunn in his notebook, "is about 1) the psychology leading to the act of sympathy. You start as the last man and end as the first man (through perceptions of the meaningless, guilt, the presence of others). [And] 2) [t]he only form in which it is possible to think of an Eden."[34]

"Misanthropos" was begun in San Francisco and finished in London a few years later in 1965. It is the poem Gunn refers to in "Talbot Road," from *The Passages of Joy* (1982), where he shows himself trying "to render obscure passages into English / as I try now."[35] The superimposition in "Misanthropos," of Ladd's Hill onto Land's End, corresponds to the synthesis of styles—of the more closed and the more open, imaginatively grounding the hyphen between *Anglo* and *American.* "My life insists on continuities—between America and England, between free verse and metre, between vision and everyday consciousness."[36] This sense of continuity best defines the modern transatlantic sensibility. Crossing and crossing back. In the imagination there is no fee for such transport.[37]

While Gunn alternated between meter and free verse starting in the 1960s, "Misanthropos" proved to be a key poem:[38] it presented him with a single narrative and philosophical occasion, yet demanded a flexible approach toward subject. Rapid shifts of form took hold within a single dramatic frame, a shift of form responsive to the shifting needs of imitating actions of consciousness (meter) and those of instinct (freer verse forms). Gunn was a transatlantic poet whose feeling of *inheritance* never hindered his *discovery system,* whose growing instinct for formal integrity within formal variety matched a developing ethical vision. To inherit a prosody of English poetry and to move to America to seek new experiences (and thus new rhythms) was certainly an act of will for Gunn. A different version from Anton Schmidt's perhaps, of not being held hostage by circumstances in the exercise of choosing.

But Gunn's growth as a poet was not a teleology parallel to the American severance from England and Europe, of a revolutionary break in style or a radical turn; his sense of growing formal inclusion does not include a renunciation of a prior formal practice—(again) he is not, in that sense, a *formalist.* "It's interesting," noted Clive Wilmer in an interview with Gunn, "that you continue to like a good deal of poetry you admired as a younger man. I know, for instance, that you're a great admirer of Edgar Bowers's new poetry, which couldn't contrast more than it does with August Kleinzahler [for whom Gunn expressed enthusiasm]." Gunn replied:

> Well, this connects with what I was saying before: that stylistic concerns are not limited to style of poetry only. They have to do with impulses and decisions in our lives in all aspects. Impulses, of their nature, are kind of

> open-ended and we have impulses all the time. We also make decisions all the time and those are closed, like closed lines in poetry, they're like metre, they're considered. Our lives are mixtures of those. So I continue to have sympathies with both kinds of poetry. I'm not surprised that I have sympathies with such a broad range of poetry: I'm surprised that everybody doesn't.[39]

3

My look at the transatlantic occasions of "Misanthropos" takes place within the bounds of creative process, while only hinting at contexts. But what were the social occasions of the poem, and how did they inform the imaginative ones? In some sense, of course, it's impossible to know, because, while the poem is fixed, the social context, like any process, is in flux and hard to see. Nevertheless, just as there are clues to the process, learning the poem's social context adds to our understanding of Gunn's transatlantic occasion.

"Misanthropos" first appeared in the August 1965 issue of *Encounter,* along with poems by (notably) Anthony Thwaite, Gavin Ewart, and D. J. Enright. Edited by Melvin J. Lasky (an American intellectual) and Stephen Spender (the British poet), the issue also included Isaiah Berlin on J. G. Herder; Barbara Rose on pop art; Arthur Lewis on African dictatorship; a dispatch by Edward Lucie-Smith on the famous Albert Hall poetry recital (Ginsberg, Lawrence Ferlinghetti, Christopher Logue, Adrian Mitchell, et al.); Walter Lippmann's "On the Importance of Being Free"; and a spirited exchange in the "letters" section on Marx and alienation.

Encounter, founded in 1953 by Spender and Irving Kristol, was a serious intellectual journal that served as the showcase for the anticommunist, antitotalitarian "Congress for Cultural Freedom"; its agenda was to promote abroad not just liberal values, such as intellectual freedom, but other American values as well.[40] "Specifically," writes Paul Giles, "the publication of *Encounter* from London coincides with a new interest in American culture within British university and political life. The British Association for American Studies was formed in 1955, only four years after the equivalent academic organization in the United States, and Marcus Cunliffe, one of the most visible forces in the British Association in its early years, was a frequent contributor to *Encounter.*"[41] So, too, reports Giles, was the Cambridge critic, Tony Tanner.

Tony Tanner was a good friend of Gunn's. They met at the University of California, Berkeley: Gunn was on the faculty; Tanner was a visiting scholar on a Harkness Fellowship (ca. 1959–1960), which was established to reciprocate the Rhodes. Tanner was one of the first to choose a West Coast university over the East Coast Ivies. He had chosen Berkeley in order to conduct research on the Mark Twain papers, under the supervision of Henry Nash Smith, having already embarked on writing his first book, *The Reign of Wonder* (1965). Though Tanner was never fully comfortable living in the States, he and Gunn shared a keen and committed interest in American literature. Gunn had begun to absorb an American influence in his poetry—his essay on William Carlos Williams, "A New World," appeared in *Encounter* a month prior to the publication of "Misanthropos" there. Tanner likewise had begun to devote himself as a scholar at Cambridge to the criticism of American literature; he had been working on his study *The Reign of Wonder,* now a classic, during his time at Cal. Tanner dedicated the book "To Thom Gunn," just as Gunn dedicated "Misanthropos" "To Tony Tanner." (Gunn would later add Don Doody, an American friend, to the dedication.) "Many of the themes and ideas in the poem," writes Gunn, "originated in, or were at least helped along by, the wide-ranging discussions between my friends Don Doody and Tony Tanner."[42] The conversation between friends across Gunn's hospital bed as he was recovering from hepatitis is carried over, as one might imagine with writers, to the rigor of the page: two British friends, each immersed, albeit differently, in the project of American literature, publishing frequently in a noted transatlantic journal, learning from their studies, and sharing their inquiries.[43]

When Gunn refers to his mentoring poets and other scholars who influenced him, he includes F. R. Leavis (British) and Yvor Winters (American), and his friends Robert Duncan (American) and Donald Davie (British). But in considering Tanner's study (subtitled, "Naivety and Reality in American Literature") one cannot but speculate on the intimacy of Tanner's dedication, "To Thom Gunn": the book is not *for* Gunn, it's *to* him. One hears such an address most clearly in Tanner's afterword, in which he criticizes J. D. Salinger for generalizing about transcendental problems without establishing a convincingly particular reality; and where he praises Walker Percy (in *The Moviegoer*—a novel Gunn admires) for dramatizing that very problem in Binx Bolling's "decision to . . . turn away from the Universal Law and seek for truth in particular instances."[44]

I may be somewhat fanciful, however, in hearing Tanner address Gunn directly, telling him that American writers cannot easily "take second steps" or arrange the vast, complex American experience they've absorbed into "some sense of ordered form."[45] Yet I can't help but hear Tanner urging Gunn to keep his eye on "architecture and not mere aggregates." "Nature organizes herself to survive," argues Tanner regarding the idea of organic form; "art is organized to discover and display meanings and values. . . . Nearly all American writers have found it difficult to move beyond the first step, to find satisfactory forms."[46] Further, "many American writers have shown persistent antipathy to 'analysis.'" Yet "without some sort of analysis there can be no second steps, no fully realized form. It is the necessary prelude to a new synthesis."[47]

If such concluding remarks were Tanner's challenge, directed publicly "To Thom Gunn" in 1965, "Misanthropos" may stand as Gunn's answer—an attempt to take the "second step," and to create an architecture for aggregate experience. For Gunn attempts, as does Percy, to dramatize the very process itself: how the "last man" will emerge from the instinctual life submerged in aggregates, to discover in his consciousness a connection between himself and others; and how a poet previously devoted to a prosodic tradition that privileged consciousness over nonverbal experience will redraw the metrical contract so as to license improvisation, and to dance according to a rhythm discovered in the moment, on "the undipped wing of the present."[48] The movement of the last man to the first man bears a crisscrossing relation to Gunn's own movement: from a poetry devoted to consciousness to a poetry that can also capture the nonverbal life of instinct. Binx Bolling's shift of commitment in *The Moviegoer* from the "vertical search" (Universal Law) to the "horizontal search" (particular instances) is not a solution, suggests Tanner, but a significant aspect of the problem in the adventure of the American imagination. We hear Gunn working out this tension between fidelity to particulars and the exigencies of an adequate architecture in the 1963 notebook (quoted above): on the one hand, Gunn criticizes the modernists for "leaping into abstraction" in a denial of "particular observations"; on the other hand, the body of a poet's work "should not be a collection of phenomena or of beautiful things, but should add up to a comment on existence." The solution lay in the discovery of new and adequate forms.[49]

One key term connecting Tanner and Gunn as transatlantic compatriots is "synthesis." "One wants a style," writes Gunn in his 1963 notebook, "that does not limit one to a specific type of experience."[50] Gunn developed such a flexible style through his synthesis of metrical and freer verse forms, but it would take years of practice before he could master it. And Gunn never flinched from admitting to himself and to others that this impelling necessity of synthesis had sometimes mixed results. In a clarifying assessment of his work up through 1971, Gunn criticizes his own volume, *Touch* (1967), which included "Misanthropos," as an effort that "doesn't come off." "I was trying," writes Gunn, "too deliberately, to synthesize the styles and meanings, in 'Misanthropos,' which goes dead at the end."[51] Thirty years after the publication of "Misanthropos," Gunn admitted "I had great difficulty in the years when I was writing the poems that went into *Touch*. . . . The book strikes me as transitional."[52] "I really wasn't quite sure how to connect the poetry of everyday life and the heroic poetry (which is greatly to oversimplify the two kinds). But I wanted to make some kind of connection. I maybe started to do so when I wrote a longish poem called, 'Misanthropos.'"[53]

Cast back to the spring of 1964, and we find Gunn in his notebook expressing with some urgency this aesthetic and ethical search for a new synthesis:

> I spend this evening looking through my poems of the last four years. Some appear better than I thought, some worse. But there seems to be no body, there seems no decisive style. They are different from the poems of my three books, but not different enough. They would be okay to support the unwritten poems.

Gunn then adds to the accounting above both "Misanthropos" and "Confessions of the Life Artist;" but, still unsatisfied, he finds that

> though there is more bulk, there is not yet what I want.—What do I want? Well, I want the new vision (I would use this word only to myself),—the new vision fastened in the material world by the style. The vision must be of the strength, variety, validity of life, implying the ethically good. The good must be in commerce with other people, in that delight at their freedom which also makes one's own freedom more precise—and the style must tie it all down to "this" & "this" & "this."

Like Dostoyevsky's conception of *The Brothers Karamazov,* "Misanthropos" and "Confessions of the Life Artist" are merely "preparations for the vision" that will push him to new ways of seeing.

> I have been making eliminations (exclusions), and preparations; but the poetry is still about the Lonely Man, suffering within his limitations or

> being consciously brave & understanding about them. The vision is of him as the same man, but among others like him, and the beauty is in his recognition of them.[54]

"I want to be through with the Lonely Man," Gunn would write a month later. What becomes clear in his further consideration is that this would require him to follow a new impulse—one that not only brings together the consciousness of meter and the instinctual process of free verse, but that also synthesizes the motives of the poet with those of the novelist. "I wonder," writes Gunn, "if what makes a man decide to be a novelist or a poet is the knowledge that he wants to write of others or of himself? I say this because I see that I want to write a kind of poetry that hasn't been much written this century." For Gunn, "technique of comprehension" (Winters) must extend the self from the experience of "Awakening," which he associated with his early poetry, to one of "Recognition," of the self in the social realm, which would constitute the growing obsession for the rest of his career. "Eliot's [poetry] is all about himself; Yeats' is even more concerned than Milton's with striking the pose of the Great Poet; Stevens lives in an inanimate universe where only he is human. Larkin's poetry is all about how he shrinks from other people; Ted Hughes writes of animals; Geoffrey Hill of Subjects. But Pound, for an instant (1919–20) writes of others, Hardy writes of relationship, and William Carlos Williams of all the living world, so some have done it."[55]

How Gunn would manage to produce "a poetry that has not been much written this century" led to the books that followed *Touch* (1967): *Moly* (1971); *Jack Straw's Castle* (1976); *The Passages of Joy* (1982); *The Man with Night Sweats* (1992); and *Boss Cupid* (2000). The significance of that transitional, transatlantic moment for Gunn in the mid-'60s would be difficult to overvalue. "Misanthropos" is a poem he never stopped criticizing, so never stopped thinking about; it was a touchstone, a reminder; a spring chapter in the story of his effort to renew poetry after the formal and ethical exhaustion of modernism. It's not just the story of a poet, though, but of a man who wanted to live the one life given to him. The poetry is not the life, never can be; yet the reader does find a life in it, that is both more and less than the life the poet lived.

Two Versions of "Meat"

THOM GUNN

Meat[1]

My brother saw a pig
rooting in a Cornish
field its eating and rooting
one athletic joy
the whole lovely body
wriggling through the mud and weed

When we the overlords
have slaughtered them we
can taste in their muscle
a delighted interest
we make into ourselves
as the cannibal Huron
digested his enemy's courage

Not like this degraded meat
is it chicken or pork
tastes only of the half-life
in the high bright tomb
echoing with nervous sounds
from the tiers of little cells
where the meat is raised
in its own boredom and shit

To make this meat
worth eating you have to

add the succulent liberties
of tomato, onion,
green pepper, the redolent
adventures of thyme
that crept where it wanted
or rosemary
                    that shook
in the world's breeze

Meat[2]

My brother saw a pig root in a field,
And saw too its whole lovely body yield
To this desire which deepened out of need
So that in wriggling through the mud and weed
To eat and dig were one athletic joy.
When we who are the overlords destroy
Our ranging vassals, we can therefore taste
The muscle of delighted interest
We make into ourselves, as formerly
Hurons digested human bravery.

Not much like this degraded meat—this meal
Of something, was it chicken, pork, or veal?
It tasted of the half-life that we raise
In high bright tombs which, days, and nights like days
Murmur with nervous sound from cubicles
Where fed on treated slop the living cells
Expand within each creature forced to sit
Cramped with its boredom and its pile of shit
Till it is standard weight for roast or bacon
And terminated, and its place is taken.

To make this worth a meal you have to add
The succulent liberties it never had
Of leek, or pepper fruiting in its climb,
The redolent adventures dried in thyme
Whose branches creep and stiffen where they please,
Or rosemary that shakes in the world's breeze.

Gunn's "Meat": Notations on Craft

JOSHUA WEINER

As of 1992, when Thom Gunn showed me the first version of "Meat," in free verse, he had been writing poems in traditional meters and free verse for close to thirty years, exploiting by turns the full range of English and American poetic forms.[1] Already an impressive poet as an undergraduate, Gunn unsettled the Oxford/Cambridge literary world of the early 1950s with tough, brainy stanzas full of syntactic vigor and verbal knottiness reminiscent of John Donne, matched to a philosophically existential sensibility. By the time he got to Stanford University and started working with Yvor Winters, Gunn's searching imagination found expression in his experiments with syllabics—a deliberate, willed attempt to teach himself the unpatterned rhythms of free verse. Since then his poems have shown a virtuosity as much indebted to American innovators such as Williams, Pound, Creeley, and Duncan, as to the poets of the English tradition. As a poet, Gunn is a master of forms: he knows what different forms can *do,* what kinds of effects they have, and how they might capture and give shape to imagination and experience. When does a poet who can write in couplets choose not to? How does the pressure of design urge life into shape?

Reading "Meat" in its early incarnation as free verse against the final, more formal version included in Gunn's book *The Man with Night Sweats* shows us how a poet gets different effects from different forms, and how those effects change our experience of the poem.

The writing in both versions of "Meat" is characteristically chaste and unadorned, the diction terse, the images concise, and the abstractions plainly elegant. About the free-verse version, Gunn says that the poem "was completely finished, no rhyme or suggestion of rhymes." Indeed, the free verse is so plain it seems quite stripped of sonic figures altogether.

The poem catches the reader initially, not through euphony, cacophony, or rhyme, but through its darting, rhythmically quick observation of physical movement:

> My brother saw a pig
> rooting in a Cornish
> field its eating and rooting
> one athletic joy
> the whole lovely body
> wriggling through mud and weed

The shift in position of "rooting" between lines 2 and 3, and the race of syntax over a two- to three-beat line that often breaks between subject and verb or adjective and noun, create the effect of muscles flexing in activity; actions are piled on top of each other without subordination, so that rooting, eating, and wriggling all happen at once, the verse movement jerking forward in its freedom from punctuation.

Observation of physical detail and its pleasures shifts to the poet's enlarging rhetoric in the second paragraph, where a full sentence runs without stalling. The action of statement then shifts again (lines 14–16) as comparison breaks into question and further assertion, lineated stiffly by phrasal blocks:

> Not like this degraded meat
> is it chicken or pork
> tastes only of the half-life

This clipped lurching is quite different from the speed of Gunn's final proposition, which slides over a predominantly two-beat line:

> To make this meat
> worth eating you have to
> add the succulent liberties
> of tomato, onion

The poem in this free-verse version is most engaging formally in the tension and release of its rhythms, the way rhetorical statement and descriptions of physical action come alive through line break and subtle modulations of tone. These effects are generally small ones, and I may be applying unfair critical pressure to them, but I do think they are the poem's real effects. It is not, however, a poem to judge so much as it is a tool to help define the formal achievement of the final version.

Where the first version of the poem seems fresh in its initial spontaneous sensuality—a sensuality that seems immediate despite the claim in the first paragraph that the description is a secondhand account—the final version contains the traditions of the art, and through the measure and rhyme of its pentameter couplets gives a more ordered shape to speech. The first lines of the free-verse poem yank one into the physical with their paratactic stacking and the way phrases trip into each other; in the metrical poem, one hears Gunn *speak* more than one sees the pig rooting—the description of physical action couples with abstraction, which is really the perception of intellect:

> My brother saw a pig root in a field,
> And saw too its whole lovely body yield
> To this desire which deepened out of need
> So that in wriggling through the mud and weed
> To eat and dig were one athletic joy.
> When we who are the overlords destroy
> Our ranging vassals, we can therefore taste
> The muscle of delighted interest
> We make into ourselves, as formerly
> Hurons digested human bravery.

Traditional measure and rhyme work harder and more effectively here toward dramatizing the action of the mind as it runs in the body of a sentence and connects idea and world—the way, for example, that "this desire which deepened out of need" links in sound to the purely physical action of "wriggling through the mud and weed." As an utterance, the metered "Meat" seems itself to exercise more "athletic joy" in the life-generating activity of its syntax. The couplets can reinforce in their end-rhymes conceptual links ("To make this worth a meal you have to add / The succulent liberties it never had"), or heighten physical experience (". . . each creature forced to sit / Cramped with its boredom and its pile of shit"). The couplets throughout are distinguished by their combination of heroic snap and a more pre-Augustan freedom of movement.

In his essay on Ben Jonson in *The Occasions of Poetry,* Gunn writes that the occasion of a poem is "a starting point to which the poet must in some sense stay true. The truer he is to it, the closer he sticks to what for him is its authenticity, the more he will be able to draw from it in the adventures it produces."[2] The occasion of "Meat" is that of a social, moral judgment publicly uttered, and as such it seems to have a fuller, more lively embodiment in pentameter couplets. One feels in the free-verse poem that the possibilities of how to shape speech are multiple and unsettled, and that the poem's closure as the penultimate line drops is groped toward or stumbled upon. By the end of the final version, one's ear is tuned to the counterpoint of rhythm playing against a pentameter line, and the anticipation of rhyme. The poem closes with an inevitability and finality that fits its occasion without stifling Gunn's subtle music.

PART THREE

In America

Summation and Chthonic Power

JOHN PECK

It is our main meaning . . .

—Gunn on eros, not agape, in "A Wood near Athens"[1]

1. Power from Force, Feeling from Impulse

Summation is powerful and mature statement, but as an organizing principle for poetry in English it has regained, long after the modernist detours around it, at best an intricately defended, half-confident status. To modify a phrase from a late poem by Wallace Stevens in "The Course of a Particular," there is a resistance involved. Thom Gunn excelled in skillfully neutralizing that resistance from the outset of his career. As for chthonic power, that phrase represents something common in literary thinking since writers began to reassess Romanticism in the wake of the depth psychologies and the ongoing demolition of traditional metaphysics. Gunn hardly walked in fear of the category, though he never employed it, as far as I know. His flexible style is one of the most conceptually discerning in the century just past, and also one of the most mature in exploring the adventures of instinct ("adventure" a term he takes from Robert Duncan). The two terms in my title, especially given Gunn's experience with hallucinogens, point to several dimensions. Consensus reality, though it has long runs and regular showings, hardly has a corner on the way things are. Also, a price is to be paid for abiding by that consensus, and another for stepping outside for a look around. Both prices are real, and each demands its own currency. Gunn's work tracks the exchange rate between them, and the cost of a round-trip transfer between these destinations.

"Chthonic" is a common adjective now in educated discourse. Recently

I came across the phrase "chthonic power" in W. S. Merwin's memoir *Summer Doorways*. Arriving at Princeton on scholarship late in World War II, the young Merwin discovered at the same time P. B. Shelley's Alastor, William Blake's Satan, and their prototype: "No one had led me to expect the resounding splendor of Milton's language, its chthonic power."[2] With ample substance in Milton's case, the adjective and noun in Merwin's usage point to the authority to rebel against authority. And they indicate linguistic earth for the later riot of Romantic foliage: in that earth stir troubled eros, enormous ambition, and philological depth. Funny thing is, all this may ride as one's youthful baggage behind the sober label *organ tones*—not in Merwin's case but in the routine dishonesty of respectable usage. Whereas if this stylistic quality is messily real in Milton, freighted with outrage, striving, and rebellion, then its kin in other poets should amount to more than decorous trials in the acoustics lab.

The topic is vast: if Milton's *serpeggiante* coils of syntax and parallel complications of rhythm compensate for the abjuration of rhyme, then rhyme must index primordial chthonic reach, along a vertical axis into depth. Osip Mandelstam's "Talking about Dante" from the early 1930s probes an overtone series of hammered rhymes woven through an orchestral fretwork of labials and dentals, as a frame for the presence of earth in heaven, and for the beyond in the here and now. Short of Mandelstam's intuition, Merwin and many contemporaries hear in Milton a resonance that Milton himself did not sense; that is, a poet today longs to sound such a basis within his own isolated venue, knowing that his audience remains wary of the full metaphysical reach of "answerable" style, whether he secretly hankers after some version of it or not. *Paradise Lost* was carried into the American backwoods, along with the Bible and Bunyan, a chthonic portage certainly, but premodern. Yet vast remains the topic: the universals in our time, the heaven of ideas, have fallen entirely into the earth of the human psyche, setting it into tumult.

The consequence for rhetoric of this metaphysical descent is very large, down to the smallest of its elements, whether Francis Ponge's homophones in "Le Pré" or Mandelstam's phonemic drifts. And so what one makes of matters as pedestrian and miniature as "the sensory detail"—Yvor Winters's phrase, redeployed by Gunn—carries heavy freight, stamped *chthonic* in the marshalling yard, and numbering everything implied by Merwin's tone of homage from our secretary for Latin to the Lord Protector Cromwell. In a poet explicitly atheist and Dionysian, as was Gunn, the charged terms of the topic are not imposed on him; indeed, they stand intrinsic to the growth of his mind and style. A treasure found in Gunn in this respect is his explicit confinement within those terms. It enforces his containment of conflict with its long train. Whatever he took and matured from Winters, who for Gunn was the bloodhound of the neglected and significant single poem rather than some system—and however he crossbred it with Romantic adventure and blur in Robert Duncan—the style that he eventually consolidated couched it once more, reshaped and retoned, as definition. (Clive Wilmer has long since indicated the pivotal place that this category holds in Gunn's thinking.[3]) Gunn wrote *Moly* aware that he was encompassing new ranges of experience, including the infrared reaches of sensing and mind, while still writing significant poetry. That consolidation of style brought more to trial and triage than the dispersed chthonic tendency in Walt Whitman: "My voice goes after what my eyes cannot reach, / With the twirl of my tongue I encompass worlds and volumes of worlds."[4] Though Whitman's polygonal voice is spookily effective in "Crossing Brooklyn Ferry," elsewhere it goes too easily everywhere and everwhen, melting solids and achieving solidarity with one sweep of its arm. Whereas the improbable descent from Milton's chthonic power through Winters's postsymbolist fusion of conceptual and descriptive registers to Gunn's own fusion style—stranger lineages have been sown!—brings home the venison.

Obviously I cannot invite Pandora with her box to tea over all this, but must tease my pair of terms into specific alignment. As for chthonic power, let me approach it at first inductively, by way of two poems from Gunn's seventh and sixth books in the *Collected Poems* (*The Passages of Joy* and *Jack Straw's Castle,* 1982 and 1976, respectively), and then more compactly in a pair of poems from *The Man with Night Sweats* (1992), "Philemon and Baucis" and "Odysseus on Hermes (his afterthought)," with a closing look at the summational poem on erotic suffering in *Boss Cupid* (2003), "A Wood near Athens."

Gunn tracks masculine growth in the first two of these books, both its high roads and its dead ends, in particular the classic road of descent into the ego's shadow realm, at times primordial and evil. Two longish poems, "Jack Straw's Castle" and "The Menace," work through a gallery of encounters with this opposite number (which is masculine but itself has a feminine counterpart, at times). I select from this extensive material only one seemingly small feature, a Baudelairean glimmer of radiance when, in the second major poem of descent, "The Menace," Gunn's fantasy opponent becomes a bed partner: in one section "a sly / gleam touches a shirt / thrown over a chair," and in the next it multiplies as great bridge piers are "being searched / by the wind, but their secrets hide / deep in the meshed gleam of the river."[5] Such a detail may gnomically stand in for much larger weaves of theme and treatment because within its descriptive and plotted context it can bear the load. The fate of the sensory detail in Gunn could occupy an essay in itself; in this essay I will focus on its luminosity, mindful of the precedent in Gunn's three favorite poems by Charles Baudelaire (for instance, in "Les petites vieilles," the eyes of old women as puddles at night or ironmongers' crucibles sequined with cooling spatter—the other two poems being "Les septs vieillards" and "Le cygne").[6]

"The Exercise" in *Passages of Joy* and the earlier "Faustus Triumphant" in *Jack Straw's Castle* illustrate a transition, one quietly and the other ecstatically, from chthonic force to chthonic power (a transition I'll characterize shortly). In "The Exercise," Gunn in his mid-fifties recalls the adolescent he once was, sensing then his different nature and drawing strength from the wind that bowled across a woodlot lake fenced in "by the Surrey commuters." That youth leaned into it among branches shaped by the same force. "Though the wind was like / impulse, it was not impulse. / If I was formed by it, I was formed / by the exercise it gave me. / Exercise in stance, and / in the muscle of feeling."[7] Is the stance one of will or something more instinctual? The mature poet has already learned, as he put it in a late interview, that at first he thought his sexuality was chosen or willed rather than discovered as natural.[8] The poem quietly yokes in matters pertinent to the soldiers or toughs idealized in Gunn's early poems but also to the induced transcendence of LSD in *Moly:* in the prose section of "The Colour Machine," detailing the drastic loss of a fellow tripper to psychosis, Gunn then wrote that although he learned to skirt the deep end of that pool, nonetheless "I am uneasy and hanker for courage and impulsiveness."[9] Gunn's connoisseurship of impulse and its consequences marked his mature appreciation of both Duncan and Basil Bunting. Duncan's Pindar poem "cultivates not only pattern but the impulsive life within that pattern," and the Law as Duncan frames it accompanies "true impulsiveness."[10] Bunting's trust in impulse as the counterpart to his search for a modernist form of containment Gunn saw leading him finally "to place the heroic and impulsive in the context of a tragic destiny."[11]

In his essay of 1993 on *The Spoils,* Gunn took the measure of Bunting's life of action, "which is ultimately I think the life of impulse," indirectly with an eye to finding a durable "container" for it not only in Bunting's work but also for his own active commitment, "spontaneous action," as that submits to Gunn's equally strong gift for evaluative summation (in

Bunting he locates two ideograms for this tension, assessor versus man of action and parsimonious versus liberal living).[12] In his finest critical essay, "Adventurous Song," on Duncan in 1991, Gunn distinguished two closely overlapping categories, the impulse of childlike adventure from the adult undertaking of exploration, his examples being Stendhal's Fabrizio del Dongo and Lewis and Clark: all adults, but the first childlike in attitude, galloping headlong through Waterloo with *fun.* Duncan called exploration adventure; Gunn bored into their overlap as would a phenomenologist. "What exploration feels like is to run into the sensory reality of something, often before knowing what it is in conceptual terms, and almost always before being able to fit it in with the already known." I would add that both the explorer and the adventurer are adult, too, in sharing experience that is *initiatic,* a necessary and regulated immersion in sensing and regression at the service of metanoia. Already in "The Exercise," ten years or more before both essays on Bunting and Duncan from the early 1990s, Gunn's grasp of the strengthening lent to him in youth by natural force, which seemed like impulse yet was not, carried long-term implications for understanding—that is, for skill in deriving power from a force whose tempo and character, with chthonic basis and flowing spirit, tests one lifelong. "The wind blew against me till / I tingled with knowledge. / The swiftly changing / played upon the slowly changing."[13]

Lodged one-third of the way into *Passages,* this poem quietly sets this developmental scrim behind the book's scenes of suicide, obsessions, comeback stories for others, examples of self-destructive decline (Elvis Presley in "Painkillers"), and quiet pockets of immersed notice (Keats's absorbing everything on his Hampstead walk back from meeting Coleridge, or a cat hearing the wind three yards off). Not "Spleen et idéal" but *hazard naturel,* the book retrospectively defines his gay masculine formation, one of those hazards being the impulse impersonally invited by his pursuit of *le paradis artificiel,* the rest displaying all those encounters with instinctual shadow that inevitably arose once he was on his way. An important trade-off gets worked into the book's design. Skill in embracing the potentially murderous inner opponent, with his change into erotic chum rather than choker ("The Menace" nuances the same drama that organized "Jack Straw's Castle"), is the reward for the loss of Gunn's deeply idealized Cambridge friend Tony White. The powerful glimpse in "A Waking Dream" makes that loss final, as if glimpsed in Plato's myth of Er in the *Republic;* "The Exercise" follows four poems later. Comparably, the long "Talbot Road" memoir, featuring Tony White again and closing with the lovely departure of an anonymous white-shirted teen youth into the greater world, Gunn's own mature freedom reborn, precedes the cabbie-monologue "Night Taxi" which ends the book on a Hermes-tour, its swift and loose connections topped off by a luminous sensory detail (again the Baudelairean flash or glimmer): "Glancing upward I see / high above the lamppost / but touched by its farthest light / a curtain of rain already blowing / against black eucalyptus tops."[14] The cabbie is Gunn's adventurer/explorer from the final essay on Duncan, *feeling* the sensory reality of the known as its luminous margin enters the unknown. To the book's entire development, its shadow encounters alongside the firming and rebirth of gay masculine spirit, the chthonic/spiritual wind writes signature.

Chthonic force describes, for one thing, then, the sexually explosive ballast of human spirit. In that vein, chthonic power is the conscious incorporation of as much of that force as one can live responsibly. Socrates spoke no less respectfully, in no less awestruck a manner, than did C. G. Jung about this theme in his memoir. Typhonic eros, potentially monstrous at every turn, is a dark god for Plato in the *Phaedrus;* and sexuality, as Jung took pains to acknowledge, moved him no less than it did Sigmund Freud in their early conversations: as a child he dreamed that a momentous subterranean phallus lifted its single eye to the beyond, and as a man he called sexuality the dark face of God. Sex is limitlessly symbolic, therefore: chthonic power expresses such range in its ramifying reach, which modulates into autochthonous loyalty to one's turf, as well as into instinctually grounded union with cosmos, the animal soul, and our own kind. Along its axis one definitely, fatefully enters the transconscious psychic realm, that is, the mysterious range of mineral, animal, and ethereal natures that our possibility somehow spans—the old chain of being rattled, within the tumbrels of instinct, by initiation.

Initiation hath many forms but only one dynamism, framed by mortal risk, loss of illusions, a shift of standpoint, and the derivation of potentially mature power from raw force. The best complementary poem to "The Exercise," therefore, occurs earlier in *Jack Straw's Castle,* where chthonic force comes not from wind but directly from self-drawn blood in the encounter with primal shadow-urges toward power and knowledge. "Faustus Triumphant," a monologue parallel to the long title poem in *Jack Straw's Castle,* dares to celebrate irruptive instinct and its drivenness. "The dazzled blood / submits, carries the / flame," whereas the youth in the later poem had stood into the wind: such is the range evoked in antiquity by complete Dionysian initiation, whose chemically by-blow offspring, equipped with a self-starter but no memory, came onstage in the twentieth century as abruptly as did the god himself at the beginning of Euripides' *Bacchae,* where he commanded the old men to dance (they did) and warned that the rigid young king must follow suit (he did not). Came abruptly, in part because the West had forgotten, in its long detour through the splendor and Gothic distortion of Jewish and Christian spirit, that it had ever known such a thing.

The Faustus monologue falls just past midpoint in *Jack Straw's Castle,* directly after "Saturnalia" and "The Outdoor Concert," one poem away from the pivotal title poem; nine poems separate it from the earlier, equally pivotal "The Geysers." This monologue asserts, years before Gunn reflected on the youthful, persistent, and quiet willing of immersion in natural force, in "The Exercise," that a headlong contract with one's whole nature, including all its shadow aspects evoked in these two books, is man's work. It also keys the feeling of sensory exploration per se to a high pitch. What the adolescent of the 1940s could not know, this monologue specifies: that nature, not as mother but father, as dire pusher rather than nurturer, demands that one shatter the tables of the law, not for knowledge as Faust construed it but for the gnosis demanded by one's whole nature, leading to the paradoxical redemption that Goethe gave to his wildered and disastrous theologian. For Gunn's fellow, redemption translates to a gamble invited by the House and assured of winnings: "For / vein and artery are not / store keepers, nor is / Nature a lawyer."[15] The monologue permits voice to exult in that crossover moment for the conscious life that breaks conventional taboos about pacts with shadow evil in order, finally, to serve the individual taboo that one dare not break. The step is perilous, paradoxical, and quite dark to ordinary mind, as Goethe's *finis* for Faust in heaven clearly signaled and as Dionysian loosenings of instinct ritually taught in antiquity. "Already vining the / arbours of my body, flame / starts from my fingers!"

I would add that Gunn's emphatic embrace of the archetypal father here, in a poem he collected in 1976, joins hands with Robert Bly's astute reading of Goethe's "Mignon" in his commentary-anthology *News of the Universe,* published in 1982; both writers anticipate a *novum,* the emergence of a guiding spiritual father grounded in nature, well past the present disrepute and shambles of the father principle, probably lying on the far side of catastrophe. Although Gunn's style flexibly and keenly defined things with Wintersian and Baudelairean accents, it also, to use Joseph Conrad's phrase, in the dangerous element immersed, enlarging firmly conceptual definition in ways no other recent poet in

English has managed to do. In closing I shall return to implications that this monologue raises for Gunn's work, especially the late "A Wood near Athens," for implication rather than complete statement takes its place in the final tally of his style. "Assertion and implication are not the same as demonstration,"[16] he gently scolded the Bunting of *The Spoils,* yet "A Wood near Athens" relies on implication to complete its demonstration. Gunn's revisions of stylistic grasp, both the quiet and the irruptive fathered by changing influxes from wind or the blood, spirit or instinct, will long repay close scrutiny.

2. A Fusion Style Almost from the Start, and the Old Lyre

The American and British 1960s and '70s root back toward German Romantic resistance, by way of holistic aesthetic *Bildung,* to the same philistine, respectable, and finally repressive opponent against which hipsters squared off in our time. The American proto-fascist reactionaries now in power still find their casus belli in the explosion of cultural change that occurred then, a matter hardly settled by a long shot. What one now makes of that tension can be clarified by seeing it through Gunn's eyes, since he grappled with it (wrestling is a persistent trope in *Jack Straw's Castle*) quite early as a matter of style. And did so in the spirit of engagement: the incisive early essays on Gary Snyder and Ben Jonson firmly set alongside each other two such standards. One is Snyder's respect for manly courage and refinement in meeting chthonic force. Snyder's clean naming and direct presentation lend force to verbs—*feeding* and *surging*—so that "when we reach them we are wholly able to interpret the italics of '*& dark here—*': it is desire-plus-terror as you get a hint to the silent, powerful and leisurely purposefulness of the large and unknown."[17] The other is Ben Jonson's measured navigation between, on one side, willed equanimity together with willed feeling about the dangers of feeling, and on the other side the *unwilled* clarity that derives from *adventure* (the same essential term in Gunn's homage to Duncan) in the spirit of complete grasp: *understanding* things as "taking them to heart, [which] means—ultimately—*acting* on them."[18] Not that even such an engaged stance was sufficient, however; Gunn goes on to infuse *understanding,* in Jonson's mixtures of the artificial with the sincere, by invoking Christopher Isherwood on High Camp. One main stimulus for Gunn at that stage was his encounter with Winters, in no way susceptible to Camp, needless to say. One does well to notice that beside Bunting and Duncan's fusion styles, which in Gunn's view reconciled William Wordsworth with Ezra Pound, and Romantic blur with modernist progression, Gunn had already met up with a fusion style in Winters's postsymbolist practice. It was less a method than a recovery from what Winters saw as persistent defects in Romantic consciousness still abroad among the "badly taught." That subtle practice nonetheless incorporated what it opposed: the pivotal "Sir Gawain and the Green Knight" remarkably ends nearly echoing the conclusion to Keats's "La Belle Dame sans Merci."

Accordingly the sensory detail, already vital for Winters, became newly vital for Gunn in carrying the freight that made definition larger; perception's wedge-function, in what Aldous Huxley called "Mind at Large," colors Gunn's short descriptive poems of immersed notice—"Grasses," "Aqueduct," "Cat and Wind," and "Fennel," among others—with the tone I have noted at the end of "Night Taxi." Initiatic explorations of induced transcendence, and transforming shadow encounters, both stretched Gunn's intellectual toughness and keenness, but also his moral strength—morale, staying power, the heart in action of which he spoke in Jonson—one of whose complements is the Baudelairean compassion constant in his work (to begin with, consider Sergeant Anton Schmidt and the traumatized protagonist in "Misanthropos," and the crone described in *Touch,* both from the mid-1960s). Another complement, however, is the spaciousness of detail in those short poems devoted to description. The fate of the quietly saturated sensory detail marks an epicenter for Gunn's own fusion style, but all these aspects are channels for chthonic power, urgent or quiet, in Gunn's expansion of definition and his measured adoption of modernist containment.

To clarify what containment might mean in Gunn, I would distinguish his interest in modernist structure, notably in Bunting's late longer poems, from containment in another sense of that term, noted by Clive Wilmer in a tribute to Gunn on his sixtieth birthday. "Thom's poems include emotion, but do not attempt to contain it. They evoke sensations, but never pretend to have captured them. He is the most modest of poets: he never allows you to forget that 'there is a world elsewhere.'"[19] Wilmer also nicely distinguished Gunn's appreciation of Winters's view of poetry as a "technique of comprehension" from the more open exploration in Gunn.[20] But in rereading Gunn's essays on both Winters and Duncan, one can see that his sustained grasp of both styles, utterly at odds in spirit, plays host with equal interest to their uses of particulars vis-à-vis the unknown. In Duncan, however dual and blurred the aim, once the embracing idea is established, "it may be extended and deepened in the sensory detail." Thus on Gunn's map, one can observe the early Winters of

"'Quod tegit omnia'"—"Adventurer in / living fact, the poet / mounts into the spring, / upon his tongue the taste of / air becoming body"—brushing Duncan's heretic elbow on the road to postsymbolist comprehensiveness. The encounter becomes intelligible.

Let two passages from *Moly* of 1971 serve as initial inscriptions for the oeuvre: the prayer that brings Gunn's first major phase to summation, "Sunlight," and the epigrammatic "Listening to Jefferson Airplane (in the Polo Grounds, Golden Gate Park)":

> Great seedbed, yellow centre of the flower,
> Flower on its own, without a root or stem,
> Giving all colour and all shape their power,
> Still recreating in defining them,
>
> Enable us, altering like you, to enter
> Your passionless love, impartial but intense,
> And kindle in acceptance round your centre,
> Petals of light lost in your innocence.

> The music comes and goes on the wind,
> Comes and goes on the brain.

Both passages define large harmonies, one differentiated, the other gnomic. Consolidating a decade of social, sexual, and drug exploration, *Moly* took both those stances toward the immeasurable "unity of unabsorbed excess"[21] invoked at the end of "Flooded Meadows." Such meadows occur at least three times in these poems. Their imagery defines the flux that reconfigures mind and poetic ambition but that also outdistances them. "On the stream at full / A flurry, where the mind rides separate! / But this brief cresting, sharpened and exact, / Is fluid too, is open to the pull / And on the underside twined deep with it" ("At the Centre—*LSD, Folsom Street*").[22] A painted board in the next stanza, and human connections in the next after, hint at this too: "The flow-lines faintly traced or understood." Any person from Porlock can make light of drug-altered perception, but they will miss the commissioning it can bring and to which Gunn attests. Hallucinogens show strange amplitudes at large within both sensing and mind, those of madness as well as the CIA's early use of LSD as a truth serum; but their workings also trail far ahead, Hermetic heralds down every road at once. As I shall note toward the end of this essay, they also ask us to reread the literary record, notably the later Pound on sensibility. A British analyst who once assisted Allan Watts used to advise his young acid-tripping patients carefully to record their experience, stow the record for twenty years, and only then digest it for meaning. To drop acid may well mean to drop down the entire gravitational curve of human development before one can actually read it.

Robert Stone has remarked in an interview that the generation subsequent to his, which he taught for a decade at Yale and which affected materialism and elegant fashion, as inheritors of 1960s culture showed little change as a consequence of that bequest. Any acceleration of sensibility, and the necessary delay in mining it, may turn into a tribal dead end. Assimilation of such sensibility is as arduous as any real and sticky shadow, a commissioning from which there is no escape. In the second of three essays on Robert Duncan in 1988, Gunn lamented the small ambitions of all Duncan's contemporaries, including, it seems, himself—perhaps, it strikes me, from his knowing all too specifically that, with Mind at Large, one's attitude, the heart that one acts upon, must go with one's skills to the school of category redefinition. Gunn's learning from contrary and ambitious fusion styles sets him apart in this respect. His fascination with Robert Duncan dwelt on the openness to procedures for venturing all over the place, poetically at risk but achieving nonetheless the *containment,* in Gunn's word for Basil Bunting, of both Romantic and modernist practices, of Romantic blur with Pound's precision. I suspect that a careful reading of "The Geysers," but also of any number of other poems both metered and in free verse, would show Gunn putting all of this study to work in relatively small compass, on the scale of the single phrase, line, and enjambment. There is also the question of the internal organization of each of the sections in his later books. *Containment* is Gunn's term for Bunting's achievement of both the cleanly defined phrase and modernist progression, first in *The Spoils* and then in *Briggflatts; "stylistic* willfulness" is one of his charged terms for Duncan's achievement in the pivotal Pindar poem, in "a field which is both an open and a boundaried place."[23] Only that poem for Gunn ranked in the same class with *Briggflatts,* the poem which for Donald Davie, too, was the century's landmark outside of parts of *The Cantos.* The yearned-for lover in "A Poem Beginning with a Line by Pindar," a motive whose lineage includes Dante and Plato, was not an object of ambition for Gunn as it manifestly was for Duncan, yet Gunn's work as a whole has been determined by a factor equally daunting in its attraction. One cannot name it with Duncan's allegorical compactness as the soul's erotic power, although eros and conviviality frame it throughout Gunn. Baudelairean compassion begins to encompass this range of feeling in his work, but my guess is that only cosmogonic eros, questioned and brought to summation in the late "A Wood near Athens," names it compactly.

Our topic is stylistic fusion, but it requires distinctions. In Duncan's Pindar poem, the beginning, like Ariadne's awakening on Naxos, is sudden and disoriented. Gradually the poem fills out the soul's yearning for its partner or lover, through a *collagiste,* Poundian trajectory of paratactic accretion and development. By contrast, both in "At the Centre" and "The Geysers," Gunn moves slowly and section by section (description supporting analysis) through an integral experience, in the second poem literally into the landscape that supports the experience, both times to epiphanies—the sublime axis in "Terror and beauty in a single board," and the dismemberment-rebirth axis in "I am / I am raw meat / I am a god"—each of which also acquires a particular social context. In "Sunlight" the discourse is meditative, analytic description—postsymbolist at maximum efficiency and depth—culminating in prayer. It is the Cleanthes hymn of our day. Gunn's essays on Duncan, Winters, Bunting, and Isherwood write the bible on these matters, but Gunn and Duncan together flank a factor that those essays do not describe: the long drama of speed and then recuperation from acceleration, of metanoia then fidelity to its consequence.

Gunn's subtle terza-rima elegy for "our Dionysian experiment," "Saturday Night" (from his last book) identifies that drama's sponsor: although Duncan's poem takes up the Cupid-Psyche myth, the double for psyche in one respect is indeed Dionysus. A peculiar abruptness marks Dionysian initiation, which plays out as union. Symbolized by marriage, it alters both partners (the god is no longer animal emotion but devoted feeling). The boisterous, disorienting, triumphal rebirth of Dionysus, with infusions of wine, signals an advance over a catastrophic, titanic instinctual fate.

Dionysian cult embraced initiation as dark-bright, initially ecstatic but then unfolding through a long chapter, which its myth turned into a love story that changes both the human ego and the divine factor. Enormous longing—Duncan's theme in the Pindar poem—is met with a tumultuous opening, a new light from the trans-conscious psyche, no longer filtered solely through the world and not to be grasped all at once. In the last of the initiatic Dionysian frescoes at Pompeii, a seated matron gazes at all the other previous scenes as if she were, as Linda Fierz-David proposes, Memory herself gathering what must be assimilated whole and in right sequence, without distraction.[24]

Another poem from *Jack Straw's Castle* installs an interlude among its initiatic descent into encounter with primal shadow. "The Outdoor Concert" invokes the softer Silenic integration as a pre-discursive opening to meaning. "At the edge / of the understanding / it's the secret. / You recognize not / the content of it but / the fact that it is / there to be recognized."[25] One no longer wrestles with content or proposition, but submits to perfused connection. This interlude from descent installs two other Dionysian dimensions of great age: the late Hellenistic presence of "the near one," whether in grotto or temple, celebrated *hupaithrion* or under "the open sky"; and then the god's initiation of women and promotion of social mixture to sponsor civic cohesion.[26] Both factors save the community in the end, though often "outside" of or no-where (u-topian) in respectability. Gunn's first elegy for Duncan in long lines from the late 1980s, "At the Barriers (Dore Alley Fair) in memory Robert Duncan," is sited behind police traffic barricades from the rest of town. Including an inset of leopard slugs on a TV screen dangling in primal sexual embrace—Typhonic eros in slo-mo, safely mediated—it plays out the Dionysian investiture of civic space with chthonically *initial* stable coherence. For even with his aura of dismemberment, *Dionysus Polites, ho pro poleōs,*[27] was civic as we are not, troubling gender separations as *the Loosener* while bonding the polis (that paradox being his forte), leading the Delphic oracle to put it in '60s Berkeley terms: he must be honored by citizens "in the streets *ammiga pantas* all mixed up together."[28] In "Outdoor Concert," the open-air, companionable dimension, the Old Lyre teaching of dithyramb and vast attunement, both matches and qualifies the rock concert scene. Thus the assignment of that lyre, as the late Hellenistic initiatic frescoes at Pompeii paint it, went to a mildly ample Silenus with the face of Socrates.

So Gunn's interlude in that book concerns, in the big picture, the Beethovenian, titanic wozzle of natural flux, sounding from the arena or the hillside on bass amps, as obligato to a subtle yet venerable discipline that must transmute large stressors. Typhonic eros stands over against the love for what Diotima carries: the one breeding raw engulfment, the other the comprehensive light of nature, but together gearing us now, *aristoi* and *demos* alike, into "our main meaning." If we get it right, we will taste through the raw the gentle, stay on our pins with the Socrates who drinks more than anyone else while staying awake, and not consign the prickles to amnesia. Those same frescoes at Pompeii show a huge winged being whipping the daylights not out of but into an ecstatic female initiate: with Dionysiac influx, in the best of all possible whirls, come both the Old Lyre and the sting of consciousness.

In one of his seminars from the early 1930s, describing processes that show crucifixion following from Dionysian initiation, Jung observed that they have us touch a bit of the "conscious experience of the totality of nature," which demands staying with life as it *is*. But if we do, then at the same moment we know joyous fulfillment and great pain. "One tries to keep them separate. But . . . in actual fulfillment, you will have seen and felt the sting."[29]

What does such initiatic sting punctuate if not mind rewritten? The narrative comes in over one's head, compactly, whose agenda must be taken as it comes, however long that takes. In the first section of Gunn's superb elegy "Duncan" in *Boss Cupid*, his description of the poet composing nonstop, as he rides the ferry back and forth across San Francisco Bay, enacts an expeditionary and endless poetics. Its loom-like action might even allude to the myths for writing in Greece and the Rig Veda (the stem for *hymnos* refers to weaving). In section 9 of "A Seventeenth Century Suite," Duncan writes, "Slow, slow, even as time alone erodes the matter, / I turn and turn upon my life."[30] At any rate, its open-field shuttling at last gets tautly straightened by life—a few lines later in that section, Duncan writes, "In the old stories, the protagonist learns / what Time has to do with him"—for here life itself spreads the page with its framing spaces, in Gunn's stirring allusion to Venerable Bede's account of the Anglo-Saxon mead hall at the end:

> He was now. . . .
> In sight of a conclusion, whose great dread
> Was closure,
>   his life soon to be enclosed
> Like the sparrow's flight above the feasting friends,
> Briefly revealed where its breast caught their light,
> Beneath the long roof, between open ends,
> Themselves the margins of unchanging night.

Gunn's own book was inscribed with subtly rewritten *definition*, early mastered but later stretched. In "Duncan" he reports that the ill and weak poet, falling down Wheeler steps at Berkeley, mythologized the event by having Gunn catch him as he fell, whereas in fact, "He fell across the white steps there alone."[31] In generous fancy Duncan assigned closure to his mishap: there it could be sweet because it honored filial love. Gunn's great tribute, by submitting the weaving motion of Duncan's poetics to the overmastering stroke of the bird's flight, does finally catch his great friend, although not physically. That stroke folds the open field of Duncan's poetics into the definitional summary of Gunn's own method, a moving closure that is also complementary and deeply relational. Another Baudelairean gleam swiftly spot-welds the effect. Though Gunn perceives Duncan as he must through his own practice, the two ways of writing converge in a totality upon which Gunn's poem also closes in, taking it up in its arms. Duncan the weaver had enlarged Gunn's practice, to be sure, yet Gunn had to be large enough to receive it with his own different, more linear grasp.

3. "Invented in the continuous revelation": The Sting of Consciousness and Staying Power

For a start on Gunn's own Dionysian practice, well along into its unfolding, I will explore two yoked poems from the 1980s. Collected in *The Man with Night Sweats* of 1992, "Philemon and Baucis" and "Odysseus on Hermes (his afterthought)" compose a virtual diptych. The first poem describes the trees that frame Ovid's telling of the myth, both separate and melded ("the two trees close together, and the union / of oak and linden in one"). The only people in Phrygia who gave hospitality to Zeus and Hermes disguised as men, Philemon and Baucis were spared the retributive flooding of their region, were made Zeus's priests, and were granted the boon of simultaneous death—which came as mutual metamorphosis into those trees.[32] Gunn's epigraph from W. C. Williams reads, "love without shadows." That ideal, since ideals are never quite human, Gunn refracts through an Ovidian fusion of opposites in the green world, alluding to the couple's normal conflicts but also transposing fulfillment, and the long term of marriage, leafward. The challenging love story of mind with chthonic love's initiating influx, a dimension of Gunn's work after *Moly*, is never far away. The poem quietly reformulates the appeal of Romantic consciousness:

> They put unease behind them
> a long time back. . . .
> . . . when each
> —Riding the other's nervous exuberance—
> Knew the slow thrill of learning how to love
> What, gradually revealed, becomes itself,
> Expands, unsheathes, as the keen rays explore:
> Invented in the continuous revelation.[33]

Sunlight here, prolonged illumination, spurs a slow invention through self-unfolding: Keats's vale of making reformed, and subversively also (in Winters's phrase) a form of discovery.

Romantic consciousness, which Gunn addressed several times at least—in the second essay from 1991 on Duncan, and in the witty sonnet "Keats at Highgate"—was of course the constant theme of Winters, who ambitiously shifted from modernist free verse to meter, mastered American, British, and French poetry, made a diagnostic study of American literature, and, as he wrote rambunctiously to Pound in 1928, claimed that "I could have done you more good than Joyce."[34] Gunn attests that he learned more about poetry from him than from anyone else, a telling testimony to the friend who sternly assessed Gunn's work in *Forms of Discovery* before his death in 1968 as often "journalistic." The younger man did not mind. The few who have read Winters usually pass over his fruitfully conflicted ways of settling the hash of modern consciousness and its Romantic antecedents. "Sir Gawain and the Green Knight" crowns his passionate engagement with the absorptive surround to human consciousness, Gunn's theme in "Philemon and Baucis," but in an agonistic key. "Philemon" converses with his teacher's green-world masterpiece across that divide of attitude, the vernal power in this poem enshrining a possible best outcome of his own risky adventure. Definition in these two poems diverges momentously, from Gunn's side toward small-scale containment in the diptych as a whole, in order to enlarge definition. *Grasp,* the term whose two meanings, holding and understanding, animate a key line in the terza rima of Gunn's late "Saturday Night"—"we translate / Our common ecstasy to a brief ascent / Of the complete, grasped, paradisal state / Against the wisdom pointing us away"—speaks for both definition and containment in view of the social failure of his band's venture.[35] Holding or containment in the diptych alludes to Duncan's role as a Coleridgean Hermes, the man whose table talk repeatedly led Gunn to run home and take notes, attempting to track the process that Michael Palmer calls "strikingly heuristic, resistant to closure, the goal a mapping of attention and a form of comprehension."[36]

Thom Gunn rewrote "Sir Gawain" at least twice: once in the pivotal "The Geysers" of *Jack Straw's Castle,* with a Dionysian embrace of transformation beyond panic, and again here some twenty years later. Eros grounds all three poems; Gunn rewrote Winters by way of relational stances that proved to be life-central for himself and life-and-death for Winters. The erotic test in "Sir Gawain" engaged human consciousness in a sensuous but heroic ordeal in the organic realm, "Where growth was rapid, thick, and still."[37] In his formative experimental phase, Winters had cultivated this state of immersed intensity and immediacy, praising it as "waking oblivion, which is the only infinity and the only rest."[38] During recuperation from tuberculosis, after what the early poetry and prose show to have been a deliberate exploration of liminal states of consciousness, Winters judged that his own equipment would disorient him were he further to pursue his fascination with process, which earlier had moved him toward microbiology. In consolidating his major, metered style around that perception, postsymbolist in his final formulation, Winters compactly rewrote the beguiling fourteenth-century Middle English romance, based on a folktale, using scholarship on the vegetation myths to strike a balance both heroic and accepting. In fact it was his own compact symbol of initiatic immersion and rebirth (Winters was thirty-seven); as I have noted, its coda indirectly signals to Keats's own such drama. In "To Yvor Winters, 1955," Gunn at thirty-four paid homage to his teacher by using Winters's own sensual and agonistic terms. The perceptions and diction mark the old threat to stable consciousness:

> Shapes combine,
> Vague mass replacing edge and flickering line . . .[39]

Yet they also anticipate Gunn's description of the joined trees in "Philemon," and then the cactus and human growths in "Odysseus," the complementary blank verse and free verse refining these yoked matters:

> Their barks have met and wedded in one flow
> Blanketing both. Time lights the handsome bulk.

> . . . in my thick maturity
> suddenly unsettled
> un-solid
> still being formed—
> in the vulnerability, edges flowing,
> myself open to the god.[40]

The older myth, Greek and Levantine, insists on the green wedding that Gunn takes care to amplify through fusion, which in his view the mind may grow into with initiated ease as well as the hero's struggle. In the rest of the tale, the pair is distinguished for hosting the unseen divine factor in an oblivious time. (Goethe lent this behavior great significance in *Faust II*, where Faust has the old couple murdered. Carl Jung inscribed the lintel at his lakeside retreat "Baucis and Philemon's Temple, Faust's Penitence.") This humble duo can pay due respect to powers that are indispensable, dangerous, envied, and ignored, which the learned often use lightly or get wrong. My guess is that Gunn, whose modesty balanced an adventurous ambition, could assess these erotic and cognitive virtues—allegorical for his own enterprise with the senses—largely because Winters and Duncan's dissonant pairing and comparably large ambitions flanked his own. If the news branches "from sense to sense, / Bringing their versions of the flower in small / Outward into intelligence" ("The Messenger" in *Moly*[41]), then the senses, like the old couple, do so generously, without ulterior motives: Thomas Aquinas's doctrine on that same traffic mindward from sensing—nailed onto the doors of the late *Cantos* by Pound—turns out to have large bearings on vitality, which rewards its humble hosts with union at the definitely un-speedy, vegetable pace of non-human life. So valuable is this green note to Gunn that one of his pointedly nasty shadow figures, the speaker of the longish "The Menace" in *The Passages of Joy*, covets just that outcome, "an unceasing thick / traffic of feeling."[42]

As for the learning that Gunn the outsider drew from Winters the maverick, it imbibed something of that mixture of gentleness with rigor that Winters did indeed communicate personally but which his poems wrap close and tight. The old pair in Ovid's tale do not know how good or loving they are; they suit Gunn's reflections in his later fifties in part for what they move beyond, or to one side of: heroic ethics and sensibility. They became fused lover-trees because they took to heart, and acted upon, hospitality to the real, immeasurable thing, quite unaware that divine powers moved *within* them (Odysseus is stirred by just that recognition). For a poet alive to that question of hospitality to the greater, the entry that their tale makes into the green world treats the Gawain-Bercelak tale as Romantic *avant le lettre* and as Greek *après:* hospitality, courtesy, limit powers, and blessing so mark it. To Winters's allegory Gunn added this archaic antiphon about the remaking of mind and heart after the long afternoon of Romantic forays into borderline consciousness.[43]

The drama in "Philemon and Baucis" therefore dovetails with the metanoia spoken in "Odysseus on Hermes (his afterthought)." In one poem Hermes is messenger, while in the other he is subject, the accent there falling on initiatic quickening—on staying open to eros while avoiding engulfment. Sustained openness calls for homeopathic wisdom, however: a greater seducer must shield one from a lesser, the guide Hermes from the temptress Circe:

> I was seduced by innocence
> —beard scarcely visible on his chin—
> by the god within.

This couplet rhyme, solitary in these nineteen lines, takes as formal counterpoint a fourfold repetition of "the god," as Odysseus likens the adolescent facial fuzz to cactus, another simile from the green world, pliant at first and then heavy. Though the god comes in for repeated mention, twice the hero elides himself, twice leaving "I was" unstated (before "still open" and "then closed"). Individual awareness visibly emerges from latent into manifest statement, the sprung grammar packing the lines with tension. And mind sums up things by gradually standing forth into the incalculable factor that has been at work inside it:

> . . . soft-green—not fully formed
> the spines still soft and living,
> potent in potential,
> in process and so
> still open to the god.
>   When complete and settled
>   then closed to the god.
> So sensing it in him
> I was seduced by the god,
> becoming in my thick maturity
> suddenly unsettled
>   un-solid
> still being formed—
> in the vulnerability, edges flowing,
> myself open to the god.[44]

The parenthetical subtitle "(his afterthought)" responds to the moment that Homer narrates in book 10, starting at line 275, and which Gunn used as the epigraph to *Moly:*

> When I was near the house of Circe I met Hermes in the likeness of a young man, the down just showing on his face. He came up to me and took my hand, saying, "Where are you going, alone, and ignorant of the

> way? Your men are shut up in Circe's sties, like wild boars in their lairs. But take heart, I will protect you and help you."[45]

The saving plant and its drug he then yanks from the earth and gives to the refugee.

This parallel visit from the gods in the diptych, and one more erotic transformation, summarize the passage from spellbound youth to requickened, mature veteran. A second pliancy submits cactus firmness to graduate, postdoc dissolution, across an unpunctuated transition: "I was seduced by the god, / becoming in my thick maturity / suddenly unsettled / un-solid." Influx makes the stiff pliant once more; the spiky old warrior faces his original passage anew "in the vulnerability." But now he is among the twice-born, for the abstract noun replaces an adjective because a condition, no mere quality of experience, has been assimilated—that is, both stably defined and flexibly contained. The poem's variable measure precisely reflects this fluid tension between states, hung between a standard trimeter measure varied by lines of shorter and longer length, and free verse, doing so to effect in the abrupt pair of lines inset far right. The final line straddles these modes.

The tension throughout—between pliant and thick, open and closed, younger and seasoned—reworks the end of Gunn's "On the Move" from *The Sense of Movement:*

> At worst, one is in motion; and at best,
> Reaching no absolute, in which to rest,
> One is always nearer by not keeping still.[46]

The initial foot in that final line may or may not count as elided; the line *contains* indeterminacy. So, *one is* and then again *one's as one is,* much as in the later "Faustus Triumphant" significance speedily moves "there" and "there": between the repeated main clauses here stirs Gunn's 1955 mode of balance, strung between his Sartrean mean and his revised Aristotelian mean, the two kinds of willing that he calibrated after meeting Winters. Balance trembles between headlong plunge and vigilant quiver, not yet the nested, budding affair to come, in which the god conjoins the generous couple and pricks renewal loose, and the wound gently open, in the man.

"Hermes" also sponsors the roving youthfulness of serial affairs right through the AIDS period. One might say that it protected Gunn from any shadow deviation into moony drifting (the dilution of guiding and messaging functions), fascinating to Gunn in "The Release," and also from Odysseus's loss of all companions, tasted as senex resignation in "The Great Dejection" (where Eliot's tone muddies Gunn's style for the first and last time). This godly drug dealer therefore keeps Gunn away from falling into sheer animality—engorgement at Circe's sty, in "Cafeteria in Boston," in the rounds of roaming, eat-you-up eros, and also, along the outermost rim of shadow possibility, in the abyssal, homicidal necrophilia of Jeffrey Dahmer, whom Gunn studies compassionately in *Boss Cupid.* "Odysseus on Hermes" marks a hinge point by defining Gunn's mature grasp of a somewhat elusive, essential agency. It has preserved him with repeated pricks of consciousness, stings that inoculate rather than kill. The monologue lets him voice this grasp as a bewildering realization of survival. Contemplation is still forming, in a Romantic redefinition of grasp. If chthonic power invents itself out of chthonic force, then the same holds for comprehension, grasp, and definition: *vulnus,* or wound, must stay open if their potential is to manifest. Chthonic power that deeply takes heart also acts on its understanding in the Odyssean warrior's way, rejoining its mate only after drastic episodes of expansion. *Moly* has grown up.

Duncan too enters this picture along with Winters. Running beneath the overt themes in the diptych is the coitus that Gunn carefully isolated by describing leopard slugs mating on a TV in "At the Barriers (Dore Alley Fair) in memory Robert Duncan," sometime after Duncan's death in 1988. Its announced "Masque of Difference and Sameness" may reach across to the Ben Jonson section 9 of Duncan's "Suite," where "The Solemnities of Masque, and Barriers" play out.

> They are hermaphroditic, equally giving and taking,
> overspread with a pattern of uneven spots, leopard-like.
> By a strong thread of mucus reaching from their tails,
> which suspends them from a branch of the Tree,
> they hang—in air—nothing impeding them
> as they twine upon one another, each body
> wrapped at every point about the other, twisting in embrace,
> in a long slow unstopped writhing of desire,
> wholly devoted to the sensual ecstasy.
> Glistening, they exude juices from their mutual pressure.[47]

Though strictly observant, this is nearly mythical, an underbelly of what oak and linden wrap into each other as fulfillment. It is us and yet not us, infrared sequestered from ultraviolet. Minus the sexual drive, "Considering the Snail" tracked a similar fascination in *My Sad Captains* of 1961. Between slug passion and the god-struck trees whose "Leaves shine / In tender habit at the extremities," Gunn had made his way, Odysseus as his warrant for mobile grasp and Hermes as the light within it. The *molü* antidote to engulfment both guides and conjoins, sanely though uncannily. Duncan had volleyed between a regenerative father in his "Suite" and a divine feminine figure whom he addressed as "a voice / brought to a barrier in marriage as upon perishing / to speak out of the cloud of Jonson's solemn masque / or from that hallucinatory court Parmenides' vision knew."[48] The union of opposites in Gunn's Baucis-Philemon theme saves him, precisely, from the *tour d'horizon* navigated by Duncan's jet airplane—that is, from the devout shuttling that bounced off the barriers it met. Gunn's masculine spirit, a soldier demobbed from his former existentialist cohort—and from furloughs for that G.I. in the Bosch-like, Renaissance-court "Fair in the Woods"—he has mustered into Hermes' green legion, swearing him to an oath of definition while pricking him with the stigmata of his own tattoo. The slowed fusion of lover-trees, a conscious counterpart to slug eros, joins Hermetic cactus in a uniting ideogram. The Odysseus in this poem is Gunn's Sir Gawain.

4. Murder Unincorporated, "inner gloss," and "Slow, accurate lips"

Gunn witnessed the social fate of the 1960s movement through its full run. His inventory of its shadow side was already vivid in "Jack Straw's Castle" and "Painkillers" by the mid-'70s; his epitaph on the movement, including a quietly defiant justification of its value, comes in *Boss Cupid*'s "Saturday Night." The shadow dynamics serve large matters. First, they step up to Robert Stone's critique in both *A Flag for Sunrise,* nearly coeval with *Jack Straw's Castle,* and the recent memoir *Prime Green.* In the novel, a onetime CIA man in Vietnam, the anthropologist Frank Holliwell, remembers an Army-Airborne officer who was convinced he could never lose. Holliwell's Looking-Glass inclusion of the officer's remote counterparts in Golden Gate Park, as doubles to the warrior-fantast, is more than glancing.[49]

> How could they convince themselves that in this whirling tidal pool of existence, providence was sending them a message? Seeing visions, hearing voices, their eyes awash in their own juice. . . . They were beyond good and

> evil in five easy steps—it had to be O.K. because it was them after all. . . . Inevitably they discovered the fundamental act of communication, they discovered murder. . . . For the less forceful, the acceptance of murder was enough. Unhappy professors, hyperthyroid clerics, and flower children could learn the Gauleiter's smirk.

Prime Green reports that a reunion with Ken Kesey's group in California posted Stone exactly above Jay Sebring's home at the time of the Manson gang's murders. Stone's former Company man concludes his analysis bleakly: "It was necessary to believe in oneself. Very, very difficult. One was a series of spasms, flashes. Without consistency, protean, infantile—but one would have to do."[50] Gunn's intelligence had steered neither around nor over these black-Bergson, flower-glower abysses. He variously submitted to Stone's acrid Holly-well test, in part by weighing spasm and flash in the late "A Wood near Athens" as biological reductions of eros, and in part by owning murder's root in one's own earth: "Jack Straw" was most likely another name for Wat Tyler, either way a rebel and wanton killer, a Manson for all seasons. By admitting that *Moly*'s passport "from sense outward into intelligence" required a thorough vetting at Murder Unincorporated, Gunn held frenzy's dire old root into the light, and penetrated collective amnesia, a forgetting longer than our decades of Prime Brown, about his particular initiation of choice.

In that light the "Dionysian experiment" that Gunn stands by, past its failure to secure a social beachhead, acknowledges the initiatic power of a natural intelligence regardless of modern forgetting. Robert Stone's lament in his memoir *Prime Green* over the naïve gift his generation made, of easy meat for the baying hounds of the reactionaries, is met indirectly by Gunn's work, though in the end probably met well.[51] As for now, however, the battered Romantic generation of the 1790s has its heirs, holing up from the rain after "providing the enemies of freedom and insight," as Stone growls, "with a drug menace to hype in their yellow press" and Ronald Reagan's venal populists with an "endless pep rally for repression."[52]

Let me amplify these matters before getting to Gunn's triangulation of Bunting and Winters in his own fusion style.

The repeated plea of Mignon to the Father in Goethe's poem is precisely the voice, "the call that one form of consciousness makes to another" in Bly's phrase, resisted stoutly by Winters but also by much else in Anglo-Saxon poetic intuition and definition.[53] The sheltering presences in the poem's second stanza ask of that intuition: "What have they done to you, poorest child?" Yet what we minimize at great danger to ourselves we cannot simply repair with verbal acknowledgments, even over the course of a poetic career: thus the blood drawn ecstatically and at risk in Gunn's monologue. Second, I would argue that the return of the redeemed father as a pattern for action and emulation, a fruitful archetype once more, likely lies on the far side of catastrophe. What Gunn enacted in the Faustus monologue, glancing over his shoulder to a myth still alive, remains anticipatory; the interesting corollary to seeing that fact is that we too remain far ahead of ourselves. But first of all we must see it, starting with that prophetic look through Goethe's eyes. And third, the ways in which, by its very nature, acid consciousness in the 1960s got ahead of itself—shuffling the cards of mature development through the deck, ahead of schedule and out of order—enacts precisely and helpfully (but only if one reads the signs) the *longue durée* of catch-up ball we must play out, as individuals with our sensibilities and as a culture with our chances for survival.

Donald Davie took the measure of "The Geysers" and its brother poems in a verse epistle to Gunn from *In the Stopping Train* of 1977, calling his friend Conquistador and Commodore, and setting aside the book's dogs and cherry trees as diversions from its Marianna-Trench sounding of "the Age of Reptiles." He finds down there what the chummier, hipper praise for Gunn's work does not: "Nothing rhymes with this / Lethal indifference that you plumbed to even / Once in a bath-house in Sonoma County."[54] Something does rhyme, though it too is indifferent: the fiery impersonal leading edge of a whole personality. The mythic process of the Mind at Large in *Moly* spanned a folklore witch's threat to identity and the Arden-like haze of a Renaissance "Fair in the Woods"—not rhyming with each other because they cannot in the course of adventure. What Davie sensed aright here needs amplifying as much as Bly's contrary perspective does, for both men smell the impersonal, collective unknown at work. What Gunn ventures to take to heart and act upon gets worn inside, zoned off as impersonally as the police barricades for a street fair, and so carried *in the open* yet hidden: the father of Daphnis in the ancient *Daphnis and Chloe* is called *Dionysophanes,* the god's epiphany right there though not apparent (he looks like you and me but knows a reality we may not). The Faustus monologue blazes with an X, and the dark, primal explorations of shadow in poems near it press that X down in, to ramify through and assimilate the Elder Dionysia. Such an initiation once shaped the culture whose psychic continuity we inherit; but we have forgotten even that we ever had it.

Therefore the heedless gift of a warrant for repression offered by the acid generation to the deacons of American power, sharply lamented by Stone, is not the possessed yet committed heedlessness of the Faustus monologue, which moves to bridge splits and have life more abundantly. Gunn wrote a Romanticism awake, in yoking the headlong Dionysian drive of Faustus with the regenerative masculinity of his cactus-Odysseus. Both figures carry the sting of consciousness that was ritually administered to Dionysian initiates, both taking that sting within for the long haul. Neither figure scants mortal risk. And both descend, to the dead or to the Mothers, before resuming with right tempo what in "Philemon and Baucis" is "invented in the continuous revelation." It continues because it has been, against the odds, *stabilized* by fusion.

How does that fusion occur? The "unabsorbed excess" of perception in *Moly* first must be scattered by dissipation, its blood gone "flamy" and submissive in "Faustus," if regenerative recovery is to store up sap for later feats of self-gathering that will *define by containing* such sensibility and the powers it encodes. Painter Thomas Chimes in the same decades invoked "The Bureau of Tempo Catastrophe," and Carlos Castaneda's Yaqui shaman, an improbable coeval for Gunn's matured Odysseus, laughingly cautioned his apprentice about the "indulgence" that the sometimes-Harpo, sometimes-Faust initiate must survive: "That's the trouble with people that go wild, they go wild both ways. Yesterday you were all questions, today you are all acceptance."[55] The entire practice at which Gunn aimed submits to many descriptions, but its communal ethos at best achieved a cultural flash in the pan. Gunn would have confuted Stone's point no more than he would have cancelled Davie's glimpse of life's deadly indifference. The push he gave to imagining his redemptive blood pact consciously accepts social failure, as the retrospective "Saturday Night" in *Boss Cupid* indeed inscribes it.[56] Thoroughly rewriting a seduction poem begun in 1975, it was completed only in 1990. Gunn's essay on it in *Shelf-Life* implies that his choice of Dante's terza rima looks far past the burned-out San Francisco Barracks bath-house, beyond not only conventional prudence but also the calendar.

If, furthermore,
Our Dionysian experiment
To build a city never dared before
Dies without reaching to its full extent,
At least in the endeavor we translate
Our common ecstasy to a brief ascent

Of the complete, grasped, paradisal state
Against the wisdom pointing us away.
What hopeless hopefulness.

That slow, heavy iambic foot in "complete, /*grasped, par*/adisal state" (the second foot here with midposition caesura) thrusts with Faust's knowledge of what he was about in the end. *Grasped* as held by experience, and also as fully understood, with no illusions.

Before going further, we would do well to take note of Gunn's reflections on Bunting published only a few years after his rewriting of "Saturday Night," because they anchor both the grasp and containing power within the sensory detail. He observed in *The Spoils* Bunting's initial struggle to fashion a durable "*container* of values with which to counter the disgust of the earlier poetry," noticing that it happens first in the line or phrase.[57] Taking the description of vultures at work on the carcass of an ass, "too heavy to fly, wings deep with inner gloss," Gunn presses down hard on that noun; in *The Spoils* "the sharply defined language had its own shiny depths," and "glosses as well were inner indeed, all of them *contained* within the phrase's outline, no fuzzy excess disturbing the cleanness of that definition."[58] The two senses of gloss converge. When Bunting's search for containing form regressed to symbol, a reverse mode of summation,[59] it did so out of imagistic desire—as if he were Pound wanting to become Yeats to avoid becoming Winters. Gunn himself practiced both strategic recoveries—the modernist one from Victorian habits and the postsymbolist one from Romantic—in a tightrope walk across the century's divide, adopting "general and defensible enough" Romantic beliefs while immunizing himself against the modernist conviction that traditional organization and summation are the great bugaboos.

Let me return to the line or phrase as the scale for containment, and to the sensory detail as it ventures out from there. Here rests Gunn's fulcrum, at least for the remaking of what intelligent light can mean within larger structures. With Bunting's vultures, gloss is both sheen and interpretable meaning. As descriptions go, that duality is contained by the phrase's outline; that is, gloss as meaning is contained within statement, a lobe of syntax, whereas gloss as light is contained by the whole poem's interactive structure of details and organizing concern, a profile close to postsymbolist description. Gunn's discernment here accounts for his mildly Wintersian stricture toward *The Spoils:* "Assertion and implication are not the same as demonstration."[60] What I would add to that picture comes from old and useful terms: gloss as meaning enclosed in statement would be the scholastic and Aristotelian light of the intellect, while gloss as sheen from details within a structure of meaning encodes the scholastic *intellectus agens,* the luminosity of event. Here enters Gunn's dare. Event or action Gunn amplified as taking values to heart and acting on them, while gloss as light, including hallucinogenic light, and gloss as comprehensive grasp he ventured to whisk, with lysergic acid and chemical speed, through Aristotle and Aquinas as news moving "outward into intelligence." Probably only the German tradition sits easily with such dares because the *lumen naturae,* coming through *Naturphilosophie* into Goethe and Romantic philosophical speculation, and into Coleridge, denoted an order of meaning *within* nature that bespeaks an intelligence wider than our own. Once one allows for this gap, the right *containment* of its value becomes a major fascination and a steady preoccupation, as worthy of note as the taboo against authorial statement in modernism. With exemplary clarity Gunn manages a slow expansion of significance and emotion around those details that carry such luminosity beyond any judicious attunement with idea (the postsymbolist balance) into occulted definition, the quietly alert aura of significance appraised as an open-air secret in "Outdoor Concert." Again, his last essay on Duncan speaks for this as what it "*feels* like" to enter a sensory manifold free of conceptual orientation. Definition in this mode shines, through the long Dionysian aftermath, with the light of nature rather than the *intellectus agens.* As for being taken to heart, that very taking is what such intuition leads one to act upon. In "Fennel" from the 1980s (a plant employed ritually in Dionysian cult), the sharpness of detail in Gunn's notice shades into buoyant release, the smell's "fierce poignancy" suspending him "as if invisible."[61] The secret has become perceptible, but awareness sinks into that secret: "I float free / Of personality, and die / Into my senses, into the unglossed / Unglossable. . . ." Here Gunn pushes through Romantic commonplace to anything but a regression. Winters valued T. Sturge Moore's "From Titian's *Bacchanal* in the Prado at Madrid" because it performed an autopsy on such blotto releases from identity, whereas Gunn finds that such immersion absorbs into itself the *containment* given by identity, defining it *within* sensibility, not swooningly but alertly: "The very agent that releases me / Holding me here as well."

While the history and psychology around these matters remains humblingly up for grabs, modestly we can still acknowledge that our topic—roughly, fusion and clarity holding hands in the light of nature—do seem to usher imploded grasp and meaning into some other zone of organization. We are back on "Jefferson Airplane": am I hearing it, and is it happening, inside or outside? Such is the mode of the Old Lyre and the Socratic Silenus; Gunn's poems of immersed notice decelerate perception to that tune. The earlier "Aqueduct"[62] tracks the slow accretions of green that later define "Philemon and Baucis" and "Odysseus on Hermes": "And green, there, seeks itself." "Jack Straw's Castle" has a comparable sensory detail marking the ranch hand's descent into shadow evil; when he coolly dares to stare at Medusa, imploding luminosity sizzles him:

> On the table
> gold hair struck
> by light from
> the naked bulb,
> a dazzle in which
> the ground of dazzle
> is consumed, the
> hair burning
> in its own gold.
> . . . .
> In her dazzle I
> catch fire
> self-delighting
> self-sufficient
> self-consuming
> till
> I burn out
> so heavy
> I sink into
> darkness into
> my foundations.[63]

A few pages earlier Faustus reverses this, into expansion: "The dazzled blood / submits . . . / till blood itself / is flamy. . . . / There is / no terror in combustion."[64] At this juncture, the fate of the sensory detail in Gunn's work makes a chthonic transit, from paralysis of feeling by terror to a fiery expansion past terror. Awareness vanishes at hazard into that light so as to stand forth within it more powerfully again: anathema in postsymbolist Los Altos, but the only way out on postsymbolist Folsom Street.

In compact terms, style's microlevels stage an initiatic cycle, and "wings deep with inner gloss" project its light. What must become sharp with definition also morphs through a Dionysian pause wherein, as

Gunn's Odysseus puts it, one meets "potency in potential." Meaning is still en route and detail has withdrawn, glowing, into the furnace of the seed. The sensory detail, at times incubating light within its own outline, begins to model processes at work on a much larger scale within styles, including Bunting's hybrid modernism and postsymbolist practice. And those processes all draw on the chthonic two-way transit, to include the ranch-hand's burnout, the slow and thick traffic of mature feeling, stable solar fulfillment, and Faustian takeoff. Does love also, like the sleep of reason, breed monsters? So it does, and Plato has told us so. Gunn's intelligence protected him from mischance through these intricate turns, as it shielded his early pair of moral values in the American essays, namely, what can be taken to heart and acted on, which in the *Spoils* essay becomes, "intensity of participation" and "something to live by."[65] Spontaneity and impulse, those long-term residents of the Hotel Romantic and Bunting's major themes in *The Spoils,* thus sought dynamic stabilization, however provisionally achieved.

In "Saturday Night," then, "brief ascent" lives with one foot in myth and the other in luck. It comes and goes on the wind of the cycles; it comes and goes on the brain. In his essay on the treatment of fertility in Eliot, Pound, and Bunting, "What the Slowworm Said" of the early 1980s, Gunn comments at length on *Briggflatts,* the late heir and fulfillment of *The Spoils,* singling out a Geordie setting in which the Matter of Fertility, in contrast to Eliot, lets Bunting "act on" his themes by lying low and paying attention "through the senses to the natural physical world."[66] Gunn's phrase about Duncan, on his reinforcement of an embracing idea through a subtle extension into sensory detail, is not far off. But clearest is Gunn's echo of his early essays on Gary Snyder and Ben Jonson (about sustaining chthonic power cleanly, and grasping things wholeheartedly), in treating a passage in which a past is "not only recaptured and reentered by the imagination but literally prolonged":

> Shepherds follow the links,
> sweet turf studded with thrift;
> fell-born men of precise instep
> leading demure dogs
> from Tweed and Till and Teviotdale,
> with hair combed back from the muzzle,
> dogs from Redesdale and Coquetdale
> taught by Wilson or Telfer.
> Their teeth are white as birch,

slow under black fringe
of slow, accurate lips.
The ewes are heavy with lamb.
Snow lies bright on Hedgehope
and tacky mud about Till
where the fells have stepped aside
and the river praises itself,
silence by silence sits
and Then is diffused in Now.

A fact in the Northumberland of the 1960s, no pastoral figment, in which

> every perception, every movement described, has the easy *exactness* of familiar recurrence—the turf *studded* with the herb thrift, men of *precise* instep, dogs with *accurate* lips: in this specific and fecund scene, seeming spontaneity is a re-enactment of tradition. [Bunting in *Briggflatts*] shows us a full reconciliation, though brief, tentative, and qualified by its own transience. Ceremony has matured to tradition; the representative man has become the specific man of autobiography; a montage of places has become one place. He does indeed show us.[67]

Without enlisting Gunn onto anyone's team, I sense that he could sustain his contemplation of a failed social revolution alongside his admiration for a continuous chthonic power that can taste summation. The durable container tracked later in *The Spoils* he already locates here, as provisionally durable. *Prolongation* in Gunn's essay of the early 1980s has all the strength and pathos of that complex achievement, whether Bunting's or Gunn's.

To my mind that achievement of Bunting's also evokes Winters's breakthrough sonnet of 1929, "The Castle of Thorns."[68] A precursor to "Sir Gawain and the Green Knight" in using romance folklore, it treasures stable recovery from the alluring unknowns that saturate sensing.

Through autumn evening, water whirls thin blue,
From iron to iron pail—old, lined and pure;
Beneath, the iron is indistinct, secure
In revery that cannot reach to you.
Water it was that always lay between
The mind of man and that harsh wall of thorn,
Of stone impenetrable, where the horn
Hung like the key to what it all might mean.

My goats step guardedly, with delicate
Hard flanks and forest hair, unchanged and firm,
A strong tradition that has not grown old.
Peace to the lips that bend in intricate
Old motions, that flinch not before their term!
Peace to the heart that can accept this cold!

Next to Gunn's essays on Bunting and Duncan, this poem confirms my sense that Gunn refined postsymbolist practice precisely within the scope of more expansive fusion styles. Winters, Duncan, and Bunting may convene in no other parliament, but they do parley here. Gunn began reading Bunting attentively in the late 1960s (*Briggflatts* appeared in 1966), before Davie's salute to that poem in *Thomas Hardy and British Poetry* in 1972.[69] As for Bunting's fusion style, it caught up stability within modernist progression, Wordsworth amazingly within Pound; the fecundity of tradition, not its ability to withstand rigors and allures, remains its focus. Through it chthonic strength threads "what is unpracticed and uncalculating . . . what acts on impulse through a trust that is source both of strength and vulnerability."[70] This observation of Gunn's cuts closer to his own ventures with impulse than to the firm, delicate, intricate, and unflinching, though he entrusted both kinds of qualities to his expanded definition. These two poems by Winters and Bunting stand either side of Gunn's path between contrasting fusion styles, a singular path in the last century. On it *inner gloss* retains sensory sheen and dense yet legible meaning, alive to chthonic staying power, strong beauty, and hard chances. From this path one looks past historically brief ascents to the much slower tempo of chthonic eros, stabilized yet still open to invention and revelation. A vision is at work, saturated with impermanence but achieving a certain ground; and I dare say that such was Gunn's summary vision. In reply to Stone's critique, it declines debate in order simply to salute a proven possibility, painted in sharply specific terms, whose guardians are at ease in their vigor and whose dogs have accurate lips.

5. Demonstrandum

In "The Lesson of *The Spoils*" Gunn left something unresolved between implicitness and demonstration. There he argued that demonstration or complete definition cannot rely on assertion and implication alone, while in the earlier essay on Bunting the sheepherding episode made for him a complete *showing* or demonstration, largely through sensory particulars.

So persuasive was this passage that Gunn underscored the plain sense of demonstration: "He does indeed show us."[71]

If demonstration were simply the logical affair of common usage, Gunn's mild contradiction would be small beer. But *de-monstrandum* carries at its center, in *monstrum* or monster, the hot focus of the shadow realm in Gunn's poetry early and late. Gunn studies his monsters carefully and with rare compassion. From Jack Straw and the Medusa whom he tries to stare down, to Faustus (the murderer of Baucis and Philmeon in Goethe), to the beggar wolfing down scrapings in a cafeteria, to murderer-necrophile Jeffrey Dahmer in *Boss Cupid,* these figures pitch our sense of the human into chthonic vertigo. Some are ominous—and *omen* describes the *monstrum* of demonstration, in fact. Without the ominous preview of a change in our understanding (that is what omen and *augsmen/auger/*augury do), one's grasp of any matter worth calling human remains dry and safe.

Even Gunn's gentle outsiders—the crone in *Touch,* the harmless drifter in "The Release," the neighborhood Vietnam vets in "'All Do Not All Things Well'"—are his urban Baudelairean bearers of omen, migrant outliers of a monstrosity that nestles smack in the middle of clear understanding or grasp.

There the monster of chthonic force is held up in the light of theoretic power. Perseus lifting the head of Medusa, of course—but Perseus was only Athene's errand boy. That goddess of swift practical mind and armed efficacy sent him out to bring back precisely this visage of paralyzed horror. Medusa, sometimes called "Queen," a mortal Gorgo-sister raped by Poseidon, went on living transfixed by the wreckage of her beauty. Athene mounted that frozen terror on her breastplate, over her heart. The myth encodes a radical integration. Athene knew that such hellishness of passion was not to be pushed away; she had to taste it sufficiently to withstand its power. She wore that crucified affect because her strength depended on such knowledge, and as proof to others—demonstration indeed—that she could meet such fear wide awake. Armed, active mind *takes to heart and acts on* chthonic terror and fixity.

I employ Gunn's own terms of value to underscore the relevance of such demonstration to his work. The difference between Athene's way with the Gorgon's head and the ranch-hand's way is striking; his "self-delighting / self-sufficient / self-consuming" response blurs into unconsciousness, resembling Dahmer's autoerotic, self-entrapping state in the "Troubadour" monologues given to him. Each is a warning, *monstrum,* about how not to engage with this power, for the hellishness of the encounter must be sustained, just as Baudelaire sustains feeling and clarity toward his monitory crones, old coots, and derelict swans in poems of urban shock.

Gunn's consistent pledge to take to heart and act upon his ethos leads to this etymological nucleus of demonstration, for Athene-Medusa as the image of *demonstrandum* suits his Dionysian initiatic ethos down to the ground.

Demonstration carries force; it claims to hold out proof. But a troubling omen, from Latin into the modern European languages, is called an *abomination.* Yet omen more generally, from *augere,* to grow or increase, sets demonstration about the business of growing new consciousness. *Monere,* to warn (from *men,* mind) joins with augury to fashion the *monstrum* (a god is speaking, and I can *prove* it to you!). Mind is warned to grow around a potent and unknown, divine factor. If we don't get it, the monster ad*mon*ishes us; the de*monstra*tor bangs on the table. Whether the effort be science, persuasion, or art, it is all about a forceful demand that new consciousness rise around something uncanny.

In that light, the induced expansion of drug experience brings its own *monstrum,* the news rising from altered sensing to intelligence. The drug revolution of the 1960s plunged mind into a fluid proof that its limits were up for revision, sensed through "unabsorbed excess." But that excess carried the entire chthonic donation, not just the gentler stuff. Thus the *monstrum,* as Stone's Holliwell reads it, leads from one's own juice straight to murder, the link that Gunn fingered scrupulously in his Jack Straw underworld descent to those "foundations," into which the ranch-hand sinks, conked out before Medusa. Gunn backs up Stone, but reflectively. As for Holliwell's contention, yes: Eibl-Eibesfeldt and other ethologists since the '80s have demonstrated that the human ego, uniquely among primate species, takes its threshold formation from the act of indiscriminate murder. As far back as one looks in the human record, he says, one sees the smashed human skull. But Gunn's reflections do not stop among that bony litter.

Imagine a diagram in which *demonstration,* the touchstone from the first Bunting essay, and *clarity,* Gunn's touchstone in his reflections on Isherwood, rest at the focus. Both men embody the autobiographical ethic close to Gunn's own central ethos of taking to heart and acting on what one most esteems. The central area, then, weds *definition to clear demonstration as known and lived.* Around that center spreads the rest of Gunn's work with shadow, fusion, stabilization, and dynamic equilibrium (terribly general terms that must serve as place-markers). What unites them is the tension between stabilization and vitality.

In one corner lodge those self-consuming powers, enclosed within sensing and the instincts, which burn out like our ranch-hand; there trauma sucks light inward upon itself. Medusa retained horrified awareness of the implosion, but Jeffrey Dahmer lay captive within it; Gunn's "Final Song"[72] in the "Troubadour" monologues has Dahmer fall into himself, his pickled trophy a depleted Medusa.

> a face stared from a shelf
> unreadable on guard
>
> connection disconnection
> between headcheese and lard
>
> only one self remained
> fresh credibly maintained.

Compassion can still find its way to Dahmer, whereas his autoerotic cousin Arthur Rimbaud, mounter of delirious demonstrations, prompts Gunn's autopsy; in "Shit" Rimbaud, convinced that he has caught supreme meaning, has only cadged it into "awful suspension, / Its whiskers quivering through the Romantic mist, / in terror that had stripped it of intention."[73] Such terror caricatures the real thing on the goddess's breastplate, for although some called Medusa invincible (useful indeed on the aegis), her name denotes the essence of alert intention: it is the Greek present participle "guarding." This capable horror protects, not paralyzes. Suspension and reiteration horrify Baudelaire in "Les septs vieillards"; such a stuttering, unconscious limit to stabilization retains a hold on life. *Nota:* the trauma response in Baudelaire; Bunting's early self-disgust, later transcended; the repetition of trashed springs named for violated nymphs in Davie's late *Three for Water Music* (one scene akin to the rapes in "A Wood near Athens"); Gunn's own fascinated disgust at wolfish appetite in "Cafeteria in Boston"—all these approach Medusa the "Indomitable" in remaining horrified at the thing one dare not become.

As long as that horror remains, one may still be mindful of the treasure lost to chthonic force. One incorporates the remonstrance or reshowing. Only a tightrope's width separates Faustus's elation from fool's mind: his cry that there is "no terror in combustion" serves only because he surrenders to an expansion that will save him he knows not how. Further along, chthonic power finds a complex hosting in the pivotal first diptych of "continuous revelation." What sustains such dynamic equilibrium, whether Bunting's pastured continuities or Gunn's mature diptych on passion, is initiated wisdom about whole meaning. Within it neither grabby instinct nor dissociated thinking obstructs what forcefully has been *shown*.

To take effect, this showing must be intolerable, as analyst Neil Micklem once wrote of Medusa's image.[74] The theme of urban shock in Wordsworth, Baudelaire, and Walter Benjamin is known ordinarily to anyone who has been impaled by a situation that stops them, until real change emerges out of that immobility, all on its own. Thus goes initiation, silently and one knows not how.

The lethal indifference glimpsed by Davie at the bottom of Dionysian initiation in "The Geysers" is also nature's shrug at erotic suffering in "A Wood near Athens." But that enormous *monstrum* of suffering is precisely the poem's sting, which demands that awareness grow. In Gunn's early Merlin poem, as in "Misanthropos," a wound to perception and feeling begins to recover; a certain profound shock thaws out. Baudelaire knew them both well. Gunn's essays on Bunting track the containment of inconsistent methods for coming to clarity of feeling against the drag of disgust and pessimism. Between these falls the green diptych, where chthonic powers either gently or prickingly nourish marriage mind and warrior mind. Autoerotic involution, dazedly demanding incorporation, writes the shadow to active mind, which incorporates abomination—the ingrown paralysis itself—as its initiatic safeguard. A certain parallel comes into view: Dionysian initiation carefully displays sexual traumata, while this parallel initiation, through demonstration of clarifying shock, seeks out self-fixated horror. Both demonstrations incorporate chthonic powers on purpose, to put appetite on notice. As for Gunn's poetry among all these demonstrations, the proof is not in the poetry. The proof is in the eating of the poetry. It does indeed show us.

6. Staying Power as the Stigma of Style

The brevity of realization for the happy few (Stendhal's ethos of elective freedom in *The Charterhouse of Parma* was another touchstone for Gunn) goes some way toward accounting for those poignant Baudelairean jabs of light when they do enter the late poems. From the rain-misted street light at the end of "Night Taxi" to scribbled light across the forest floor in "A Wood near Athens" (the title borrows a stage direction from *A Midsummer Night's Dream*), such luminous detail grows rare. Between these poems streaks the light caught on the breast of Bede's bird in the elegy for Robert

Duncan. But even in Gunn's strong and lovely second diptych of melded erotic instinct, about the braided flows of Arethusa and Alpheus ("through dark tons / barely swaying / they shoot"), no Baudelairean gleams mark this, his final enlargement of fusion.[75]

The light of nature in effect goes out around chthonic ecstasy in later Gunn. The gleam scribbled through the agonized wood of desire in "A Wood" signals its farewell, marking the "conflicting trails" of biological necessity, routinely deadly rivalry, tragic family loyalties, the Hebrew creation myth as narcissistic love story, suffering lovers from fiction, Dahmer's erotic obsession: the "beautiful and ridiculous" pursuit that, nonetheless, "is our main meaning." What compensates that disappearance of natural light is vision; thus the *Paradiso*'s high wattage in closing, unnamed as Dante's, a generic light. But how so?

The inquest set up in "A Wood near Athens" carefully erects a mental theater for its ruminations. A stage manager, as it were, haunts the vast set after hours, imaginatively blocking his figures and commenting on their performance. The smother of chthonic force he notes early on: "We thought we lived in a garden, and looked around / To see that trees had risen on all sides."[76] Against this encirclement he eventually asserts not chthonic power but the artful balancing of dance and a remembered, poignant interview.

Twice Gunn has invoked the cosmic solar blossom at climax moments, in "Sunlight" for *Moly* and here in "A Wood near Athens." In the first a composed realism about actuality and the force of attraction issues into prayer with no allusions to art-making; in the other some thirty years later a sophisticated realism about eros, in a Lucretian-Darwinian framework, calls on many witnesses to art-making and one spotlit vision. Their testimonies sum up the conflicting understandings we bring to instinctually driven process, through science, great art, and jolted common sense. The summary, however, writes a groping demonstration. If Bunting's theme was the relation of love and poetry, Gunn's work fills the same bill, with the addition of one more theme, the pursuit of new consciousness.

The sunlight of Gunn's summary poem in *Moly*, and the creation of the cosmos in Dante's solar rose, put emerging consciousness in cosmogonic frames, the one scientific and devout, the other phrased by wondering skepticism about the place of human love in nature. Both poems put me in mind of Jung's remark in his *Visions Seminars* from the 1930s (devoted to the active-imagination protocols of Christiana Morgan), that the "creation of a new conscious world is really a cosmogonic miracle, it is like the Indian cosmogonies."[77] Yet new consciousness barely shines through in the later poem, for the cosmogonic factor enters as allusion, one more in the array, though taking pride of place above this forest of pained errantry. As if the solar blossom of "Sunlight" had withdrawn into Dante's vision, this glimpse of comprehensive light enters between implied quotation marks, seeming to leave Gunn's argument somewhat up in the air.

Yet, realistically so, it may be. Although "Saturday Night" had inventoried a colossally destructive chapter for eros, the shadow energies of destruction demanded more of Gunn's honesty. The two crucial "Philemon" and "Arethusa" diptychs about chthonic process and fusion, across a decade, remained mythical. Love without shadows and rape without tragedy indeed require myth. Left to acknowledge, then, was the shadow to mythical assertion, in a demonstration that would indeed show—hold up the *monstrum* steadily—the place of love in a strictly naturalistic accounting. Thus "A Wood" rolls out the spectacle of panoramic waste and grotesquerie in nature's use of love as fuel. Art will enter the dock with science; the court wants all the evidence, it presses for a tough research program, it tallies prodigies of pain and instinct, Dahmer's necrophilia among them. In *Boss Cupid* exhibits already lay near at hand, in the five poems in "Troubadour: Songs for Jeffrey Dahmer," which examine the grisly archaic root parallel to the wild hunt, the primal omophagy that is nowhere the product of later Greek Dionysian religion. Such involutional horror haunts human eros; no one identifies with an abomination that all are prepared to invoke with fascinated revulsion and, thus, just barely, to admit as the absolute shadow to their passions. Like the thought-experiment in "Misanthropos," which asked if relational feeling could survive catastrophic impact, this poem inquires: What shall we make of love's ecstasies, blind drama, and grotesque dead-ends? "It is ridiculous, ridiculous, / And it is our main meaning. / . . . / Beautiful and ridiculous. . . . / But who did get it right?"[78]

That question summarizes the tone that I might call, taking a cue from Gunn on Duncan, conceptual rather than sensory exploration. The mood and procedure—earnest, comprehensive, baffled—preside over inquest nearly to the end. They are what hold the poem together, even to ushering in Dante's vision. In his third essay on Duncan, Gunn referred to Alighieri as "Dante the knower," the antitype to Duncan as adventurer into the unknown. If anyone ever got it right, then, it would have been Dante. Thus the form in "A Wood near Athens" is being stretched. But in what direction?

No Dionysian experiment, this form quietly displaces Dionysian initiation to the plane of reflection; sexual drives and traumata were classically part of such initiation for women, but here they, too, yield to inquest. Yet the Shakespearean frame introduces the Masque element of choreography, and then a close-up exchange. Between the rational inquest and the concluding slab of vision Gunn blocks out sections of a dance troupe. The first is, "Cadets and skinheads, city boys, young Spartans," as painted by Atilla Richard Lukacs, who stand as if waiting to join the corps de ballet made up of "Alyosha, Catherine Earnshaw, Jeffrey Dahmer." The second is Gunn himself speaking with the young man who had been seduced at thirteen by his mother's boyfriend. Gunn asks, "'Were you confused?— 'No, it was great,' he said, / 'the best thing that had ever happened to me.'" Together, the painted group, the remembered young man, and the older bisexual who callously initiated him summarize the failed drive of chthonic force toward the light of conscious strength. Intervening between the skinheads and the young man's story are these lines:

> They that have power, or seem to,
> They that have power to hurt, they are the constructs
> Of their own longing, born on the edge of sleep,
> imperfectly understood.[79]

Or seem to: does the hurt acquire other meaning in another light? And *imperfectly understood* by themselves, or their victims? Thence to the remembered conversation, across that divide of flawed understanding: "Once a young man / Told me my panther made him think of one / His mother's boyfriend had on *his* forearm." One of Dionysus's great cats hosts this exchange, while already in the young man's fate it had marked his seducer.

The structure for these last blocks of material pivots around the tattoo's sting of consciousness. *Sting* derives from *stigma,* as does *style.* A breakthrough to fulfillment usually isolates its bearer; it inscribes; and it distinguishes. Here the envelope of understanding gets pushed because the great cats take different roads. Not only do those who hurt others fail to understand, and perhaps their victims with them, but the writer trying to know more continues to seek. The *monstrum* of vast suffering hangs before us in the demonstration. But can mind also expand around it?

That sting goes on working under the skin, keeping the wound Hermetically open (to the poignant summary of pain) and therefore also to a larger view. The poem's structure at this point stretches the mind around two teams of contrasting partners: Gunn and the seducer make up one, while the wandering wounded in their dark wood and the high-wattage performers of the cosmos "distinct in brightness and function" compose the other. These pairs suit the two-team destiny of eros, which strays through the world's costly generation of life, but dances above it as creator, abruptly visible as its Shiva-like turbine.

In the Godhead blossom seen by Dante, however, the saints and angels glad in their *giochi e canti* may or may not be dancing. The notion of a universe enacted by such dance is nowhere in sight. But Dante's thrice-repeated gesture (this is the second one) serves Gunn: "*Io levai li occhi* . . . (I raised my eyes . . .). And at that center, with their wings outstretched, I saw more than a thousand angels celebrating (*ciascun distinto di fulgore e d'arte*), each one different in brilliance and in manner." As for cosmogonic power, Alighieri's Prime Love, Prime Mover, and Divine Mind are one and the same centrality, translating roughly into Gunn's last line below in his scoping of the bit from Canto 31.[80] New understanding moves there. But a coordinating conjunction ushers it in swiftly and democratically, as one more attempt at definition and enactment from sufferers in the *selva oscura* ("But who did get it right? Ruth and Naomi, / Tearaway Romeo and Juliet, / Alyosha, Catherine Earnshaw, Jeffrey Dahmer?").

> And once, one looked above the wood and saw
> A thousand angels making festival,
> Each one distinct in brightness and in function,
> Which was to choreograph the universe,
> Meanwhile performing it. Their work was dance.
> Together, wings outstretched, they sang and played
> The intellect as powerhouse of love.[81]

This cosmogonic Masque comes through Dante but not from him. That fact may account for Gunn's tactic of anonymity; Dante framed the vision, but dance fills it out. Close at hand are Shakespeare's wedding entertainment and Attila Lukacs's city boys waiting "To join the balance of the corps in dances / Passion has planned. They that have power, or seem to. . . ."[82] And there are the great cats, mascots of the free dance of bacchic rite.

The end of this poem takes on an extraordinary character once the question of conscious expansion opens up. The *monstrum* of erotic suffering and confusion, its blundering pavanes and galliards in our chthonic cellar, anticipate the visionary cotillion. What crosses the bridge of Gunn's "And" is a cue to that effect: one dancer cuts in on two others in the classic waltz of incest.

Once a young man
Told me my panther made him think of one
His mother's boyfriend had on *his* forearm
—The first man he had sex with, at thirteen.
"Did she know about that?" I asked. He paused:
"I think so. Anyway, they were splitting up."
"Were you confused?"—"No, it was great," he said,
"The best thing that had ever happened to me."

And once, one looked above the wood . . .[83]

The tattooed panthers of Dionysus inaugurate this exchange, while Gunn's questions to the young man speak for our ordinary sense of the mess, our social worker's questions about it (was the youth defensive?). But his happy non sequitur is left just so, indeed is granted its full dignity as it squires in the vision. Dante and his loss go unnamed; one startling implication of the sequence is that the young man's happiness implicitly stands as analogue to all that celebration encircling the Godhead. If we mutter to ourselves, "Why, it's Dante," then our next inference just might be that between Dante's loss and the young man's violation a parallel holds; in each case a blow has led to happiness. In any event, the drastic change of partners and its outcome blur into that dance of the astral troupe: how confusing, indeed irrelevant, to ordinary inspection can *not* getting it right become?

View changes in this poem, but around the irreparable. Each story is allowed to be what it is; the fearsomeness of eros is let be, for there is no way to get it right. Dante's long trek through the worlds leaves it be—*Guarda, e passa*—in the same spirit; soul is not our domain to rule but a reality that fulfills itself through us. Thus totality, and thus, even, Socrates' long echo: "To hell with the Ego-world!" roared Jung in a late letter, as if he were the old Greek: "'Listen to the voices of your *daimonion*. It has a say now, not you!'"[84] Our symptoms would initiate us; they would demonstrate to us how to see. Depth comes over us, and in it we look up. Depth burns all the way around suffering and causal thinking, for visionary powers do not stitch events together, but make them transparent to whole light.

Those synchronistic panthers are mascots of this changed view, for their silent omen argues that chthonic force will necessarily make its way onto the scene and insist, regardless of the outcome, on becoming a power active in the final reckoning. It too seeks light, errantly or accurately, but irrepressibly moving toward investiture as chthonic power, wherever it may find purchase. When I met Gunn at Princeton in the late 1970s, he remarked in tribute to Yeats, "*Dance* is a difficult word to use now in a poem, isn't it!" But on certain occasions it cannot be avoided. The *demonstrandum* here required it if the sad content of suffering were to change, crossing to greater understanding and burning there.

That is, *implicitly* mind takes up chthonic force and shapes it into power. Reflective in tonal range, stalked by the specter of rational stymie and despairing shrug, the poem builds a mood that it also aims to break through. The shadow of clear judgment, a clear-cut relativism, stalks this forest, but its mood, meeting summational power, is broken by performed ideogram rather than postsymbolist definition. Rational irony is not allowed to harden, nor do statement and particulars simply trade in the "subtle penetration"[85] that Gunn learned from Winters. Full definition is nowhere stated, and explicit questions get no direct answers. Not that our questions don't count, but that the young man's testimony cannot be entirely discounted, and, right or not, it has entered into the dance.

My guide here is Gunn on *The Spoils:* the end of this poem composes an ideogram. The clarity of its demonstration is tied not to assertion but to stymied questioning. It is also Dionysian demonstration, a womb for "the continuous revelation" carrying the impact of suffering's glaring omen upon rational mind and feeling. Metanoia quietly pours across a coordinating conjunction and a doubled signature tattoo. Those panthers on Gunn and the other man are dance masters; sleekly they demonstrate a packed little initiatic *monstrum,* expanding definition, padding past what otherwise must remain perfectly understood, couching confused and confusing suffering in their movement. And all this in service to Gunn's fullest grasp of compassion, which is Baudelairean in kind but not in derivation. As definition widens, full understanding remains partly mum, the poem's tone of pained rational feeling silently opening to its staying power. The bleak carries the radiant.

And not only that. This enlargement takes up a gesture that Gunn has used before to end a poem: the simple act of looking up to another, expansive plane. Recall "Night Taxi," in which the Hermetic boundary-crossing cabbie, completing his run through 'Frisco "loose but in control," feels a sprinkle on his knuckle: "Glancing upward I see / high above the lamppost / but touched by its farthest light / a curtain of rain already blowing / against black eucalyptus tops."[86] This release through a luminous sensory detail miniaturizes "The Outdoor Concert" from the mid-1970s ("At the edge / of the understanding: / it's the secret")[87] and lifts sight across a sensory threshold where "what exploration *feels* like" heralds a "luminous intersection." At the end of "A Wood," the details come from visionary reportage, but their light concerns definition itself, its distinct wattages and functions. The whole image delivers access to something normally invisible, just past something nearly intolerable: part of the originating secret, whose tact in summary draws on twenty-five years of practice.

The parchment in "Wrestling" close by "Outdoor Concert" supplies the final antecedent for illumination in "A Wood near Athens." There the vellum's indentations were held into the light: you "see / the discourse / where the stylus pressed / the fat. . . . / like a high / window you never noticed / it lets in light / continual discourse / of angels."[88] The syntax in "Wrestling," ecstatically wobbly in Duncan's way, stuttered over sources for "beginnings," the elusive cosmogonic power whose hum concludes "A Wood." While expanded definition is the business of both poems, the stylus in "Wrestling" had not yet begun to press into what the later poem tattoos. But the stitch is worth marking. From at least the early 1970s, against the thrusts of both chthonic force and the light within sensing, Gunn had asked sensory detail, syntax, and statement to grow and stretch in concert. Yet advance is heralded by the sensory detail, in Gunn's fusion style as in Winters's, reviving the Romantic/anti-Romantic tension around definition, in this poem earmarking the Dionysian sting, stigma, and style by wedding the known to the unknown with the *numen* of monstrous hurt. For demonstration *au fond* is both a comprehensive round-up of actual growth, and a lab equipped for taking to heart and acting upon paradoxical fulfillment, its sting with its staying power. In this poem that power demonstrates both a bleakly compassionate inquest and a stinging tattoo gnosis which silently breaches it. The drama of failed social experiment in "Saturday Night" gains here its tragic partner, both poems laying claim to staying power only implicitly; in "A Wood" the sting goes in all the way.

To conclude, then. Those who decline to feel such a *monstrum* come home miss out on something large; on visiting Kesey's band in Mexico, Stone observed that "the concept of real life was elusive."[89] The implicit charge lodged by Winters's stance—that psychedelic experience could not inform significant poetry, present already in his praise for Sturge Moore's poem on Dionysian release—was not narrowly intended. Its wider sense would seem to be underwritten by Stone; to parallel a phrase from *Prime Green:* there was more blooey than Blake in tripping because, in moving from seeing auras around things to changing them, what mattered was character, not the color machine. Comrades in one's arms start becoming comrades-in-arms only when consensual reality stops slipping around the corner. Its sharpened definition in the dust of battle actually becomes *fun,* as Gunn said near the end in a note on *Buddenbrooks.*[90] Stendhal's aristocrats of freedom in *The Charterhouse of Parma* remained adult while improvising intelligently, acting on their sensibility in tune with the tactical intuition already in mind for Gunn in "At the Barriers" near the beginning of our Brown Decades; "All this good will seems easy, but it is set apart."[91] A prudent *cordon,* or powerlessness? Gunn's fusion style carries the tension of that ambivalence without acceding to marginality. In his third essay on Duncan, Gunn's old Jonsonian touchstone, wholehearted grasp, meant to live fully and be the better for it. And that meant pushing definition as amply as sensibility could push experience. The entire modern-to-modernist-to-postsymbolist ethos in that sense is indeed set apart, its sensory details a spot-welder's genealogy: Baudelaire's flash or glimmer in episodes of traumatic shock-response; Pound's comparable glimmers in the Paris Metro or senescent Venice; Winters's gleaming wine-smeared boot; Eugenio Montale's electrical sizzles; and Bunting's gloss.

As for investing crucially in sensibility while banking it in a matter-spirit union, Gunn has a counterpart in the Pound of "Rock-Drill." (Gunn reviewed those Cantos aggressively as a young man, later repudiating the piece.) Incarcerated at St. Elizabeth's Hospital in D.C., Pound adopted the classic Confucian ideogram LING in the second tone as the hinge-icon of his practice.[92] He translated it as "sensibility." The visual roots—sky, cloud, three drops of rain, and ritual performance—Mathews in his Chinese-English dictionary[93] renders as "The spirit of a being which acts upon others. . . . Supernatural. Efficacious," while Du Cange's Latin lexicon adds this sidelight: *sensus* and *sensibilitas* are cognate with *intellectus* and *cognitio.* Both Leibniz and Matteo Ricci read LING as an *active* parallelism between matter and spirit. How Pound would have abominated Berkeley's *paradis artificiel,* yet how much we miss if we overlook the old fascist and Taoist's program next to Gunn's: from opposed ranges of stylistic temper, social outlook, and politics, two attempts to write well against the grain of their time while defending vision and acknowledging defeat.

What the Reagan crowd faced with smiling plywood now wears the Captain Midnight gabardine of the smart bomb and the dumb counterfactual. What then took aim at denying a lost war and a cultural upheaval has now, in its gilded hardening, killed a republic. Against this charade of moralistic clarities—transatlantic by the 1980s and flourishing at the end of Gunn's life—Gunn's fidelity to the styles of clarity in Isherwood and brief continuity in Bunting set its steady course. The new consciousness at which he aimed was for individuals, who would build the world at home, yet build it sincerely around an odious monstrosity.

Thus the *Phaedo* feels contemporary. When Socrates paid his respects to Apollo in taking up the stylus, he whispered to Dionysus. Gunn's work spans precisely the period of ascendancy for capitalist ideology over its adversaries. In retrospect, Gunn's Arden, its fair in the woods cordoned off by traffic barriers, planted a tattered guidon for the demoralized social thinkers who now try to imagine community past anything on offer in the last century. Already such writing carried the mythic yearning one hears in the contemporary French rock group Anabase ("Sous mes pieds, des jardins imaginaires," in "Le Bonheur flou") and thus reaches to our own long up-country march. Gunn's mature reflection marks a surprising turn (which I can scan only sketchily here); it zones out the false Silenus of his era, the late Presley "Fatty in gold lamé"[94] who betrayed his earlier Dionysian art, while it banks on a sensibility that dresses on Isherwood and Stendhal, improvisational and self-recognizing, as the more reliable measure past those ashes at the Barracks bathhouse. From Stendhal to Isherwood in Gunn's happy few, then, runs the counterpart of stabilized, fragile tradition in that stylistic touchstone, Bunting's shepherds.

But here a tough-minded critic might object: the Socratic Silenus painted at Pompeii may look above the fray, past Typhonic eros to attunement, but such initiatic analogies, he might say, only veil the elder Gunn's fallback to nuclear eros in a finely furnished bunker of style! Yet surely "A Wood near Athens," rather than falling back, remakes Gunn's Arden as his laboratory for testing the foundation and prospect of vision. To my mind, "Saturday Night" and "A Wood" together weigh vast social trends in the scales of utopian and Typhonic suffering, and evoke Jung's testimony to the piercing sting that comes with a real taste of fulfillment. Yes, the original vision in "Fair in the Woods," "Outdoor Concert," and "At the Barriers" touched back to those Renaissance and Baroque courts that fostered *Midsummer Night's Dream* and the operas of Lully and Rameau. But "A Wood near Athens," completing the inquest begun in "Saturday Night," sweeps all those settings into a dark forest where Gunn pays the price for new awareness and compassion. The world-shaping miracle that makes new mind lends people a basis for founding communities but also, after failure, buffers their unmaking. Much remains unstated in "A

Wood" because its stinging totality remains at the edge not of a secret but of our day's unutterable summation.

Such intricate clarity looks to no guarantees. Its subtly sweeping view is what the adjective "Dionysian" identifies: acquainted with the worst and singing past that, it calmly fosters new bonds. Gunn's poem "Iron Landscapes," about the Statue of Liberty's double aspect, from one angle that copper maiden disclosing a revolutionary posture, quietly speaks from the Dionysian corner when it eulogizes watery flow, "Cool seething incompletion that I love."[95] Hardly in head-on confrontation with the "hard" forces it identifies, nonetheless it meets them in clear and celebratory stance. Gunn's work therefore likewise indirectly acknowledges Robert Stone's scathing critique of his generation's naïveté. Asserting a modern version of the dialectical Silenus, that sober drunkard, the earthy musician in the fresco who looks above the wood, Gunn's oeuvre says lucidly but subtly: it is better if you follow me into death as soon as possible—that is, die to your normal grasp of things. In "A Wood near Athens" Gunn's demonstrative clarity found an apex in visionary gesture. Without mimicking Yeats's dancer, that poem propels mature statement to explore its own outer limits, through an ideogram designed to enlarge and enact meaning. And so it does.

Our Dionysian Experiment: Three Theses on the Poetry of Thom Gunn

BRIAN TEARE

> A literary influence is never just a literary influence. It's also an influence in the way you see everything—in the way you feel your life.
>
> —Thom Gunn, ca. 1970 notebook (BL)

1. Prologue

There's a story about literary history I keep returning to, an anecdote as sharp as a paradigm.[1] In 1944, *Kenyon Review* editor John Crowe Ransom rejected Robert Duncan's "African Elegy"—a poem he'd "previously admired and accepted for publication"—in reaction to Duncan's outing himself in the essay "The Homosexual in Society," first published in Dwight MacDonald's monthly *Politics*.[2] Though Duncan in a footnote appended to the essay in 1959[3] very tactfully gives neither the name of the journal nor its editor—I got the skinny from Michael Davidson's study *The San Francisco Renaissance: Poetics and Community at Mid-century*—he does reprint a lengthy excerpt from the letter in which Ransom recants his acceptance on the grounds that,

> with your permission, I [now] read the poem as an advertisement or a notice for overt homosexuality, and we are not in the market for literature of this type.
>
> I cannot agree with you that we should publish it nevertheless under the name of freedom of speech; because I cannot agree with your position that homosexuality is not abnormal. It is biologically abnormal in the most obvious sense. I am not sure whether or not state and federal law regard it so, but I think they do. . . . There are certainly laws prohibiting

> incest and polygamy, with which I concur, though they are only abnormal conventionally and are not so damaging to society biologically.[4]

To type out this fraction of Ransom's letter wrests me from dis-ease and sentences me to disease. What I mean is: Imagine picking out from an average day's mail a business envelope. You recognize the journal's return address; indeed, it could be the proofs you were expecting. Imagine opening it, unfolding a few sheets of heavy cream-colored paper and, in reading their contents, receiving against you the eugenicist judgment implicit in Ransom's final sentence. It's the kind of swift kick that lingers in the ribs for years. Even as stalwart a soul as Duncan would, more than two decades after Ransom's rebuttal, seven years after Stonewall, insist, "As for 'homosexual literature' in America, even now the word *homosexual* has not yet transcended prejudice where you can write about your gay life because it is a human life and not a bizarre anomaly."[5]

I repeat his statement here because I'd like to foreground the lingering psychological inhibitions brought about and reinforced by such prohibitions as Ransom's, given that, for Thom Gunn as for Robert Duncan, there have been many such public judgments brought down upon his work. I'm also not sure Duncan's statement doesn't retain the bracing flavor of more than a pinch of truth; he made it, after all, not very long ago in historical terms. Has "homosexual literature" in only thirty years managed to transcend prejudice? Has the default universality that characterized New Critical definitions of "poem" and "poetry" been sufficiently troubled by situating the genre within its dependency on historical contexts? And does not the subtle, stubborn residuum of heterosexist thought still inhibit the liberatory potential of even our most thoughtful critical discourses? I ask because I'm afraid that what Robert K. Martin asserts in his introduction to *The Homosexual Tradition in American Poetry*—published in 1979—is still for the most part true, even if it seems awfully belated to insist that "[m]ost writing has traditionally been heterosexual, not by declaration but by implication. . . . And heterosexual assumptions are presumed to be universal . . . for the homosexual man, who must repeatedly observe the differences between his own sexuality and the prevailing assumptions about 'everyman,' sexual definition is a matter of individual struggle and personal decision."[6]

I ask because when I write "gay poetry," the phrase immediately, anxiously separates into critical questions: What exactly is "gay"? How do I define "poetry"? When these words are yoked together, what kind of writing practice or practices do they signify, and do they in fact remain anomalous? And, perhaps more important, with what intentions do I go about reading this obvious, elusive category of literature?

I'd like to attempt to answer these questions, no matter how indirectly or provisionally, by examining the creative and critical oeuvre of Thom Gunn, with particular emphasis on his notebooks and his work's critical reception, which, when read side by side, allow us to witness a kind of interior/exterior dialectic concerning the terms "gay" and "poetry." Ultimately, it's my contention that, when taken together—Gunn's publication record and its critical reception, his development in his notebooks of a distinctly gay poetics, and his relationships with mentors Yvor Winters and Robert Duncan—all tell an exemplary story about the tension created, sustained, and sometimes resolved by the close proximity of "gay" to "poetry." And though this essay is foremost a story about Gunn's own poetry and his development as a gay poet, this story might also be read as representative of aspects of both poetic and gay histories in twentieth-century Anglo-American literature.

For it's a late-twentieth-century or contemporary oeuvre's ability to register, to make legible and productive, the tension between the terms "gay" and "poetry" that defines a practice of gay poetry, which, though it might be marked by the record of homosexual desire or subjectivity, is *not* defined by it alone. Gay poetry is not constituted solely by the content of a poem, nor is it simply a poetry "that lends itself to the hypothesis of a gay reading, regardless of where the author's genitals were wont to keep house."[7] Gay poetry at this point in literary history defines itself by the way *a body of work* acknowledges the tension between the historicized gay subject and traditional poetic practice and fashions itself in response to this tension. "Gay poetry" is foremost characterized by this intentionality, by a poet's recognizing the paradox of his or her own implausible practice and leaving this conflict inscribed within a poetics, on the body of their work. If earlier in the twentieth century this inscription was often implicit in the conspicuous absence of material, physical, and historical traces of gay desire, as in the work of W. H. Auden or the lesbian poet Elizabeth Bishop, a parallel practice has tended to highlight evidence of the work's historicity, its struggle between a genre defined by New Criticism and a sexuality always already defined by its relationship to sociohistorical conditions, for example, the poetry of Robert Duncan, or Adrienne Rich, or Thom Gunn.

Gunn's career lends itself to the argument and themes of this essay because the radical shifts in critical favor that attended both the changes in his formal practice and the gradual entrance of the gay subject into his work act as a kind of dye injected into the vascular system of literary history. Given their figurative status as blockages in or obstructions to literary discourse by virtue of their uniquely embattled status, the terms "gay" and "poetry" are defined and made readable by Gunn's critical reception, which is employed here in a stint as a kind of part-time vascular imaging system. For instance, when Gunn turns from employing exclusively accentual-syllabic measures to utilizing syllabics in *My Sad Captains* (1961), a sample of the critical discourse shows that "poetry" is acutely in need of diagnosis: "In spite of Gunn's rimes," said Yvor Winters, "I can detect no pattern that I can recognize as that of verse; the poems move like dead prose."[8] Likewise, when *The Passages of Joy* (1982) appears, the withering tone of some reviews—such as Ian Hamilton's patronizing *TLS* review, in which he carps that "[m]uch of this . . . is done with the relish of one who has for years believed that he would never get to write about such things"—reveals that "gay" causes pain to the critical system.[9] And it's also equally instructive that not until the more explicitly "out" *Jack Straw's Castle*—published in 1977—does *The Advocate* begin to review Gunn's work, a trend that continues through the 1993 article "Top Gunn," a tribute to Gunn's career on the occasion of his being awarded a MacArthur "Genius" fellowship after the publication of *The Man with Night Sweats* (1992).

In light of this dialectic between the evolution of Gunn's work and its interpretation by his critics, I'd like to suggest that Gunn's career so expertly elicits from twentieth-century critical discourse the shifting historical definitions of "gay" and "poetry" for the following three reasons:

1 His early fame as a British poet was concomitant with both a metrical verse and a closeted sexuality that he later challenged after a decade's residence in the U.S. With each subsequent publication after 1961's *My Sad Captains*—the book in which he most extensively introduced syllabic verse—Gunn's work became increasingly critically embattled. The syllabic and free-verse poems that followed in its wake were seen by some UK and U.S. critics as "tainted" by American influences, especially since the poems' subjects include, without being limited to, San Francisco street life, gay sex and sexual identity, LSD, and S/M subculture. However, starting with *Jack Straw's Castle*, published in 1976, he steadily gained gay readership and exposure in the gay press.

2 Gunn's publishing career spans almost fifty years, from 1954 to 2000, seismic decades in the U.S.: McCarthyism, Civil Rights, Gay Liberation, AIDS, "Don't Ask, Don't Tell," and both Bush eras. Excluding selected and

collected poems, he published roughly five full-length collections of poetry before Stonewall and five afterward, two of those after the full onset of the AIDS epidemic. Though many critics—especially in the gay press—associate the gradual relaxation of his formal choices with the dual influences of U.S. culture and the opening of his closet door, an examination of Gunn's notebooks reveals a more complex and ambivalent portrait of his relationship to pre- and post-Stonewall ideas of gay identity and community than a liberationist reading of Gunn's work would suggest.

3 Gunn had two major mentors, the first straight and the second gay, and the character of his relationships with each speaks to the vicissitudes of his simultaneous development as poet and as gay man. Yvor Winters, with whom Gunn studied at Stanford in the 1950s, oversaw and influenced the poems of Gunn's second book, *The Sense of Movement* (1957), but deeply and publicly disapproved of his move to syllabics in his third. Robert Duncan, whom Gunn first met in the early 1960s, wrote a series of poems in response to Gunn's sixth, LSD-inspired book, *Moly* (1971), while Gunn went on to write several poems dedicated to Duncan as well as three inspired and lengthy essays concerning his poetry, the earliest being "Homosexuality in Robert Duncan's Poetry." His reciprocal and mutually influencing poetic relationship with Duncan acts as a gay alternative to heterosexual models of imitation and "influence," one based on desire, elective identification, and collaboration rather than on anxiety, disidentification, and apprenticeship.

Having spent several afternoons in UC Berkeley's Bancroft Library reading Gunn ephemera alongside his poetry notebooks—which, when they contain prose, are as full of reactions to literary criticism as they are of diary entries, side notes on his evolving poetics, and his own rehearsals for essays—I'm acutely aware of his ambivalent, often antagonistic feelings toward literary criticism. For instance, an inscribed and annotated copy of his 1987 chapbook *Night Sweats* includes an occasional poem—uncollected by future editions—entitled "Hatchet, the Reviewer," the entirety of which is as follows:

> A drunkard, come to think of it,
> Is Janus-faced: Hatchet was too.
> The man you met, charm tempering wit,
> Was courteous and considerate:
> When he reviewed you, though, he'd switch
> From gentleman to envious bitch.

And the real article? You knew
He must be one of them, but which?[10]

This particular copy of *Night Sweats* happened to have the name "Ian Hamilton" written in Gunn's hand above the poem's crossed-out title, and given both Hamilton's reputation as a hatchet man and his homophobic review of *The Passages of Joy*, we might well understand Gunn's thoroughly personal, pointed retaliation. Having himself practiced the art with so much precision, intelligence, and integrity while being subjected to egregious misreading after egregious misreading, Gunn was, later in his career, thoroughly disenchanted and not a little hostile, as this unpublished notebook draft, "Lit Critics 1994," attests:

The reason I detest you,
for your interpretations of poems you have made your own property
—the true proprietor, the poet, would not be delighted,
not that you care, you are showing how smart you are—
is the same reason I detest Charles Manson,
for his interpretations of songs on the White Album. . . .

But he was less cynical than you,
he believed in his interpretations, he acted on them.[11]

This is merely the prosy first draft of a poem that, though he takes it through at least a half-dozen more ever-tightening revisions, he never finishes; however, its rhetoric survives each draft and stands in the end as a concise statement of his deeply moral stance toward criticism: that it should be accurate to the intention of the poet him or herself, and not consist of "proprietary" gestures of intellectual and/or aesthetic ownership that merely promulgate the critic's own views. Free of pretension, this criticism should also be willing to roll up its sleeves and act upon the accuracy of the interpretations it puts forth, as well as to embody a theory of reading that is able to distinguish between its own aims and those of the poet. To aim for less than that, he implies by analogy, would be in some ways a criminal act.

Gunn's ambivalence and occasional hostility toward literary criticism mirror his relationships to academe and literary journalism. Several times early in his career, he avoided making deeper commitments to the academy and the university, choosing first in 1958 to discontinue his studies toward a PhD in English at Stanford, and then in 1966—one year after receiving tenure—abandoning his professorship at UC Berkeley in order to experiment with LSD, to more fully embrace the gay and youth countercultures of San Francisco, and to write the poems that would become *Moly.* This decision came a couple of years after he stopped reviewing regularly, a time during which he'd become "more and more dissatisfied with the business of making comparatively fast judgments on contemporary poets. . . . I felt more and more that I had to live with a book for some time before I could really find out its value *for me.*"[12] After that point, it's safe to say Gunn became a professional adjunct: he taught only enough to make what money he needed to live on, and though he continued to write reviews and criticism, they were "only about poets I liked."[13] He seems to have done so in spurts, perhaps spurred on as much by economic necessity as enthusiasm for individual poets; whatever his reasons, the late 1970s and late '80s seem to have been particularly generative times for critical activity, and his two collections of criticism seem to stem from these years.

Despite his continued critical practice, he came increasingly to distrust academic discourse concerning poetry; indeed, in the '80s especially he used literary criticism mainly as a forum to discuss and pay tribute to those poets whose work interested and nurtured his own. In a 1989 interview with Jim Powell, Gunn reveals both his distaste for literary criticism qua literary criticism—"theory is . . . simply boring"—and his own criticism's increasingly crucial function as a method by which he can better understand the work of his peers.[14] And if at first he claims he's "interested in individual poets, not in poetics . . . I'm interested in writing poetry and not very interested in the theory of poetry," later he argues that "[m]aybe a tradition that's able to take account of the avant-garde and the traditional is necessary. That's what was so wonderful about Duncan."[15] And it seems that he did attempt, within the boundaries of his own inclinations, to form just such a theory, for example, in the criticism collected in 1993's *Shelf-Life.* Between 1988 and 1992 he published a comprehensive, instructive review of *New Oxford Book of Sixteenth Century Verse* and sympathetic essays about the poetry of Janet Lewis and Allen Ginsberg, as well as his final two essays on Duncan, "The High Road: A Last Collection" and "Adventurous Song: Robert Duncan as Romantic Modernist," both of which contain intricately detailed explications of Duncan's erudite, complex poetics as well as traces of the effect Duncan had on Gunn's own understanding of poetry.

Perhaps because he set such clear parameters around his criticism, Gunn's singular practice of attention, respect, and affection toward the work of a fellow gay poet—his three exquisitely wrought and deeply thought essays on Duncan's poetry—serves for me as an example of the kind of dialectic gay poets can set up between one another's work. Duncan is not quite a model for Gunn; rather, as he says in a notebook, he is "a source."[16] Additionally, the ambition and scope of his work serve less as examples than as interlocutors for Gunn's own emerging practice as a gay poet. I hope, in what follows, to live up to Gunn's high standards of self-knowledge, self-possession, and generosity even as I fashion for myself answers to questions he himself endeavored to answer.

2. Ugly Feelings

I haven't always had such admiration for Thom Gunn's work, much less an understanding of its historical context or its relationship to gay authorship. In fact, for much longer than I'd like to admit, I never bothered to read his work. Why? When I was nineteen and twenty—the years right before I thought of "becoming a writer"—my first encounters with reading poetry were through identity-themed anthologies, the most important of which was Carl Morse and Joan Larkin's *Gay and Lesbian Poetry in Our Time: An Anthology.* Hungry for the information I could get only through poetry, I read then that kind of anthology the way a Southerner hits a potluck buffet on Sunday after church: relentlessly, pausing only for a change of plate or a drink of water. I'd end up absolutely stuffed, curiously overexcited. But why was I drawn back time and again to perusing *Gay and Lesbian Poetry in Our Time*? What kind of information did I find there?

I've just pulled my beat-up copy off the study shelf; I bought it during a time when I was still careless with books, so its paper covers bear scrapes, tears, stains, folds, and rubbing I'd never subject a book to now, especially one bearing the autograph of the first out queer poet I met: Minnie Bruce Pratt, who was born and raised in Alabama and graduated from the same state university I was attending when the student-run Gay/Lesbian/Bisexual/Transgender Alliance invited her to read. Yet the book's battered aspect is an integral part of its history: these marks testify to its own part in my story, the one in which, as I learned the exigencies of craft and the vicissitudes of the writing life, I began to see a book as vulnerable, as needing protection, because authorship itself is both valuable and precarious. And thus the book's state is eidetic in the way only things that have witnessed the attainment of a large portion of our hopes and desires can be.

And yet I can't remember reading its brief selections of Thom Gunn's poetry, four poems now familiar to me: "Courage, A Tale" (from *Jack Straw's Castle*); "As Expected" and "The Cherry Tree" (from *The Passages of Joy*); and "Lament" (from the then-unpublished book *The Man with Night Sweats*). Honestly, I think this lapse speaks to the fact that for me at that age, reading poetry by queers was as erotic as it was political, and these particular poems by Gunn neither turned me on the way some gay men's work did, nor did it, as feminist lesbian work tended to, lend me a sociopolitical framework within which to read. I was political and horny and I *loved* the "wild cooking pederasty and intoxication" of reading Allen Ginsberg's "Howl" as much as I identified with these lines from Minnie Bruce Pratt's "The Child Taken from the Mother": "Lesbian: no. / Put that outside the place of the poem. Too / slangy, prosy, obvious, just doesn't belong. / *Why don't you: Why didn't you: Can't you / say it some other way?*"[17] It strikes me now that reading queer poetry was as much about my own desire as it was about the internalization of others' prejudices against it: both were rendered nearly unspeakable, absolutely invisible by the society I lived in, just as both desire and prejudice continued to thrive behind the psalm-printed paper fans of Southern manners. To read about them seemed the very essence of what I'd need to survive, and in what work of Gunn's I'd read, there was no recognition of the emergency my life seemed to me to be—I judged him then and didn't reopen the case until over a decade later.

However, as Eavan Boland writes in *Object Lessons*, "Young poets are like children. They assume the dangers to themselves are those their elders identified; they internalize the menace without analyzing it."[18] In this, I was like any young poet, and I understand now that though the dangers Pratt and other queer poets like her identified were indeed similar to the ones I faced—discrimination, homophobic violence, periods of isolation and lovelessness, difficulty in accepting oneself, AIDS—there lay ahead of me a more difficult and intransigent danger: authorship. Impossibly, it was possible that a boy could, first of all, grow up to be gay, and after that, become a writer; it never occurred to me that I'd have to ask myself what relationship my sexuality would have to my writing. It never occurred to me that, rather than providing me with answers to this question, *Gay and Lesbian Poetry in Our Time* provided only examples of *other* poets' answers to this question; it only occurs to me in writing this that each answer was provisional, subject to change, and as hard-won as any other aspect of their craft. Had I access to each of Gunn's books and to his notebooks as well, I could've read my way to an understanding of how I might slowly negotiate a relationship first with being a poet, and later, a gay poet, a process as much of revaluation and integration as celebration and liberation. I might've had the chance to fall in love with patience, as well as witness the pain of integrating oneself fully into one's craft—a process that took Gunn almost thirty years.

Though fifteen years ago I was unable to imagine developing such a relationship with Gunn's work, it seems particularly fitting that I revisit it in light of my earlier self who was so unaware of the dangers that lay ahead. To attempt as it does a history of desire, writing gay literary history is a practice particularly marked by unstable relations between past and present, by cross-temporal identifications as political as they are erotic. As Robert L. Caserio writes in "The Mortal Limits of Poetry and Criticism," the gay critic writing about gay poetry is, at least in part, "a critic whose reading of his subject's way of loving is simultaneously the defense of the critic's own way," and for that reason I'd like to suggest that to write about Gunn (or Duncan) is essentially to write about aspects of myself, not just those of the poet, but also those of the citizen, the lover, and the beloved.[19]

Historically, gay writers have read each other's works not only for aesthetic kinship but also in search of identity and community models, to see how others like themselves have fashioned their lives and relationships. This kind of reading has almost always been fraught, made complex both by the coded writing practices queers have often undertaken as well as by pedagogies that have removed their texts from historical and/or biographical contexts. Thus Thom Gunn, in a 1977 interview with *The Advocate,* mentions the internal prohibitions he faced when desiring the satisfaction of this kind of gay reading, saying, "I thought I was reading things into writers like Marlowe and Forster and others whom I later found to be gay. I'd no idea that my favorite poet, Auden, was gay."[20] It's also true that gay writers have read texts written *about* gays for ways to articulate their own desires and to have their own desires affirmed and inflamed; if they've read to escape the moral judgments of their societies, they've also looked to see what their own fates might be. In a 1976 interview with Robert Peters, Robert Duncan discusses the fruits of his own particular method of gay reading:

ROBERT PETERS: Apparently you didn't sit around in the libraries as I did reading Krafft-Ebbing to educate myself and understand that I wasn't the only male in the world suffering sexual turmoil.

ROBERT DUNCAN: Oh, no. I did read Krafft-Ebbing, and I've seen my own life in terms of those case histories. . . . Though I used to go to the Krafft-Ebbing volumes to search for myself, as I'm sure you also did, I didn't find much help. The self I sought, I knew, was not really different from the self I was in the family I grew up in. I was looking for another story, possibly, and certainly took a long time before I was comfortable living that story, a homosexual one.[21]

It's clear that gay writers like Gunn and Duncan began reading in the hopes of identification with a possible self in a possible future, and if they often finished a gay text fueled with communion—or even the suspicion of communion—they just as often finished their reading disenchanted with the prospects revealed to them. And if with similar hopes and desires I likewise came to the work of Gunn and Duncan—both appear in *Gay and Lesbian Poetry in Our Time*—I did so after two very marked historical shifts in gay community politics: Gay Liberation and AIDS. Just as it's historically instructive that I—like Gunn—turned for evidence of gay life first to literature rather than psychology—as Duncan had—so my own inability as a young poet to find what I desired in Gunn's work informs me of the ways in which political history determined what I'd be looking for.

Following the work of Christopher Nealon's *Foundlings: Lesbian and Gay Historical Emotion before Stonewall*, I'd like to suggest that because Thom Gunn's poetic career splits almost evenly between pre- and post-Stonewall publications, a distinct and distinctly ideological shift informs not only his critical reception, but also his own conception of poetry, its formal and material possibilities. However, given Gunn's characteristic care, caution, and discretion, a pre-/post-Stonewall divide indicates neither a swift nor an absolute break between say, 1967's *Touch* and 1971's *Moly*, but rather the instigation of a slow evolution that over time results in books like *Jack Straw's Castle* (1977) and *The Passages of Joy* (1982). Indeed, notebooks from both 1974 and 1979 contain abandoned drafts titled "Gay Rights Parade (NY, 74)" and "The Gay Parade,"[22] and though he was never able to finish his own Gay Liberation poem, it's clear from others of Gunn's poetry notebooks that as early as 1970 he was attempting to write openly about gay sexuality and identity in drafts of poems from *Moly*. The series of "centaur poems" that later becomes "Tom-Dobbin" goes through titles of varying thematic explicitness, one string of which heads an early draft: "The Centaur/Being Queer/ Making Love/We Are (All) Centaurs."[23] And though an additional early draft of the poem's fifth section clearly sets a scene and describes the speaker's role in a sexual act with another man, this same draft contains a fairly finished version of the last stanza, next to which is written: "maybe just/last stanza?":

> Ruthlessly gentle, gently ruthless (we) move
> As if thro water with delaying limbs
> We circle each around an unseen/unmapped center
> Gradually closer, till we enter
> Light's cove, together and clasping—which is me, which him?—
> Selves floating in the one flesh we are of.[24]

In revision, it does indeed become the *only* stanza of section five and the close of the series itself; in editing what was once a depiction of gay sex down to this lyrical evocation of the subjective morph and merge that can happen during fucking, Gunn emphasizes the theme of transformation—a move typical both of his native discretion and of his preference at this stage for privileging the thematic work a poem does over its narrative qualities. Thus the centaur's specifically gay symbolic nature remains mostly subtext in the final draft, leaving the themes of the poem less specific to gay sexuality. In a book that Gunn sees as being "about metamorphosis, change in the human being toward (his sources/the primitive and irrational),"[25] it even makes political sense, then, not to characterize gay sexuality as primitive or irrational, but to focus on sexuality qua sexuality as constituting a more primordial kind of consciousness.

This example illustrates that the shift toward openness in Gunn's work is deliberate and slow: he lays groundwork years before he's able to fulfill his plans. Thus the metamorphosis and change, the opening of consciousness in the *Moly* poems—which reflect the deliberate mind-altering he was pursuing at the time—prepare the way for *Jack Straw's Castle,* the first book in which his oeuvre opens onto the wider horizon of "gay poetry," an epithet which for me carries no tinge of the pejorative but instead characterizes "a struggle to find terms for historical narration that strike a balance between the unspeakability of desire, especially punishable desire, and group life."[26] The book's title poem explicitly wrestles with bringing the gay subject into the poem, into *poetry,* and only through a fairly hellish struggle against internal prohibitions and deep-seated fear achieves both poetic closure and triumphant success: "And even if he were a dream / —Thick sweating flesh against which I lie curled— / With dreams like this, Jack's ready for the world."[27] That this gesture was made possible for Gunn by virtue of historical context he makes clear in a 1977 interview with *The Advocate.* In response to "Has the gay movement helped him, as a writer?" Gunn suggests:

> Yes, very much I think. In my early books I was in the closet. . . . I figured it didn't matter, it didn't affect the poetry. But it did. Later I came out. . . . I wouldn't have expected it to make so much difference as it did. In the title poem of *Jack Straw's Castle* I end up in bed with a man, and I wrote this quite naturally, without a second thought. Ten years ago, I doubt if the incident would have appeared in the poem. It wouldn't have occurred to me to end it in that way.[28]

Seen from the vantage point of both his notebooks and his published writings, the arc of Gunn's career clearly illustrates what Christopher Nealon suggests was "a movement . . . from isolation to peoplehood" that characterized homosexuality's mid-twentieth-century shift from a discourse of inversion to one of ethnicity: "We may think of the inversion model of homosexuality—the idea that homosexuals are people whose souls are trapped in the body of the 'other' sex—and of the ethnic model—the idea that gay men and lesbians, either separately or jointly, constitute a people with a distinct culture—as two poles between which the history of U.S. lesbian and gay sexuality was shaped in the twentieth century."[29] Though its influence can be seen in the subtle articulations of Gunn's own self-awareness as well as in the more dramatic rhetoric of some of his critics, Nealon himself would be the first to remind us that texts such as those of Gunn and his critics "illuminate the *tension* between [inversion and ethnicity]," *not* a complete acceptance of one model over another (my italics).[30] And while it is true that "the inversion model enjoyed dominance in the first half of the century, while the ethnic model rose to prominence in the second,"[31] it's important to remember, as David M. Halperin would have us do, that "earlier forms of sexual discourse are not superseded by later ones . . . and continue to appear within the discourses of homosexuality."[32]

Indeed, when Gunn's midcareer work is set next to that of his critics, or when his own notebook entries or drafts are compared with his published poetry, temporal "folds"—"outdated" paradigms existing anachronistically inside of or next to more progressive strands of thought—are often created, and these "folds" might appear to indicate "a definitional incoherence at the core of the modern notion of homosexuality."[33] However, as Halperin suggests, this temporal simultaneity is merely a sign of homosexuality's "historical evolution," and should notions of inversion continue to appear within the discourse of the ethnicity model, then "there are good historical reasons for that."[34] The tension inherent in this historical evolution is more than apparent in the relationship of Gunn's work to its critics—the constant negotiation and renegotiation of terms of identity and politics within the gay community since Gay Liberation has paralleled an analogous definitional struggle within poetry since entering postmodernity.[35] Because of these parallel evolutions, I'd argue that not only did *Gunn* not always think of—and for—himself as a poet and gay poet but because of the time it took for his own thinking to come to fruition, critics often thought and wrote about his work either nostalgically, as the poet he *once was,* or futuristically, as the poet *he was to become.*[36]

This kind of nostalgic lag in critical acumen is evidenced by a journal like *Critical Quarterly,* which has published a total of five essays about Gunn's work—one each in 1961, 1971, 1977, 1987, and 1993—and of these five, only Bruce Woodcock's 1993 "'But oh not loose': Form and Sexuality in Thom Gunn's Poetry" considers Gunn's work in light of gender or sexuality. This is perhaps understandable in essays published in or before 1971, years in which Gunn had yet to publish *as* a gay poet, years in which the discourse about gay identity coined by Gay Liberation had not yet penetrated academe. However, as Gregory Woods points out, gender is nonetheless notable as absent in the critical discourse, given that, as reviewers of the first three books "concentrated on the apparently violent aspect of his subjects, and on his conception of men's *will,* one might have expected them to begin to analyze the erotic vision to which these themes adhere."[37] What begins as an egregious oversight in 1977 becomes something more like irresponsibility in 1987, considering that, as Woodcock writes of *The Man with Night Sweats,* "the developments . . . emerged from directions his work was already taking and tensions which were already present."[38] And yet if some critics—such as Alan Bold in his 1976 study *Thom Gunn and Ted Hughes*—would persist in referring to all "the loved ones in the poems as female," gaining visibility as a gay poet was not necessarily to Gunn's advantage among gay critics, who judged the work before *Jack Straw's Castle* according to ideologies his work had not yet had time to absorb, interrogate, and interpret back to the gay community.[39]

Thus early studies of gay poetry—Robert K. Martin's 1979 *The Homosexual Tradition in American Poetry* the first among them—understandably spare very little approbation for Gunn's early work, of which Martin says,

"Gunn clearly feels guilt and unhappiness about his homosexuality, and these feelings pervade his poetry. He cannot reconcile the needs of the body with the claims of the mind."[40] While it's true that Martin's Gay Liberation politics inhibit his ability to see Gunn's early work as anything but symptomatic, he does write mostly of books and poems in which Gunn is not writing *as* a gay poet per se, books that—as Gunn himself would wish—should be judged accordingly. Thus Martin, like many early gay academic critics, remains deeply ambivalent or even confused by Gunn's early poetry, not sure if it's simply the work of an invert or an actively anti-gay poet; Martin often resorts to judgment, deeming the poems "quite clear on a number of points that one can most charitably call morally dubious," a stance usually reserved for Gunn's straight critics.[41] "The need for the homosexual to react against the effete and decadent" and his eroticization of a butch, macho style of masculinity, Martin argues, link "the erotic and the violent," a gesture which "make[s] his vision suspect."[42] Martin posits this before also going on to suggest that Gunn's "lyrical treatment of sadomasochism" is actually intended "to demand of homosexuals that they not relegate their sadistic or masochistic brothers to the inferno of scorn where once all homosexuals lived."[43] Definitional incoherence aside, if Martin sees the work from *Moly* and *Jack Straw's Castle* as exhibiting "a growth toward community and the development of a newer, more androgynous self," it should be noted that these *are* volumes Gunn wrote during and after the years of his experiments with LSD and participation in Gay Liberation: years that most involved Gunn in a gradual unfolding of self-knowledge, volumes whose ideological values are much more befitting post-Stonewall politics than those of the neoclassical, existential lyrics of Gunn's first three books.[44]

But what of *Fighting Terms, The Sense of Movement,* and *My Sad Captains*? What are the best ways to read them now, knowing what we do about Gunn's development as a gay poet? Before I could get access to the Fantasy Press edition of 1954, I read the version of *Fighting Terms* Gunn presents in his 1994 *Collected Poems;* aside from order, it hews fairly closely to the 1958 Hawk's Well Press edition, which also removes from the first edition two poems—"A Village Edmund" and "Contemplative and Active." Upon my first reading the *Fighting Terms* of 1994, my critical method operated much along the lines of Martin's in that I could only see the closet at work—in my early notes I wrote things like "'Anxious' and 'studied' are good words to describe his early work's insistence on a superficially masculine heterosexual identity," and though this isn't necessarily a wrong impression, it's certainly only a surface one. After reading the earliest editions of his first three books, I'd say they in fact record a fascinating oscillation between disclosure and the closet—rather than being simply closeted—and that the poems themselves, to greater or lesser extent, partake of the strange pervasive atmosphere of a nearly thwarted sexuality that results from such open ambivalence. But what was it about these editions that helped to challenge and deepen my first impression?

When I finally opened the canary-yellow-covered boards of the Fantasy Press edition of *Fighting Terms,* I was surprised to find the dedication, "To Mike Kitay," and even more puzzled to find it followed by the famous poem of sexual duplicity and humiliation "Carnal Knowledge." Though I'd known before that Gunn met Kitay at Cambridge, the fact that his name prefaces a book I'd previously thought of as exclusively "closeted" changed my working definition of the closet to include Gunn's *active* knowledge of his own homosexuality. But how did recognizing the active status of this knowledge change my reading of Gunn's early work? Next to the dedication to the man who would be Gunn's lifelong partner, "Carnal Knowledge" suddenly seems decidedly about *sexual,* not existential, identity and rejection; in the *Collected Poems,* Gunn shifts the poem to the middle of *Fighting Terms,* where it seems less ambiguous, more hetero.[45] When in its original context I read, "Even in bed I pose, my self is not like my body, bare," the rhetoric seems newly revelatory, as though the speaker were admitting this, *in front of his male lover,* to a woman.[46] Thus when he says to the addressed, "I am not what I seem, believe me," it's almost funny; when he says, "You know I know you know I know you know," it's simply hilarious.[47] But the difficult thing about reading "Carnal Knowledge" now is that we know both that (a) the poem portrays the speaker as heterosexual and (b) he's deadly serious—as G. S. Fraser writes in "The Poetry of Thom Gunn," the early Gunn "has plenty of wit of the severer kind, but almost no humor."[48]

If my first impression is still right, if Gunn's severe speakers utilize a "superficially masculine heterosexual identity," then the right question to ask is: what were the uses of this disguise? In his 1961 essay Fraser calls "Carnal Knowledge" "a more awkward, a more undergraduate poem than the others" in *Fighting Terms,* and goes on to say that this is due not so much to "the callowness of the attitude as the weakness of the writing . . . the conscious manly toughness . . . and the at once coy and trite narcissism."[49] Keeping in mind that Gunn's speakers were indeed able to pass as hetero *because* of this "conscious manly toughness," I'd like to recuperate the camouflaging sexual gestures of Gunn's early work as examples of savvy survival techniques. If the world-weary "carnal knowledge" of their poses accomplishes anything, Gunn's early poems—many of them in actuality love poems to Mike Kitay—create a homosocial relationship between the speaker and the reader based on an alleged shared knowledge about and conspiratorial "callowness of attitude" toward sex, including the female partner in a heterosexual coupling.[50] Even if a single poem is itself vague about a beloved's gender, other poems in Gunn's first three books specify her, "any Miss Brown or any Miss Jones," and thus create a general heterosexual context tending to stabilize localized gender ambiguity and safeguard the relationship Gunn's speaker has created with his reader.[51] And yet, as one gay critic suggests, there is also a subtext created by many of Gunn's poems, which also often attempt to accomplish homosocial "male bonding" by presenting paeans to an iconic, idealized masculinity that the reader—like the poet—is supposed to identify with: "images of discipline and will: soldiers, leather-armoured motorcyclists, tattooed arms, historical toughs like Alexander."[52]

In these gestures of disclosure—often simultaneous with the disguises of the closet—lie the *true* ambiguity of Gunn's speakers' poses. As Eve Kosofsky Sedgwick notes, there is a "potential unbroken . . . continuum between homosocial and homosexual—a continuum whose visibility, for men in this society, is radically disrupted," and the deep identification with the masculine icon that many of Gunn's early poems perform fully *restores* the visibility of this continuum between homosocial and homosexual.[53] These "outward and visible signs of a drive towards self-definition" are—any gay man could tell you—telltale: a man's supposed to want to *be* the tough, not to fuck him.[54] Hence the strained atmosphere that attends the oscillating sexual identity of Gunn's early poems: if, as one gay critic writes, "Identification is desire,"[55] then it's clear that the intensity of identification in Gunn's early poems leads another gay critic to say of them that "[t]he homosexual feeling was obvious, if never overt."[56]

Keeping in mind that Gunn was *not* publicly out in 1961, two further comments by Fraser are worth mentioning, as much for their anachronistic irony as for the kind of unintentional cruelty the assumptions of a heterosexual critic can deliver: "Gunn is never quite at his best when he writes of personal relationships";[57] and, of another Gunn poem in which "two men have been sharing a bed (or the two men may be different aspects of the poet's one personality)," he claims: "When the speaker turns on his pillow at the end, he may perhaps be turning not toward the exhaustion of sleep but to make love. . . . But the love, as between two men, would be, by definition, sterile. This seems to me one of the most powerful of Gunn's earlier poems, with an almost Dantesque quality of visionary horror."[58] Censure aside, Fraser's last comment is worth noting because, though Gunn's early critics assume his and his speakers' identities to be heterosexual, there do exist early poems of Gunn's in which an oddly uncanny, almost gothic power derives from a meeting between the homosocial and the homoerotic, usually in a doppelgänger figure, as in "The Monster" from his third book, *My Sad Captains.* Even though at first it appears to be a textbook rendering of a Sedgwickian erotic triangle in which a woman is exchanged between two men—two men meet by chance outside the window of a female lover—it's notable for the powerful way in which its narrative situation turns away from this trope to become instead possible code for one man's negotiation between his heterosexual and homosexual identities.

The poem takes place in a foreboding Gothic landscape of ruin, "Where the carved cherub crumbled down," on a night when the speaker takes "the turn I had renounced" to arrive at "the cul de sac" and, surprised, finds "an unmoved waiting back." "How had she never vainly mentioned / This lover, too, unsatisfied?" the speaker asks. "Wide mouth ugly with despair," the rival "monster" the speaker confronts could be read as the figure of the invert, "gloating over / a grief defined and realized, / And living only for its sake."[59] However, because "It was myself I recognized," because the speaker, "Standing before this man of mine, / The constant one I had created," admits to the part he's played in nurturing and sustaining the misery of his double, he can see clearly the dilemma presented by his divided self:

> What if I were within the house,
> Happier than the fact had been
> —Would he, then, still be gazing here,
> The man who never can get in?
>
> Or would I, leaving at the dawn,
> A suppler love than he could guess,
> Find him awake on my small bed,
> Demanding still some bitterness?[60]

You could say that the invert, like "the monster," is made ugly by its marriage to impossibility, to a pathology that ensures eternal internal division, damned to being "the man who never can get in." It seems completely plausible to read the poem as a kind of allegory about the divided consciousness of the closet. However, you could also say that the poem impeccably maintains a level of exclusively homosocial reading—a poem perhaps about sexual jealousy and rejection, of seeing reflected in a rival one's own ambivalence about a sexual partner. Others can become symbolic for us and inform, even structure our definitions of selfhood; thus, even after he's been left behind, "the man who can never get in" might yet demand reparation, "some bitterness," from the man who can.

Just as it's difficult to distinguish between the real and symbolic functions of the allegorical doppelgänger of "The Monster," Gunn's early style maintains a highly sophisticated form of sexual camouflage. This becomes particularly clear in *The Sense of Movement,* in which the insistent macho posturing of his first book is both further necessitated and justified by the tonal and subjective detachment of his Winters-influenced neoclassical formality. The persona of this book, necessarily distant from everything—but seeming especially anxious to distance itself from anything overtly gay—deflects suspicion aesthetically and existentially, as in the infamous heroic couplets of "Lines for a Book": "I praise the overdogs from Alexander / To those who would not play with Stephen Spender."[61] I'd like to suggest that though Spender *is* a figure of ambiguous sexuality, the insult is more than just Augustan or Sartrean bluster. Rather than simply embodying a desire to shock the older generation, it's the highly stylized credo of a gendered existential philosophy, a fact whose effects he discusses in a 1977 interview with *The Advocate:* "I honestly don't think I was attacking the homosexual element in Spender's lines; that I would never have done. I was against a certain namby-pambiness . . . which has no more to do with homosexuality than heterosexuality. But I can't defend my poem. It was fascistic and foolish and I wouldn't publish it now."[62]

But it's hard to believe Gunn completely when he says "a certain namby-pambiness . . . has no more to do with homosexuality than heterosexuality," especially because we know effeminacy is de facto a discourse about masculinity. And while in terms of antiessentialist logic he's absolutely right, streetwise we know better. The continuum between homosocial and homosexual, Sedgwick would remind us, remains ruptured for a reason; in our homophobic society, fey equals gay; and such a formula makes a clear distinction between gay male sexuality and male heterosexuality. To put the argument about Gunn's style another way, the distinction between homosocial and homosexual is "a strategy for making generalizations about, and marking historical difference *in,* the *structure* of men's relations with other men."[63] Gunn's early poems certainly and quite consciously participate in this strategy; they elicit a homosocial relationship between their speakers and their readers, both of whom the poems presume to be heterosexual men.[64]

It's just possible that the eventual alignment of Gunn's work with Gay Liberation identity politics and its relative comfort with the ethnicity model has obscured the ingenuity and innovation of the disclosing disguises of Gunn's early poems. *Gay and Lesbian Poetry in Our Time* was able neither to include work that participates in such disguise nor to celebrate this kind of gesture, but one result of this was that I—and perhaps others of my generation—wasn't at first able to see how hard-won Gunn's later poetry really is. Similarly, it's possible that the rearrangement within and selection of Gunn's *Collected Poems* obscures both some of the felicities and the missteps that illuminate the deliberate development and deployment of his strategic camouflage. Having solved the particular problems of authorship that faced a gay poet of his generation perhaps gave him the permission to create out of his oeuvre what Jonathan Dollimore calls a narrative of "pathology to politics," one in which *The Man with Night Sweats* forms the crucible that fuses deepest expression of communal solidarity to a metrical verse tradition.[65]

Don't get me wrong: it's not as though I *want* to celebrate what in Gunn's poems could be read as the effects of homophobia on the poet's art. But it would also insult Gunn to reduce his early work to pathology or simple self-hatred when in fact much of his camouflage was not only deliberately chosen from among a variety of possible solutions but also cleverly conceived and executed. Indeed, the terrible cold lucidity of his early love poems, the way within context they reveal and sorrow in their own emotional duplicity, strikes me now as a kind of wayward honesty, the result of "feeling the fullness of [his] powers / at the precise moment when [he] must not use them," to rewrite Adrienne Rich's "I Dream I'm the Death of Orpheus." Time and time again in interviews, Gunn emphasizes the fear of retribution that surrounded his sexuality during the 1950s; he reports, "People say, 'Why didn't you come out of the closet, publicly, sooner than you did?' I would never have got to America, for one thing. I would never have got a teaching job, for another thing. And I would probably not have had openly homosexual poems published in magazines or books at that time, in 1954."[66]

But of course material limitations are not the only censures used by society to restrain and shape gay sexuality; within the realm of literature, criticism serves just as well. We've only to look back into recent twentieth-century Anglo-American literary history to see the deeply ideological conflict that arises for some straight critics when setting the word "gay" beside "poetry." Gunn himself reports the fact that, in the 1950s, "[h]omosexuality was held in peculiar horror even by liberals who would not have dreamt of attacking other minorities," and goes on to relate an anecdote about Yvor Winters, his mentor during that time, who, when asked by Gunn "why he did not like Whitman's poem about the twenty-eight young men bathing . . . replied that the homosexual feeling of the poem was such that he could not get beyond it."[67] And just when we assume that the intervening decades might have changed the intellectual climate, a critic as intelligent as Donald Davie suggests that "it is disconcerting to reflect that any poet who wanted in his or her verses to promote such causes [as homosexual liberation] would, it seems, have to make the same sacrifice that Gunn made in *The Passages of Joy:* the sacrifice, that is, of any profound resonances from periods earlier than the eighteenth century."[68] In this comment of Davie's, we have a really helpful example of the varieties of Logos straight critics call upon to undermine gay poets:[69] if "poetry" is defined by its ability to refer to a historicized tradition of English poetry, then this English tradition, by virtue of one particular reading of history and ideology, automatically excludes gay poets. Further, if for Davie as for John Crowe Ransom, gay subject matter is equal to a kind of advertisement for or promotion of a homosexual lifestyle, then its presence turns the poem into a disguised form of prose, thus simultaneously discounting its artistic merit and its claim to any legitimate tradition of poetry. This final connection between Davie and Ransom is important, for it shows that, even twenty years after Stonewall, homophobic prejudices survive by calling upon their own "profound resonances": uninterrogated and inexcusable rhetorical tropes that can—and do—impinge upon the intellectual acuity, efficacy, and verity of literary criticism.

Why give so much of this essay over to caution, doubt, and unease? Because, as Sianne Ngai suggests in her brilliantly canny book *Ugly Feelings*, anxiety, like other "ugly feelings," "can be thought of as a mediation between the aesthetic and the political in a nontrivial way."[70] Because he attained fame early on and remained for almost half a century in the critical light of two countries, there have been hundreds of reviews and articles written about Gunn's work; because early in his career, each of his books was scrutinized for its aesthetic value, and later in his career, each was pored over for both its emerging aesthetic *and* ideological values; it can justifiably be said that he deserved to be anxious, especially when, in the early work, there *was* something to hide. In writing so much about desire and love when unable to admit to his desire's true love object, Gunn's early poems do indeed convey, according to Catherine R. Stimpson in 1977, "violence, guilt, fear of subordination and passivity, retreat" exactly *because* they are designed to be "discreetly evasive," their "topography blank or opaque, the sex of the lovers unknown."[71] In addition to the negative emotions they report—frustration, anxiety, boredom, a sense of duplicity—the emotions Gunn's early work evokes in me—embarrassment, irritation, uncomfortable laughter, suspicion, sadness—are in and of themselves *political* feelings: they describe the difference between the Gay Liberation ideal I inherited from such anthologies as *Gay and Lesbian Poetry in Our Time* and what Gunn, with his own inheritance, was able to achieve at the time.

I've given over so much of this essay to uneasy or "ugly" feelings because to write about gay poetry is to write about literature's connection to the sociopolitical history of a highly variegated and often internally divided community, which is to say that ugly feelings are a fact and product of the gap between how gay history is lived and how it is written. The presence of anxiety, discomfort, or anger helps reveal to us how such history reappears *as* the present in both individual expression (poems) and the collective imagination (politics); often the presence of "ugly" feelings is in fact a *product* of the tension between the individual and the collective and helps describe the terms of that conflict. As Duncan, in his 1959 introduction to "The Homosexual in Society," says of his essay and the difficulty he had in writing it: "the work often has value as evidence in itself of the conflict concerned and of the difficulty of the statement then just where it is questionable. . . . I had a likeness to the public and shared its conflicts of attitude."[72] Given the constant interplay between the individual and the collective that informs the sociopolitical construction of literature, Gunn's own slow, slightly asynchronous cultivation of a gay literary politics is a good example of how, during a time when Gay Liberation reigned supreme, earlier modes of thinking and writing about gay literature and experience were kept alive in a dissenting discourse aimed at amending the mainstream.

Another way of spinning this historicism is perhaps more cautionary, but no less trenchant: earlier forms of homophobic discourse are not necessarily superseded by later, less homophobic ones, and continue to exert force and influence within the present, no matter how much we wish they didn't. Which is why, even after drafting and attempting the gay poetry that would become the expanded-consciousness-centered "centaur poems" in *Moly,* even after marching—on LSD and in full leathers—in New York City's 1974 Gay Pride Parade, Gunn still had difficulty placing the terms "gay" and "poetry" next to each other without the terms canceling each other out. And yet, as a gay man born in 1929, as a poet who had already published four books, in 1966 he gave up tenure, took acid for the better part of a decade, and thrived in San Francisco during Gay Liberation. Apolitical as he professed to be, he nonetheless took note of and actively participated in the historical changes around him.

What relationship to the tradition of poetry did such lived historical experience have for him? Were I following the New Critical paradigm of ultimate textual authority, it would be unfair to expect Gunn's poetry to answer such a question. And yet, in its own way, because he was not in the end interested in any one critical paradigm, his poetry does tell a fabulously multifaceted story about the historical and cultural changes in the gay communities of San Francisco in the 1960s, '70s and '80s. However, the story that Gunn's *Collected Poems* doesn't tell—and which I longed to find out—is how he came *to be able* as a poet to write books such as *Jack Straw's Castle, The Passages of Joy,* and *The Man with Night Sweats.* That he underwent such a change is obvious—we have the poems—but what was it that altered in Gunn's conception of authorship to enable him to become a gay poet?

3. Hesitation

> Perhaps the hesitation may be diagnosed simply as a form of being disappointed or as a fear of losing one's pleasant sense of expectancy even though the expectancy may have been an illusion.
>
> —Thom Gunn, ca. 1970 notebook (BL)

How and why does conflict arise when twentieth- or twenty-first-century literary critical discourses attempt to address "gay poetry"? Even now, the presence of "gay" and "poetry" together suggests a paradox: for at its most descriptive, "gay" is neither apolitical, ahistorical, nor morally neutral, even as, at its most politicized, "poetry" can never not refer to specific traditions whose tropes and values are paradoxically alleged to transcend historical time. Even if they are bound as much to upholding cultural norms and values as they are to underwriting large historical shifts and flux, even if these terms often come to represent ideological stress points within literary critical discourse, their presence together still has the power to unsettle what assumptions we hold both about what it means to write and read poetry and what constitutes gay identity. In fact, what's most interesting

> about the proximity of "gay" to "poetry" is how each must shift definition to accommodate the other.

Writing the above paragraph blocked me from further writing. Though I dutifully eked out a few more anemic pages of notes, what I'd really penned was an impasse symptomatic of my dual education as critic and poet. As a gay critic introduced to literary criticism through the feminist and queer theories of the mid-1990s, I'm deeply suspicious of the ideologies that adhere within New Critical practices, which predicate literary value on a poem's ability to present poetic form as a "universal" aesthetic experience divorced from historical period and context.[73] As a gay poet educated in the United States during the 1990s, I attended graduate creative writing workshops whose basic tenets were New Critical, workshops whose reaction to my poems ranged from moral hostility to mere tolerance, and which only rarely indicated familiarity with gay literary history, much less an objective sympathy with or appreciation of the project of engaging that history. Because to write gay poetry refutes boundaries between history and poetry, New Criticism just doesn't *like* gay writers; New Criticism might like a writer *who happens to be gay,* or a writer with a *gay sensibility,* but it's a fine rhetorical line we're drawing here between life and art, and my hand isn't steady when the stakes are so high. After all, in my own life and writing practice, I experience no psychic conflicts between the categories of "gay" and "poetry"—in fact, they look quite comfortable there, right next to one another on the page: *gay poetry.* Why is this not so when I'm writing criticism?

I brought this impasse to the "Thom Gunn" Gunn recorded in his poetry notebooks at Bancroft Library on the Berkeley campus of the University of California. Aware that I needed a kind of mentoring, I was hoping what traces of himself Gunn had taken care to leave behind might serve as a kind of map—one, I might add, that would help me navigate over, through, under, or around what blocked my path. After all, Gunn had been educated at Stanford by Yvor Winters—a mind so fiercely, idiosyncratically conservative that Cleanth Brooks in *The Well-Wrought Urn* judged Winters's arguments to be as exasperating and dogmatic as his persona was intimidating—and had nonetheless gone on to write *The Passages of Joy.* Not knowing exactly what I was looking for—other than what working notes and drafts I could find for the opening poems of *Moly*—I chose a notebook at random and opened it. For the first hour, each time I opened a book I seemed to find some track or trace indicating a direction, some gesture of potential escape past an impasse that I felt increasingly I had not made but had stumbled upon, and whose nature I was in the process of discovering:

(1) from his September 28, 1981–October 1983 notebook:

> Why is my impulse to write poetry so closely connected—so much a part of—my sexual impulse? When I feel one, I feel something very similar to the other. I don't like this too much—I mean I like it somewhat, but I feel it necessary sometimes to steer my energy into nonsexual subjects almost by an act of will, since I don't believe all the important parts of life are sexual. And when I succeed in doing so, I'm quite often successful. Yet it does, even then, derive from an energy that is sexual energy—it's quite the same kind of concentrated excitement that lights up everything in a limited area (as a flashlight lights up everything in the circle it makes). I wonder where this comes from . . . I wonder how many other poets this happens to. . . . It's my limitation.

(2) from his September–November 1968 notebook:

> I pass the romantic impulse through the classical scrutiny. The scrutiny is both the experience and the poem's form. It is destructive . . . of all that is not hard and genuine in the impulse . . . examples of the impulse: fantasy; sexual fantasy; themes of liberation from authority; the decorum of naturalness; repossession of innocence . . .

(3) from his May 4, 1980, notebook:

> I do believe in poetry as an activity reflective of one's life at its fullest—not only reflective, but it actually can *be* one's life at its fullest.

(4) from a notebook of 1950:

> Sexual fetichism [*sic*] is not really hard to explain. Ejaculation must take place in a normal human body because it is a physical necessity. But what it is associated with is dictated by chance. Convention says that it shall be women, but in Greece convention said that it should be men and it attached itself to that idea equally easily. Again, though convention says it shall be women, chance may bring it about that it is associated with men, objects, or animals.

(5) from his September 28, 1981–October 1983 notebook, an entry of January 7, 1983:

> The issue of *Salmagundi*[74]: the straight contributors, good liberals all it seemed (or perhaps ex-liberals), confronted with homosexuality. And their great horror was promiscuity. What form that promiscuity took, how it worked out in real lives, they didn't bother to find out: the closest they came to being specific was with Genet, but the complication with Genet was that he was another generation—one I have found largely pessimistic of the possibilities of a happy homosexual life (except Isherwood and Duncan), and so he acted out the role of poete maudit. (Homosexuality to him was no more "life-affirming" than stealing or murder.) But these high-minded professors, Herb Blau, etc.—perhaps they stuck their heads in a gay bar some time and carried away the impression of the hysteria of the damned—some masque of the Red Death orgy or sumpin'. They have no idea of how their abstraction breaks down, of how we really do live our lives. Here is a sequence of pictures: 1) the high-minded rhetoric of Herb Blau 2) the complex web of specific life, e.g. the monogamous lovers 3) the non-monogamous lovers 4) the importance of friendship, which may well have emerged from tricking in the first place 5) the constants of promiscuity—it is not all self-regarding, self-satisfying—joy, entering other lives (homes, etc.), visiting inside other lives, an entrance into all humanity. There are constants everywhere.

At this point—after copying everything down, after reading the phrase "They have no idea how their abstraction breaks down, of how we really do live our lives," and feeling gratefully chastened for having been so long caught up in abstraction—I had to stop and sort through what I'd learned so far.

On the one hand, Gunn's own words affirmed for me a sense of the centrality of his own life experience to his work, and that, for him, the line between life and art is consistently blurred, both deliberately and, at times, helplessly: "I do believe in poetry as an activity reflective of one's life at its fullest—not only reflective, but it actually can *be* one's life at its fullest." His notebooks also affirm the sense that poetry's *being* life at its fullest means that the poet's creative and sexual energies are intertwined, and that, for Gunn, "When I feel one, I feel something very similar to the other." Thus the reader of Gunn's notebooks can trace from 1950 onward a growing acceptance within Gunn of the centrality of sex and sexuality to his identity, as well as a preoccupation with their relationship to his writing. If at age twenty-one he's anxiously figuring out how to talk about his sexuality, and justifies it via an ill-formed notion of Greek cultural life and homosexuality's place within it, we also know he's yet to go to Cambridge, where he'll meet his lifelong partner Mike Kitay, and where, as he'll later put it in an interview, "Everything happened to me. . . . I found myself as a poet. . . . I met and fell in love with the guy I still live with. . . . Everything good happened to me."[75] And if at age fifty-four he's articulating a transcendent theory of promiscuity as a form of secular humanism, of "joy, entering other lives (homes, etc.), visiting inside other lives, an entrance into all humanity," as Gunn himself suggests, "There are constants everywhere."

On the other hand, even amid this constancy, there are signs of conflict between his sexuality and the practice of poetry. Even if poetry "can actually *be* one's life at its fullest," Gunn's definition of poetry is stringent: he must "pass the romantic impulse through the classical scrutiny," and if his romantic impulses include "sexual fantasy" and "themes of liberation from authority," then it must have taken an enormous amount of psychic strength and artistic stamina to strain every "romantic impulse" of imperfection, of "all that is not hard and genuine." And indeed, his notebooks are a testament both to his stamina and his immense dedication to craft, as each contains an astoundingly large number of drafts for almost every poem. Some pages fairly reel with ideas for scansion and/or stanzaic forms, some shift a draft's balance between rhetoric and narrative, some merely offer line edits, and some introduce an entirely new structuring conceit—but all prove the intensity and duration of his classical scrutiny. And though each successive draft struck me as cause for admiration, each one also made me wonder, in the words of another critic, "if the forces of sexuality can't be tamed without there being a horrible penalty[.] What if it turned out that domestication of sexuality is a measure compromised?"[76]

It's no wonder Gunn doesn't like it "too much" that his "impulse to write poetry" is "so much a part of—[his] sexual impulse," an impulse he ironically characterizes in the wonderful poem "Sweet Things" as greedy and in his notebook entry as promiscuous: one way to subject the romantic impulse to classical scrutiny is to force himself to "steer [his] energy into nonsexual subjects almost by an act of will." No wonder he sees this single source for both creative and sexual energies to be "my limitation." I do wonder, however, how deeply indebted to heterosexist definitions of artistic universality Gunn's "classical scrutiny" is, given that, as a young poet, his formative relationships were with F. R. Leavis and

Yvor Winters, both of whom he describes as "formidable" father figures. Is it any accident two of the romantic impulses Gunn was taught—taught himself?—to scrutinize so deeply are "sexual fantasy" and "liberation from authority"?

It turned out that blocking my way was an impasse not solely mine, but an unfortunate inheritance, part of the history of being gay and a poet, passed down by one's elders, each successive generation adding its own discoveries and ideas without actually getting past the problem. I put "gay" next to "poetry" again, and the same thing happened: in my own psyche, there was no discord; in my critical mind, the categorical problems remained. This impression of inheritance was certainly redoubled by opening another notebook, this one from "May 4, 1980." Not far in I found a list—Gunn was in his notebooks, among other things, a great keeper of lists—of poems and prose to be written in the coming months: among the commissioned essays and reviews already earmarked for specific publications was an essay about "Poetry and Gay Poets," promised to no one. Perhaps he aimed to write it for his own edification? I was very excited. A few pages later, there began a draft of that very essay:

> Very few poets have ever set out to be Gay Poets. The dedication of poets is a large one, perhaps one of the most enormous—as our subject matter we aim at nothing less than everything and the idea of our initial dedication settling for anything less. . . .
>
> Why settle for part of the world when you can lay claim to the whole of it? When I started writing poetry I wanted to be Shakespeare, and from my reading of the lives of poets I don't think the ambition is an uncommon one. Of course, I rationally knew it was unlikely I could be Shakespeare, but I wanted the best, and to have accepted a smaller ambition would have been to want less than the best. By now I know that I will never be Shakespeare, but I also know that I can be more than one kind of poet. A career, if it is to be a happy one, can be a series of breakthroughs into fresh territories, and to limit oneself permanently to one style or subject matter for more than one duration of an individual project would be stupid.
>
> I am fully aware of the usefulness of literary classification. To miss the gay elements in say Marlowe's or Whitman's work has resulted in not only unbalanced views of them but in [illegible word] misreadings. But to treat them exclusively as Gay Poets is also unbalanced . . .

The draft broke off there, only to be followed on the facing page by what seemed to be a first draft, more fragmentary in form and vocally far less sculpted for the public. If there's one certain thing I learned from reading the earlier draft, it's that when Gunn's "romantic impulse" is put under his "classical scrutiny," a great deal of bare emotion is removed: anger is tempered; sarcasm and scorn are lightened. His tone does indeed become more "balanced" as his argument becomes more reasonable and his critical stance attains the defined edges of the authorial voice of his published essays. Here follow a few paragraphs—in sequence, but with some interstitial material removed—from that initial draft:

> To be a poet is more important than to be a gay poet. So when WW says "I am the poet of the man and I am also the poet of the woman," he is *not* being dishonest. He was not as good about women as he was about men, but this was a weakness in his realization, not in his intention. . . . Did Auden . . . "change" *he* to *you*? I would not think so: that is not the way any halfway responsible poet works. The decision to suppress the pronouns . . . preceded the inception of any specific work, I would guess*: it became part of the conditions within which he happily worked, as Shakespeare's primitive [illegible] was part of his conditions and limitations.
>
> *no such poem would have been [illegible] anyway

What became clear to me from reading the drafts of this essay is that Gunn himself came in 1980 to the very same impasse I'd reached, and at that moment chose a path I'm not willing to take. Gunn presents the question simply, "Why settle for part of the world when you can lay claim to the whole of it?" and gives his judgment baldly: "To be a poet is more important than to be a gay poet." In these statements he unfortunately seems to privilege New Critical notions of poetry as something always already apart from gender, sexuality, and history, and in doing so figures it as some transcendent signifier floating out there in the humanist yonder. However specious I find the arguments in both drafts, I did find myself in total agreement with the notion that "to treat [poets such as Marlowe or Whitman] exclusively as Gay Poets is also unbalanced," as I, myself, have cringed when being read this way. I also found myself in partial agreement with some critical comments in the earlier draft, concerns regarding a friend's reading of "On the Move," the justifiably much-celebrated first poem of *The Sense of Movement:* "Guy's comment on my sexual feeling in 'On the Move'—yes, I was sexually excited by the subject matter, but . . . sexual excitement is not my *subject,* I want the excitement to come over but if anybody misses the sexual overtones they are missing nothing important to the poet." While I'd completely disagree were Gunn suggesting as universal tenet the idea that if a reader "misses the sexual overtones they are missing nothing important to the poet," I would certainly agree that "On the Move" has far less to do with "sexual feeling" than it does with articulating a gendered notion of existential agency. If the motorcyclists' "hum / bulges to thunder held by calf and thigh," they also "strap in doubt—by hiding it, robust": the first image could be said to sexily suggest a merge between the motorcycle's power and an equally "bulging" male agency, while the second reveals itself as a deliberately chosen masculine posture, a surface gesture indicating a deeper philosophy. In the end, the stance of the motorcyclists is inseparable from their masculinity, suggesting a "solution, after all" of self-definition, of power and control over their lives' meaning that is—remember it's a poem published in 1957—concomitant with their gender.[77]

However, the sentence "To be a poet is more important than to be a gay poet" dogs me. It's a highly ambiguous statement—a fact that, at first, escaped my attention. And though a heterosexist essentialism might in fact lurk behind its assignation of value, here's an anecdote that changes the meaning behind the sentence, shifts its context to the year 1980, post–Gay Liberation, just on the cusp of the AIDS epidemic. It comes from a 1985 interview with Robert Duncan: "At the beginning of the gay liberation readings, Thom Gunn and I were sitting there, and the new writers were reading poems that were hair-raising; and Thom said, 'I feel so old-fashioned and embarrassed, I don't mention anything but love.'"[78] This anecdote reminds us that Gunn was born in 1929: he was forty the year of Stonewall. It also reminds us of the fact that he, like Duncan who was born in 1919, had created a way of thinking and writing about being gay that was likely challenged by the tenets of Gay Liberation, and that perhaps neither of them, at least initially, relished that challenge very much. As Gunn would have us remember, in publishing "The Homosexual in Society," Duncan "had won himself an interesting artistic freedom: he could speak about his sexuality openly but with barely any twentieth-century tradition of such openness behind him. He had to create it for himself."[79] But what, exactly, was the nature of this tradition of openness he created?

In his essay "Homosexuality in Robert Duncan's Poetry," Gunn suggests that, though "homosexuality is as central to Duncan's poetry, to its origins and realizations, as it was to Marlowe's or Whitman's . . . he is no more than they *merely* a Gay Poet."[80] Duncan did, of course, out himself in "The Homosexual in Society," and his bravery serves as a part of the essay's rhetorical ethos: it's a credo *against* partisan identity politics, and argues that the homosexual should *not* separate himself off from broader political goals and communities: "Almost coincident with the first declarations for homosexual rights was the growth of a cult of homosexual superiority to heterosexual values; the cultivation of a secret language, the *camp*, a tone and a vocabulary that are loaded with contempt for the uninitiated."[81]

What's fascinating about Duncan's argument is that, while of course society must "recognize homosexuals as equals, and, as equals, allow them neither more nor less than can be allowed any human being," he's equally adamant that each member of the gay community recognize his or her own share of injustice toward others in "one's battle against the inhumanity of his own group . . . in this special case—the homosexual cult."[82] In coming out to his audience in this fashion, he dares them to respond in kind with an equal gesture of generosity and ethical open-mindedness. Even if Duncan's phrasing is at times commensurate with how political conservatives might have seen (and some continue to see) *all* homosexuals—they're a cult! they eat babies!—it's no less notable for how his argument also sternly refuses at all times to engage the then-dominant Freudian discourse of "inversion" or legal victimization to plead his case: "There are no special rights."[83] Gunn in his essay reminds us of a fact that Duncan couldn't, given the ethos of his argument: he'd done this thinking in the context of no public discourse, at the expense of what gay community he'd found.

Revisiting Duncan's anecdote of their shared shock in the face of Gay Liberation poetry and rereading "The Homosexual in Society" reconfirms my instinct that perhaps implicit in Gunn's statement "It is more important to be a poet than to be a gay poet" lies the same kind of insistence against gay insularity and longing for a more inclusive unity. Perhaps this stemmed from Gay Liberation's borrowing of the ethnicity model from other civil rights movements—something they might have seen as creating a unified gay community at the expense of a human community. My sense that this is true is bolstered by the closure of Gunn's essay concerning Duncan's poetry and homosexuality—published in 1979—in which his praise of Duncan's accomplishment greatly echoes Duncan's own political and aesthetic sentiments in both versions of "The Homosexual in Society":

> Duncan started with little modern American precedent for speaking openly about homosexuality. There is now a way of speaking about it, and

> we may thank Duncan's continued example more than any other that it is not a specialized speech, it is not separated from the heterosexual's tradition. It is due more to Duncan than to any other single poet that modern American poetry, in all its inclusiveness, can deal with overtly homosexual material so much as a matter of course—not as something perverse or eccentric or morbid, but as evidence of the many available ways in which people love or fail to love.[84]

Despite his gorgeously phrased and persuasive rhetoric, I still have my doubts about the gist of this argument. Not that I don't in large part agree with Gunn about Duncan's achievement, but all I have to do is read an excerpt from a review of Gunn's *The Passages of Joy*—written in 1983 by no less a critic than Terry Eagleton—and my doubts are renewed: "Gunn's recent collection . . . has little to recount beyond casual encounters and homosexual gossip, depressingly thin and banal for a poet who at one time promised to be the most intellectually resourceful of the younger English writers."[85] (Sigh.) I type "gay" next to "poetry" and ask myself why the utopian rhetoric of Gunn and Duncan doesn't work: after reading Eagleton, "gay" looks "thin and banal"—is that better than "perverse or eccentric or morbid"?—and "poetry" looks all transcendently unsullied by gay community gossip and promiscuous, casual sex.

Perhaps my impasse is in fact distrust disguised as healthy skepticism? With Eagletons and Hamiltons and Davies and Ransoms around, the deep sense of trust that both Gunn and Duncan show not only the language itself but also their often-hostile readers is an example of generosity anyone would do well to imitate. And though both Gunn's and Duncan's aesthetic practices *as gay poets* embody that desire for larger community they both so value, it's perhaps pragmatic to ask "to what extent are the ideals of sexuality and community actually compatible?" as Bruce Boone does in his essay "Robert Duncan and Gay Community: A Reflection."[86] Boone's question stems from the fact that "Duncan's particular, effective brand of combining gay emphasis with universalist humanism deserves real consideration" despite that, "[i]nsofar as it comes firmly down on the side of breaking down barriers between gay and non-gay . . . Duncan's breakthrough took place at the cost of a break with the then-existing gay community."[87] It's the very fact that "it's not 'gay-community' minded" that "Duncan's work is a good place to ask questions like this," because, as Boone suggests, "the hope is dark to keep it from being naïve."[88] I like Boone's reading of Duncan's politics because, while I too "like the sense of conflicts not resolved," I share Boone's very legitimate concerns:

> Is it possible, one wonders, without rolling back advances for gays in the form of rights, social cohesiveness and a greater, earned sense of self-esteem—to push out the boundaries of our identification so they can apply less narrowly, more generally? . . . the corollary for gays: how to go beyond *separatism* without negating its advances?[89]

This, then, is the inheritance left the twenty-first-century gay poet by the gay poets of the twentieth. If it seems at first a paradox, upon second thought it suggests not an impasse but rather a wider range of possible relationships to history. It implies that though poets like Gunn and Duncan were bound up in the historical categories that defined the times and communities in which they lived, they were not necessarily bound *by* them. Interested in literary and sexual communities and ways to construct and sustain them, yet often tangential to prevailing political and/or literary ideologies, they chose to move differently through history. If at times their mutual emphasis on an inherited universal humanism does in fact seem to negate an active relationship to the then-newly minted ethnic model of gay community, if they seem simultaneously old-fashioned and radical, this may in fact be evidence of homosexuality's "historical evolution."

In fact, when reading mid-period Gunn or Duncan's work from the 1950s (such as *Caesar's Gate*), I'm often seized by the sense that the poet has put down the given maps and his individual compass and is making his way through history's open field by virtue of careful intuition—a journey that is, at first, as often blunder as success, as much candor as calculation. In the brief essay, "Two Saturday Nights: Rewriting a Poem," Gunn beautifully illumines a suggestive, fugitive line from his 1974 notebook—"Folsom Barracks: a gloss on the angels of Dante"—by explaining that after reading Dante's terza rima, he attempts "a poem about the Barracks" but that he "never published this poem because something dissatisfied [him] about it."[90] He goes on to say, "In 1975 I had been granted a new subject matter. . . . It was still the time of Gay Liberation, a phrase which now has a quaint but worthy ring to it. There was talk of a 'gay community,' something I doubted existed. But community it was . . . we were part of a visionary carnal politics! . . . At the baths, or in less organized activity, there was a shared sense of adventure, thrilling, hilarious, *experimental*."[91] This sense of experiment is best represented by the attitude Gunn ultimately takes toward categorical thinking, the fixity of whose categories tradition depends on both for meaning and for stable values; this explains, for example, how in a 1982 *Advocate* article, "In

Search of a Muse: The Politics of Gay Poetry," Steve Abbott can report that "Gunn prefers not to be labeled as 'a gay poet for the same reason that I don't want to be labeled a nature poet or a city poet. I'm an everything poet.'"[92] However, this distrust of labeling ultimately results *not* in a refusal of community but in a pleasing and informative categorical fluidity.

Thus the most common way for experiment to enter a later Gunn poem is when a traditional verse form contains not only "a new subject matter" but a new *experimental* consciousness, one that is often conscious of its participation in a gay community—this is how he finds Dante's rhythms and rhymes alive and well in the Folsom Barracks. Gunn also often ensures—via site names, dates, and/or dedications—that this new subject matter and consciousness are markedly historical and context-dependent, which stretches and extends the tradition that gives articulation to the poem's form. It is perhaps Gunn's greatest gift to what might otherwise have remained culturally conservative verse forms: a new future that might itself be called subversively visionary, as this passage from the final draft of "Saturday Night" makes clear:

> If, furthermore
> Our Dionysian experiment
> To build a city never dared before
> Dies without reaching to its full extent,
> At least in the endeavor we translate
> Our common ecstasy to a brief ascent
> Of the complete, grasped, paradisal state
> Against the wisdom pointing us away.[93]

That this city is both literary—a New Jerusalem—and literal—gay San Francisco or New York—is the crux of Gunn's mid-career and late poetics, which insist on fusing the world the poet finds outside himself with the world he makes so that there is *no discrepancy of values* left between them. As he writes in a notebook entry of 1977:

> Writing about the Mine Shaft or the Barracks it is easy to fall into Baudelairian melodrama, but that is untrue to the experience: they are places of joy and excitement, not of despair, or rather they are places to which we bring what we want them to be. . . . They are like a country walk, enlivening each sense again, making the mind fresh and body fresh firm with its powers.[94]

Only integrating his sexuality into poetry could have allowed for Gunn this reciprocal, clear-eyed relationship between verse and the world, as it indicates (a) the poet's *deliberate* choosing of how and when his sexuality enters or influences his work; and (b) no existing a priori moral gloss on this sexuality. In other words, Gunn's later verse fully embodies the gendered existential vision of "On the Move" in the sense that "Men manufacture both machine and soul, / And use what they imperfectly control / To dare a future from the taken routes."[95] In Gunn's maturity, the world and his verse are coextensive, generously intertwined, and mutually annotative; as he writes in the opening section of his "centaur poems," "Tom-Dobbin":

> light is in the pupil
>   luminous seed
> and light is in the mind
>   crossing
> in an instant
>   passage between the two
> seamless
>   imperceptible transition. . . .
>
>   there is the one
> and at once it is also the other.[96]

This position—toward the role of queer consciousness in mediating the relationship of verse to the world—would have been not only unthinkable but also unattainable by the young Thom Gunn, whose poems could but dream about self-determination forging the shape of his future. Remember that it had been a crucial exercise for the early Gunn to subject to classical scrutiny his fantasies "of liberation for authority," as he realizes in a notebook from 1968. Perhaps Duncan, in tandem with Gay Liberation, allowed Gunn to find a home in a different tradition and community outside of the "authoritative" ones that elicited from him a need for distance and liberation. Perhaps he made a move from a poetry defined almost exclusively by classical ideals to a poetry defined as much by local prerogatives—as Gunn himself says, "I like the word *community,* I don't like the word *universal.* I've always hated it, since it struck me as a word that high-school teachers use to fob off the criticisms of their students."[97] Or perhaps the kinds of permission given by Duncan and the gay community enabled him not to escape authority at all, but rather to relocate it in a source with which he felt less of a discrepancy in values: himself.

4. Our Dionysian Experiment

> I was fond of saying at one time that I was the only poet who'd dedicated poems to Yvor Winters and Robert Duncan.
>
> —Thom Gunn, in Campbell's *Thom Gunn in Conversation with James Campbell*

In later life Gunn relished recounting what happened when Elizabeth Bishop lived in San Francisco for a year—1969—and during that time met Robert Duncan: "They got on terrifically well," he tells Christopher Hennessy. "They would talk and gossip together and laugh."[98] Obviously delighted each time he relates the story of what's supposed to seem an unlikely friendship—"the poetics behind their two projects were fundamentally opposed in a way that their personalities were not"—Gunn spins it wittily, subsequent accounts differing only in the ratio of summary to scene and specificity of detail.[99] In one version Bishop baked Duncan a wicked batch of pot cookies "because he didn't know how to inhale," and "both afterwards described with glee" how, as a consequence of her recipe, he'd been "reduced . . . to a mass of giggles on the carpet."[100] In others, Gunn "asked each of them separately what they thought of the other's poetry, and each of them said the same thing: 'Oh I can't read it. It means nothing to me at all.'"[101] However, each version is in fact pretense, a disguise for a pointedly didactic parable concerning "literary reputation" and tradition, and the moral Gunn draws from it never varies: "You do not have to choose between Bishop and Duncan any more than you have to choose between William Blake and Samuel Johnson."[102]

I frame my discussion of Gunn's mentors with this dictum because, given the larger-than-life personalities and critical reputations involved, it's all too easy for one or the other of them to seem the villain or the hero. Nonetheless, it's useful to remember we don't have to choose between Yvor Winters and Robert Duncan any more than Gunn did. He was equally influenced by Winters, with whom he studied at Stanford in the 1950s, and Duncan, whom he first met in San Francisco in the early '60s. At first their equal influence on Gunn seems implausible: Winters was straight, a neoclassicist most famous for his unusually strict and fiercely defended system of literary and moral criticism; Duncan was gay, a neo-Romantic best known for his modernist erudition and wide-ranging cosmological poetics. But Gunn not only insists that Duncan is "besides Winters . . . the poet who meant most to [him] in [his] life," he somewhat glories in the fact that Duncan and Winters "didn't like each other, though they never met. Each stood just for the kind of thing the other disliked most: Winters for authority and Duncan for anarchy."[103] Indeed, what's so wonderful about Gunn's relationship to Winters and Duncan is what makes his work so disconcerting to categorization: stylistically he often appears to practice a neoclassical, Wintersian verse; however, the consciousness at work underneath the verse style—and sometimes at odds with it—is one that often draws upon a source closer to Duncan's. Gunn neither chose between them personally—he would never have done so—nor chose between them aesthetically—for though his ear and ironies might be Wintersian, the larger architecture of sequences such as "Jack Straw's Castle" and "The Geysers" belies a different mind at work. Rather, he chose between the respective *readings of poetic tradition* they each represented.

As outlined in the preface to *In Defense of Reason,* a collection of the criticism Winters published from 1937 to 1943, Winters as a thinker operates in a mode whose suppositions and sympathies constitute a "didactic theory of literature" familiar to us from poets such as Pope and Dryden; accordingly, for Winters the function of literature is to "offer . . . us useful precepts and explicit moral instruction."[104] The moral certainty he so prized in Ben Jonson he posits counter to the "hedonistic" moral relativism he sees in Romanticism in general and in Emerson, Whitman, Walter Pater, and Hart Crane in specific, all writers emblematic of "a general deterioration of poetry since the opening of the eighteenth century."[105] Though Winters is most famous for the broad sweep of his rhetoric, he reads specific poems with an absolutist, nearly Platonic operating theory, not only of poetry, but also of the good and great, or "ideal," poem:

> The poem is a statement in words about a human experience. . . . The poem is good insofar as it makes a defensible rational statement about a given human experience (the experience need not be real but must be in some sense possible) and at the same time communicates the emotion which ought to be motivated by that rational understanding of that experience. . . . Rhythm, for reasons which I do not wholly understand, has the power of communicating emotion; and as part of the poem it has the power of qualifying the total emotion. . . . These aspects of the poem will be efficient insofar as the poet subordinates them to the total aim of the poem.[106]

Thus while Winters, on the one hand, judges the content of a poem against theological and moral paradigms, believing as he did the "clerisy he traced from Aristotle to Aquinas . . . [was] the appropriate response to man's isolation in the universe,"[107] on the other, he evaluates a poem's form against "certain poetry of the sixteenth and seventeenth centuries," poetry that "approximates most closely the qualities that seem to [him] the best."[108] While it was oft maligned during his lifetime and since his death has been largely obscured by its reputation for cantankerousness and conservatism, there is much to admire in Winters's critical position: its adamantine authority, rhetorical and moral clarity, and consistent logic, whose thoroughgoingness allowed him to read everyone from William Shakespeare to Louise Bogan with the very same set of expectations.

"Reason and the ideal," Duncan writes, as if to chide Winters's defense of classical precepts, "are futile if they have not admitted to the full range of our human experience."[109] And yet Duncan as a critic presents us at first with qualities strikingly similar to Winters: he, too, possesses an authority as much moral as it is scholarly, and if his rhetoric at times lacks Winters's crystalline focus, its wide horizon allows us to see exactly where in the sky of history each of his ideas sits, and with what other ideas it constellates. However, Duncan quickly differentiates himself from the academic Winters by engaging in a critical practice founded on and necessitated by his identity as a poet—an identity he sees as primary—and a body of knowledge predicated on appetite and visionary ambition. And further: where Winters would describe himself as a moral, rational philosopher from whose stoicism stem both his poetry and criticism, Duncan in *The Truth and Life of Myth* sees himself first a "Romantic spirit" whose primary métier is cosmology, a poet for whom myth "is not only a story that expresses the soul but a story that awakens the soul to the real persons of its romance, in which the actual and spiritual are revealed, one in the other."[110]

Drawing upon psychologists as different as Freud and Jung, as well as from disciplines as various as comparative religion, folklore, and anthropology, Duncan as poet-critic is interested in revealing already-present and dynamic continuities between disciplines, cultures, and cosmologies and argues that men who live myth "live in its history, in its living changes and permutations, not its petrifications."[111] However divergent Duncan's reading of theology might be from Winters's, he is rather paradoxically concerned with eternal forms, with distinguishing truth from falsehood, and in his Neoplatonic gnostic way claims "to raise . . . a theater, a drama of Truth" in place of "a dialectic, a debate, toward what [Philosophy] calls Truth."[112] This theater, too, need be a didactic forum, given that "when we are concerned with Poetry, we are faced, as men in religion are faced, with violent operations of words. A mistake is a mutation altering the life of the spirit."[113] If Winters's whipping boy is Romantic relativism, Duncan would single out for drubbing the demythologized "modern man," who

> has labeled whole areas of human thought and feeling sentimental and over-charged with improper emotion or emoting in order to escape from the threat of discomposing images or affections . . . has erected an education of sensibility, class spirit, or team spirit, argument and rationalization, designed to establish himself in a self-protective world of facts and problems stripped of their sympathies, in the real business of making money.[114]

Emphasizing the almost sidereal power inherent in language-as-gateway to greater consciousness, Duncan sees the formal qualities of the poem as intricately tied to its ability to represent an accurate cosmology. True to his purview, the poem is a revelation of gnosis that can be gotten only through an interior struggle that is as engaged with the psychoanalytic possibilities of linguistic slippage and homophonic play as it is with the suggestions of deeper consciousness thereby revealed. Thus if Duncan seeks "to go as deep into . . . the soul as the sense of relations and ratios can carry me" so that "in the composition of the poem, powerful impulses toward pattern energy along lines of felt relationship," he must first "wrestle with the syntax of the world of my experience to bring forward into the Day the twisted syntax of my human language."[115] With his goals for poetry so grandly ambitious, it's no wonder that Gunn once wrote of Duncan that "he was a daredevil rather as a cat is, jumping down into wells of obscurity or on to formidable spiked fences where no reasonable creature would have ventured."[116]

But the mature Gunn wrote of both mentors with sympathy and admiration, and what makes his position between them so complex and subtle is that he sides with the inclusivity of Duncan's poetic tradition—his appreciative criticism spans from Jonson, Greville, and Hardy through Whitman, Pound, Williams, Duncan, and Ginsberg—even while creating an important link *in practice* between Duncan's Romanticism and Winters's classicism: he carries Winters's Renaissance practice of *imitatio* into postmodernity by marrying it to what Duncan calls "derivation." As noted by Stefan Hawlin in his essay "Epistemes and Imitations: Thom Gunn on Ben Jonson," Dryden in "The Preface to Ovid's Epistles" characterizes *imitatio* as a kind of translation based primarily on stylistic imitation, in which "the Translator . . . assumes the liberty not only to vary from the words and sence, but to forsake them both as he sees occasion: and taking only some general hints from the Original."[117] *Imitatio,* Hawlin argues, is closely related to Duncan's practice of derivation; indeed, in "A Seventeenth Century Suite in Homage to the Metaphysical Genius in English Poetry,"[118] Duncan engages the practice of *imitatio* by "printing original and 'imitation,' 'derivation' or 'variation' side by side" so that the reader "reads . . . how particular lines and tropes have been 'translated' and so that 'the exchange between anterior poem and imitation ensures that the [original] remains as a critique of Duncan's . . . viewpoint.'"[119] If this is not exactly the practice that Jonson advocates for in *Discoveries*—"To make choise of one excellent man above the rest, and so to follow him, until he grow very Hee; or so like him, as the Copie may be mistaken for the Prinicipall"—the fact that Duncan, by printing the Metaphysical original next to its gnostic derivation, instigates a dialectic between model and derivative nonetheless keeps his practice in active dialogue with *imitation.*[120]

Winters would, of course, have original and imitation mirror each other's viewpoints, or at the very least enact a kind of epistemological rhyme: he was attracted to and privileged in contemporary verse what he perceived as an ethos particular to the Renaissance, not just the "clarity, definition and language that was wholly apposite to the subject" of the sixteenth-century plain-style poem.[121] And while Hawlin would place the emphasis of Duncan's practice on its stylistic similarities with *imitatio*—his "most achieved imitations . . . take significant license with their originals," but are, "in Renaissance terms . . . effective reworkings of style and meaning"[122]—Michael André Bernstein would have us see Duncan's derivation as a "*process* of discovery" whose emphasis is "on the ways in which he himself has been moved to a new understanding by an unexpected source."[123] As process rather than objet d'art, derivation differs from *imitatio* in that it doesn't aim for the achievement of accuracy and wit, though it might in fact contain those qualities; as Bernstein explains, derivation is a "gradual, often hesitant and incomplete, working-through," and thus the result is "that the distinction between the psychological and the textual, between a strictly personal quest and the discovery of communal values in different traditions is collapsed."[124]

Given that, as Hawlin notes, Gunn in *The Man with Night Sweats* explicitly engages several of Jonson's poems in imitation, it's clear that during the instability and trauma of the AIDS crisis, he felt it necessary to leave temporarily his mid-career free-verse derivations from the poetics of Williams and Duncan for the Renaissance models he'd first emulated in his youth (1520–1521). But even when most deeply engaged in *imitatio* in the 1980s and '90s, he didn't stop thinking and writing about Duncan's practice of derivation, and indeed, it seems he began to think of derivation and imitation as inseparable, one informing the other. The most explicit elision Gunn makes between derivation and imitation comes in the opening of "Adventurous Song: Robert Duncan as Romantic Modernist," an essay he published in 1991: "Robert Duncan was proud to call himself a derivative poet. We are all, of course, derivative, but most of us try to cover up our debts when we are aware of them, and to present our work as self-sufficient and self-originating. . . . Duncan too fed on those he admired, but like a true cannibal he digested their virtues and made them his, and they rose in him with a fresh life, both recognizable and altered."[125] Cannibalism here serves for Gunn as trope for the process by which a poet derives his own work from that of a precedent poet, and if the simile startles us as much for its vividness and implicit violence as for its rightness of fit, there are other even more compelling reasons for its interest and appropriateness.

The phrasing of "Adventurous Song" recalls that of an essay on Duncan that Gunn wrote four years before, "The High Road," in which Gunn claims Duncan "was proud to proclaim himself a 'derivative' poet, refusing to see the word as pejorative. We all derive, of course, we choose our own tradition, we have our influences."[126] It's important to note that, despite the similar phrasing, Gunn does not yet call upon cannibalism as a trope to describe derivation. That there was an earlier iteration of the passage from "Adventurous Song" means that Gunn—who was in fact careful not to repeat himself in print—had been for some time thinking about imitation in relation to Duncan. However, that the added trope of cannibalism is in itself an imitation makes the reiterated passage as subtle theoretically as it is vivid imagistically: "The third requisite in our *Poet,* or Maker, is *Imitation,* to bee able to convert the substance, or Riches of another *Poet,* to his owne use. . . . Not, as a Creature, that swallows, what it takes in, crude, raw, or indigested; but, that feedes with an Appetite, and hath Stomacke to contoct, divide and turne all to nourishment."[127] That passage comes to us from Ben Jonson's *Timber; or Discoveries,* a text that enunciates most thoroughly a Renaissance theory of *imitatio.* Though *imitatio*'s original function was explicitly didactic—Jonson remarks that "[t]he mind, and memory are more sharpely exercis'd in comprehending an other mans things then our owne"—and its aim an embodiment of its model's values—"[f]or as in an Instrument, so in style, there must be a Harmonie, and concent of parts"[128]—Gunn saw that derivation in fact "modifies" its source text by putting it in conversation with "all the other poets Duncan made out of his diet," much the way that Gunn's ingesting of Duncan's poetics permanently altered Winters's influence on his work.[129] The presence of Jonson's tropes beneath Gunn's second discussion of Duncan's derivative practice not only confirms Gunn's own ingenious linkage of derivation to *imitatio,* but also suggests that this connection might have come to him in the four years between 1987 and 1991—years during which, as we will see later, he was thinking of Duncan a great deal in connection to his own writing practices.

If in the 1960s Duncan introduced into Gunn's writing crucial ideas that altered his conception and practice of poetry, then what idea(s) about poetry did Gunn begin to bring into question, and what role did Winters have in shaping them? Did Gunn in fact agree with the didactic moral theory of poetry put forward in *In Defense of Reason*? If he did, and endeavored to practice *imitatio* and embody in his poetry those ideals Winters held highest, what relationship did Gunn's gay sexuality have with Winters's morality? We might take *The Sense of Movement* as an answer to these questions.

It was written almost exclusively under Winters's tutelage and, as a whole, tends, like Winters himself, to "a predisposition on behalf of the hard, the brave, the reticent, and the stoical."[130] Its forms are largely those Winters favored—now heroic couplets, now quatrains, now sonnets, all ably rhymed and accented. Broadly put, its subjects might be said to be a man's capacity to define himself on his own terms and the ways in which he's best able to do so—ironic, given the context in which it was written. Its narratives might take place in the moment during which the protagonist prepares himself for a defining action, as in "Market at Turk" or "Before the Carnival"; or they might show him "self-created, astride the created will," in action that, as in "The Unsettled Motorcyclist's Vision of His Death" and "On the Move," allows the protagonist to "join . . . the movement in a valueless world."[131] When action ceases, however, the less well-articulated tensions of the book arise: between outward appearance and the interior life of the protagonist lies a meditative miasma, as in "A Plan of Self-Subjection." Its tone alternates—now caustic, dispassionate, self-hating, rueful—between protective stoical ironies and self-analysis whose candor might seem to enable its speaker to "dare a future" as the motorcyclists do, but which in fact seem at best mostly preparatory or potential, and at worst, self-lacerating or -inhibitory:

> I put this pen to paper and my verse
> Imposes form upon my fault described
> So that my fault is worse—
> Not from condonement but from being bribed
> With order: and with this it appears strong,
> Which lacks all order that it can exist.
> Yet before very long
> From poem back to original I twist.[132]

If the title "A Plan of Self-Subjection" sounds like a euphemism for one of those Christian programs contemporary gays enroll in to become born-again heterosexuals, at this distance it's as much an ambitious poem as a symptom of psychic and aesthetic impotence, a stalemate between anachronistically expressed ideals and lived subjectivity. The poem suffers—as do a few others in the book—as Winters's later poetry does, from a problem Robert Hass diagnoses in his incisive, sympathetic essay about Winters, "What He Did": "What is damaging about the later work is that, in addition to adopting the forms and themes of the English poets, he adopted their diction. He never solved for himself the problem of getting from image to discourse in the language of his time, and instead borrowed the solution of another age."[133]

During the '60s Gunn himself would, with the work of William Carlos Williams as example, fully redress this problem for himself; in 1957, however, an equal number of his poems are elegantly disguised by stiff diction as are comfortably clothed in contemporary speech. The interesting thing about "A Plan of Self-Subjection" is that the failure of its archaic diction seems to indicate that the moral universe of *imitatio,* the one in which the imitator aspires to the values of the classical age, is one whose design ensures Gunn's failure: "And yet however much I may aspire / I stay myself—no perfect king or lover / Or stoic."[134]

For if "traditional poetry in general aims," as Winters also suggests in *In Defense of Reason,* "to adjust feeling rightly to motive . . . and a just evaluation of feeling,"[135] then where does that leave the gay subject who must evaluate and adjust his feeling according to moral and aesthetic codes defined by heterosexuals? Can he or she even enter the poem? Perhaps Gunn himself answers this: "Here is most shade my longing, from the sun / And that hot hell beneath. / My circle's end is where I have begun."[136] Indentured to the mores of another age, the speakers throughout *The Sense of Movement* remain discreetly closeted, even during a "First Meeting with a Possible Mother-in-Law," even when having "Thoughts on Unpacking" in a new apartment shared with a lover—and who can blame them? Though Gunn was able, with the aid of the book's general style, to articulate the kind of existential philosophy he wished would shape his verse and life, he could not in fact fully embody this shape in the consciousness or structures of the poems themselves: like Ouroboros, he finds his mouth always obstructed by his own presence.

Clearly Gunn was attracted to the restraints Winters favored—*Fighting Terms* is, after all, a much more clumsy deployment of them—but what was it exactly about Winters's insistence on imitating classical virtues that allowed Gunn in his verse to articulate, but *not* to develop or fully inhabit, himself? It might be true that the classical virtues Gunn's technique displays in *The Sense of Movement* are, as both Gunn feared and Martin Dodsworth argues in "Gunn's Rhymes," both help and hindrance, in that elements such as persistent monosyllabic rhyme have "something to do with considered decisiveness for its own sake," *not* self-determination in the more existential sense that actually underwrites Gunn's worldview.[137] I'd speculate, along with Dodsworth, that under Winters's influence, Gunn's early work shows how too dear a "fidelity to past practice" can be "a sign of strength *and* weakness": "It is akin to that other fidelity he shows, a fidelity to 'his' subject matter: adolescence, existential isolation, the exercise of will, the creation of identity. He has saturated this subject-matter with Gunnian feeling, and the result is a poetry of great power. At the same time, his *oeuvre* suffers from a lack of spaciousness. Movement, like development, is difficult."[138] Though I'd vehemently part ways with Dodsworth in characterizing Gunn's midcareer and late work as lacking in spaciousness, his reservations are instructive when applied to Gunn's first three volumes: they embody a "fidelity to past practice" that might have at that point in his career been an inhibiting influence—a source of anxiety rather than creative power. And though Renaissance *imitatio* and the Bloomian idea of Romantic influence don't in most logical systems stem from the same epistemology, the fact that Winters provoked an anxiety about imitation not just in Gunn but in his other students points to a contradiction fostered by the pedagogy through which Winters modeled a poetics.

Though Winters's critical practice eschews the kind of Sturm und Drang that characterizes Romantic theories of "influence" by placing its emphasis on imitation of eternal verities, his effect as a teacher might have undermined the practice of *imitatio* by placing its moral system within the highly emotional power dynamic of teacher and student. That Gunn recognized early on this risk in studying with Winters is clear, as he speaks often of the emotional effect of Winters's simultaneously forceful intellectual presence and inhibiting categorical narrowness. "I hoped I was tough enough to use what he had to offer me," Gunn writes in the essay, "On a Drying Hill," "and still where necessary resist him . . . without becoming an imitator."[139] And though Winters's insistent valuation of poetry and poets was often counterbalanced by his personal generosity, Gunn was very aware that, in the end, he'd be judged for his poems—and, more than that, "I knew that my poetry would sooner or later disappoint Winters."[140] The pressure must have been immense, given that Winters defined "traditional poetry" by modeling a canon of greatness. Gunn reports that, for Winters, "the word *great* . . . was meant to indicate a carefully assembled canon of acceptable poems" and that Winters's "canon became shorter as the years passed, and both individual great poems and great poets got eliminated from it."[141]

So while, on the one hand, Gunn "was glad to spend a year of apprenticeship, fancying [him]self as the modern counterpart of some young painter in Florence apprenticed in the workshop of a master painter," on the other hand, he was also witness to Winters's relentless winnowing of his canon, and "Winters's mind-changing was hard on some of those who got demoted and confusing to those who witnessed the demotions."[142] From the beginning of their relationship, the personal terms of this critical practice were as clear to Gunn as the high stakes Winters set by virtue of his very narrowness: "He would feel affection for me," Gunn writes, "only as long as he could approve of my poetry and my ideas."[143] Thus, though Winters's "formulations provided a refuge, a harmonious world where everything had already been decided in accordance with certain rules," Gunn admits that, because of the pressure from Winters to accept and follow his model, "I started to become wary . . . I deliberately began to go more and more seldom and ended by not attending his class at all."[144]

Given the affective disjunction between Winters's critical theory and pedagogical practice, I'd like to suggest that the reciprocal, mutually influencing "derivative" poetic relationship Gunn later had with Duncan acted as a queer alternative to the model of poetic "influence" proffered by Winters's insistence upon imitation of greatness. While the former is based on desire, elective identification, and collaboration, the latter draws upon anxiety, enforced identification, and apprenticeship and, ultimately, produces in Gunn the effect so well-expressed in "A Plan of Self-Subjection": "Each tainted with the other / Becomes diseased, both self and self's ideal."[145] If I posit a theory of poetic "influence" as heterosexual and one of "derivation" as homosexual, it's because influence's psychoanalytic framework is almost exclusively heterosexual—the relationship between a father and a son. And if I posit Winters not as a critical practitioner of but as a *pedagogical participant in* a theory of "influence," it's because Gunn himself says, "It is no loose Freudianism to say that for many students he was a father figure . . . the man himself . . . attracted them, as he did me as well."[146] Indeed, in reporting that some of these "students became disciples in a literal sense, limiting themselves to another man's world," Gunn recognizes the dangers of framing poetic practice exclusively in terms of either imitation or influence: "another man's world . . . is always smaller than the world you can discover for yourself."[147]

In a key poem from *The Sense of Movement,* "To Yvor Winters, 1955," Gunn generously and unsentimentally translates his ambivalent relationship to Winters's pedagogy of influence into a wonderful *imitatio* meant "to suggest [Winters's] own later style."[148] I'd like to stress that Gunn's ambivalence toward Winters isn't deliberately revealed in the poem; in fact, it reads to me as a poem wholly intended as tribute. Rather, its argument reveals the paradox implicit in their relationship: the poem's heroic couplets appropriately contain as much gratitude as good-bye, written when Gunn "could see an end in sight even while [he and Winters] achieved the point of greatest symbolic attachment."[149] This wobble between grateful *imitatio* and rueful farewell to an influence is present at the close of the poem, even as it hews closely both to Winters's key critical precepts and some of his favored themes:

> You keep both Rule and Energy in view,
> Much power in each, most in the balanced two:
> Ferocity existing in the fence
> Built by an exercised intelligence.
> Though night is always close, complete negation
> Ready to drop on wisdom and emotion,
> Night from the air or the carnivorous breath,
> Still it is right to know the force of death,
> And, as you do, persistent, tough in will,
> Raise from the excellent the better still.[150]

Gunn does indeed convincingly represent reason's necessary relationship to and intimacy with death, and engages this content with the knowledge that "Winters always praised most highly those poems that look directly and without flinching at the loneliness of human death."[151] Gunn also interprets "tradition" with an emphasis on force and will, moral rectitude, and a classical balance between "Rule" and "Energy," all key aspects of Winters's critical and poetic practices. It's in the poem's final couplet, however, that Gunn, by virtue of a play on words, wittily reveals the way in which, for Winters, morality and the pedagogy of influence are inseparable: Winters the teacher—who is also a breeder of dogs—by force of reason "raise[s] from the excellent the better still." If it seems odd at first that the closing line fuses pedagogy with genealogy, it's by this very analogy that Gunn reveals the implicit influence of Winters's pedagogy:

> . . . the Airedales you have reared
> With boxer's vigilance and poet's rigour
> Dog-generations you have trained the vigour
> That few can breed to train and fewer still
> Control with the deliberate human will.
> And in the house there rest, piled shelf on shelf,
> The accumulations that compose the self—
> Poem and history: for if we use
> Words to maintain the actions that we choose,
> Our words, with slow defining influence,
> Stay to mark out our chosen lineaments.[152]

Yes, there's classical "rigour" and "vigour," but there's also the fact that to "breed" for Winters is synonymous with to "train," with "control" and "will." Thus we can see that to "raise from the excellent the better still" is in fact a neat summary of the pedagogy of influence *and* a recipe for literary quality: it's at once a commentary on the breeder's skill in selecting the traits that will be passed on and then training those into prominence in the next generation *and* a metaphor concerning both teaching and writing poetry, actions in which chosen words constitute a "slow defining influence" that might contribute to some permanence of "our chosen lineaments." All of this order contrasts with the more abstractly rendered second stanza, in which Gunn portrays the unreason against which Winters is training Gunn to use both his logic and his language: "Continual temptation waits on each / To renounce his empire over thought and speech."[153] Given that in ten years Gunn not only would be experimenting with free verse but would quit a full-time commitment to the academy, it's not for nothing that the poem begins with farewell: "I leave you in your garden."

But what makes Winters so troubling for Gunn is that *imitatio,* when paired with the affect of influence, assumes a variety of further limitations inherent in their location within the heteronormative family: there is only *one* lineage (national and/or aesthetic) to which a poet best belongs; there are appropriate and inappropriate relations between poets; there is a power differential between father and son; the precedent poet is the originating source of power; "influence" extends in one linear direction and is nonreciprocal; the narrative between the poets consists of two poles in constant tension; and so on. In *The Anxiety of Influence: A Theory of Poetry,* Harold Bloom lends the relationship its more qualitative feel, one no doubt similar to the atmosphere Winters created for his students: "Between Ben Jonson and Samuel Johnson filial loyalty between poets had long given way to the labyrinthine affections of what Freud's wit first terms the 'family romance.' . . . To be enslaved by any precursor's system, Blake says, is to be inhibited from creativity by an obsessive reasoning and comparing, presumably of one's own work to the precursor's. Poetic Influence is thus a disease of self-consciousness."[154]

Just as Winters's moral criticism left room neither for what he called Romantic "moral relativism" nor for homosexuality,[155] Bloom's seductive and totalizing reading of influence—and by extension, tradition itself—leaves absolutely no room for viable alternative models. Or, I should say, his theory leaves no other viable model for being what he calls a "strong, authentic poet." If a poetic practice is characterized by emotions *less* than anxiety and a terror of the precursor's overwhelming power, then the poets in question "are minor or weaker." "It does happen that one poet influences another . . . through a generosity of spirit, even a shared generosity," Bloom admits. "But . . . the more generosity, and the more mutual it is, the poorer the poets involved."[156] Thus Gunn's characterization of Duncan's practice of "derivation" would likely count for Bloom as an example of profound weakness:[157] "Duncan's influences are not of the *fathers* but rather of *allies.* He finds his allies up and down history (Dante is one, Rumi another), but what makes him unusual is the makeup of his particular home-circle of influences, which are picked equally from the Modernists and from the Romantics."[158] Duncan's derivation—a matter of *allies* rather than *fathers*—invokes a completely different set of tropes than that of either influence or *imitatio,* and it's attended by an equally different set of affects: rather than a patriarchal structure over which the son has no control and against which he anxiously struggles for an impossible autonomy, derivation's alliances are elective and based on consonances and mutuality. The beneficent implications of an ally allow for a horizontal *as well as* a vertical relationship—between historical periods (Dante), national traditions (Rumi), generations (Duncan and Gunn), etc.—thus diffusing the hierarchies implicit in both *imitatio* and influence, and creating a potentially queer alternative to tradition, one that's based largely on attraction and affinity. That later in life Gunn found this model personally liberating is undoubted: at the end of his review of Duncan's final book, *Ground Work II: In the Dark,* he suggests that "[h]aving digested [his list of suggested poems], readers might then care to go on to whole books. They will find they have discovered a poet who alters their idea of the way it is possible to write in their lifetime."[159] But what exactly was it about Duncan—as mentor and poet—that allowed the younger Gunn safe passage into a different consciousness of himself as gay man and poet?

Perhaps the best answer to that question lies in Duncan's relationship to Gunn, while first admitting to the significance of the fact that a reader can examine this relationship in a depth he or she can't with Winters's relationship to Gunn. Because Duncan defined himself as ally while Winters positioned himself more as model and judge, Winters's relationship to Gunn is found exclusively in his criticism. Written at least five years after their relationship formally ended, the brief discussions of Gunn's work in Winters's final book of criticism, *Forms of Discovery,* alternate between very high praise and—as Gunn predicted they would—clear condemnation. Of "In Santa Maria del Popolo," the opening poem of Gunn's third book, Winters writes:

> The poem is remarkably vigorous; it is far better than anything by half a dozen poets of this century who are commonly called great. . . . Gunn, as a rule, has a dead ear, and the fact makes much of his work either mechanical or lax in its movement, but here the movement is excellent. . . . Like many of Gunn's poems, it exists on the narrow line between great writing and skillful journalism. Gunn's poems seem to me to come just a shade too easily.[160]

Remember, this is written of a poem in *My Sad Captains,* a book whose first half, as Gunn points out, contains the culmination of that Wintersian style, while its second famously contains his brief shift to syllabics, for which, a few pages later, Winters rejects him and his work almost completely: "the poems move like dead prose."[161] This severing, rather punishing gesture seems quite significant coming from a man who, as Gunn says, "didn't relish such a [paternal] role at all" and "was not interested in having a following."[162] Whatever Winters's reasons for dispensing such sharply meted judgment against a former intimate and student, it's clear that an emotional severance had occurred for Gunn long before 1967, when *Forms of Discovery* was published: "Once in the sixties when I sent him a group of poems, he wrote back that they were simply journalistic and maybe I should try to learn how to write prose instead. The letter came as no unexpected blow. I had been anticipating something like it for years, and I wasn't going to fight him about it. If he had a streak of brutality in him, I had a streak of sentimentality."[163]

To look at Duncan's poetic relationship to Gunn is to look at a dynamic altogether different, one that participates in a definition of and reflection on his practice of "derivation": first, it occurs outside of an official institution; and second, it takes place between mutually sympathetic poets. Third, because his "texts often engage another male in acts of literary intercourse that transform the source text into a more dialogical entity," as Michael Davidson argues in *Ghostlier Demarcations,* derivation "refigures the tradition as sexual," and few of Duncan's texts do so as explicitly in terms of his own homosexuality as does the one he derives from Gunn's work.[164] However, the major material indication of difference between Winters's and Duncan's relationship to Gunn is that the most public, extended record of Duncan's response to Gunn's work is neither criticism nor based in valuation—at least not in the traditional sense.

Poems from the Margins of Thom Gunn's "Moly," a serial poem Duncan began in April 1971 on a bus from New Haven to Portland, Maine, and finished in San Francisco in October of the same year, was first self-published and circulated by Duncan in a typescript edition in 1972, and later collected in the first volume of *Ground Work: Before the War,* published by New Directions in 1984. The first notable fact about the series is that it was *literally* written in the margins of *Moly,* which suggests that Duncan "uses the physical boundaries of a book," Davidson writes, "in order to record a scene that instructs even as it receives instructions."[165] The second notable fact about the series is that the typescript contains at least two crucial elements that the final version doesn't: (1) after the first section, "Interrupted Forms," Duncan places the "moly" passage from book 10 of the *Odyssey* as translated by Alexander Pope et al.; and

(2) directly facing this text (from which Gunn's own book springs) is Duncan's "preface," here titled "Preface to the Suite *Translated* from Thom Gunn's *Moly*" (italics mine). Placed so deliberately in proximity to Pope's *Odyssey,* the title not only explicitly links Duncan's derivations to classical practices of translation but in itself constitutes the signal difference of Duncan's derivative practice: he's not only willing to turn to the work of a younger poet for textual sources, he's also willing to receive formal and thematic limitations from the text of such a poet—a stunning reversal of the usual course of power in both imitation and influence.

Further, Duncan places himself in a specifically uncertain, vulnerable, and highly eroticized position toward Gunn's text (and perhaps Gunn the poet), so that there's a recognizable tension and confusion between identification with and desire for the addressed that activates the syntax and grammar, as in the opening of the series' first section, "Interrupted Forms":

> Long slumbering, often coming forward,
> haunting the house I am the house I live in
> resembles so, does he recall me or I
> recall him?   Seeing you the other day
> long I lookt to see your face his, longing
> without reason.   I meant to tell
> or spell your name, to dwell in the charm . . .[166]

The difficulties the speaker records here in making distinctions significantly inscribes, within the syntactical, figures of a desire intense enough to shatter reason: which is house and which, self? Who recalls whom? You or him? What is telling and what spelling and dwelling? Given Gunn's own 1970 notebook description of *Moly* as "a book about metamorphosis, change in the human being toward (his sources/the primitive & irrational)," it seems only appropriate to note that Duncan locates in his response to it not only his own attitude toward his sources of poetic power but a reminder of their sexual, at times irrational, origins. Taking advantage of the blurring in proscribed boundaries desire creates, "Interrupted Forms" enables a highly charged erotic atmosphere in which a kind of triangle between *I, he,* and *you* emerges. Though the players' identities are indistinct, the poem develops its own complex and engaging set of intrinsic relationships that play out more in theme and architecture than in direct explication. Nonetheless, given that *Moly* itself constitutes the series' occasion, instigates its writing, and dictates its form, *Poems from the Margins of Thom Gunn's "Moly"* leaves the reader implicated and involved in the highly suggestive extrinsic relationship between text and text:

> . . . the cold awakening
> I meant to tell you of, as if telling could reach you,
> at last come into your embrace again,   my arms
> hold you, mounting, coming into your life
> my life and interruption of all long lasting
>   inertia in feeling,
> arousal.[167]

For a reader unfamiliar with Gunn's *Moly*, the question begged by Duncan's response might be: What on earth did Gunn write to suggest such heavy petting? Is Duncan's an "appropriate" response? It's interesting to note that, given the section titles as well as the textual echoes within the sections, Duncan *seems* to be responding almost exclusively to the first three poems of *Moly*—its untitled proem, "When I was near the house of Circe," "Rites of Passage," and "Moly" itself—though without access to the original volume in which he wrote, it's hard to know exactly how far into the book itself his own text ventures, and thus whether it is indeed a holistic or a partial response. But given the highly eroticized nature of Duncan's text, it's fascinating to read the first three poems of *Moly*, which could be said to

1 set up the book's relationship to Homer (specifically to book 10 of *The Odyssey*) via a first-person retelling of Odysseus's meeting with Hermes, who warns him concerning Circe, and gives him Moly to protect him from her power;
2 introduce the theme of transformation in the figure of a speaker who turns centaur and, as a result, challenges his father to a duel in what seems to be, for him, an adolescent "rite of passage"; and
3 elaborate the theme of transformation and its link to "primitive" or "animistic" consciousness, as the poem is spoken in the voice of a man under the spell of Circe, a man, who, in thrall to his instinctual state, prays to the gods for Moly, for transcendence.

It's not only Duncan's titles that suggest his series is limited to a "reading" of these three poems. It's the fact that, taken as a whole, *Poems from the Margins of Thom Gunn's "Moly"* could be said to be a reading of Duncan's own sexual maturation narrative as prompted by Gunn the poet and *Moly* the book, in which the poet confronts the Oedipal order straight on: "For you, Old Man, no other . . . I stamp upon the earth. . . . And then I lower my horns."[168] Duncan's book seems to be spoken first in the voice of a poet looking back on his own adolescence[169] and second in the voice of a middle-aged man experiencing the kindling throes of passion for an unattainable young man. Indeed, perhaps in reaction to Gunn's relative youthfulness and the coming-of-age/coming-to-consciousness narratives of *Moly*, Duncan's speakers as often take on the self-conscious role of instructor—both Hermes and the father figure whose son challenges him to a duel—as they do of frustrated and turned-on courtier or wise witness to the struggles with consciousness Gunn's speakers undergo.

What's perhaps most moving about the series is how two sections spoken by an older, desiring man to a younger, indifferent one—both sections are titled after and respond to Gunn's "Rite of Passage"—take the "rite" out of the Freudian, heterosexual paradigm of Gunn's original and into an explicitly homosexual one by virtue of its simultaneous recognition of and attraction to the power the youth possesses. "Dark Satyr, / your blood is like a / light behind an / almond bough," Duncan writes in explicit echo of Gunn's "Rites of Passage," and further—this speaker admits to his physical arousal, his sexual renewal in the youth's presence. The power he borrows from the youth shifts the direction in which traditional "literary" influence flows: "now / something is taking / place in me— / all nature awaits," he confesses, "behind the trembling / tapestry of leaves / and buds, of / hidden, about-to-be- / awakened birds." Duncan's series also tellingly rewrites traditional romantic poetic tropes—"What is Spring / that everywhere bursts upon my world"—folding convention into derivation in ways that change and further convention while also charging the derivative with familiarity.[170]

If Duncan's text begins in the stir of eros created by a triangulation, an eros which triggers a revisiting of the speaker's own adolescent sexual awakenings, the emotional piquancy of the series stems mainly from the way in which these older men are vulnerable to the youths to whom they speak, and this authorial vulnerability—crucial to the dynamic of reciprocity—is another signal difference in derivation: "You bristle where my fond hand would stir / to stroke your cheek. I do not dare." Finally, it's the recognition of and respect for not only subjective difference but the inevitable rites of aging, of one generation replacing another that makes Duncan's series so tender and humane. If the speaker recognizes that "[i]rregular meters beat between your heart and mine," he also accepts the fact that "where my youth was, now the Sun in you grows hot, your day / is young, my place you take triumphantly. All along / it's been for you." The rueful acknowledgment of this gift that, as it's given, undoes the sexual ascendancy of the one who gives it, is accompanied by the equal sweetness of its essential generosity. As Winters's rejection of Gunn reminds us, such a gift needn't be willingly given, though if it isn't, it will nonetheless be taken in the very course of time.[171]

But what of Gunn's relationship to Duncan? Did it reflect the ambivalence and tension of *Poems from the Margins of Thom Gunn's "Moly"*? In answer we might simply look to the sheer volume of Gunn's critical writing concerning Duncan, about whom he wrote more than any other single author. We might go to the numerous poems he wrote to or for him—including "Wrestling," from *Jack Straw's Castle;* "At the Barriers," which was its own limited-edition chapbook in 1989; and "Duncan," the elegy which begins *Boss Cupid.* Or we might go to his notebooks, which throughout the 1970s report on Duncan, his conversations and ideas, and during the '80s both record his eventual decline and death from kidney failure and track the inception and initial development of a "Duncan book" or long "Duncan project" he planned to write in the wake of mourning, but which eventually became the long free-verse series "At the Barriers" and the metrical elegy "Duncan."

Perhaps the notes for this project hint most deeply at the legacy Duncan gave to Gunn, weaving together as they do the many threads, both aesthetic and political, that lead from Gunn's mid-career volumes into his final one. By virtue of the notebook's date, they also possess the virtue of contextualizing the urgency and emergence of Duncan's legacy within Gunn's writing: "1988 July 29–1989 Jan 5." During this time, Gunn finished *The Man with Night Sweats,* the AIDS crisis had taken most of his circle of gay friends, and Duncan died. If in a 1986 notebook he writes that "I am surrounded by shipwrecks, friends dead and dying of AIDS[,] of the effects of old age, poets I admire and novelists, acquaintances, dead and dying," then the significance of his July 2, 1989, entry lies in the fact that we know this barrage of death and dying didn't let up but only intensified during the intervening three years:

> The next book to be about my idea of aliveness—not of getting on with life, mostly, but of the intensity of lives in past and in present. The gay revolution—its essential subversiveness & emphasis on the individual—to be clarified, if I can, by instance and anecdote, all the more in that so many of those who have been a part of it are dead and will die soon. If we are a

> dwindling minority, all the more reason to state its values, to emphasize the libertarian aspects, the euphoria, and the way we have tried to "make it up as we go along." . . . The tragedy of loss—which has been inevitable anyway, though who would have dreamt so dramatically—is so great because of the essential optimism of the enterprise. . . . The possibility—what is sketched out at the end of the sixties and embodied in the seventies is still alive, and it is up to me to record it, as well as I can. I would like to be able to address such subjects as: the Parades, the same-sex union as a[n] (unsolemnized) marriage, bathhouses, the Castro, gay political power, etc. I am not good at dealing with such straightforward didacticism, and will probably have to do what I can indirectly as heretofore, but I'd like to . . .[172]

After this devastatingly articulate and hopeful passage, the next entry, "July 3," suggests that "I could start by combining this with the Duncan project." And indeed, after his notes reel back and forth between verse and prose drafts of what would indeed become the poems "Duncan" and "At the Barriers," a few pages later he stops and takes stock, wondering if he should "try to absorb a lot in a Duncan project," or perhaps attempt a "Duncan omnibus poem." As always when he's trying to collect himself and establish footing imaginatively, he makes a list of what such a project might include:

> poems about him directly
> poems using the opposition of open and closed in the deepest senses
> poems about ways in which the tradition is furthered by subversion
> poems about gay life as a shared exploratory project

What hits me hardest about this list is that while it clearly articulates the values that Duncan stood for—subversion, open form—there is room both for what Gunn's relationship to Duncan evoked—a conversation about closed and open form, subversion as a *furthering* of tradition—and his own extension of *the form of that relationship* toward others, the sense of gay community being "Our Dionysian experiment." This is the mature thinking that prepares Gunn to write "At the Barriers" as well as the deep gossip of *Boss Cupid*, and it serves as a grand summation of his evolution from the twenty-one-year-old novice novelist of 1950 who writes in his notebook, "Homosexuals are always flattered by the attention of females . . . because they feel that they are more 'normal' after all."[173] It's also the thinking that so beautifully and simply resolves many of the conflicts in suspension for Gunn since 1980, when he attempted to write his essay addressing the paradox of being a gay poet, stating, "To be a poet is more important than to be a gay poet." It's not that in 1989 he might not still in some small sense agree with that statement, but that the paradox, the tension between "gay" and "poet," simply disappears by virtue of his lived experience. After his fruitful, reciprocal, decades-long relationship with Duncan and the communal devastation of AIDS, experience renders the question academic, suggesting that perhaps some conflicts in *value* might get resolved only off the page, and that Gunn in the end did as Duncan was taught by him to do: he accepted that, when struck full force by the passage of time, when mired in its radically relational context, the thing to do is give—and give way to others.

However, I'd like to end this essay elsewhere in Gunn's passage, with a poem written before both Duncan's death and the devastation of his immediate community, a poem that, if it weren't for the context I first read it in, I might never have realized was written "to" Duncan: "Odysseus on Hermes." First published in the fall/winter 1985 issue of *Sagetrieb,* a Robert Duncan special issue, and later collected in *The Man with Night Sweats* where its context alters its sense greatly, the poem returns to the characters of *Moly,* the very characters whose relationship Duncan uses as objective correlative for the desires stirred in him by *Moly.* Remember that Gunn speaks only once in the voice of Odysseus—in the proem—and never in that of Hermes; after the proem, he's careful to inhabit only the bewitched sailors or the centaur: not heroes, but creatures struggling for freedom, toward a higher consciousness. In this later poem—subtitled "his afterthought"—he again takes on Odysseus's voice, but this time he inhabits not just the character Duncan's speaker so fervently desires, he actually speaks *from within* the relationship Duncan creates, responding boldly to the erotic atmosphere and dynamics Duncan set going and which are clearly still active for Gunn fourteen years later.

Given that, as the Homeric "Hymn to Hermes" reminds us, the god Hermes is "versatile / and full of tricks, a thief, / a cattle-rustler, a bringer of dreams, / a spy by night, a watcher at the gate, / one who was destined to bring wonderful things / to light," Gunn's poem recognizes the multiple psychological and aesthetic roles Duncan played in his writing life.[174] The tribute paid to Duncan's mentorship seems especially poignant given that, in book 10 of the *Odyssey,* it's Hermes who acts as Odysseus's protector, arming him with Moly against the witchcraft of Circe; and though Duncan wasn't the Hermes of Gunn's *Moly,* he's certainly the Hermes of "Odysseus to Hermes," which fittingly makes the poem a derivation of Duncan's derivation of Gunn. It's also Gunn's most directly erotic engagement with Duncan's literary presence, and, as such, it could be said to fulfill the reciprocity of Duncan's derivation by making it truly dialogic. A response made a little over a decade after Duncan's—written at roughly the same age Duncan was when he first wrote to Gunn—Gunn's poem takes up the relationship again with the advantage of having inhabited both sides: of having been the youth, "in process and so / still open to the god," and of being middle-aged, "thinking back . . . to renew that power."[175]

In another sense, the poem is also about what Gunn took to be Duncan's greatest lesson and challenge for him: "The poem written in open form is meant to be viewed less as an artifact than as part of a *process* . . . which may take directions unanticipated in the original conceptions."[176] In "Odysseus on Hermes," Gunn begins to see this aesthetic idea of "process" in terms of lifespan and sexual maturation—the way Duncan does in *Poems from the Margins*—and equates "the incompletion of youth" with being "potent in potential" while the "complete and settled" quality of middle age suggests being "closed to the god."[177] What interests me here is the fact that the poem's narrative presents a reversal of the relationship Duncan's speaker so despaired of; here, Hermes is powerful because Odysseus "was seduced by innocence / —beard scarcely visible on his chin"—he was "seduced by the god within":[178]

> So sensing it in him
> I was seduced by the god,
> becoming in my thick maturity
> suddenly unsettled
>   un-solid
> still being formed—
> in the vulnerability, edges flowing,
> myself open to the god.

Perhaps Gunn—who was just over forty at the time—himself felt renewed by Duncan's erotically freighted aesthetic reaction to *Moly*, as well as by the deepening of their relationship that it prompted: it's certainly true that it's in the next few books that Gunn becomes the poet we know him to be, and that it's in these books he both establishes a practice as a gay poet and forges his trademark flexible plain style that alternates as easily between free and metrical verse as it does between lyrical, unpunctuated fragment and highly narrative, discursive hypotaxis. As Duncan was by *Moly* made aware of "the force of a rime impending" and "forebodings at the edge we are in ourselves," so Gunn's speaker admits that he too was transformed by "vulnerability, edges flowing / myself open to the god," qualities Gunn's work did not always have permission to possess, given Winters's extreme "reservations about poetry" that is "'soft' and 'gentle.'"[179]

In 1985, when the poem was first published, Duncan had already experienced the kidney failure that put him on home dialysis and which would kill him in 1988. So in that sense, like "To Yvor Winters, 1955," "Odysseus on Hermes" is as much an expression of gratitude to a mentor as it is a gesture of good-bye; its status as an afterthought concerning a project that formalized their relationship gives it further weight in these capacities, though of course following Duncan's death, Gunn will write the far weightier and lengthy memorial of "At the Barriers." The poem's final stanza, however, stands in many ways as the most concise poetic summary of his literary and personal relationship to Duncan, whose combined roles as mentor and source, as well as friend and conspirator, amounted to his being an incomparable and irreplaceable guide to the transformations Gunn believed as central to being as to verse. The stanza manages to capture both the goad to risk that Duncan could be for Gunn, as well as the trust implicit between them—as implausible, hopeful, erotic, experimental, tricky, and mutual as it was. This is the *true* inheritance Duncan and Gunn have left gay poetry, and I can leave the reader with nothing better than what I myself have been given in the course of writing this essay, which is the future, the ongoing possibilities for poetry created by the reciprocity and respect between these two men:

> I took his drug
> and all came out right in the story.
> Still thinking back
> I seek to renew that power
> so easily got
> seek to find again that knack
> of opening my settled features,
> creased on themselves,
> to the astonishing kiss and gift
> of the wily god to the wily man.[180]

PART FOUR

Of the World

Thom Gunn's New Jerusalem

TOM SLEIGH

A year before Thom Gunn died in 2004, he told me about going to visit a sex club—he wrote about such experiences, so I don't think there's any reason not to speak about them. Since I'm straight, he described it with all the precision of someone describing the more technical aspects of going rafting down the Colorado River—the club had two floors, one for gays, one for straights, and if you were gay you could pay a little more and descend among the straights, but if you were straight, you couldn't ascend to be among the gays. There were little tents to go into when you'd found someone, and of course there was more. I like to check myself on stories told to me by friends, and when I went online to find out more for this essay, I found a place in San Francisco called the Power Exchange that answered to some of what I remember him saying. But not all. There are different floors, but there's a bottom floor with a dungeon and bondage room, for a total of three floors, not two. And there was no mention of tents, but rather theme playrooms: among others, an ancient Egyptian room, a boxing ring, and a series of cubicles that would seem to form a maze called Asshole Alley. There is different pricing, but not as straightforwardly gay/straight as I remember. And of course, it's possible he was talking about a different club altogether. What I'm certain of is this: regardless of the no drugs or alcohol policies, Thom talked about the drugs people were on: Viagra, obviously, but more to the point, speed (methamphetamine), PCP (aka angel dust), and ecstasy, though it was Thom's impression that more straights were into that.

That sex and drugs go together should be no surprise to anyone, and in Thom Gunn's poems they become dual aspects of eros: on the one hand, drugs and sex can open us up to vistas of human freedoms and discoveries; and on the other, they can lead to darker recognitions about the world and ourselves. Gunn's poems explore both aspects in a way that is compassionate, nuanced, and wide-ranging in scope. So let's start with Gunn's attitude toward drugs. I had long known that he used them—for that matter, so had I, speed, heroin, marijuana, a lot of psychedelics—and drug use was one of the bonds of our friendship. I don't mean that we did drugs together, for we weren't friends in that way. But I mean the psychological predisposition behind our drug use, the kinds of assumptions we shared about what drugs could teach you, how they opened up avenues of self-knowledge and wide-ranging spiritual and social understandings that would ordinarily be closed to you. You always took drugs for pleasure, of course, but part of that pleasure was the possibilities they gave you to test what it meant to be a human being. You might say that Gunn disagreed with Samuel Johnson when Johnson said that you didn't need to experience evil in order to shun it—though Gunn never thought of drugs as evil: rather, drugs were part of the pleasure of people who have a romance with experience and, for better and worse, take seriously the choices and obsessions that such a romance involves you in, willy-nilly.

In a Jefferson Airplane song that was something of a psychedelic anthem, Gracie Slick's exhortatory, I'm-verging-on-ecstatic, sand-paper growl spoke to the feeling of transformative power that drugs held for a certain kind of user:

> One pill makes you larger,
> and one pill makes you small,
> and the ones that Mother gives you
> don't do anything at all.
> Just ask Alice
> when she's ten feet tall . . .

These lyrics convey a disinterested, deeply curious fascination with the nuances of human personality as it's illuminated by drugs. In Gunn's poem "Listening to Jefferson Airplane,"[1] the physical phenomenon of the music, as it "comes and goes on the wind," is mirrored by its psychological effect as it "[c]omes and goes on the brain." In that sense, you could say that using drugs at a concert was a kind of laboratory to learn about human behavior and the workings of your own mind; hanging out with friends and the subtle and not-so-subtle transformations that you and they underwent was one of the things about drugs that Gunn most liked and that these lines, in both the song and his poem, point to.

And along with his attitude toward drugs, there was an ethos about erotic play that he wrote about in an essay, "My Life Up to Now," in which he discusses what his experiences in the 1960s and early '70s had meant to him: a communitarian ethos of pleasure and of how pleasure and social equality were based on the freedom to give our sexual natures and desires full expression. As Gunn wrote of the Geysers, a hot-springs area in Sonoma County north of San Francisco:

> Everyone walked around naked, swimming in the cool stream by day and at night staying in the hot baths until early in the morning. Heterosexual and homosexual orgies sometimes overlapped: there was an attitude of benevolence and understanding on all sides that could be extended, I thought, into the rest of the world. When I remember that small, changing society of holidays and weekends, I picture a great communal embrace. For what is the point of a holiday if we cannot carry it back into working days? There is no good reason why that hedonistic and communal love of the Geysers could not be extended to the working life of the towns. Unless it is that human beings contain in their emotions some homeostatic device by which they must defeat themselves just as they are learning their freedom.[2]

This was before AIDS, of course—but I remember even after the Plague, as it came to be called, had claimed many of Gunn's friends, he still insisted that he believed deeply in those values; and he once told me that he doubted he could really trust or be good friends with anybody who didn't share them. Not that he didn't have a profound understanding of the workings of the less savory aspects of sexual self-knowledge and becoming—and his image of a homeostatic device of the emotions displays a profound pessimism at the heart of his generous, radically visionary view of sexual pleasure as a revolutionary force. But a force also accompanied by depression, paranoia, self-suspicion, self-alienation, jealously, and despair.

His poetic sequence "The Menace" deals with all these emotions, in which "[i]n a theatre of reflection / I encounter again / the exemplary figure" who is "inducted by himself / into an army of fantasy" and is at once

guard	father
executioner	angel of death
delivering doctor	judge
cop	castrator

the-one-who-wants-to-get-me[3]

As a form of paranoid projection, "the menace" "leaps from the night / fully armed, a djinn / of human stature" whose "hands hang heavy / gloved for obscure purpose," and the lovers, in the course of the poem, give their bodies, too: "his arms / were our arms, his sperm ours. / His terror became / our play." In these lines, the menace goes from being a djinn to a threatening, heavy-gloved figure, to a composite figure of both their bodies, in which, during sexual play, they become one inside the body of love, their sperm and arms fusing into the act of making love, both love as sexual pleasure as well as the founding of a new identity. And so "the-one-who-wants-to-get-me" starts out as a paranoid projection and by poem's end has metamorphosed into "a cheerful man in workclothes" who "stumbles off grinning / 'Bye babe gotta get to the job.'" The menace as a projection of the speaker's paranoid consciousness becomes assimilated into the dailiness of domestic routine.

This transformation of terror into play and the consoling rhythms of domesticity suggest that however much our sexuality is tied in to our darker emotions, "[t]he great communal embrace" of the Geysers has the power to remake the way we envision our desires as we project them onto others and experience their projections onto us. At the same time, the communality of the embrace stands apart from the "tea for two, you for me, me for you" trope of monogamous, exclusive, heterosexual love. In fact, as Gunn says, such an embrace brought back from holiday would change "the working life of the towns." The subversiveness of the notion and the political implications of that subversion are wide sweeping. If the basis of democracy is the body and bodily pleasure, as the image of a communal embrace at least partly suggests, then why shouldn't sexual hedonism become one of the central values of the democratic contract? And why shouldn't drugs be one of the tools that help the body politic to achieve that contract's fulfillment?

Certainly Gunn is speaking as poet and not prophet (orgies fueled by poppers in the Bank of America bank vault come to mind!), but the ideal of this embrace exists as an abiding conviction and underwrites all Gunn's poetry. For the poet, "the passages of joy," in Samuel Johnson's phrase, are not only erogenous but civic as well. And lest this seem too utopian, not to say soft-headed, a conviction, I want to again stress that Gunn was all too aware, even at the height of his "belief in the possibilities of change," that "we all continue to carry the same baggage: in my world, Christian does not shed his burden, only his attitude to it alters."[4] But as he also says, his life "insists on continuities." And so even though the "great sweep of the acid years" has been denounced by conservatives and liberals alike for its embrace of drugs and hedonism, I deeply admire Gunn's faithfulness to that vision: "Everything that we glimpsed—the trust, the brotherhood, the repossession of innocence, the nakedness of spirit—is still a possibility and will continue to be so."[5]

At the same time, his need for domesticity is an inherent part of that vision, as suggested by how "the-one-who-wants-to-get-me," in all its erotic thrill and chill, becomes the ordinary man whom Gunn sleeps next to, his body cupping "the fine warm back, / broad fleshed shoulder blades." So just as Gunn puts a premium on sexual freedom, he evinces an equal need for domestic stability. And while Gunn speaks about the dangers of using a poet's biography to narrow the meanings of his poems in a way that diminishes them, I think it's instructive that his home life also reflected his communitarian spirit: he lived in a group house, with housemates, in which each in turn cooked dinner on assigned nights of the week. It was a remarkably stable arrangement and lasted from 1971, when Gunn bought the house on Cole Street in the Haight, until his death in 2004. During that time, Gunn had many lovers and sexual partners, but he also spent thirty-three years with the same housemates. Sex, drugs, and rock 'n' roll—as Gunn says in his poem "Transients and Residents,"[6] "I like loud music, bars, and boisterous men"—aren't necessarily incompatible with personal loyalty, homebodiness, and domestic stability.

Of course, I'm betraying typical heterosexual, basically monogamous biases/hangups here: whoever said that domestic life and sexual freedom are opposed? Well, to take an extreme, let's look at this quote from Pat Robertson, host of the Christian Right's *700 Club.* As he said in the *Washington Post,* August 23, 1993: "[T]he feminist agenda is not about equal rights for women. It is about a socialist, anti-family political movement that encourages women to leave their husbands, kill their children, practice witchcraft, destroy capitalism and become lesbians." While this is inadvertently comic, and easy and obvious a target though Robertson is, it should be noted that his particular brand of paranoia, in its fear of same-sex eroticism as a destroyer of hubby's happy home, is one that's shared, in a much more tamped-down style, by a lot of straight men and women, particularly if children are involved. On the other hand, one wonders what Robertson would make of Family Day in Provincetown, Massachusetts, where gay couples wheel baby carriages down Commercial Street amid a generally party-hearty atmosphere, and where, as far as one can tell, no knife-wielding, capitalist-hating, depraved lesbos are slitting their babies' soft little throats and dancing to old Black Sabbath tracks at a witch's coven. But I bring up these issues not to debate the merits of monogamy, patriarchy, or black magic, whether practiced by gays or straights, but to stress the depth of Gunn's social and poetic commitments: as Keats would say, Gunn proved them on his pulses, and in his life and in his work he shows how pleasure and eroticism and domestic stability were, for him, a seamless continuum.

This is no common perception. As a matter of fact, when you survey literary tropes associated with love poetry in English going all the way back to Thomas Wyatt, it turns out to be a highly original one, at least as far as literature is concerned. Wrack my brains as I might, I can't come up with a single straight writer of the twentieth century or, for that matter, any century who develops this trope such that all three of these qualities seem mutually entailing. When I mentioned this to an extremely well-read, female straight friend, she, too, was unable to come up with a single name; and though she did suggest Rumi, we both agreed that he fudged the issue by making the beloved synonymous with God. Several other names, Edna St. Vincent Millay, late Yeats, were quickly dismissed. And after a moment or two of silence, my friend said, "Actually, it's kind of sad." Sad that eroticism and pleasure and domestic stability are seen as antithetical, at least as a poetic convention for straight writers. And so it's no exaggeration to say that Gunn's development of this trope of seamless connection among eroticism, pleasure, and domestic stability is one of the deep sources of his originality.

As regards Gunn's originality, I think my friend also meant that it was sad because of the limited repertoire of roles that straight people feel are available to them, as well as the constraint on feeling that these roles impose on the conventions of heterosexual love poems. I don't for a moment think Gunn is advocating that heteros expand the range of those roles—he never expressed any sentiment about other people's sexual desires, except to say, quite sensibly, that everyone should do whatever turns them on. Which is simply to say, again, that Gunn's vision, his "community of the carnal heart,"[7] is the vision of a poet and not a social reformer: it isn't a poet's duty to preach, or to do anything at all but write the poems that come his or her way. But it's one of the inadvertent pleasures in reading

Gunn to discover in his imagination a passion to propose new forms of human relation, at least as far as the straight world is concerned, through the practice of his art. This is what I mean when I say that Gunn's vision is socially radical in its implications. It isn't just Pat Robertson and his fear of slinky witches dancing around in the latest from Victoria's Secret: it's the conflicted, and conflicting ways gay and straight conceive of their sexual freedoms and constraints when you compare Gunn's version of community through sexual connection, and the typical conventions that surround heterosexual passion as it gets expressed through love poetry in English for the past five hundred years.

Gunn writes very movingly of the vicissitudes of his particular kind of domesticity in "The Hug," a poem addressed to his longtime partner, Mike Kitay. In the poem, their "grand passion" has grown so familial that when he wakes to find his partner hugging him from behind, he says:

> It was not sex, but I could feel
> The whole strength of your body set,
> Or braced, to mine,
> And locking me to you
> As if we were still twenty-two
> When our grand passion had not yet
> Become familial.
> My quick sleep had deleted all
> Of intervening time and place.
> I only knew
> The stay of your secure firm dry embrace.[8]

The dryness of the embrace marks the transition from sexual to domestic love, from the physical joy of sex to the physical joy of being held by someone with whom a life has been shared. Now, what heterosexual male poet would celebrate such a transition? Presumably, that poet would say how sexual attraction was attendant on the hug; or else the poet would lament the passing of such passion. But Gunn does neither—or if there is a touch of melancholy, it is balanced by an equal sense of triumph. To make the point even clearer, and to ground it in the differences between Gunn's version of domestic love and the hetero "tea for two" version, allow me once again to resort to biography. Bill Schuessler—a friend whom Gunn and Kitay met in 1967, the Summer of Love—moved in with them in 1971. According to Schuessler, "It was the happiest time in my life, really. It was a wonderful time to be alive in San Francisco. But it was more than that: I was wildly in love with Mickey [Kitay]. And Thom became almost like a father figure to me because he was always looking out for me. Which was incredibly strange—or nice—given that Mickey was his lover. It sounds like incest, but we all got along together."[9] The sexual mores that govern how we act out our carnal fates are obviously beyond the bounds of this essay, but how many straight households, how many Elizabeth Barretts and Robert Brownings, could adjust to the addition of a third wheel, with or without a night out at the Power Exchange, with or without a handy supply of mood-inducing drugs?

Not that maintaining this continuum between carnality and domestic life doesn't present difficulties. And many of Gunn's best poems, especially during the height of the AIDS epidemic, attempt to preserve that continuum against not only biological forces, but against the less tolerant, more repressive social forces in the culture that both the Right and the Left have fostered. This is especially apparent in his great, late poem "Saturday Night," a Dantesque version of a night spent in the Barracks, a famous San Francisco bathhouse—Dantesque because not only is it written in terza rima but it takes the decor of Dante's Hell and makes it emblematic of paradisal aspirations accomplished, of course, through eros, and drugs as an aid to eros:

> I prowl the labyrinthine corridors
>   And have a sense of being underground
> As in a mine . . . dim light, the many floors,
>   The bays, the heat, the tape's explosive sound.
> People still entering, though it is 3 a.m.,
>   Stripping at lockers and, with a towel tied round,
> Stepping out hot for love or strategem,
>   Pausing at thresholds (wonder never ends),
> Peering at others, as others peer at them
>   Like people in shelters searching for their friends
> Among the group come newest from the street.
>   And in each room a different scene attends:
> Friends by the bedful, lounging on one sheet,
>   Playing cards, smoking, while the drugs come on,
> Or watching the foot-traffic on the beat,
>   Ready for every fresh phenomenon.
> This was the Barracks, this the divine rage

In 1975, that time is gone.
All here, of any looks, of any age,
Will get whatever they are looking for,
Or something close, the rapture they engage
Renewable each night.
If, furthermore,
Our Dionysian experiment
To build a city never dared before
Dies without reaching to its full extent,
At least in the endeavor we translate
Our common ecstasy to a brief ascent
Of the complete, grasped, paradisal state
Against the wisdom pointing us away.[10]

The vision of social equality that emerges from these lines, in which "All here, of any looks, of any age, / Will get whatever they are looking for," posits a world where glam girls and glam boys are no more privileged than the ordinary-looking Jos and Joeys. All of us are entitled to our desires, and all of us will have them fulfilled. And if not fulfilled—for what desire can ever be absolutely satisfied?—then we will get "something close," and in such a form that "the rapture" we engage is "renewable each night." And part of this renewal, of course, is the shared commonality of "[f]riends by the bedful, lounging on one sheet," as opposed to couples on separate beds on separate sheets; and even the card game, with its connotations of domestic familiarity and friendship, shows the continuities between the civic and the erogenous that Gunn is so deeply committed to.

Of course, as ever in Gunn's vision, drugs are a part of the rapture, the facilitator of the "divine rage," the catalyst that helps trigger the "Dionysian experiment" and the "brief ascent" to "the complete, grasped, paradisal state." In an epigram called "The 1970s,"[11] Gunn speaks of the different varieties of New Jerusalem, the political and pharmaceutical kinds, and tells us how "I've visited most of them." But the only one he'd care to return to is "the sexual New Jerusalem," because it "was by far the greatest fun." And so in "Saturday Night," you can see Pat Robertson's worst nightmare come true: not only does Gunn appropriate the holy city's name to describe the nonmonogamous, noncompetitive, noncapitalist polis of carnal desire, in which everyone gets what they want, but there are no losers and hence no winners either in this New Jerusalem. In the New Jerusalem that the Barracks represents, "fun" is sufficient reason for pleasure: there are no bosses calling the shots (at least in Robertson's understanding of the word "boss" or, for that matter, "shots"), no divinely ordained patriarchal arrangements about whose body gets to use whose. Of course, there are conventions of sexuality that the Barracks adheres to; but since the Barracks represents a free choice—you can choose to enter or not enter, in all the myriad associations of "enter"—the coercive nature of Robertson's vision is exploded by the Barracks' Dionysian energies. And these energies don't simply devolve into chaos but represent a collective effort to discover "a common ecstasy" despite "the wisdom pointing us away."

But here Gunn hesitates: at the same time as he articulates his vision of building "a city never dared before," he seems completely cognizant that it's doomed to failure:

> What hopeless hopefulness. I watch, I wait—
> The embraces slip, and nothing seems to stay
> In our community of the carnal heart.
> Some lose conviction in mid-arc of play,
> Their skin turns numb, they dress and will depart:
> The perfect body, lingering on goodbyes,
> Cannot find strength now for another start.
> Dealers move in, and murmuring advertise
> Drugs from each doorway with a business frown.
> Mattresses lose their springs. Beds crack, capsize,
> And spill their occupants on the floor to drown.
> Walls darken with the mold, or is it rash?
> At length the baths catch fire and then burn down,
> And blackened beams dam up the bays of ash.[12]

The "homeostatic device" that regulates human behavior and emotion has clearly undergone a readjustment: the sexual New Jerusalem falls both from without and from within: from within because "the community of the carnal heart" loses faith in its vision of sexual freedom as civic freedom; and from without, because Pat Robertson's capitalist ethos debases drugs into just another commodity to be sold with a "business frown," and because god biology, in the form of AIDS and the social consequences that AIDS unleashes, combines to turns against the carnal heart and overwhelm the community with flood, fire, mold—and that most ominous of all these apocalyptic forces, the harbinger of disease, rash. But despite the failure of the sexual New Jerusalem, it still exists in Gunn's poem as a human possibility that can again be incarnated. It's not that the poem goes back on the revolutionary nature of the vision—it's that the human reversion away from rapture, coupled with social and biological forces, eventually overwhelmed what Gunn presents as a heroic adventure into extending the range of what we mean when we say that we are human.

The "hopeless hopefulness" that is this poem's emotional signature presents a darker vision than the untrammeled and orgiastic celebration of sex and drugs that characterizes Gunn's experiences at the Geysers. And while the terza rima is an obvious homage to Dante, the other, more skeptical intelligence that presides over the poem is Baudelaire. Gunn's take on the sublime and sinister aspects of this New Jerusalem, in its druggy, hallucinatory intensities, shares many affinities with Baudelaire's hashish dreams of Paris, especially as he depicts the city in *Parisian Scenes*. And in Gunn poems like "A System" and "Sequel"—two poems that chronicle a friend's progress into addiction to angel dust and then back out into the world again, as well as in "Saturday Night," all from his last book, *Boss Cupid*—you can see how Baudelaire's nightmare cityscapes and spookhouse interiors seem to haunt Gunn's all-night drug parties, orgies, and vividly recalled sexual encounters. All three of these poems speak of the psychic and social costs that are oftentimes the unexpected consequences of visionary moments of orgiastic release—a dynamic that parallels Baudelaire's longing for perfect worlds of pleasure that give way to his fascination with murderers, gamblers, whores, and debauched aesthetes as harbingers of what he simply called "The New." In Gunn's iteration of this dynamic, though, the poet has a profound sympathy for the world of the street—and this sympathy can be traced back to the communitarian ideals that drug use once promised and, in Gunn's poems, more often than not, successfully sponsor.

You can see this ethos in its public application in a poem like "'All Do Not All Things Well,'"[13] in which the poet takes sides with some "Auto freaks" who have an auto repair business going in their driveway, against an "officious / Realtor" who "threatened them / For brashly operating / A business on the street." The realtor, who wants them evicted, wants "the neighborhood neat / to sell it." It's easy to see how the social vision of the New Jerusalem of sexual ecstasy, in which all "get whatever they are looking for," with drugs as part of the sacred ritual, also extends to the lives of the street and a desire for social equality in the world at large. As Gunn says about these "gentle joky men," lamenting their eviction: "Such oily-handed zest / By-passed the self like love. / I thought that they were good / For any neighborhood."

That love should bypass the self comes as no surprise if you consider how Gunn characterizes "the divine rage" encountered in the Barracks and the erotic, impersonal ecstasy of "The Geysers," a poem based on his orgiastic experiences at the place itself.

> green moonlight, smell of dope
> the shining arms and eyes
> staring at me without surprise
> I am trapped
> It will begin
> pubescent girl and bearded boy close in
>
> I give up
> hope as they move in on me
>
> loosened so quickly from it I am free
>
> I brace myself light strong and clear
> and understand why I came here
>
> entering their purpose as they enter mine
>
> I am part of all
> hands take
> hands tear and twine . . .[14]

Gunn's recognition that our sexual and social interdependence, in which we cannot help but enter other people's purposes if we are to be in relation to them, is a fact that the Pat Robertsons, the dealers with their business frowns, and the officious realtors don't seem to comprehend, or are eager to blot out of consciousness by thinking that their social exchanges always have to be on God's terms or on business terms—which is to say, their terms alone. Again, the recognition of our mutuality isn't free of anxiety. And in these lines, both in the way the couplets keep falling apart, and in the distanced, rigorous cool of the speaker's self-observations, Gunn beautifully embodies, in both the verse form and the point of view, his fluctuations between fear and ecstatic anticipation.

This isn't to say that Gunn's use of fixed forms and free verse—as is often claimed, sometimes by Gunn himself—neatly correlates to a contrasting tension between the liminal nature of doing drugs and trying to capture that through a fixed form, or using free verse to give ordinary life a more dreamlike texture. LSD-induced or not, the poem is a poem, not an acid trip. And however acid trips may feel when you are *on* them, the poem is based on conventions. I have no doubt that Gunn used couplets as a way to order the experience; but the experience we are talking about, in addition to the orgy, is the experience of writing a poem. And that's a literary experience, not a druggy one. What the poem actually dramatizes is how the mind, as it experiences a loosening of its own contours, reacts against such loosening by fastening onto some detail of landscape, or sense perception, that will once again ground it. And it's interesting to note that for a poem that claims to be about visionary experience, the poem largely consists of naturalistic description. The color of the moonlight may be green, but that is as much a characteristic of Gunn's accuracy of perception, as an indication of a disordered mind. And "the smell of dope" is also a way to ground, in naturalistic detail, the closing in of the girls and boys. Plus, the way the poet's lineation fragments the syntax before it resolves into coherent phrasing makes the falling apart and regrouping of the couplet a drama in itself, one that the reader directly participates in just as the speaker in the poem dramatizes his participation in the orgy.

That said, when I read this poem, I do in fact experience the couplet as a way to make order come out of disorder. And this dynamic is also present in the kind of free-verse line that the poet learned from William Carlos Williams and Basil Bunting. Gunn's free-verse poems are structured in ways that dramatically embody the desire for spontaneity and openness in life, while acknowledging the need for meaningful pattern. In both modes, and particularly in these lines from "The Geysers," Gunn seems to have been aiming at maximum hardness of execution accompanied by maximum fluidity of conception—and in the case of the communitarian ethos I've been speaking of, the hardness of execution is Gunn's acknowledgment of the limits of his own experience—the vision is only his vision, after all, he is the one who is "light clear and strong"; others may be experiencing something radically different. And the fluidity of conception suggests Gunn's relation to language is an open-ended process of discovery; which is why the modified couplet form is beautifully appropriate for his purposes: the poet both nods to the couplet's traditional form of closure and steps away from it in order to signal the liminal and shape-shifting nature of consciousness.

This fluidity is made all the more credible in "The Geysers" by the way Gunn's voice functions at a remove—a remove, in fact, that is a kind of courtesy to his readers, striking a balance between the intensities of druggy fantasy bordering on the dangerous, and the need to be a reliable and companionable guide. The poem isn't written for a coterie audience of druggies, it's written for anyone who wants to understand the way boundaries of experience fall away and then reassert themselves. So even as the sequence seems to be pushing toward some ecstatic revelation, Gunn's curiously intellectualized understanding of eros makes it seem as if the speaker is at once there and not there, a part of the action but separate from it, a participant in his own sexual appetites but also a witness to them—and a witness with an uncannily dispassionate eye.

This need to establish the proper distance from which to view the action is also dramatized by Gunn's movement back and forth between verse and free verse in which his use of rhyme and meter establishes a certain kind of performative norm that nonetheless allows for the felicitous local freedoms and improvisations that make rhyme and meter no more constricting than any other way of writing poetry, whether in antinarrative fragments, associative glissades, or methods of juxtaposition, collage, and cut-up. In other words, Gunn's alternations between free verse, on the one hand, and rhyme and meter, on the other, correspond to his need for continuities within the freedoms he has chosen and that the social world makes available to him.

In a wider sense, what this means is that Gunn's vision of community through eros, and his attendant, almost Virgilian role of guide and spokesman for that vision, in part determines the poet's faithfulness to language as primarily referential, and therefore social—Gunn, like Virgil, is no symbolist, and if he traffics in allegory, the allegory has a key and definite meaning. So that the community will better understand that meaning, words must be reliable and mean what they refer to; and narrative, too, on the whole, should be a reliable mode of inquiry. Though the experience in "The Geysers" may partake of the visionary, the description throughout, I repeat, is grounded in naturalistic detail. Furthermore, for Gunn, poetic language is what W. H. Auden said it was: "memorable speech";[15] and Gunn's fundamental orientation, in regard to his use of poetic diction, is toward speech as a kind of common civic glue that helps make a community happen, even as it serves as an instrument to explore, criticize, and memorialize it.

Gunn's understanding of speech as both an instrument of inquiry and a form of civic bonding mirrors the typical Gunn persona, one—split between the performing and the observing of actions—that creates the community. As we saw in "The Menace," the observing self watches the participating self play out a drama in which drugs and eros become the agents of paranoid self-confrontation. I see a continuum between this kind of confrontation and how it gets expressed through Gunn's sense of identity as roles to be played through, from the paranoid "the-one-who-wants-to-get-me" to the self anticipating entering into an orgy: "I brace myself, light strong and clear." The observing self watches the participating self feel the need to brace against the risk of merging identities, and also bodies, as the pubescent girls and bearded boys close in on him. But that anxiety is balanced by the speaker's feeling "light strong and clear." These liminal shiftings between sexual creature and intellectualizing watcher, between dreamer and day-to-day doer (what Yeats called "the bundle of accident and incoherence that sits down to breakfast"),[16] parallel the way altered states of consciousness in Gunn's poems can lead to the New Jerusalem of gratified desire, but also to dealers in bathhouses selling drugs with "a business frown." The sexual creature and the dreamer engage ecstasy; and the intellectualizing watcher and the day-to-day doer observe how "the community of the carnal heart" responds to the inexorable forces of money, disease, and the way time itself changes the nature of our desires as we age. But even if we "lose conviction in mid-arc of play," that doesn't negate the vision of the speaker in "The Geysers" who feels "I am part of all." And though the ominousness of "hands take / hands tear and twine" is unmistakable, the act of taking and tearing isn't simply a rending asunder of identity; it's also an acknowledgment of our mutuality: we are all taken and torn by the grip of sexual ecstasy, what Gunn calls "the divine rage."[17]

The experience of this divine rage, as it gets articulated and acted out in our various social roles, and as those roles shape our civic understandings and misunderstandings, is part of the continuum between bodily joy and spiritual insight: the shock of being taken and torn is also part of twining together. And while "business frowns" and dealers are indeed the dominant note of our commercial culture, there are also counter forces at work. The Barracks and its "community of the carnal heart," though it has gone down in ashes, was, nonetheless, as Gunn says in his little essay about the writing of "Saturday Night," "a visionary carnal politics. . . . As hippies were the indirect heirs of the communists between World Wars, so we were the direct heirs of the hippies, drug-visionaries also."[18]

The "we" Gunn refers to as the hippies' direct heirs was the specifically gay male community that Ellen Willis described in a *Village Voice* article in 1989, from which Gunn quotes: "The lesbian movement of the '70s was not primarily about liberating desire . . . but about extending female solidarity; for the gay male community solidarity was, at its core, about desire."[19] The sexual politics of this distinction is a salient one from the point of view of the economic and social inequities that exist between men and women, and if there's any myopia in making desire the core for community solidarity, it's perhaps in the incommensurability of desire from one person to the next. Be that as it may, Gunn's version of those carnal politics, in which sex and drugs and pleasure took on civic meanings, fiercely challenges the prevailing ethos of the officious realtors and dealers who, with their business frowns, only see in a community something to be cleaned up and sold.

I remember the last time I visited Thom at his house on Cole Street. We talked for a long time about how the Haight had changed and was changing ever more rapidly into a well-to-do neighborhood, and about how he himself was changing, taking long naps, finding it difficult to write. And later, when we walked to get lunch, he told me little spicy stories about people whom he knew that certain houses or shops reminded him of, back in the day, before the neighborhood had gone upscale. He was dressed in a black sweatshirt that sported an image of Bluto (Popeye's rival in the Popeye comic strip and cartoons), black motorcycle boots, black jeans, and an earring that gave him an air of piratical suavity and grace. He spoke about how the last time he'd been to a sex club, everybody had been speeding their brains out, and how it hadn't been much fun. But he said it in such a way that you knew that this was all part of the adventure, part of his lifelong romance with experience that would end a few months later with him pronounced dead, according to the autopsy report, from "acute polysubstance abuse." Whatever you make of his death, Thom was a true servant of eros. And in keeping with that devotion, his New Jerusalem was an open one in its generous conviction that the ecstatic could become a communal property, open to anyone, an apocalyptic city of carnal fulfillment and desire, in which his work will forever be one of the cornerstones.

Domains of Ecstasy

DAVID GEWANTER

1. Prelude

How can the body find ecstasy? How can it survive it? For some Romantic poets, moments of bliss may come to a solitary explorer who "wanders lonely as a cloud," then finds a new flower or ocean. Yet the obdurate materials and boundaries of Thom Gunn's urban world resist such moments of sensation and access, and the simple naturalism of first-person change. His boyhood home of postwar London is the gray city of Dickens, not Keats; his second home of San Francisco, though streaked with Ginsberg's hallucinogenic "Blake-light," is still plagued by Blake's "mind-forged manacles" and "harlot's cry."

Wordsworth, "bewildered" and "[d]ragged by a chain of harsh necessity" of betrayal and murder in revolutionary Paris, returned to England's "breast of Nature" still holding "all my resolutions, all my hopes."[1] Thom Gunn's postwar emigration to San Francisco also brought access to a new, naturalistic trust. In the environs of San Francisco, the people of Gunn's poems traveled "darkened stairs" to a place of revelation or love, even as they were relegated, finally, to the delimiting and dispirited "common ground above."[2] Gunn's city-dwellers—men at bars, homeless teens, neighborhood car-freaks, travelers, gym-rats, lovers, and betrayers—seek ways to "stretch the self," and to escape, sometimes briefly, sometimes tragically, the dooms of physical limit, shallow domesticity, social custom, and personal fear. The harsh demands of the city, and of other people, put this explorer in danger; if he grows against them he may sense the lineaments of a new self, and beyond that, a new community. But then, with a kind of impersonal, but gathering vengeance, the central gravities of the mundane world fall upon him. Can he grow, even as he is broken, blunted, or killed off?

In Gunn's early poems, the self's expressions—flesh, vision, speech, imagination—reach outward, hesitantly, through the barricades and armor of its surface. In the 1960s, a willed recklessness of Gunn's poetic forms and of personal experiment begins to puncture and tear at these surfaces. New identities flower and die back into the self, which grows more ample and undefended with each adventure. In Gunn's later poems, the porous body becomes more fully open to passion, impulse, lust, and drug. Yet by now, the body's welcomed hosts—its guests and enemies—have taken up residence in the body's lush and open environs. In late poems such as "Lament," and in the monumental elegies of *The Man with Night Sweats* (1992), Gunn shows an extraordinary mix of frustration, clear sight, and acceptance; this heralds the end of the body's adventure, as it becomes a necropolis.

2. The Armored Body

Gunn's *Collected Poems* (1994) opens with his famous portraiture of postwar fatigue, "The Wound" (1954), where the contours and villages of the mind show marks of battle. The Achillean speaker's self-containment—"I was myself"—allows for Britain's war to be replayed, existentially, in the mind. Yet the mind offers no truce: when the speaker "called for armour," his wound reopened. "Over again / I had to let those storm-lit valleys heal."[3]

The hermetic early verses are admired for their strictures: in disciplined form, in the speaker's realization of his limits, and in the cost of trespassing them. Gunn's second book, *The Sense of Movement* (1957), quotes from Pierre Corneille's heroic boast "Je le suis"—which, in *Cinna,* follows the claim "Je suis maître de moi comme de l'univers." In this second volume of poems, though, a nomadic motorcyclist, however self-mastering, acknowledges that the frontiers of a solitary sense have become a doom: stasis.

> I used to live in sound, and lacked
> Knowledge of still or creeping fact,
> But now the stagnant strips my breath,
> Leant on my cheek in weight of death.[4]

By the end of the poem, the "Unsettled Motorcyclist" must acknowledge a second mastery, one that spins downward from himself. He estimates the gifts that the self-in-motion can offer the grasping, generative world:

Cell after cell the plants convert
My special richness in the dirt:
All that they get, they get by chance.

And multiply in ignorance.[5]

Open movement brings danger and choice; it forces the will either to act or to withhold action. In San Francisco, such new freedoms are first admired from the middle distance. At the provocative-sounding street corner of "Market at Turk," Gunn finds an American Achilles hunched and ready: "he presides in apartness, / not yet knowing his purpose / fully, and fingers the blade."[6] Gunn's early romance with San Francisco is figured in many quick portraits, of muscle contracting the body inward, of the body coiled and protective. At "Taylor Street" a man's "small eyes watch / what he is not living." We gaze upon

his big crumpled
body anxiously cupped
by himself in himself, as
he leans over himself not
over the cold railing.[7]

The streets of Gunn's new city provide a voyeur's "self generated glare," a gallery of still lifes where, it may be, "active love is in the past."[8] Gunn's solitary, existential heroes—such as the protean, difficult "last man" of his long poem, "Misanthropos"—walk through bleak landscapes and lurking menace, but find their measure in the city. The man of "Misanthropos" wears dark glasses as a buffer: "Nobody in the street could / see if my eyes were open"; yet without social recognition he may remain only a "presence without full / being."[9]

From "the streetcorner," Misanthropos asks if he has become "spy or spied on, master / or the world's abject servant?"[10] One answer is embodied nearby, in the "silent garrison" of men loitering in (the poem) "Pierce Street":

They are the soldiers of the imagination
Produced by it to guard it everywhere.
Bodied within
the limits of their station
As, also, I am bodied in my skin.[11]

Our minds and impulses flare out but are held in check by physical determinants: the flesh; our separateness; identity subsumed by one's infinite desires or by another's infinite demands. Then, in mid-1960s San Francisco, Gunn found the means of "raying out from the private"[12] and of discovering "new territories that were being opened up in the mind": LSD. Taking LSD, "trusting Eden in the human," Gunn remembers, was "of the utmost importance to me, both as a man and as a poet": "almost all of the poems" written for *Moly* (1971) "have in some way however indirect to do with it."[13] Gunn describes the acid trip as "unstructured" and "essentially non-verbal": "you hanker after the infinite." Yet even as he tripped in Golden Gate Park or "on rooftops, at beaches, on ranches," and attended "the opera loaded on acid," Gunn needed "to give myself . . . control over the presentation of these experiences, and so could be true to them."

Thus, drawing perhaps from the minimalism of his early poetry, and perhaps from the habits of his English-Scottish family, Gunn found that "[m]etre seemed to be the proper form for the LSD-related poems." The openness of public space; openness of feeling and adventure; a liquid-ease of movement; easy, trusting contact with lovers or strangers—all these infinities were "render[ed] . . . through the finite, the unstructured through the structured."[14]

3. The Puncture

Thus, the voyeur of the book *Moly*, however "[h]ot in his mind," to some extent becomes, rather simplistically, what he glimpses: "Tom watches Dobbin fuck, / Watches, and smiles with pleasure, oh what luck, / He sees beyond, and knows he sees."[15] In this "centaur poem," whose form varies between split pentameters, couplets, blank verse, and free, Tom moves in from the margins and

> plunges into orgy. It moves about
> him in easy eddies, and he enters their mingling
> and branching. He spreads with them, he is veined
> with sunshine.[16]

Desire, experiment, and new lovers stretch Tom beyond his barriers; he grows liquid, arboreal, a centaur. The poem is titled "Tom-Dobbin": "dobbin" is an English term for a real or pantomime horse. Its last stanza eddies in a centrifuge, rhyming ABCCBA, and shows

an unmarked centre
Gradually closing in, until we enter
The haze together—which is me, which him?
Selves floating in the one flesh we are of.[17]

A sweet ending, though awkwardly expressed. In another poem, members of a newly formed "speed-family" swirl in a woodland "Landscape of acid," embracing a Yeatsian dancer: "They raced toward stillness till they overlapped, / Ten energies working inward through the one."[18] A fluid melding of bodies helps to define and express the self:

Though in the river, I abstract
Fence, word, and notion. On the stream at full
A flurry, where the mind rides separate![19]

The hit of drug, the surging lover, the wash of epiphany. Gunn's fantasy, unlike Coleridge's in "Kubla Khan," serves to contain him: "By / means of such promiscuity I can keep myself intact."[20] Yet this generous love may become the domain of bliss: many of *Moly*'s poems drift, immutable and suspended, out of time. Meanwhile, a community of interpenetrating people is forming, one that delights in this transcendent social contract. In his memoir, Gunn finds "no good reason why that hedonistic and communal love of the Geysers [a free-love hot spring north of San Francisco] could not be extended to the working life of the towns." Unless, he admits, that people somehow "must defeat themselves just as they are learning their freedom."[21]

For the poem must end, the world continue, and the laws of consequence, like a mindless twitch, will have us serve out their sentence. A Keatsian "fragrant zone" allows brief enslavement by "La Belle Dame Sans Merci," then relegates the knight-errant to the "cold hill's side." Near San Francisco dwell the "dreamers," their "faces bobbing round me on the heat / green moonlight, smell of dope."[22] But in San Francisco dwell the dealers, murmuring their "Street Song" on Market Street:

My methedrine, my double-sun,
Will give you two lives in your one,
Five days of power before you crash.[23]

Here, time's removals and their human meaning are sometimes articulated (as Keats did) in natural forms. The dealer's coin of bliss is a blasting double-sun; yet with a survivalist's instinct, we set our time according to just one of these suns. The "concentrated fires" of "Sunlight," Gunn observes, "Are slowly dying   the image of persistence / Is an image, only, of our own desires."[24]

Our bodies' bright moment flashes briefly, even as desire, drug, and nature's energy continue. And below this trinity, perhaps, there continue the impoverished forms of the city's social contract—a coin of trust that must be credited on the street, in bars, and in bedrooms. For in the city, the romantic ideals of Rousseau meet an unsentimental education written by Thomas Hobbes. From the gush of *Moly*'s "Geyser," then, we land upon the more finite "The Road Map" in Gunn's next book, *Jack Straw's Castle* (1976):

> Now my mind catches up and looks back.
>
> And wreckages of trust litter the route
> each an offence against me.
> I gaze back
>   in hardened innocence.[25]

The body's trust is broken, marked like a map of neighborhood crimes; yet the speaker does not gaze back in bitterness or retreat. Innocence becomes tense, but so as to endure. Earlier, in *Moly*'s poem "Rites of Passage," new selves had turned fluid; they "break loose" of tensile constraints, then "harden / toward a completion," which is simply named "mine."[26] In Gunn's poems of the 1970s, an identity may brace against new experience, but also tries to maintain its shape and integrity of surface. Will the city allow it? The bad boys of the city, the rogue and romantic transgressors who fascinated Gunn all his life, betray these new communities and the old hippie grace. Meanwhile, they mouth whatever song helps them puncture the barriers, and then escape. In "The Idea of Trust," we meet one such manipulator:

>   he said
> that trust is
> an intimate conspiracy
>
> What did that
> mean? Anyway next day
> he was gone, with

all the money and dope
of the people he'd lived with.[27]

Gunn is intrigued both by the crafty contrarian remark and by the betrayal; his laconic, unsentimental transition—"Anyway"—offers no moral heat. He then imagines the man—identified in the poem and essay as "Pretty Jim"[28]—slyly probing through everyone's private belongings, enjoying his own trickery:

I begin
to understand. I see him
picking through their things
at his leisure, with
a quiet secret smile
choosing and taking,
having first discovered
and set up his phrase to
scramble
that message of
enveloping trust.[29]

This trickster delights in using rhetoric to break down the shield-wall of trust. The new community's embraces have become restrictive and suffocating, perhaps another means of "being trapped in your own skull."[30] Pretty Jim's subversive "counter-poetics" and theft, then, nourish impulse and desire. They grow against the bonds of communal trust. Through betrayal, Gunn supposes, Pretty Jim is "getting / free":

His eyes
are almost transparent.
He has put on
gloves. He fingers
the little privacies of those
who acted as if there
should be no privacy.

They took that
risk.
Wild lilac
chokes the garden.[31]

The community pays for its presumption and daring. The revenge is not cast as Hobbesian civil war but as the natural order of things—more specifically, as nature's fructifying energy as it overwhelms our human designs. This is not an unwelcome defeat.

Gunn's ability to hold and respect competing interests here shows a growth from his advocacy of free-love communities and a recognition perhaps that our wildness and vitality, coursing through the veins of hoodlum and helpmeet, are themselves powered by nature—and that they will, in their demise, supply the raw matter for nature. Against "the water's motion," the lovers' "stringy bodies" can only briefly manage the "full caught pause of their embrace."[32]

Gunn's slowly developed prismatic understanding of the love union and its defeat prepared him, sadly, for the harrowing destruction of his San Francisco community in the AIDS epidemic in the 1980s. His responding poems in the volume *The Man with Night Sweats* (1992) constitute the greatest elegiac sequence since Thomas Hardy's *Poems of 1912–13*. With unblinking clarity and earned wisdom, they show the body's adventure, as it leaves its barricades to find human contact in the city. Grown open and porous to intimate love, the body later provides a new home to a lethal disease, which gains its own kind of health in betraying its host.

4. A Welcoming City

The Man with Night Sweats, who had "Prospered through dreams of heat," must now "Wake up to their residue, / Sweat, and a clinging sheet."[33] As in Gunn's early poem "The Wound," the domains of the body are once again shown as a field of combat, where one must first trust oneself. The man had carried the means to venture out: "My flesh was its own shield: / Where it gashed, it healed."

> I grew as I explored
> The body I could trust
> Even while I adored
> The risk that made robust,
>
> A world of wonders in
> Each challenge to the skin.[34]

In the next poem, the explorer meets two "fiercely attractive men / who want me to stick their needle in my arm."[35] "They tell me they are called Brad and John," Gunn continues flatly, "one from here, one from Denver." The speaker admits,

> I love their daring, their looks, their jargon
> and what they have in mind.
>
> Their mind is the mind of death.
> They know it, and do not know it,
> And they are like me in that
> (I know it, and do not know it)
> and like the flow of people through this bar.

Brad and John "get restless" and "move off into the moving concourse of people" who carry "the news of life and death." The speaker admires them for pushing beyond the body's frame:

> Brad and John thirst heroically together
> for euphoria—for a state of ardent life
> in which we could all stretch ourselves
> and lose our differences.

A seductive ideal. But the flexing body can exceed its limits. As the Man of the title poem understands,

> The given shield was cracked
> My mind reduced to hurry,
> My flesh reduced and wrecked.[36]

Waking from his sweat-soaked bed, he literally catches himself:

> Stopped upright where I am
> Hugging my body to me
> As if to shield it from
> The pains that will go through me,
>
> As if hands were enough
> To hold an avalanche off.

The flow of change, earlier figured in the Geysers and in centripetal dances, now brings Gunn's people to confront a cold, final state. In their last moments, as the virus renders the body open and defenseless to a world of other diseases, they gracefully step back through the stages of personal growth. One man is made mute (though expressive): "He still found breath, and yet / It was an obscure knack," since a breathing tube has "his mouth enclosed / In an astonished O."[37] Another man, near death, visits a feverous friend:

> You climbed in there beside him
> And hugged him plain in view,
> Though you were sick enough,
> And had your own fears too.[38]

And there is yet another man who, "fleshed out again" ten days after his death, "hugged us all round."[39]

But of all the portraitures, Gunn's magnificent elegy "Lament" most fully depicts the way disease flourishes inside the body, so that the dying body, finally, offers it a new and welcoming place. "Your dying," "Lament" begins, "was a difficult enterprise"; the experience is cast not solely as deprivation or loss but as a kind of achievement. The poem refuses its valid rights to moral complaint, to bemoan someone who "falls upon the thorns of life," as Shelley said. Here,

> . . . petty things took up your energies,
> The small but clustering duties of the sick,
> Irritant as the cough's dry rhetoric.[40]

The snap of the couplet, like the foreknowledge of the plot, puts a quiet irony to the man's gathered resolve:

> In hope still, courteous still, but tired and thin,
> You tried to stay the man that you had been,
> Treating each symptom as a mere mishap
> Without import. But then the spinal tap.

With this puncture, the man leaves "the normal pleasures of the sun's kingdom"; his failing body begins to give his disease a new vitality:

> No respite followed: though the nightmare ceased,
> Your cough grew thick and rich, its strength increased.

His death-shape begins to reveal itself: in his cheek "appeared the true shape of your bone / No longer padded" by healthy flesh.[41] "Still hungry for the great world" he is losing to death, he faces the enterprise of dying by attempting to "make of it a life." To make a life of your dying is, truly, to achieve a kind of ecstasy; however, it does not create a second, mirroring self. Other things take over. His body's previous health had impeded the functioning of the machines attached to him:

> Meanwhile
> Your lungs collapsed, and the machine, unstrained,
> Did all your breathing now. Nothing remained
> But death by drowning on an inland sea
> Of your own fluids.[42]

In this ecstasy, the body becomes a home and garden-soil courteously welcoming the virus, which now continues life in a new domain—the body's necropolis. After the attractions, after the trust, the commingling, the breakthroughs: a person becomes a place, a city of the dead.

> You never thought your body was attractive,
> Though others did, and yet you trusted it
> And must have loved its fickleness a bit
> Since it was yours and gave you what it could
> Till near the end it let you down for good,
> Its blood hospitable to those guests who
> Took over by betraying it into
> The greatest of its inconsistencies
> This difficult, tedious, painful enterprise.[43]

Though the arc traveled by Gunn's adventurers—discovery; contact and conflict; and lethal resolution—accords with romanticist stories of the rebel, who finds voice in an isolate *cri du coeur,* Gunn's works turn from both the poetics of confession and the outsized claims of American individualism. Instead, they coolly appraise the enterprise and outcomes of these outcast-heroes and establish a kind of *locus aemenis*—a domain of ecstasy, brief safety, and transformative death—for those who will not or cannot swim the mainstream.

Thus, Gunn's achievement in lyric poetry offers an alternative to what may be called a poetics of bliss, as found in Coleridge's "Kubla Khan,"

Yeats's "Among School Children," or even Elizabeth Bishop's "At the Fishhouses." Though poetic bliss (and its shadows, voyeurism and pornography) is difficult to define, we know it when we feel it—in its registry of intense, internal feeling, one that survives its causes. A romantic singer may depict this feeling as a private and inward experience, a moment out of Frank Sinatra, "only for the lonely"—or as Wordsworth, returned to the "breast of Nature," admitted in the *Prelude:* a way to become "A Poet only to myself, to men / Useless."[44] The asocial quality of ecstatic experience pushes us toward self-reflection, a second self. Rather than discovering a new frontier, our vision can prompt a solipsistic doubling, a triumph of self-regard. But Gunn's explorations, his ecstasies, betrayals, and broken finales all draw their energy, and agency, from the social.

In postwar America, other poets of Gunn's generation sought bliss in drug, drink, and flesh; but whether through Ginsberg's "Blake-light tragedies" or Robert Lowell's dramas of mania and incarceration, they put the primacy of individual vision before such stable observations of the social world as Gunn's unfevered and unsentimental poetry shows. His work provides, then, a brave alternative to some of twentieth-century poetry's muddy experiments in "personhood."

The punctured self finds access to bliss; the world in turn demands its pound of flesh. Many lyrics use hit-and-run tactics—the quick sketch of personal experience, a flutter of thoughtful-sounding phrases, paper-boat images—to defer this Faustian burden. Gunn's late poetry, by observing our demise and derangements from the inside and outside, by seeing us as both person and place, more fully keeps the contract.[45]

Considering "Considering the Snail"

PAUL MULDOON

"Considering the Snail"[1] was one of the first poems by a contemporary poet I read in my high school, in or around 1967, not that I knew when I first read it that it had been written by Thom Gunn. It had been given to us by our teacher Jerry Hicks by way of preparation for that section of the A-level examination in English, in which one was faced with a piece of writing by an anonymous author and had to respond to it as best one could. It was, in other words, a life lesson.

Much of the impact of the poem, which had been collected only five or six years earlier in 1961's *My Sad Captains,* would have been construable even to the sixteen-year-old boy I then was. Hicks had taught us, in the best Leavisite tradition, to try to bring the text under the kind of scrutiny under which the snail itself was about to be brought. I would almost certainly have recognized something of the resonance of that first word in the title of the poem, the definition of "consider" in the *Oxford English Dictionary* being "to view or contemplate attentively, to survey, examine, inspect, scrutinize."[2] I would have recognized, in the best Leavisite tradition, that there were echoes already of the phrase "*consider* the lilies of the field"[3] from Matthew 6:28, particularly when the fact that they "toil not" is immediately set against the laborious movement of a snail that "pushes through." I would have recognized the echo of Milton's "On His Blindness":

When I *consider* how my life is spent,
Ere half my days, in this dark world and wide,
And that one Talent which is death to hide,
Lodg'd with me useless . . .[4]

The "dark world" of Milton is carried over into the world of the snail, "where rain / has *darkened* the earth's *dark,*" while one meaning of "lodg'd" is "to throw down on the ground, lay flat,"[5] a description of rain- and wind-beaten crops that is picked up in the fact that the "grass is heavy / with water." The snail, meanwhile, is notable for its own poor sight, a fact that is reflected, say, in Marianne Moore's focus on "the curious phenomenon of your occipital horn" in her address "To a Snail." I'll come back to Marianne Moore a little later. Let me continue to consider the "consider" in the title of Thom Gunn's poem, summoning up as it does another famous animal poem, Christopher Smart's "Jubilate Agno," with its litany of reasons why its speaker might announce, "For I will *consider* my cat Jeoffrey." There's another Geoffrey lurking in the title, by the way, *Geoffrey* Hill, whose "Merlin" was collected in his 1959 volume *For the Unfallen:*

> I will *consider* the outnumbering dead:
> For they are the husks of what was rich seed.
> Now, should they come together to be fed,
> They would outstrip the locusts' covering tide.
>
> Arthur, Elaine, Mordred; they are all gone
> Among the raftered galleries of bone.
> By the long barrows of Logres they are made one,
> And over their city stands the pinnacled corn.[6]

It seems that something of this system of imagery, of the "galleries" and "long barrows" and the corn that stands "over," has been taken over by Gunn in his vision of the grass that "meets over / the bright path he makes" and "the blades above / the tunnel" through which the snail pushes.

Now, this would be an appropriate moment at which to remind oneself that the title of this poem is no longer "Consider the Snail" but "Consider*ing* the Snail." I say "no longer" because it turns out that, for most of its earlier drafts, the title was indeed "Consider the Snail."[7] The strongest argument for that change of title may have been the downplaying of the very associations I've just listed, so weighty a cargo might they seem to be for such a comparatively frail vessel. The definition of the gerundival "considering" as "taking into account, having regard to, in view of"[8] suggests both a longer drawn-out process and the drawing of a conclusion, an action upon which further action might be based. This reading also begins to take into consideration the meaning of "consideration" as "regard for the circumstances, feelings, comfort etc. of another; thoughtfulness for another; thoughtful kindness,"[9] which, again, suggests a response of an emotional, perhaps even ethical, kind. The musing of the speaker of "Considering the Snail" turns into a moralizing method. Something of this resonance may be traced back to the root of "consider" in the Latin verb *considerare,* that *sidus* referring specifically to a "star or constellation," which, according to the *OED,* "might thus be originally a term of astrology or augury."[10] Those stars show up in the title poem of *My Sad Captains* ("who turn with disinterested / hard energy, like the *stars*") as well as "Blackie, the Electric Rembrandt," the poem immediately following "Considering the Snail" in the collection:

> We watch through the shop-front while
> Blackie draws stars—an equal
>
> concentration on his and
> the youngster's faces. The hand
>
> is steady and accurate;
> but the boy does not see it
>
> for his eyes follow the point
> that touches (quick, dark movement!)
>
> a virginal arm beneath
> his rolled sleeve: he holds his breath.[11]

"Blackie, the Electric Rembrandt" mimes something of the action and something of the vocabulary ("concentration," "touches," "movement," "dark") of Ted Hughes's celebrated poem "The Thought-Fox," collected in *The Hawk in the Rain* (1957), Hughes's concluding image of "the page is printed" given a little twist by Gunn, in which the "virginal arm" is somehow "printed":

> . . . Now that it is finished, he
> hands a few bills to Blackie
>
> and leaves with a bandage on
> his arm, under which gleam ten

stars, hanging in a blue thick
cluster. Now he is starlike.[12]

The couplets of "Blackie, the Electric Rembrandt" allow the reader to fairly readily take in the light, but legible, rhymes on "he" / "Blackie," "on" / "ten", and "thick" / "starlike." Were it not for the contextualization of "Considering the Snail" among other so lightly rhymed poems one might miss its own stanzaic rhyme scheme of ABCABC in "green" / "heavy" / "over" / "rain" / "he" / "desire." This is a far cry from the full-throated rhymes of a poem like "The Byrnies" in the first part of *My Sad Captains:*

  Thus for each blunt-faced ignorant one
The great grey rigid uniform combined
  Safety with virtue of the sun.
Thus concepts linked like chainmail in the mind.

  Reminded, by the grinding sound,
Of what they sought, and partly understood,
  They paused upon the open ground,
A little group above the foreign wood.[13]

The setting of the "rigid" byrnies against the "open ground" might be said to be a drawing up of battle lines between the traditional formalism that characterized Gunn's first two books, *Fighting Terms* (1954) and *The Sense of Movement* (1957), and the new rhymed seven-syllable line that was coming more and more to the fore, between the "deliberate progress" and "slow passion" exhibited by the snail itself. It had been a combination of a somewhat fuller rhyme and six-syllable line that was evident in a related poem published in 1928, the year before Gunn was born, entitled "Slug in Woods":

For eyes he waves greentipped
taut horns of slime They dipped
hours back   across a reef
a salmonberry leaf[14]

This poem, complete with its Anglo-Saxon fire-break in the middle of the line, was written by Earle Birney, the Canadian poet's name a homophone of the word for "a cuirass, corslet, coat of mail"[15] we met earlier in "The Byrnies." I propose, in my predictable way, that Gunn is carrying over a sense of Birney's name into the title of that poem, one of the first he wrote after beginning to teach at the University of California, Berkeley, in 1958, the Berkeley where Birney had himself been a student thirty years earlier, just as he's carrying over something of the snail-like slug to the sluglike snail:

> What is a snail's fury? All
> I think is that if later
>
> I parted the blades above
> the tunnel and saw the thin
> trail of broken white across
> litter, I would never have
> imagined the slow passion
> to that deliberate progress.[16]

An earlier version of these lines reads:

> All I can say is that when some
>
> human lover parts the blades above
> your tunnel . . .[17]

These lines are from a manuscript of "Considering the Snail" held at the University of Maryland, and they introduce us to a character who doesn't quite make it into the published poem. The "human lover" is implied, perhaps, as she or he might be in a poem by Marianne Moore, a poet whose conflation of the amorous and the armory is carried over by Gunn no less evidently into the "chainmail" of "The Byrnies" than is her trademark combination of syllabics and slight, slant or—imagine it—*silent* rhymes into "Considering the Snail." The idea in Earle Birney's poem that the snail is "himself his viscid wife" is evident in Gunn's representation of the erotics of the seemingly erratic, the "foreign wood" at the end of "The Byrnies" turning out to be "a *wood* of desire." The description of the snail as being "drenched there / with purpose" is somewhat contextualized by a phrase in "Adolescence," also from *My Sad Captains:*

> I pass foundations of houses,
> walking through the wet spring, my knees

> *drenched from high grass* charged with water,
> and am part, still, of the done war.[18]

A poet whose very name might be read as a near version of Thom(p)son (submachine) Gun(n)—he was christened only one year after the famous model of 1928—might think of himself as being "part, still, of the done war" in a very particular sense, of course, but this war is also a form of sexual combat, Gunn's heroes and sad captains in the military sense, their trenches and tunnels transmogrifying into *The Passages of Joy,* the title of his 1982 collection, which includes "The Miracle":

> "Right to the end, that man, he was so hot
> That driving to the airport we stopped off
> At some McDonald's and do you know what,
> We did it there. He couldn't get enough."
> —"There at the counter?"—"No, that's public stuff."[19]

Here Gunn's combination of strict rhymes and iambic pentameter with the most prosaic matter is quite masterful, taking as it does an unexpected turn:

> "Then suddenly he dropped down on one knee
> Right by the urinal in his only suit
> And let it fly, saying Keep it there for me,
> And smiling up. I can still see him shoot.
> Look at that snail-track on the toe of my boot."

It's as if the five-line ballad form were fused with bathhouse, Gunn's beloved Thomas Hardy with hard-core. The clever enjambment on "knee," where the leg (*jambe*) is literally bent, echoes the "*knees* / drenched from high grass" in "Adolescence," while the "snail-track" would have forced both Jerry Hicks and perhaps even my adolescent self to revisit the ramifications of the image in "Considering the Snail" of what appeared in early manuscripts of the poem as "a broken / trace of white"[20] but became "the thin / trail of broken white" in the final version as a description of ejaculate. Some readers might be tempted to read the "white" as a version of Tony *White,* the name of Gunn's fellow Cambridge undergraduate who does indeed appear as late as in "A Waking Dream" in *The Passages of Joy* and to whom Gunn uselessly calls out "Tony." "Talbot Road," meanwhile, also collected in *The Passages of Joy,* is written "in memory of Tony White":

He wondered aloud if he would be happier
if he were queer like me.
How could he want, I wondered,
to be anything but himself?[21]

Tony White is also associated with the "viscid" and "boots" in "Innocence," the poem from *My Sad Captains* dedicated to him:

When he stood near the Russian partisan
Being burned alive, he therefore could behold
The ribs wear gently through the darkening skin
And sicken only at the Northern cold,

Could watch the fat burn with a violent flame
And feel disgusted only at the smell,
And judge that all pain finishes the same
As melting quietly by his *boots* it fell.[22]

We may fast-forward from the jell on the "boots" in "Innocence" to the jism on the "boot" in "A Waking Dream," taking time to pause only at "Considering the Snail" itself, thereby gaining a sense of the continuity of Gunn's sense of the sacred in what's secreted from the body. I must have had some, very partial, sense of this as I read "Considering the Snail" in 1967, particularly since in the following year I wrote a poem rather blatantly entitled "Snail":

I guessed the letter must be yours.
I recognized the cuttle ink,
The serif on the P.
I read the postmark and the date.
I would not open it just yet,
Impatience clamped beneath a paperweight.
I took your letter at eleven
To the garden with my tea.
And suddenly the yellow gum
Secreted halfway up a damson bush
Had grown a shell.
I let the folded pages fall
And took a stick to break its hold.
I turned it over through the grass
To watch your mouth withdraw.

This poem, a version of which I almost certainly presented at my first reading in Dublin in the very early 1970s (with, as it happens, the aforementioned Earle Birney), is no less influenced by or indebted to "Considering the Snail" than is "The Miracle," which ends with an extraordinarily charged image of renewal, perhaps even the endless renewal of which a poem, like love—perhaps even love for the unsounded "White" in the litany of "night" and "sight" and "right"—is capable as it lingers over and wonders at the connection it has just made:

> —"Snail-track?"—"Yes, there."—"That was six months ago.
> How can it still be there?"—"My friend, at night
> I make it shine again, I love him so,
> Like they renew a saint's blood out of sight.
> But we're not Catholic, see, so it's all right."[23]

Thom Gunn's "Duncan"

WENDY LESSER

Perhaps one of the many reasons I love this poem is that I was present at the final moments of its gestation: I actually saw it in embryo, just before its birth.

And yet pregnancy seems precisely the wrong metaphor to use for Thom Gunn's writing process. He was always the most masculine of men. There was nothing "sissy" about his homosexuality, as he might have put it—no desire to imitate the female of the species, no particular bond with the feminine. This had its virtues but also its disadvantages. Of all the poets I have known, he was perhaps the least introspective. (That could have been due to his Englishness, of course, as well as his boyishness—and also to the horror of his adolescence, by which I mean his beloved mother's suicide.) Thom was a great one for keeping things bottled up or tamped down. He was resolutely chipper even in the face of darkness, and he chose, at least in my presence, to skate across the surfaces of things, allowing all the scary stuff to proceed elsewhere, frozen fathoms below.

But he did, that one time, show me a poem before it was completely finished. I was always hounding him for new work to publish in *The Threepenny Review*—not that I had to hound very hard: he would as easily give a new poem to me as to the *New Yorker* or the *TLS*, since he had very little regard for either status or money and a great regard for friendship and loyalty. This time, after one of our intermittent lunches at Zazie's or wherever it was we were meeting for lunch in the late 1980s, he invited me back to his house to look at the manuscript of a poem he described as nearly done. I say "manuscript," but of course I mean typescript: everyone who knew Thom knew the squarish face of his old manual typewriter almost as well as we knew the tiny italic-cursive of his handwriting.

And in fact both were in evidence here, for the typescript of the nearly finished "Duncan"—a poem, it turned out, about his friend and fellow poet Robert Duncan, who had died earlier that year—was marked in a few places with his handwritten emendations. But those were not what he wanted my opinion on.

"It's this last line," he said. "I can't decide whether it should be 'unchanging night' or 'changeless night.'" That, at least, is what my memory tells me he said. But now, rereading the poem, I see that it must have been "*a* changeless night" or "*the* changeless night"; otherwise the line wouldn't have scanned. No matter: the verdict was for "unchanging." His verdict, I am pretty sure—I can't imagine I would have had the nerve to express a definite preference, since I am not and have never been a poet. And even if I did venture an opinion, Thom would surely have been sensible enough to follow his own better judgment if it differed from mine. It's odd, though, that I can't remember my answer. All I remember is the thrill of being asked.

Just before the final line of Thom's poem, with its possibly changeable last words about unchanging night, came a series of lines referring to a bird's flight under a long roof, over a table filled with feasting friends. "Do you know that passage from the Venerable Bede?" he said to me. "About the sparrow flying through the banquet hall?" I did not, until he told me; but like all Thom's allusions, this one could be picked up or let alone without any serious alteration to the poem. When he gave readings, he would explain to the audiences whatever he felt they needed to know to understand the reference, whether it was to a Greek myth or a piece of rock music history or an obscure geographical location in California. It was nice to know these things, but it was not essential. I always felt the explanations were mainly his way of getting from one poem to the next without seeming nervous or artificial or abrupt. They weren't *just* this, though, or he wouldn't have bothered to include some of them as endnotes in his printed books. To his poem, for instance, about Sid Vicious's murder of his girlfriend—the one that ends "Poor girl, poor girl, what was your name?"—he appended the note "Her name was Nancy Spungen."

The specificity of the dead was very important to Thom, and this is why he was a great poet about death. Death, as he knew, is not an impersonal entity that exists in the world, like air or dirt, but a very particular experience that happens to each person in a different way. One does not get used to it. One does not get over it. It is always a shock, even when it is expected. "Lament" may be his greatest poem in this vein, but "Duncan" is surely one of the runner-ups, and they share a number of qualities, including the strictness of their rhyme schemes and their casual use of medical phrases like "home dialysis." (His rhyme for that, in "Duncan," is "his responsiveness.") I know Thom would be annoyed at me for using words like *great* and *greatness* in conjunction with his poetry—he was very cutting about such terminology, particularly in his early satire of Stephen Spender's "I think continually of those who were truly great"—but I can't help it. At Thom's memorial service, Jim Powell, searching for consolation, suggested that we who survived Thom were the first generation to see the work whole, as a completed body of writing. This is true, and what I see, more and more as time goes by, is its greatness.

"Duncan" is of course about many things other than death. Since it is about a poet who was a good friend of Thom's, it is also about poetry, and about friendship, and even a little about Thom.

> Down Wheeler steps, he faltered and he fell
> —Fell he said later, as if I stood ready,
> "Into the strong arms of Thom Gunn."
> Well well,
> The image comic, as I might have known,
> And generous, but it turns things round to myth:
> He fell across the wide steps there alone,
> Though it was me indeed that he was with.
>
> I hadn't caught him, hadn't seen in time,
> And picked him up where he had softly dropped,
> A pillow full of feathers . . .[1]

This must be one of the few places in all of Thom Gunn's poetry where he makes an appearance by name, and under his full name at that. Turned into an almost imaginary figure by Robert Duncan's subsequent retelling of the fall, Thom can for once see himself from the outside, as a person whom others might love and depend on—though he undercuts any potential sentimentality or self-glorification both by blaming himself ("I hadn't caught him, hadn't seen in time") and by exhibiting his trademark clarity of vision, his childlike capacity for cold truth ("A pillow full of feathers"). He attributes the "generous" behavior to Duncan, but it is Thom's generosity I hear in these lines. I also hear his voice, particularly in that "Well well"—not that he would have used such a phrase in conversation, necessarily, but I can still recall the intonation he gave those two words whenever he read the poem aloud. *Self-deprecating* does not begin to cover it.

Besides being about a particular person, the poem is also about a very specific place at a specific point in time. Or rather, two points in time: first, the moment—a very extended moment—at which Robert Duncan discovered his poetic talent—

> When in his twenties a poetry's full strength
> Burst into voice as an unstopping flood,
> He let the divine prompting (come at length)
> Rushingly bear him any way it would
> And went on writing while the Ferry turned
> From San Francisco, back from Berkeley too,
> And back again, and back again. He learned
> You add to, you don't cancel what you do.[2]

—and second, the much later period—"[f]orty years later," as the poem precisely tells us—when the terminally ill Duncan gave his final reading at Berkeley and fell down Wheeler steps. (There is also an implied third period, which follows shortly on the second one: the period during which the poem was actually written, sometime after Duncan's death in February of 1988 and before the end of that year, when Thom first showed it to me.)

In the forty years that separated the events in sections one and two, the ferry that Duncan rode in his youth had ceased to run between San Francisco and Berkeley, as Thom, an inveterate taker of public transportation, would have known. He doesn't mention this in the poem, but the disjunction is an important part of his period portrait, as is the fact that the Berkeley English Department, where Thom taught for many decades, was and still is located in Wheeler Hall. Thom was the kind of writer who particularly valued in other writers their connection to the details of time and place. As he said in his deeply appreciative essay about Christopher Isherwood's novels, "It is surely of permanent interest that reading them we may imagine exactly what it was like to live in the Berlin of the early 1930s or the Los Angeles of the early 1960s."[3] Thom's poems do much the same thing for the Bay Area of the 1950s through the 1990s, and the achievement is all the more surprising in that most other poets of that period did not see themselves as having this recording function.

We do not glimpse much of the new millennium in Thom's work, though he didn't die until 2004. By that time he too had, in a way, become the kind of "posthumous poet" he saw in Duncan:

> He was now a posthumous poet, I have said
> (For since his illness he had not composed),
> In sight of a conclusion, whose great dread
> Was closure,
> his life to be enclosed
> Like the sparrow's flight above the feasting friends,
> Briefly revealed where its breast caught their light,
> Beneath the long roof, between open ends,
> Themselves the margins of unchanging night.[4]

I cannot read these last lines of the poem without, now, applying them in part to Thom himself. He did not die of an illness like Robert Duncan's kidney disease, and he did not kill himself overtly, as his mother had. But he did allow himself, in his midseventies, to drift into a situation where dying was one of the likely risks. His death, the medical examiners said, was due to drugs, and in his last few months he had been taking a lot of speed—a dangerous load even for a much younger heart. I think he died in part from boredom. He was no longer teaching (he had finally retired from the university a year or two before), and he found himself unable to produce any poems. "I'm not writing," he would mention frequently, even if you didn't ask, and though he never seemed to be complaining about it, it was clear that the inability tortured him. He did not live only to write poems—Thom had always lived mainly to *live*—but when it turned out that he could no longer write them, something essential went missing from his life.

But even before that last long drought, when no poetry would come to him for months or even years, he had been through phases that other poets would have called writer's block—periods that even he, when they were over, would describe in this way. So when he wrote about Robert Duncan's inability to write poems, it was not just a prescient forecast; he was bringing to bear on Duncan's situation his own very specific memories of the same problem. As he pointed out to me more than once, you never knew which blockage would be the last one—that is, you never knew, until it was over, whether any of these painful periods of non-writing would end before you died. Thom felt that his own blocks often coincided with the publication of a book, and so he got in the habit, later in his life, of finishing the next book of poems before he would allow the last one to be published. Even this strategy, though, faltered toward the end: he had almost nothing up his sleeve when *Boss Cupid* came out in 2000, and the poems he finished after that can be counted on the fingers of one hand.

Unlike Duncan, Thom did not "dread" closure. He had taken its measure, and it had become familiar to him. At an early age, he grew far more intimate with the closure that is death than anyone would willingly choose to be. On top of his mother's suicide, there was the sudden death of one of his dearest college friends, Tony White, in a freak accident during their twenties; and then there were all those later, much more numerous deaths caused by AIDS, of which he became the chronicler. But closure of a different sort was also something Thom sought out and felt comfortable with—I mean the closure of formal structures in his poetry, and of domestic patterns and habits in his daily life. Such patterns reassured him with their repetitions and their predictabilities. Thom valued openness enormously, and he strove for it, in his life and in his work, but his natural tendency was toward something much harder and firmer and more self-contained, and it was this combination, of the desired improvisatory openness with the underlying dependence on structure, that made both his personality and his poetry so interestingly and appealingly contradictory.

Robert Duncan, on the other hand, was notable for his openness as a poet. In contrast to Thom, who favored set measures and older forms, Duncan worked mainly in an expansive free verse. But he was a rigorous poet and an extremely knowledgeable one, and Thom admired him hugely. Their shared homosexuality, in a San Francisco that had made them feel welcome, was also a bond, though each had a different relationship to gayness. For Duncan, it offered the possibility of a fey flirtatiousness, a chance to mimic femininity ("in which he might adopt / The role of H.D.," as Thom says in "Duncan"), whereas Thom, a decade younger, came from the generation that adopted leather and motorcycles and Marlon Brando. Hence the inside joke—the mutually approved, mutually reinforcing story, told by Robert Duncan when he was alive and then by Thom after his death—contained in the lines about Duncan's falling into "the strong arms of Thom Gunn." But it is much more than a joke, because the poem itself has now become the strong arms in which the memory of Duncan lies, the structure that encloses his once unenclosable self.

Thom is very aware of this, and he ventures into this violation of Duncan's essence (if it is indeed a violation) with his characteristic delicacy and respect. I have said that Thom was the least introspective poet I ever knew, but I was referring to the man only; the poet, in his poems, knew everything that mattered about himself in relation to other people. In this poem, he brings to bear his own poetic personality on Duncan's and asks us to consider them side by side, in a way that is neither churlish nor self-serving nor falsely modest nor smarmily worshipful. It is a very difficult thing to pull off, this giving full due to a poetic talent completely unlike one's own, but Thom manages it here, and we are left with a heightened sense of both men's talents and virtues. To encase the late Robert Duncan in strongly metered, rhymed verse could easily have seemed a somewhat hostile act, but in Thom's hands the gesture is both a tribute and an acknowledgment of his own limits ("limits" being a Gunn sort of thing and not at all a Duncan sort of thing). There is something tender in the gesture, too, as if Thom were composing a lullaby with which to sing Duncan into that unchanging night.

If there are limits in this poem, there are also, very pointedly, margins. The "margins of unchanging night" in the last line echo the margins of Duncan's own writing, as Thom had described it in the second stanza:

> Between the notebook-margins his pen travelled,
> His own lines carrying him in a new mode
> To ports in which past purposes unravelled.
> So that, as on the Ferry Line he rode,
> Whatever his first plans that night had been,
> The energy that rose from their confusion
> Became the changing passage lived within
> While the pen wrote, and looked beyond conclusion.[5]

But now, in the last stanza, Duncan is "in sight of a conclusion." Thom's feeling of sympathy with him is so powerful that he breaks his own line in the middle—

> was closure,
>   his life to be enclosed

—as if to give Duncan a little escape hatch, a space between. And then he gives him another gift, the best he has to offer, in the last four lines about the sparrow's flight.

I had never, until I sat down to write this essay, looked up the reference in the Venerable Bede. (In fact, I hadn't even correctly remembered the authorship as Bede's: my mistaken memory was that it was St. Augustine, and my more scholarly friends had to set me straight.) But now I did look it up, and learned that the original passage was both strikingly like Thom's use of it and yet crucially unlike it. The analogy between the brevity of life and the quick flight of the sparrow is there in the original; so are the feasting friends and the open-ended banquet hall. But the Bede version, which is meant as an argument in favor of Christianity, emphasizes the coldness and wetness of the wintry night outside, and the pitifulness of the sparrow's fate—in other words, "See how brief this pleasant life is, compared to the discomfort of all eternity? If you want to come in out of the cold permanently, you must embrace God."

Thom's version is much more complicated, much less pointed. There is no sense, in his rendering of the story, that the sparrow is any happier indoors than out. It is just passing through. "Briefly revealed where its breast caught their light": this image is Thom's alone, and it somehow transfers the pathos and the longing from the bird itself to the men down below. There is something wonderful and moving and free about Thom's sparrow, flying "between open ends" like Duncan's pen flying across the page on the ferry—and then he is out, into "the margins of unchanging night," as if he has flown off the page and out of the poem.

If this were a seventeenth-century metaphysical poem of the sort Thom much admired, the analogy between the two kinds of margins would be exact, like a pair of compasses, and tight logic would prevail over wild improvisation. But Thom, in paying this final tribute to Robert Duncan, has let in some of the fruitful "confusion" that gave Duncan's own work such energy, and so the reappearance of the word *margins* is also a transformation of the very idea. It is not just that the margins have changed their color (from the white of paper to the black of night) and their geometry (from the two dimensions of a notebook to the three dimensions of a building); it's that the margin itself has become permeable. Something that cannot be breached by writing itself—that is, the space on either side of the written or printed line, which is by definition its edge, its limit—is broken by that sparrow's flight. So the closure that Thom Gunn has imposed on "Duncan" the poem, with those resounding end-rhymes of *friends* and *ends, light* and *night,* is at the same time a movement toward openness, a freeing gesture that Duncan the man would no doubt have appreciated.

And whereas Bede's version of the story is a markedly Christian one, Thom's is that of an agnostic—or, better yet, a Lucretian, for whom the darkness that precedes life is no different from the "unchanging" darkness that follows it. This may be cold comfort for those of us left behind, but that in no way diminishes the idea's beauty, nor its truth.

Coda:
Thom Gunn, Inside and Outside

ROBERT PINSKY

Donald Davie, an old friend and longtime admirer of Thom Gunn, once described Thom as being at his core, under the sometimes wild exterior, "the sensible Englishman with his pipe."

Davie, himself a frequently sensible Englishman (and yes, sometimes with a pipe), knew what he was talking about. However, the proposition is reversible: sure, Thom the drug-taking, club-cruising leather-boy kept, under that surface, his center of shrewd, conservative good judgment and fine, traditional good manners. But it is equally true that under the surface of an earnest, conscientious, and polite university instructor, or an astute literary man, Thom kept his center of wild recklessness. Neither set of qualities was merely affected—just as both were genuinely visible and exterior, both were profoundly interior.

Inside and outside, prudent and crazy—this doubleness is more than a matter of personality, and beyond gossip, more than simply psychological or social: because as an artist, too, Thom Gunn is all-of-the-above. To see only the meticulous prosody or only the flamboyant sexuality, only the scholarship or only the hedonism, only England or San Francisco, only literature or only gay life—or to see only stereotypes of these categories—is to misperceive Gunn's genius.

The doubleness is more interesting, more organic, than a simple contrast between form and material. It has been often noted that *Moly* is a learned book in rhyme and meter about the experience of LSD, but the dualities go far deeper than that. Oedipal father and son, man and beast, transformed and the same—in a Gunn poem, with each situation, each character, the sympathy or one-ness prevails over polarities of judgment or detachment. His kind of poetic immediacy, a negative capability of the psyche, accords with the notion that in dreams the dreamer is every character, the reborn and the old, the son and the father, Greytop and horned one, the first person and the other person:

Rites of Passage

Something is taking place.
Horns bud bright in my hair.
My feet are turning hoof.
And Father, see my face
—Skin that was damp and fair
Is barklike and, feel, rough.

See Greytop how I shine.
I rear, break loose, I neigh
Snuffing the air, and harden
Toward a completion, mine.
And next I make my way
Adventuring through your garden.

My play is earnest now.
I canter to and fro.
My blood, it is like light.
Behind an almond bough,
Horns gaudy with its snow,
I wait live, out of sight.

All planned before my birth
For you, Old Man, no other,
Whom your groin's trembling warns.
I stamp upon the earth
A message to my mother.
And then I lower my horns.[1]

This sexual and myth-ridden imagining, alert to all sides and all directions, has a mild, social counterpart in my memory of Thom Gunn's conversation. A funny, alert disher and observer of personality, he also had a deep, not perfunctory need to correct what he said about others with a balancing declaration of his own imperfections. If it was some professor's tedious mannerisms, after dissecting them Thom needed to observe with a grin that his own mannerisms probably annoyed the scholar equally.

This quality, distinct in his art and his conversation, reminds me of the epigraph Thom chose for the second part of *Jack Straw's Castle,* from Dickens:

> . . . and when he pictured in his mind the ugly chamber, false and quiet, false and quiet through the dark hours of two nights, and the tumbled bed, and he not in it, though believed to be, he became in a manner his own ghost and phantom, and was at once the haunting spirit and the haunted man.
>
> —*Martin Chuzzlewit*

The poems of the section that follow are all explicitly about sex, sometimes in detail. Few poets have attended so carefully to the sensations involved in fucking, and few have so consistently put that experience into its social context.

Sometimes, it is even a historical context, apparently. But context is not as accurate as simultaneity; this is equally Rome and California, as it is equally objective and inside a skull:

Saturnalia

The time of year comes
round, the campagna
is stone and grey stalk

Once again outlaws
in majority, the throng
bursts from street to
street
          one body
no longer creeping through
a conduit of mossed stone
or marble it is a
muscled flood, still
rising still reshaping

licence awakes us

finding our likeness in
being bare, we

have thrown off
the variegated stuffs that
distinguished us one from
one
      here in orgy
a Laocoön of twined
limbs, in open
incest reaching through to
ourselves in others

beloved flesh
the whole body pulses
like an erection, blood
in the head and furious
with tenderness
                  the senses
mingle, before returning
sharpened to their homes,
they roam at play through
each organ as if
each were
            equally
a zone of Eros[2]

This poem is interior thought and exterior behavior; it throws off "the variegated stuffs that / distinguished us one from / one"; and at the end it lets a synesthesia of orgasm metaphorically describe—and be described by—good citizens returning to their separate houses refreshed by the experience of communal orgy. The blended senses and the mass-coupled citizens are metaphors for one another.

This many-mindedness in Gunn's work rises above attempts to put him in one category or another. His gaze is more clear than those sentimental about the streets would like, and more generous than judgmental souls would like. Meticulously, always, he reserves scorn for himself only, while seeing others clearly but without facile superiority. Nor has any writer been less of a show-off about his capacities for sympathy. He observes this life of another by giving it a thorough, and thoroughly quiet, investment of imagination, tucking the word "ungiving" into the poem like a joke on itself:

Improvisation

I said our lives are improvisation and it sounded
un-rigid, liberal, in short a good idea.
But that kind of thing is hard to keep up:
guilty lest I gave to the good-looking only
I decided to hand him a quarter
whenever I saw him—what an ugly young man:
wide face, round cracked lips, big forehead
striped with greasy hairs. One day he said
"You always come through" and I do, I did,
except that time he was having a tantrum
hitting a woman, everyone moving away,
I pretending not to see, ashamed.
Mostly
he perches on the ungiving sidewalk, shits
behind bushes in the park, seldom weeps,
sleeps bandaged against the cold, curled
on himself like a wild creature,
his agility of mind wholly employed
with scrounging for cigarettes, drugs, drink
or the price of Ding Dongs, with dodging knife-fights,
with ducking cops and lunatics, his existence
paved with specifics like an Imagist epic,
the only discourse printed on shreds of newspaper,
not one of which carries the word improvisation.[3]

The poet's criticism of his own glibness on the final word is not perfunctory nor rhetorical: it is thoroughgoing, with a merciless though amused quality that Thom Gunn seemed never to direct anywhere else.

Thom's literary essays, too, benefit from his viewpoint inside the art as a poet and outside the little sandpit of professional literary criticism. His essays on William Carlos Williams, on Fulke Greville, on Robert Duncan, on Thomas Hardy and the Ballad, are models of insight, economy, and knowledge of an art applied by a master artist. The essays are collected in the volume *The Occasions of Poetry*—a slim and invaluable book. Young poets should study it, and pedants should be shamed by it.

But literary criticism was far from his favorite mode or métier. "You poor man," says the note from Thom that I find in my copy of his Faber and Faber *Collected Poems.* "I hadn't realized until a few days ago that you had to write a Piece on me for the Nation." He describes the book as "a paperweight," a touch that like the initial cap on "Piece" catches something about his laughter—the serious man's freedom from solemnity about his art, to which he was devoted, and about the world of Pieces, to which he was not. (The absence of underlining for the *Nation* magazine—the occasion was an essay to mark the Lenore Marshall Prize for *The Man with Night Sweats*—is likely part of the joke, too.)

Davie's word "sensible" might seem to apply to the self-deprecating joke about the "paperweight" more than to "Rites of Passage," "Saturnalia," or "Improvisation": these brilliant evocations of how life is ruled above all by needs and senses, not good sense. But it is a shrewd, informed vision—generous in all senses—that perceives itself in the horned and hoofed offspring behind the flowering almond tree, the orgiastic cluster, the feral panhandler. That cool understanding of one's own heated imperfections is the highest form of good sense. The maker of these poems, by not presenting himself as more sane or less driven than anyone else, attains the rarefied ground where reasonableness merges with charity.

NOTES

INTRODUCTION

1. Thom Gunn, *Collected Poems* (New York: Farrar, Straus & Giroux, 1994), 401 (hereafter referred to as *CP*).
2. Personal correspondence, undated, circa 1989.
3. Thom Gunn, *Boss Cupid* (New York: Farrar, Straus & Giroux, 2000), 111 (hereafter referred to as *BC*).
4. Thom Gunn, "An Anglo-American Poet: Interview with Jim Powell," in *Shelf-Life* (Ann Arbor: University of Michigan Press, 1993), 227 (hereafter referred to as *SL*). I am correcting here an error I made in a symposium essay that appeared in *The Threepenny Review* (Summer 2005), in which I quote from faulty memory and so paraphrase words that Thom never spoke.
5. Thom Gunn, "My Life Up to Now," in *The Occasions of Poetry*, ed. Clive Wilmer (New York: Farrar, Straus & Giroux, 1982), 195 (hereafter referred to as *OP*).
6. Thom Gunn, Notebook V, 9/5/69–2/28/70, Bancroft Library, University of California, Berkeley (hereafter referred to as BL).
7. An English translation, *The Poetry of Thom Gunn*, is forthcoming from McFarland as we go to press.
8. Personal correspondence, 2001.

ALL THAT YOU PRAISE I TAKE

1. Philip Levine, "A Symposium on Thom Gunn," *The Threepenny Review*, Summer 2005, 6.
2. Thom Gunn, *Fighting Terms* (Oxon: Fantasy Press, 1954), 19 (hereafter cited as *FT*). *CP*, 9.

YOUNG GUNN

1. Jack W. C. Hagstrom and George Bixby, *Thom Gunn: A Bibliography, 1940–1978* (London: Bertram Rota, 1979), 13 (hereafter cited as *TGB*).
2. Michael Wishart, *High Diver* (London: Quartet, 1977), 30.
3. Thom Gunn, *The Sense of Movement* (London: Faber, 1957), 11 (hereafter cited as *SM*); *CP*, 39.
4. *TGB*, 13.
5. Ibid., 14.

6. Ronald Hayman, ed., *My Cambridge* (London: Robson, 1977), 135.
7. Thom Gunn, *The Missed Beat* (Sidcot, UK: Gruffyground Press, 1976), unnumbered pages.
8. *TGB*, 17.
9. Hayman, *My Cambridge*, 140.
10. Ibid., 141.
11. The home secretary at the time, David Maxwell Fyfe, and the director of public prosecutions, Theobald Mathew, oversaw an antihomosexual purge that resulted in a wave of prosecutions for "gross indecency": among those convicted were the actor John Gielgud in 1953 and, the following year, Lord Montagu of Beaulieu, Michael Pitt-Rivers, and Peter Wildeblood, who were jointly charged with conspiracy to induce two serving members of the Royal Air Force to commit indecent acts.
12. *Thom Gunn and Craig Raine*, Faber Poetry Cassette, 1984.
13. *TGB*, 15.
14. *Fighting Terms* (London: Faber, 1962), 9 (hereafter referred to as *FT*); *CP*, 3. (Page references to *FT* in this essay are to this third revised edition.)
15. *Troilus and Cressida*, 3.3.226–28. References are to act, scene, and line.
16. Ibid., 3.3.219–20.
17. Hayman, *My Cambridge*, 137.
18. W. I. Scobie, "Gunn in America," *London Magazine*, new series, 17, no. 6 (December 1977): 9.
19. See Neil Powell, "Real Shadow: Gunn and Caravaggio," *Agenda* 37, no. 2–3 (Autumn-Winter 1999): 57–63.
20. *FT*, 14–15; *CP*, 10.
21. *CP*, 15.
22. *TGB*, 26.
23. *FT*, 21; *CP*, 15.
24. *FT*, 30–31; *CP*, 27.
25. *FT*, 27; *CP*, 23.
26. *FT*, 28; *CP*, 24.
27. *FT*, 18; *CP*, 13.
28. *FT*, 35; *CP*, 31.
29. *A Midsummer Night's Dream*, 5.1.21–22.
30. Thom Gunn, "Ralph's Dream," *London Magazine* 2, no. 1 (January 1955): 50.
31. Gunn, *The Missed Beat*, unnumbered pages.
32. G. S. Fraser, "The Poetry of Thom Gunn," *Critical Quarterly* 34, no. 4 (Winter 1961): 363.
33. *OP*, 53–54.
34. Sir Philip Sidney, "Astrophel and Stella," in *The Oxford Authors: Sir Philip Sidney*, ed. Katherine Duncan-Jones (Oxford: Oxford University Press, 1989), 165.
35. *TGB*, 16.
36. Christopher Isherwood, *Christopher and His Kind* (London: Methuen, 1977), 10.
37. *SM*, 12; *CP*, 40.
38. See Eric Partridge, *Shakespeare's Bawdy* (London: Routledge, 1968), 81, 115, 218–19.
39. *SM*, 28; *CP*, 54.
40. Thom Gunn, *My Sad Captains* (London: Faber, 1961), 29 (hereafter cited as *MSC*); *CP*, 108.

41. *SM*, 31; *CP*, 57.
42. John Fuller, untitled review of *FT*, *The Review* 1 (April/May 1962): 30.
43. Kenneth Allott, ed., *The Penguin Book of Contemporary Verse* (Harmondsworth, UK: Penguin. 1962), 374.
44. *SM*, 30; *CP*, 56.
45. Stephen Spender, *Collected Poems, 1928–1985* (London: Faber, 1985), 23.
46. *SM*, 36. Gunn did not include "The Beaters" in the *Collected Poems.*—Ed.
47. *SM*, 45; *CP*, 70.

EXISTENTIALISM AND HOMOSEXUALITY IN GUNN'S EARLY POETRY

1. Jean-Paul Sartre, "Existentialism Is a Humanism," lecture given in 1943, published in *Existentialism from Dostoyevsky to Sartre*, ed. Walter Kaufmann (Cleveland, OH: Meridian, 1989).
2. "Cambridge in the Fifties," in *OP*, 159.
3. *OP*, 161–62.
4. Ibid., 163.
5. Ibid., 173.
6. Ibid., 177.
7. See Gunn's interview with Jim Powell, "An Anglo-American Poet," in *SL*, 222.
8. Christopher Hennessy, *Outside the Lines: Talking with Contemporary Gay Poets* (Ann Arbor: University of Michigan Press, 2005), 15.

GUNN, SHAKESPEARE, AND THE ELIZABETHANS

1. *CP*, 43.
2. Ibid., 239–46.
3. For Hawthorne's *Tanglewood Tales* and *A Wonder-Book for Boys and Girls*, see Thom Gunn (interviewed by Clive Wilmer), "The Art of Poetry LXXII," *Paris Review* 135 (Summer 1995): 168. The whole issue of Gunn's childhood reading is a fascinating one. In *OP*, 170–71, he says: "The books that meant most to me . . . were prose romances." In 1993, I sent him a copy of William Morris's prose romance *News from Nowhere*, which I had edited. He had not thought himself an admirer of Morris, but he wrote back full of enthusiasm for the book, which depicts a world that has something in common with *Moly;* Gunn and Morris, it might be said, were both looking for "Eden in the human" (*CP*, 212). *News from Nowhere* is a socialist utopia, and E. Nesbit, who was also a socialist and who met Morris through the Fabian Society, was probably influenced by his ideas. Gunn admired his mother's left-wing politics and often described himself as a socialist, sometimes as an old-fashioned utopian socialist. See *Thom Gunn in Conversation with James Campbell* (London: Between the Lines, 2000), 20.
4. *Paris Review*, 156–57.
5. *CP*, 21–22.
6. Ibid., 3.
7. Ibid., 29.
8. Ibid., 26–27.
9. Ibid., 24.
10. August Kleinzahler, introduction to *Thom Gunn*, by Thom Gunn (London: Faber, 2007), ix.
11. Michael Schmidt, ed., *Eleven British Poets: An Anthology* (London: Methuen, 1980), 146, 4.

12. "I consciously wrote my poem with such a poem as Dowland's in mind." Gunn quoted in Geoffrey Summerfield, ed., *Worlds: Seven Modern Poets* (Harmondsworth, UK: Penguin, 1974), 266.
13. John Dowland, "The Second Book of Songs or Ayres" in *English Madrigal Verse 1588–1632,* 2nd ed., ed. E. H. Fellowes (Oxford: Clarendon, 1929), 424. The quality of Dowland's anonymous lyrics is so high that one must suspect them to share a common author. Drawing the obvious analogy with Thomas Campion, Winters guessed the author to have been Dowland himself; I have a feeling Gunn agreed with him.
14. Yvor Winters, "The Audible Reading of Poetry," in *The Function of Criticism* (Denver: Alan Swallow, 1957), 99 (79–100). The whole essay is of enormous significance in the development of Gunn's poetry, especially as regards his metrical practice.
15. "I've always been interested in the life of the street. I suppose it's always seemed to me like a kind of recklessness, a freedom after the confinement of the home or the family. This goes way, way back to my teens even. There was a poem which started with the words 'Down and out,' that being (I thought romantically) a kind of freedom" (Gunn, "Art of Poetry LXXII," 186–87).
16. Fellowes, *English Madrigal Verse,* 365. Fellowes gives the poet's name in its alternative spelling: Campian.
17. *The Winter's Tale,* Arden edition, ed. J. H. P. Pafford (London: Methuen, 1963), 4.4.26–32.
18. *CP,* 183.
19. Ibid., 207–8.
20. Ibid., 454.
21. Ibid., 355–56.
22. Ibid., 326–28.
23. Ibid., 280–81.
24. John Donne, *The Poems of John Donne,* ed. Sir Herbert Grierson (London: Oxford University Press, 1933), 46.
25. "Have you not noticed how the Rhône changes its westward course to run towards the south, just to unite with its [tributary the] Saône and flow to the sea together, where both of them will die?" Quoted in Ian Fletcher, "Lionel Johnson: The Dark Angel" in *Interpretations: Essays on Twelve English Poems,* ed. John Wain (London: Routledge, 1955), 177. My attention was drawn to this by Robert Wells.
26. *Twelfth Night,* Arden edition, 2nd ed., ed. J. M. Lothian and T. W. Craik (London: Methuen, 1975), 1.5.89.
27. *CP,* 39–40.
28. Ibid., 108–9.
29. Ibid., 168.
30. Shakespeare, "Venus and Adonis," in *The Poems,* Arden edition, 3rd ed., ed. F. T. Prince (London: Methuen, 1960), 11.
31. *CP,* 61.
32. *BC,* 87–94.
33. Fellowes, *English Madrigal Verse,* 354. For Gunn's admiration, see, for example, *SL,* 13–14, and his use of a line from the poem as a title, "All Do Not All Things Well" (*CP,* 456–57).
34. "I'm not aiming for central voice and I'm not aiming for central personality. I want to be an Elizabethan poet. I want to write with the same anonymity that

you get in the Elizabethans. . . . At the same time, I want to write in my own century." (Quoted in Kleinzahler, *Thom Gunn*, xv.)

35. I am indebted for much of this paragraph to conversations with Michael Vince. Gunn identifies a comparable "reminiscence" of Elizabethan style and versification in a free-verse poem of Robert Creeley's (*SL*, 87–88).
36. Donne, *Poems*, 7.
37. See "The First Anniversary" (Donne, *Poems*, 213).
38. *CP*, 169.
39. *OP*, 159.
40. Gunn, "Art of Poetry LXXII," 148.
41. *OP*, 173.
42. Ibid., 162.
43. *As You Like It*, Arden edition, ed. Agnes Latham (London: Methuen, 1975), 2.7.142.
44. *OP*, 162.
45. Ibid., 170.
46. Colin Falck, "Uncertain Violence," in *Three Contemporary Poets: Thom Gunn, Ted Hughes & R. S. Thomas; A Casebook*, ed. A. E. Dyson (Basingstoke, UK: Macmillan, 1990), 37–38.
47. *CP*, 30.
48. *Troilus and Cressida*, Arden edition, ed. Kenneth Palmer (London: Methuen, 1982), 3.2.79–82. Gunn has slightly adapted the quotation, which should read: "This is the monstrosity in love, lady: that the will is infinite and the execution confined: that the desire is boundless and the act a slave to limit."
49. *CP*, 85.
50. *Troilus and Cressida*, 3.3.215–40.
51. Ibid., 5.1.16.
52. Ibid., 3.3.221–24n.
53. Donald Davie, *Under Briggflatts: A History of Poetry in Great Britain, 1960–1988* (Manchester: Carcanet, 1989; Chicago: University of Chicago Press, 1989), 180.
54. Gunn, "Art of Poetry LXXII," 180.
55. Gunn's aversion to gay men who "seemed to be parodying femininity" is explored in the essay "Homosexuality in Robert Duncan's Poetry" (*OP*, 124–25).
56. Ibid., 162.
57. *CP*, 483.
58. Gunn, "Art of Poetry LXXII," 158–59.
59. *Coriolanus*, Arden edition, ed. Philip Brockbank (London: Methuen, 1976), 5.6.88–101.
60. In "Homosexuality in Robert Duncan's Poetry," Gunn refers to "manifestations of [the] mother-goddess-muse in [Duncan's] *The Opening of the Field*" and adds: "presumably in the twentieth century I don't have to explain the relevance of them to the title of this essay" (*OP*, 130). I discuss Gunn's relationship with his mother, and the whole question of appropriate names, in "The Self You Choose," *Times Literary Supplement*, April 25, 2008, 15–17.
61. *CP*, 185.
62. *Coriolanus*, 5.3.124–25.
63. *CP*, 15–16.
64. Ibid., 26–27. Gunn greatly admired Stephen Greenblatt's *Renaissance Self-Fashioning* (Chicago: University of Chicago Press, 1980).

65. *Fighting Terms* (Oxon: Fantasy Press, 1954), 16.
66. *CP,* 29.
67. Ibid., 73–74.
68. Ibid., 46–47, 87–88, 111, and 129, respectively.
69. Ibid., 56 and 172. "From an Asian Tent" was written in the same period as much of *My Sad Captains* but was not included in the book. It first appeared in *The Observer,* September 24, 1961, 28.
70. Gunn, "Art of Poetry LXXII," 154–55.
71. Gunn commented: "The metaphor is a very Elizabethan one, I guess, a funny thing to find in a modern poem." *Thom Gunn in Conversation with James Campbell,* 27.
72. *The Taming of the Shrew,* Arden edition, ed. Brian Morris (London: Methuen, 1981), 4.1.175–85, 197–98. According to Morris's notes, "sharp" means famished, "to stoop" is "to descend swiftly on the prey," a "lure" is "the apparatus used by a falconer to recall his bird," to "man my haggard" is to "tame my wild hawk," to "watch her" is to "keep her awake," and to "bate and beat" means to "flutter and flap."
73. *Much Ado about Nothing,* Arden edition, ed. A. R. Humphreys (London: Methuen, 1981), 3.1.34–36.
74. *Othello,* Arden edition, ed. E. A. J. Honigmann (London: Nelson, 1997), 3.3.264–67. According to Honigmann's notes, "jesses" are "straps, fastened round the legs of a hawk, attached to the falconer's wrist," and "Hawks were sent off with a whistle, against the wind in pursuit of prey, with the wind when turned loose."
75. *OP,* 128.
76. *BC,* 114.
77. *CP,* 374–75.
78. Jorge Luis Borges, *Other Inquisitions, 1937–1952,* trans. Ruth L. C. Simms (New York: Washington Square Press, 1966), 113; T. S. Eliot, *Selected Essays,* 3rd enlarged ed. (London: Faber, 1951), 15.

THOM GUNN: THE PLAIN STYLE AND THE CITY

1. This essay first appeared in *The Threepenny Review,* Winter 1995, 14–17.—Ed.
2. In San Francisco.—Ed.
3. This "line on Gunn's poetry" was popular in Britain, and perhaps still is.—Ed.
4. Edward Lucie-Smith, ed., *British Poetry since 1945* (London: Penguin, 1970), 143.
5. Kenneth McLeish, *Companion to the Arts in the Twentieth Century* (Harmondsworth, UK: Penguin, 1986), 105.
6. The "plain prose" translations are by Francis Scarfe (London: Penguin, 1961, 196–200, 209–11). Kleinzahler has lineated them himself.—Ed.
7. Neither the author nor the volume editor was able to track down this citation.—Ed.
8. The reviewer is Michael Fried in "Approximations," *The Review* 25 (Spring 1971): 59–60. Kleinzahler elides in the quote in order to join a sentence that occurs early in the review with two sentences that occur at the end.—Ed.
9. The quote from Greville can be found in Gunn's edition, *Selected Poems of Fulke Greville,* edited with an introduction by Thom Gunn (London: Faber, 1968; Chicago: University of Chicago Press, 1968, reprinted 2009 with a new afterword by Bradin Cormack), 35–36.—Ed.

THOM GUNN AND ANGLO-AMERICAN MODERNISM

1. Jim Powell, "An Interview with Thom Gunn," *PN Review* 70, no. 16.2 (Autumn 1989). Reprinted as "An Anglo-American Poet" in *SL*, 218.
2. *CP*, 489.
3. The phrase "the two poetries" is from Marjorie Perloff's introduction to a special issue of *Contemporary Literature* published in 1977. See "The Two Poetries: An Introduction," *Contemporary Literature* 18 (1977): 263–78.
4. Robert Potts, "Moving Voice," *The Guardian*, September 27, 2003, http://www.guardian.co.uk/books/2003/sep/27/featuresreviews.guardianreview13 (accessed July 4, 2007).
5. *SL*, 218.
6. There are other English poets of Gunn's generation whose work is a hybrid of English and American traditions—Roy Fisher and Charles Tomlinson, for example, to name two of the better known among them—but for the most part these poets did not begin as Gunn did, which is to say as a poet whose practice was antimodernist. Donald Davie is like Gunn in having come to admire varieties of modernist poetry after publishing in his first prose a critique of modernism, but Davie arguably had less success in incorporating modernist technique in his poetry. In "Duncan" (*BC*, 3), Gunn writes, "You add to, you don't cancel what you do." Gunn seems to have viewed his own development as a poet, from English to "Anglo-American," as equally unremarkable. See Keith Tuma, *Fishing by Obstinate Isles: Modern and Postmodern British Poetry and American Readers* (Evanston, IL: Northwestern University Press, 1993).
7. *CP*, 14.
8. *BC*, 85.
9. Blake Morrison, *The Movement: English Poetry and Fiction of the 1950s* (Oxford: Oxford University Press, 1980), 42–54.
10. See Andrew Motion, *Philip Larkin: A Writer's Life* (New York: Farrar, Straus & Giroux, 1993), 344.
11. *SL*, 225.
12. For Andrew Duncan's foldout poster "Styles of British Poetry 1945–2000," which attempts to map the field without including Gunn (and many others) as part of it, see *Chicago Review* 53, no. 1 (Spring 2007).
13. Langdon Hammer, "The American Poetry of Thom Gunn and Geoffrey Hill," in *Something We Have That They Don't: British and American Poetic Relations since 1925*, ed. Steve Clark and Mark Ford (Iowa City: University of Iowa Press, 2004), 122.
14. Ibid., 118–19.
15. Philip Larkin, "Introduction to *All What Jazz*," in *Required Writing: Miscellaneous Pieces, 1955–1982* (London: Faber and Faber, 1983), 297.
16. Donald Davie, "The Spoken Word" (1950; review of *Poems for Speaking: An Anthology*, ed. Richard Church; and *Poets of the Pacific*, second series, ed. Yvor Winters), in *The Poet in the Imaginary Museum* (Manchester, UK: Carcanet, 1977), 3.
17. Thom Gunn, "My Life Up to Now" (1979), in *OP*, 186.
18. Those readers who noticed the press accounts of recent joint readings by British poet laureate Andrew Motion and American poet laureate Donald Hall, readings designed to affirm the "special relationship" of the two nations by circulating what little symbolic capital poetry has on offer, heard both poets waxing

nostalgic about a time before the 1960s when "English and American poetry used to know each other better than they do now." See Elizabeth Kelleher, "Poet Laureates of Two Nations Reach across Atlantic" (USINFO press release, http://london.usembassy.gov/gb054.html [accessed July 5, 2007]). Motion is also heard admitting that British poetry has ignored its modernists. That is certainly true, but I am not persuaded that there was a time before the 1960s when British poets were, as a rule, significantly engaged with American poetry. There are individual cases to consider, but I would argue that British poets have been *more* engaged with American poetry *since* the 1960s, whereas the opposite is true of American poets. Contemporary British poetry has largely disappeared from American maps since the 1960s, with the work of a few poets such as Gunn, Ted Hughes, and Larkin or, for those interested in experimental poetry, Tom Raworth, standing in for a larger field of practice.

19. Davie's critical study *Thomas Hardy and British Poetry* (1972), a book intended for audiences on both sides of the Atlantic, later defended what current British poet laureate Andrew Motion and others sometimes refer to as the "English line," which names as central to British poetry an English tradition running from Hardy and Edward Thomas up through Larkin and beyond him. In some of his earliest critical work, Davie praised a poetry of "chaste" diction and a similarly restricted mode of practice, its exemplary figures minor Augustan poets, as he promoted an "Arnoldian tone of the centre" to serve the needs of liberal democracy in post-imperial Britain. See Donald Davie, *Purity of Diction in English Verse* (London: Chatto and Windus, 1952), 5–17, 26–27.
20. See Ella Whitehead, *John Lehmann's "New Writing": An Author-Index 1936–1950*, Studies in Comparative Literature 13 (Lewiston, NY: Edwin Mellen Press, 1990).
21. Hayden Carruth, "2,000 Poems, Mostly Good" (review of *The Criterion Book of Modern American Verse*, ed. W. H. Auden; *The Mentor Book of Religious Verse*, ed. Horace Gregory and Marya Zaturenska; *The Silver Treasury of Light Verse*, ed. Oscar Williams; *Invitation to Poetry* by Lloyd Frankenberg; *Fifteen Modern American Poets*, ed. George P. Elliott; *Poetry Now*, ed. G. S. Fraser; *New Lines*, ed. Robert Conquest; and *Mavericks*, ed. Howard Sergeant and Dannie Abse), *Poetry* 91, no. 2 (November 1957): 124.
22. Ibid.
23. Ibid., 131.
24. Ibid., 132.
25. Samuel French Morse, "A Transatlantic View," review of *Collected Poems 1930–1955* by George Barker; *The Collected Poems* by Norman Cameron; *Visitations* by Louis MacNeice; *Not Waving but Drowning* by Stevie Smith; *The Stones of Troy* by C. A. Trypanis; and *The Sense of Movement* by Thom Gunn, *Poetry* 92, no. 5 (August 1958): 328.
26. Frederick Eckman, "Neither Tame Nor Fleecy," review of *The Maximus Poems 11–22* by Charles Olson; *The Improved Binoculars* by Irving Layton; *Howl and Other Poems* by Allen Ginsberg; *The Wrath Wrenched Splendor of Love* by Judson Crews; *To Wed beneath the Sea* by Judson Crews; *Superman Unbound* by Harold Witt; *River Full of Craft* by Felix Stefanile; *Light and Dark* by William Bronk; and *Adam's Footprint* by Vassar Miller, *Poetry* 90, no. 6 (September 1957): 386–94.
27. Thom Gunn, "Eight Poets," review of *The Forms of Loss* by Edgar Bowers; *The Battlement* by Donald F. Drummond; *A World of Saints* by Thomas Cole; *Three Priests in April* by Stephen Stepanchev; *Poets of Today III: The Floating World and*

Other Poems by Lee Anderson, *My Father's Business and Other Poems* by Spencer Brown; *The Green Town* by Joseph Langland; and *Villa Narcisse* by Katherine Hoskins, *Poetry* 89, no. 4 (January 1957): 245.

28. Ibid., 250.
29. Thom Gunn, "Book Reviews." *London Magazine* 3, no. 2 (February 1956): 70–75; *Critical Essays on William Empson*, ed. John Constable (Aldershot, UK: Scholar Press, 1993), 327–33. I should point out that by no means did Gunn admire the poetry of Dylan Thomas.
30. Ibid., 331.
31. Thom Gunn, "The Calm Style," review of *Brutus's Orchard* by Roy Fuller; *The Open Sea and Other Poems* by William Meredith; *Home Truths* by Anthony Thwaite; and *The Forever Young and Other Poems* by Pauline Hanson, *Poetry* 92, no. 6 (September 1958): 378.
32. Ibid., 378.
33. Ibid., 384.
34. Donald Davie, "Remembering the Movement" (1959), in *Poet in the Imaginary Museum*, 72–73.
35. Davie, "The Spoken Word," 3.
36. Gerald L. Bruns, preface to the new edition, *Modern Poetry and the Idea of Language: A Critical and Historical Study*, 2nd ed. (Normal, IL: Dalkey Archive Press, 2001), vii.
37. *SL*, 218.
38. Thom Gunn, "A New World: The Poetry of William Carlos Williams" (1965), in *OP*, 24.
39. Thom Gunn, "Adventurous Song: Robert Duncan as Romantic Modernist" (1993), in *SL*, 143.
40. *OP*, 35.
41. Thom Gunn, "Hardy and the Ballads" (1972), in *OP*, 100.
42. *CP*, 315–16.
43. Ibid., 77.
44. Ibid., 244.
45. *The Passages of Joy* (New York: Farrar, Straus & Giroux, 1982), 28; *CP*, 337.
46. Ibid., 338.
47. *CP*, 253.
48. Ibid., 329.
49. Ibid., 297.

FROM LADD'S HILL TO LAND'S END (AND BACK AGAIN)

1. *SL*, 222.
2. *OP*, 190.
3. While Gunn's use of fictive technique to renew poetic form is of particular interest to this essay, the essay can't accommodate a detailed demonstration of how specific ideas in particular twentieth-century novels influenced Gunn's own thinking: that must be left to another occasion. However, in the notes that follow I make some connections to suggest correspondences between some of the novelists Gunn mentions and the existential ideas in "Misanthropos."

   Gunn mentions, for example, William Golding's *The Inheritors* (1955) in *OP* (190): one senses the influence in how Golding imagines the small Neanderthal tribe as both "first man," in their primitive existence, and "last man," in their encounter with the Cro-Magnon tribe that leads to their extinction. In the notebooks, Gunn also names as a source Golding's novel *Pincher Martin* (1956), about a British naval officer pitted against the elements in his struggle to survive on a bare rock in the middle of the sea (HL, Notebook 9/63–1/64, series 1, box 4). One could also point to *Lord of the Flies* (1954), which takes place in the wake of nuclear war; and *Free Fall* (1959), in which the narrator, Mountjoy, attempts to define the pattern of his existence in a condition of literal darkness and isolation.

The sources Gunn lists for the poem "Misanthropos" also include a set of works of great variety, historically and of genre: Andrew Marvell's mower poems; Elizabethan echo poems; Virgil's *Ecologues; Sidney's Arcadia; Robinson Crusoe; Timon of Athens; King Lear;* and Kafka's story, "The Burrow." (HL, Notebook 9/63–1/64, series 1, box 4.)

4. BL, Notebook VIII, 12/29/70–3/13/71.
5. Gunn's notebooks are not personal diaries, but working notebooks, in which he explores ideas, begins essays, speculates, questions himself, and reflects on poetry and its place in his life. In the archives at Bancroft and Hornbake libraries, one finds materials that Gunn himself prepared for preservation. Some of the notebooks have pages ripped out of them, presumably containing materials that Gunn considered too personal to leave for snoops; other folders contain pages that have literary interest ripped from notebooks that one presumes held by and large contents too personal. One is well-reminded that all the opinions and arguments in the notebooks must be understood as provisional; yet the notebooks do serve as a kind of window into Gunn's attitudes and ideas during this period of composition. (HL, Notebook, series 1, box 4.)
6. Because syllabics is a measure based only on syllable count, and not the number of accents, nor the relation of accented to unaccented syllables, there is such rhythmic freedom that one cannot *hear* the measure, hence Gunn's sense that there was no real difference between syllabics and free verse: Gunn's apprehension is of rhythm. Later, he would characterize the problem in larger terms: "What I most want [to continue to do]: pass the romantic impulse through the classical scrutiny [n.b., Gunn's echo of the title of Leavis's critical journal, *The Scrutiny*—Ed.]. The scrutiny is both the experience and the poem's form. It is destructive (or should be) of all that is not hard and genuine in the impulse." (BL, Notebook I, 9/4–end of Nov. 1968.)
7. Thom Gunn, from the introduction to *Ben Jonson,* ed. Thom Gunn (London: Penguin, 1974; 2005), ix.
8. *OP,* 106–7.
9. The poem was initially titled "For the Survivor." Other titles Gunn considered: "In the City of Kites and Crows" and "From the Green Tower." (HL, series 1, box 1.)
10. HL, series 1, box 4.
11. M. L. Rosenthal and Sally Gall, *Modern Poetic Sequence* (Oxford: Oxford University Press, 1983), 7.
12. *OP,* 190.
13. *CP,* 133–34.
14. *OP,* 190.
15. N.b. the following well-known passage from Golding's *Free Fall:* "I have hung all systems on the wall like a row of useless hats. They do not fit. They come in from outside, they are suggested patterns, some dull and some of great beauty. But I have lived enough of my life to require a pattern that fits over everything I know;

and where shall I find that? Then why do I write this down? Is it a pattern that I am looking for?" The systems here are social systems and systems of thinking, but they suggest aesthetic ones as well, as the self-reflexive question casts into its frame of inquiry the very act of writing. (Harcourt Brace, 1959; 1967), 2.

Thinking about the importance Gunn places on his early reading of R. L. Stevenson and the like, one suspects that he found in a novel such as *Lord of the Flies,* Golding's most famous work, an example of how existential questions can provide the philosophical foundation for a new kind of adventure story, of conscience, and of *poeisis.*

16. *OP,* 197.
17. HL, series 1, box 1.
18. *CP,* 134.
19. An anonymous reader for Chicago has suggested that Gunn may be responding directly to George Herbert's poem, "Heaven," "effectively re-secularizing and turning into a counsel of despair, what in Herbert announces the 'perseverence' of another, better world." This connection may very well be a right one, born out not only in Gunn's theme, which is a kind of inversion of Herbert's, but in the quality of his echoing rhymes, some of which resemble Herbert's: in both poems, the echoing rhyme word is sometimes a truncated acoustic repetition of a longer prerhyme (in Herbert's poem, consider the rhymes "high/I," "know/no," "abide/bide," "wholly/holy," "delight/light," "enjoy/joy," "pleasure/leisure," and "persever/ever." In Gunn's use of homonym and straight repetition, his echoing is also similar to Philip Sidney's in the second eclogues of "The Old Arcadia."
20. *CP,* 134–35.
21. Ibid., 135.
22. Gunn is drawing most directly here from *Crusoe* and Golding's *Pincher Martin.* It's worth noting that persistence of this kind of Crusoe myth in science fiction remains strong. Take, for example, its most recent appearance in the form of the film *I Am Legend* (2007), starring Will Smith: a science fiction/vampire story penned by Richard Matheson in 1954, it was first adapted for the movie *The Last Man on Earth* (1964), starring Vincent Price, then remade into *Omega Man* (1971), starring Charlton Heston. The hook-line for the most recent remake, "The last man alive on earth is not alone," is an accurate enough tagline for Gunn's poem.

Given Gunn's interest in science fiction, one wonders if he knew of Cousin de Grainville's *Le Dernier Homme* (1805), the novel that inaugurates the "Last Man" subgenre, itself a prose work that, in its division into "cantos," evokes epic poetry. In English, the "Last Man" verse narratives span the first half of the nineteenth century (by Thomas Hood and Edward Wallace, among others); find incarnation on the stage; in apocalyptic paintings by John Martin; and include Mary Shelley's novel *The Last Man* (1826), republished after more than one hundred years of being out of print, in 1965, the publication date of "Misanthropos." See I. F. Clarke's introduction to Cousin de Grainville's *The Last Man* (Middleton, CT: Wesleyan University Press, 2002). Nineteen sixty-five appears to have been a good year for "Last Man" narratives, including, as it does, *Dr. Bloodmoney, or How We Got Along after the Bomb,* a post–World War III survivalist story that takes place in Berkeley and East Bay environs, by Philip K. Dick, a favorite of Gunn's.

And considering Gunn's sense of William Golding's growing achievement in the novel, one is drawn, as well, to the corresponding passage in *Free Fall,* in which Mountjoy, coming out of solitary confinement, has a mystical vision about human connection: "This substance was a kind of vital morality, not the relationship of a man to remote posterity nor even to a social system, but the relationship of individual man to individual man—once an irrelevance but now seen to be the forge in which all change, all value, all life is beaten out into a good or a bad shape. This live morality was, to change the metaphor, if not the gold, at least the silver of the new world" (170). Though not a sci-fi work, by any means, the visionary tone of such passages in Golding share something with the subgenre.

23. *CP*, 135–36.
24. Hannah Arendt, *Eichmann in Jerusalem* (New York: Viking, 1963; revised ed., 1965), 230. Gunn cites the book in his note to the poem.
25. *CP*, 144.
26. Gunn's rank in the British Army, sergeant, was the same as Schmidt's, thus another kind of rhyme, of historical correspondence. I thank Clive Wilmer for pointing this out (personal correspondence, June 13, 2008).
27. A question remains about the placement of the Anton Schmidt epitaph in the narrative sequence, a question regarding the voice of the poem; for one hears the speaker of this epitaph through the voice of the poet—that is, the *I* does not register here as the first-person protagonist of "Misanthropos." In fact, this "epitaph" poem stood separately in another collection, a chapbook published by Richard Gilbertson titled *The Explorers* (Devon, UK: Crediton, 1969).
28. Poem 10, *CP*, 143.
29. *CP*, 137.
30. Poem 16, *CP*, 151.
31. Poem 17, *CP*, 151.
32. Poem 12, *CP*, 145.
33. *CP*, 151.
34. HL, series 1, box 1. The question of sympathy runs through Gunn's later work. In light of this notebook entry, consider this culminating passage from Camus's *The Plague* (1947; 1948): "After a short silence the doctor raised himself a little in his chair and asked if Tarrou had an idea of the path to follow for attaining peace. 'Yes,' he replied. 'the path of sympathy'" ([New York: Viking, 1975], 254). Such sympathy prompts D'Arrast, the protagonist of Camus's story "The Growing Stone," to physically share the burden of carrying an enormous stone in a village ritual. The protagonist's movement from observer to participant leads to the making of a place for him at the table with other villagers. Gunn's notebooks indicate the story made an impression on him. Camus, *Exile and the Kingdom* (1957), trans. Justin O'Brien (New York: Viking, 1958).
35. Clive Wilmer remembers hearing Gunn read in Cambridge in autumn 1964; Gunn talked on that occasion about working on "Misanthropos" before he read a few sections of it (personal correspondence, June 13, 2008).
36. *OP*, 194.
37. Gunn considered as epigraph for "Misanthropos" a piece of dialogue he read, as spoken by a character in a Truffaut short: "The very fact that I say something means that there is a link with what I said before" (quoted in *Sight and Sound*, Autumn 1962, 170). In the "complete draft, 3rd" (in HL), the epigraph runs before poem 2, in the echo form, which in that draft opens the sequence; the second poem is poem 1 in the published version.
38. Reading over the reviews of *Touch* (1967), the volume that included "Misanthropos," it's fair to say that reception of the poem was mixed at best. On

the positive side: "As for the long poem, 'Misanthropos,' this belongs with Gunn's most impressive work" (Martin Dodsworth, *The Listener*); "Mr. Gunn's other manner, grander and much more attractive, is that of the longest, most ambitious poem in the book, *Misanthropos.* Here he writes with assurance and impact. . . . One cannot but wish that Thom Gunn would develop more of this vein of purest silver. . . . [He has] the power and authority of an imagination that has as much in common with Rilke's as with Genet's" (Daryl Hine, *Poetry*).

To capture the flavor of the negative response, consider: "He is desperately tenacious of humanism, and yet finds it a burden he can barely support" (Robin Skelton, *Kenyon Review*); "a mysterious, oppressive poem" (John Press, *Punch*); "it hovers uncertainly between the God's-eye view of character and the character's view of himself" (Ronald Hyman, *Encounter*); "The sequence 'Misanthropos,' which runs through an impressive variety of forms, is an honest, civilized treatment of the themes of isolation and loneliness, but where he attempts to reach beyond the self this 'tough' poet's emotion tends to drift into sentimentality" (Michael Thorpe, *English Studies*); "There is an increased dependence on abstraction which debilitates many of the poems here and, in *Epitaph for Anton Schmidt,* the effect is disastrous. . . . This tendency, so recurrent in *Misanthropos,* spoils the sequence since its oddities . . . as with *Paradise Lost* [!!—Ed.], make us so conscious of the narrator's methods we have no chance to believe the convention of first or last people on earth" (Peter Dale, *Agenda*).

Most acutely, Laurence Lieberman in the *Yale Review* identifies in Gunn a struggle he shares with Charles Tomlinson, to work out an answer to "the problem of evolving an Anglo-American poetics. . . . Gunn is developing a strangely impressive hybrid prosody. . . . But in *Touch,* he seems unable to sustain this quality through a single whole poem."

And most curiously, Hayden Carruth, in the *Hudson Review,* mistakes a note in the book acknowledging a performance of the poem for the BBC (Third Programme, March 8, 1965) as indication (false) that it was commissioned for the broadcast: "The poem is skillful, parts here and there are interesting, but it lacks real impetus, even real structure, and I can't imagine a radio audience attending all the way through." In fact, the BBC audience report was equally mixed to negative, between "thought-provoking," "of great relevance to the human condition," "accomplished" in its rhythms and rhyme, with a "tremendous theme" and "wonderful economy," and those who found the poem to be "an irritating mixture of the mystical and mundane," with a "very complex meaning" that remained "elusive."

The Audience Research Department concluded that "'Misanthropos' seems to have impressed many as admirable in its vocabulary, form and success in arousing emotion, even when its precise meaning was not immediately apparent." (Gunn did not read the poem himself; it was performed by Alan Dobie and Julian Glover; he was aware of the response, however, as the confidential report is among his papers at Hornbake Library.)

Other volumes in the omnibus reviews include Kingsley Amis, *A Look round the Estate;* Ted Berrigan, *The Sonnets;* Alan Bold, *To Find the New;* Edward Braithwaite, *Rights of Passage;* Peter Dale, *The Storms;* Robert Duncan, *Bending the Bow;* John Fuller, *The Tree That Walked;* Allen Ginsberg, *TV Baby Poems;* Anthony Hecht, *The Hard Hours;* Philip Hobsbaum, *In Retreat;* Richard Howard, *The Damages;* Ted Hughes, *Wodwo;* Ronald Johnson, *The Book of the Green Man;* P. J. Kavanaugh, *On the Way to the Depot;* Thomas Kinsella, *Night Walker;* Philip Levine, *Not This Pig;* Robert Lowell, *The Old Glory;* W. S. Merwin, *The Moving Target;* Howard Nemerov, *The Blue Swallows;* Kenneth Rexroth, *The Garden's Heart;* Anne Sexton, *Live or Die;* W. D. Snodgrass, *After Experience;* Mark Strand, *Reasons for Moving;* Rosemary Tonks, *Illiad of Broken Sentences.*

39. Clive Wilmer, *Poets Talking* (Manchester, UK: Carcanet, 1994): 7.
40. It was later discovered to be funded by the CIA, much to the surprise of its editors and contributors.
41. Paul Giles, *Virtual Americas* (Durham, NC: Duke University Press, 2002), 186–87.
42. *OP,* 190.
43. The conceit and the history of transatlantic movement in the case of "Misanthropos" is heightened by the account of Marcia Tanner, to whom I'm indebted for biographical information about Tony Tanner and his friendship with Gunn. Marcia (née Albright), an American, met Tony Tanner as an undergraduate at Cal Berkeley (1959–60); they became engaged in 1964, and she joined Tanner in Cambridge that April. By fall she had found a job as editorial assistant at *Encounter* in London, working for Stephen Spender. "Misanthropos," she writes, "languished on his pile for months. Having read the poem myself, and thinking it was brilliant, I finally asked Stephen how he would feel if he'd been the editor who passed up 'The Waste Land'? This nudge worked and 'Misanthropos' finally appeared in the journal" (personal correspondence, July 23, 2008).
44. Tony Tanner, *The Reign of Wonder* (Cambridge: Cambridge University Press, 1965; New York: Harper and Row, 1967), 353.
45. Ibid., 357.
46. Ibid.
47. Ibid., 359.
48. One finds Gunn's dedication of the poem to Tony Tanner in the notebook drafts of fall 1963. It's easy to imagine Gunn and Tanner discussing not only Gunn's poem, but their shared interest in American literature over the course of years (HL, series 2, box 2, 9/63–1/64). Marcia Tanner suggests as much as well (personal correspondence, July 23, 2008). Gunn liked to make lists of poems in his notebooks, as he considered how poems worked together, suggesting the evolving form of a book. In such a poem-list one finds the title "The Last Man" appearing as early as February 1958 (HL, series 2, box 1).
49. N.b. this passage, as an example of Gunn's thinking about how rhythm and image, here in Williams, express the new searching: "for Williams anything that renews is an instrument for the exploration and definition of the new world, which he labors both to 'possess' and be part of. For possession of the details is achieved not through the recording of them, but through the record's adherence to his feelings for them. The process is not of accumulation but of self-renewal" (*OP,* 34).
50. HL, series 1, box 4.
51. BL, Notebook X, 12/29/71.
52. Thom Gunn (interviewed by Clive Wilmer), "The Art of Poetry No. 72," *Paris Review* 135 (Summer 1995): 169. As indication of Gunn's mixed feelings about the poems of *Touch* (1967) and "Misanthropos," consider that in his *Collected Poems* (1994), the volume *Touch* is not represented as part of the publication record; rather its binding is undone: twelve of its seventeen poems are absorbed into a section designated "Poems of the 1960s" ("Bravery," "Breakfast," "Snowdrift," "The Girl of Live Marble," and "The Produce District" are cut loose).

"Misanthropos" (1965), however, is given its own place in the record, between the volumes *My Sad Captains* (1961) and *Moly* (1971). A prior *Selected Poems 1950–1975* (1979) contains eight poems from *Touch*, including "Misanthropos" (n.b. August Kleinzahler's selection of Gunn's work [2007] cuts it down to two poems from *Touch* and eliminates "Misanthropos" altogether).

53. Gunn (interview), "Art of Poetry," 152.
54. HL, series 1, box 4.
55. HL, series 1, box 4.

TWO VERSIONS OF "MEAT"

1. These two poems first appeared side by side in *AGNI* 36 (1992): 300–302.—Ed.
2. *TMNS*, 47. *CP*, 451.

GUNN'S "MEAT": NOTATIONS ON CRAFT

1. A version of this essay first appeared in *AGNI* 36 (1992): 303–6.
2. *OP*, 106–7.

SUMMATION AND CHTHONIC POWER

1. *BC*, 102.
2. W. S. Merwin, *Summer Doorways: A Memoir* (Emeryville, CA: Shoemaker and Hoard, 2005), 42.
3. Clive Wilmer, "Definition and Flow: A Personal Reading of Thom Gunn," *PN Review* 5, no. 3 (1978): 51–57. See also a revised version in *British Poetry since 1970*, ed. Peter Jones and Michael Schmidt (Manchester, UK: Carcanet, 1980). Cf. his introduction to *OP*, 15–16.
4. *Leaves of Grass*, section 25.
5. *CP*, 342–43.
6. *SL*, 22. The texts of all three poems are available in Angel Flores, ed., *An Anthology of French Poetry from Nerval to Valery*, new rev. ed. (New York: Doubleday, 1958).
7. *CP*, 331.
8. From a 2003 interview with Christopher Hennessy in *Memorious* 5 (2004).
9. *CP*, 205.
10. *SL*, 166–67.
11. Thom Gunn in "The Lesson of *The Spoils*," *Parnassus* 17, no. 2 / 18, no. 1 (1993): 29, 38.
12. Ibid., 26–29.
13. *CP*, 332.
14. Ibid., 388.
15. Ibid., 268.
16. Gunn, "Lesson of *The Spoils*," 36.
17. *OP*, 39–40.
18. Ibid., 110, 116–17.
19. Clive Wilmer in Douglas Chambers, ed., *A Few Friends: Poems for Thom Gunn's 60th Birthday* (Walkerton, ON: Stonyground Press, 1989), 63.
20. *OP*, 15–16.
21. *CP*, 215.
22. Ibid., 220.
23. *SL*, 167.
24. See Linda Fierz-David, *Women's Dionysian Initiation: The Villa of Mysteries in Pompeii*, trans. Gladys Phelan (Dallas: Spring, 1988), 141–43.

25. *CP*, 263.
26. See Albert Henrichs, "'He Has a God in Him': Human and Divine in the Modern Perception of Dionysus," in *Masks of Dionysus*, ed. T. H. Carpenter and C. A. Faraone (Ithaca, NY: Cornell University Press, 1993), 41.
27. Richard Seaford, "Dionysus as Destroyer of the Housefold: Homer, Tragedy, and the Polis," in *Masks of Dionysus*, 134.
28. Ibid.
29. Claire Douglas, ed., *Visions: Notes on the Seminars Given in 1930–1934 by C. G. Jung*, Bollinger Series 99 (Princeton, NJ: Princeton University Press, 1997), 2:760–62.
30. Robert Duncan, *Ground Work: Before the War—in the Dark* (New York: New Directions, 2006), 88.
31. *BC*, 4.
32. See Ovid's *Metamorphoses*, trans. Rolfe Humphries (Bloomington: Indiana University Press, 1955).
33. *CP*, 416.
34. Yvor Winters, *The Selected Letters of Yvor Winters*, ed. R. L. Barth (Athens: Swallow/Ohio University Press, 2000), 119.
35. *BC*, 43.
36. Duncan, introduction to *Ground Work*, ix.
37. Yvor Winters, *Selected Poems*, ed. Thom Gunn (New York: Library of America American Poets Project, 2003), 111.
38. Yvor Winters, *Uncollected Essays and Reviews*, ed. Francis Murphy (Chicago: Swallow, 1973), 195.
39. *CP*, 70.
40. Ibid., 416–17.
41. Ibid., 217.
42. Ibid., 229.
43. The themes of sensibility and/or "spirituality," as well as the *monstrum* of the Medusa discussed here in section 5, I develop further in "From Nightmares to Spiritual Responsibility: Several Useful Monsters," in *Spirituality and Depth Psychology*, ed. Sudhin Kaban (London: Routledge, 2009 [forthcoming]).
44. *CP*, 417.
45. Ibid., 183.
46. Ibid., 39.
47. Ibid., 399.
48. Duncan, *Ground Work*, 90.
49. Robert Stone, *A Flag for Sunrise* (New York: Vintage/Random House, 1992 [1981]), 244–45.
50. Ibid., 245.
51. Robert Stone, *Prime Green: Remember the Sixties* (New York: Ecco/HarperCollins, 2007), 199–200.
52. Ibid., 225.
53. Robert Bly, *News of the Universe: Poems of Twofold Consciousness* (New York: Random House, 1982). See especially "The Attack on the Old Position," 28ff.
54. Donald Davie, "To Thom Gunn in Los Altos, California," in *Collected Poems* (Manchester, UK: Carcanet; Chicago: University of Chicago Press, 1991), 294.
55. Carlos Castaneda, *Tales of Power* (New York: Simon and Schuster, 1974), 227.
56. *CP*, 43–44.

57. Gunn, "Lesson of *The Spoils*," 29.
58. Ibid., 20.
59. Ibid., 30.
60. Ibid., 36.
61. *CP*, 391–92.
62. Ibid., 179.
63. Ibid., 273.
64. Ibid., 267–68.
65. Gunn, "Lesson of *The Spoils*," 24 and 35, respectively.
66. Basil Bunting, *Briggflatts V*, in *The Complete Poems* (New York: Oxford University Press, 1994), 61.
67. "What the Slowworm Said," in *OP*, 157.
68. Winters, *Selected Poems*, 66–67.
69. As reported by August Kleinzahler, through Mike Kitay and Joshua Weiner: my thanks to all three.
70. *OP*, 156.
71. Ibid., 158.
72. *BC*, 92.
73. Ibid., 37.
74. Neil Micklem, "The Intolerable Image: The Mythic Background of Psychosis," in *Spring, 1979: An Annual of Archetypal Psychology and Jungian Thought* (Dallas: Spring Publications, 1979), 1.
75. *BC*, 26–27.
76. Ibid., 102.
77. Douglas, ed., *Visions*, 2:1001.
78. *BC*, 102–3.
79. Ibid.
80. Paradise, Canto 31, *The Divine Comedy*, trans. C. H. Sisson (Manchester, UK: Carcanet, 1980), 445–46.
81. *BC*, 104.
82. Ibid., 103.
83. Ibid., 103–4.
84. C. G. Jung, January 9, 1960, to Hugo Charteris (in English), in *Letters*, ed. Gerhard Adler (Princeton, NJ: Bolingen, 1975), 2:532.
85. Gunn, "Lesson of *The Spoils*," 38.
86. *CP*, 388.
87. Ibid., 263.
88. Ibid., 260–61.
89. Stone, *Prime Green*, 154.
90. Thom Gunn, "Symposium on *Buddenbrooks*," *The Threepenny Review* 24, no. 2 (Summer 2003): 12.
91. *CP*, 400.
92. See Maria Luisa Ardizzone, "Pound's Language in *Rock-Drill:* Two Theses for a Genealogy," *Paideuma* 221, nos. 1–2 (1992): 1–2.
93. R. H. Mathews, *Mathews' Chinese-English Dictionary* (orig. 1931; rev. American ed. Cambridge, MA: Harvard University Press, 1966), 586.
94. *CP*, 361.
95. Ibid., 231.

OUR DIONYSIAN EXPERIMENT

1. For help with locating hard-to-find Gunn materials, props go out to Jeff Maser. Many thanks to Bancroft librarians David Kessler and Dean Smith for incomparably flexible, generous, and irreplaceable help. Two critics and colleagues deserve special mention: Margaret Ronda generously read an early draft of this essay, and her careful and considered critical praise made this a more rigorous affair. Eirik Steinhoff both pointed me toward crucial essays by Gunn I had overlooked and provided a wonderful sounding board for ideas about Winters and Gunn's relationship.
2. Robert Duncan, "The Homosexual in Society," in *A Selected Prose* (New York: New Directions, 1955), 43.
3. Ibid., 42.
4. Ibid.
5. Robert Duncan, "Interview with Robert Duncan," interview by Robert Peters and Paul Trachtenberg, *Chicago Review*, Fall 1997, 2.
6. Robert K. Martin, *The Homosexual Tradition in American Poetry* (Iowa City: University of Iowa Press, 1998), xvi–xvii.
7. Gregory Woods, *Articulate Flesh: Male Homo-eroticism and Modern Poetry* (New Haven, CT: Yale University Press, 1987), 4.
8. Yvor Winters, *Forms of Discovery* (Denver: Alan Swallow, 1967), 350.
9. Quoted in James Campbell, *Thom Gunn in Conversation with James Campbell* (London: Between the Lines, 2000), 109.
10. Thom Gunn, *Night Sweats* (Florence, KY: Robert L. Barth, 1987).
11. BL, May 23, 1994–January 30, 1997 notebook.
12. *OP*, 178–79.
13. Ibid.
14. *SL*, 227.
15. Ibid., 228.
16. BL, "R.D. // is a source" was written on a loose sheet tucked into his September 30, 1986–August 26, 1987 notebook.
17. Carl Morse and Joan Larkin, eds., *Gay and Lesbian Poetry in Our Time: An Anthology* (New York: St. Martin's Press, 1988), 325–26.
18. Eavan Boland, *Object Lessons* (New York: W. W. Norton, 1995), x.
19. Robert L. Caserio, "The Mortal Limits of Poetry and Criticism: Reading Yingling, Reading Gunn," in Thomas E. Yingling, *AIDS and the National Body*, ed. Robyn Wiegman (Durham, NC: Duke University Press, 1997), 162.
20. Tony Sarver, "Thom Gunn," *The Advocate* 220 (July 27, 1977): 40.
21. Duncan, "Interview with Robert Duncan," 1.
22. Because the first draft was begun in such close proximity to the march itself, the second is both more polished and more clearly indebted to the rhetoric of Gay Liberation. Consider, for instance, the following lines: "It is not the influence it may have on others, finally, / it is rather the influence it has on myself. . . . I am testifying, myself, about what I used to be scared of, / I am telling my dead parents" (BL, May 29, 1979–May 1980 notebook).
23. BL, February 28, 1970–May 1970 notebook.
24. Ibid.
25. Ibid.
26. Christopher Nealon, *Foundlings: Lesbian and Gay Historical Emotion before Stonewall* (Durham, NC: Duke University Press, 2001), 13.

27. Thom Gunn, *Jack Straw's Castle* (New York: Farrar, Straus & Giroux, 1976), 56. *CP,* 297.
28. Sarver, "Thom Gunn," 39.
29. Nealon, *Foundlings,* 2.
30. Ibid., 8
31. Ibid.
32. David M. Halperin, *How to Do the History of Homosexuality* (Chicago: University of Chicago Press, 2002), 12.
33. Ibid.
34. Ibid.
35. As Lisa Sewell points out in her introduction to the anthology *American Poets in the 21st Century* (Middleton, CT: Wesleyan University Press, 2007), while "the task of delineating, naming, and defining either the important movements in twenty-first century poetry or its central figures is nearly impossible [because] the field is so 'atomized, decentralized, and multifaceted' that 'no one can pretend to know what is out there' [Hank Lazar, "The People's Poetry," *Boston Review* 29, no. 2 (April–May 2004), 1]," it is also true that criticism "glances backward, encompassing a sense of relation and origin, insisting on indebtedness to the poetry movements and schools of the late twentieth century, from the Confessional poets to the Black Arts movement, from the Beats to Language poetry" (1).
36. It wasn't until *The Man with Night Sweats* (1992) that the neoclassical poet of Gunn's first two books fully fused with the gay poet of *Jack Straw's Castle* (1976) and *The Passages of Joy* (1982); they found their common horizon in metrical verse elegies occasioned by the AIDS crisis.
37. Woods, *Articulate Flesh,* 212.
38. Bruce Woodcock, "'But oh not loose': Form and Sexuality in Thom Gunn's Poetry," *Critical Quarterly* 35, no. 1 (Spring 1993): 60.
39. Woods, *Articulate Flesh,* 212.
40. Martin, *Homosexual Tradition in American Poetry,* 180.
41. Ibid., 182.
42. Ibid.
43. Ibid.
44. Ibid., 190.
45. In a postscript to his essay "My Life Up to Now," Gunn addresses the fact that some readers aware of his sexuality might "infer . . . the thing 'known' is the speaker would prefer to be in bed with a man. But that would be a serious misreading, or *at least a serious misplacement of emphasis*" (*OP,* 188, my italics). The ambiguity of this statement—that it wavers between disclosure and concealment—is a telling and characteristic gesture.
46. *FT,* 1. *CP,* 15.
47. Ibid.
48. G. S. Fraser, "The Poetry of Thom Gunn," *Critical Quarterly* 3, no. 4 (Winter 1961): 363.
49. Ibid., 362–64.
50. The homosocial is what Eve Kosofsky Sedgwick in *Between Men: English Literature and Male Homosocial Desire* (New York: Columbia University Press, 1985) defines as "social bonds between persons of the same sex . . . such activities as 'male bonding,' which may . . . be characterized by intense homophobia, fear and hatred of homosexuality" (1).

51. The text of "La Prisonnière," for example, leads us logically to infer a heterosexual context for the poem's apostrophe—if the speaker feels compelled to reassure that he won't be out with Miss Brown or Miss Jones, then the addressed must be a (potentially jealous) woman as well—while its title infers a much more ambiguously queer context: the first of Proust's three "Albertine" novels.
52. Sarver, "Thom Gunn," 39.
53. Sedgwick, *Between Men*, 2–3.
54. Catherine R. Stimpson, "Thom Gunn: The Redefinition of Place," *Contemporary Literature* 18, no. 3 (Summer 1977): 393.
55. Halperin, *How to Do the History of Homosexuality*, 15.
56. Sarver, "Thom Gunn," 39.
57. Fraser, "Poetry of Thom Gunn," 362.
58. Ibid., 363.
59. *CP*, 96.
60. Ibid., 97.
61. *SM*, 56. *CP*, 56.
62. Sarver, "Thom Gunn," 39.
63. Sedgwick, *Between Men*, 2.
64. As Catherine R. Stimpson acutely notes in her sympathetic and perceptive essay "Thom Gunn: The Redefinition of Place," "Gunn rarely writes about women. When he does, he is conventional. Women are fertility goddesses; rural Phaedras; warriors in a sexual battle; sexual objects" (400).
65. Jonathan Dollimore quoted in Nealon, *Foundlings*, 7.
66. Campbell, *Thom Gunn in Conversation*, 26.
67. *OP*, 119.
68. Donald Davie, *Under Briggflatts: A History of Poetry in Great Britain, 1960–1988* (Chicago: University of Chicago Press, 1989), 180.
69. Though Davie was, according to Gunn, "quite a close friend . . . one of the poets I've been closest to in my life" (quoted in Campbell, *Thom Gunn in Conversation*, 25), and was "consistently supportive, very kind to" Gunn, he was also someone Gunn knew to be "very against queers," who "spoke to other people with distaste for it" (quoted in Christopher Hennessy, *Outside the Lines: Talking with Contemporary Gay Poets* [Ann Arbor: University of Michigan Press, 2005], 12). Given this distaste, his critical practice must be held accountable for what resultant rhetorical distortions have passed as logical argument.
70. Sianne Ngai, *Ugly Feelings* (Cambridge, MA: Harvard University Press, 2005), 3.
71. Stimpson, "Thom Gunn: The Redefinition of Place," 393.
72. Duncan, *A Selected Prose*, 39.
73. "The New Critics rarely look at American poetry per se, because they do not, finally, see it as having its own history separable from the English tradition," writes Alan Golding in *From Outlaw to Classic: Canons in American Poetry* (Madison: University of Wisconsin Press, 1995), 73. Further, he says, "[s]ince these critics were generally skeptical of a national poetry, it is especially revealing to examine their reading of that self-consciously national poet, Whitman" (p. 87). He also suggests that their dismissal of Whitman—whose influence they use to excoriate and damn Hart Crane—is indicative of the New Critics' "resistance to nationalism and to Romanticism, their generally conservative politics" as well as "their hidden homophobia, their not so hidden masculine biases" (71).
74. Coedited by George Steiner and Robert Boyers, this Fall 1982–Winter 1983

special issue is entitled "Homosexuality: Sacrilege, Vision, and Politics." It almost goes without saying that, for Steiner and Boyers, "Sacrilege" went before "Vision" when it came to gay and lesbian politics, but to gain a further idea of the general "high-minded" tone that enraged Gunn, one need go no further than Steiner's "In Lieu of a Preface": "When I suggested this special issue to Robert and Peggy Boyers, my motive was straightforward. . . . We *know* so little. Our sense of a homosexual presence in specific spheres of modern sensibility and intellect . . . is emphatic" (5). It's the implicit heterosexuality of "we" and the equally implicit obscurity of the "homosexual presence" that's characteristic of the issue, a dialectic of the hetero-normative and morally dubious. The rest of the issue ranges from Catherine Stimpson's "The Beat Generation," a sensitive, smart, compelling reading of gay male sexuality in Beat lit, to the outrageous moral recoil of Herbert Blau's "Disseminating Sodom," whose overheated rhetoric harks back to that of the "pink scare" paranoia of the Cold War. The contributions by gay writers—interviews with Michel Foucault and Martin Duberman, an epistolary correspondence by Paul Robinson, for example—favor the academic rather than the activist community-centered discourse Gunn might have appreciated at this time.

75. Gunn in Campbell, *Thom Gunn in Conversation,* 21.
76. Bruce Boone, "Robert Duncan and Gay Community: A Reflection," *Ironwood* 11, no. 2 (Fall 1983): 74.
77. *CP,* 39–40.
78. Robert Duncan, "Interview with Robert Duncan," interview by Michael André Bernstein and Burton Hatlen, *Sagetrieb* 4, nos. 2–3 (Fall/Winter 1985): 108–9.
79. *OP,* 119.
80. Ibid., 128.
81. Duncan, *A Selected Prose,* 41.
82. Ibid., 45, 48.
83. Ibid., 45.
84. *OP,* 134.
85. Terry Eagleton quoted in Campbell, *Thom Gunn in Conversation,* 109. *Stand* 24, no. 3 (1983).
86. *Ironwood* 11, no. 2 (Fall 1983): 81.
87. Ibid., 74.
88. Ibid., 81, 82.
89. Ibid., 81.
90. *SL,* 214.
91. Ibid., 215.
92. Gunn quoted in Steve Abbott, "In Search of a Muse: The Politics of Gay Poetry," *The Advocate* 342 (May 12, 1982): 26.
93. *SL,* 217.
94. BL, May 15, 1977 notebook.
95. *CP,* 39.
96. Thom Gunn, *Moly* and *My Sad Captains* (New York: Farrar, Straus & Giroux, 1973), 20. *CP,* 200.
97. Thom Gunn, "An Interview with Thom Gunn," interview by David Gewanter, *AGNI* 26 (1992): 298.
98. Thom Gunn in Christopher Hennessy, *Outside the Lines: Talking with Contemporary Gay Poets* (Ann Arbor: University of Michigan Press, 2005), 18.

99. *SL*, 129.
100. Ibid.
101. Gunn in Hennessy, *Outside the Lines*, 18.
102. *SL*, 130.
103. Gunn in Campbell, *Thom Gunn in Conversation*, 137.
104. Yvor Winters, *In Defense of Reason* (Denver: Alan Swallow, 1947), 3–4.
105. Ibid., 13.
106. Ibid., 11–12.
107. Dick Davis, *Wisdom and Wilderness: The Achievement of Yvor Winters* (Athens: University of Georgia Press, 1983), 214.
108. Winters, *In Defense of Reason*, 13.
109. Robert Duncan, *The Truth and Life of Myth: An Essay in Essential Autobiography* (Fremont, MI: Sumac Press, 1968), 15.
110. Ibid., 42.
111. Ibid., 48.
112. Ibid., 11.
113. Ibid., 49.
114. Ibid., 28, 29.
115. Ibid., 14, 15.
116. *SL*, 130.
117. Stefan Hawlin, "Epistemes and Imitations: Thom Gunn on Ben Jonson," *PMLA* 122, no. 5 (November 2007): 1519.
118. Though *A Seventeenth Century Suite* was first issued as a chapbook in 1973—one of a series of self-published books Duncan circulated within the poetry community during his self-imposed hiatus from commercial publishing during the years 1968–1984—and collected in 1984's *Ground Work: Before the War*, Duncan chose to title the 1968 British edition of his selected early poems *Derivations: Selected Poems 1950–1956*. It's clear that he saw himself as practicing derivation throughout his career, though for readers it's also obvious that the formal terms and seriousness of intent informing the practice changed as Duncan matured. Compare the endearing, embarrassing derivations of 1969's *Play Time Pseudo Stein* with the terrifying sequence "To Master Baudelaire"—especially the chilling, gorgeous "Toward His Malaise"—part of 1988's *Ground Work II: In the Dark*.
119. Hawlin, "Epistemes and Imitations," 1520.
120. Quoted in Hawlin, "Epistemes and Imitations," 1519.
121. Davis, *Wisdom and Wilderness*, 219.
122. Hawlin, "Epistemes and Imitations, 1519.
123. Michael André Bernstein, "Robert Duncan: Talent and the Individual Tradition," *Sagetrieb* 4, nos. 2–3 (Fall/Winter 1985): 187.
124. Ibid.
125. *SL*, 143.
126. Ibid., 131.
127. Ben Jonson, *Ben Jonson*, ed. C. H. Hereford, Percy Simpson, and Evelyn Simpson (Oxford: Oxford University Press, 1947), 8:638.
128. Ibid., 8:616–17.
129. *SL*, 143.
130. Ibid., 206.
131. *CP*, 40.
132. Ibid., 46.

133. Robert Hass, *Twentieth Century Pleasures: Prose on Poetry* (New York: Ecco Press, 1983), 148.
134. *CP*, 46.
135. Winters, *In Defense of Reason*, 150.
136. *CP*, 47.
137. Martin Dodsworth, "Gunn's Rhymes," *PN Review* 16, no. 2 (1989): 33.
138. Ibid., 33–34.
139. *SL*, 207.
140. Ibid., 209.
141. Ibid., 204.
142. Ibid., 206–7, 204.
143. Ibid., 209.
144. Ibid., 208–9.
145. *CP*, 46.
146. *SL*, 207.
147. Ibid.
148. Ibid., 208.
149. Ibid., 210.
150. *CP*, 70.
151. Hass, *Twentieth Century Pleasures*, 146.
152. *CP*, 69.
153. Ibid.
154. Harold Bloom, *The Anxiety of Influence: A Theory of Poetry* (Oxford: Oxford University Press, 1997), 28–29.
155. In fact, it's important to underscore that in his essay "The Significance of *The Bridge* by Hart Crane, or What Are We to Think of Professor X?" Winters insidiously conflates his moral disagreement with Romanticism with a distaste for homosexuality, pinpointing Whitman's influence as Crane's downfall. His normally lucid prose fills with a level of euphemism that does nothing but register his homophobia: "But *The Tunnel* offers a kind of ugliness which is not justified by the Whitmanian theme and so cannot be treated in terms of the theme. It was an ugliness Crane experienced, in part as a result of his acceptance of the theme and the fallacies of the theme, but to treat it in these terms he would have had to have understood the fallacies and what had happened to him as a result of them" (*In Defense of Reason*, 597).
156. Bloom, *Anxiety of Influence*, 30.
157. It's instructive to note that while Bloom, in *The Western Canon*, does in fact count Duncan's *Bending the Bow* among those volumes in his contemporary canon, Gunn's work is absent. Perhaps it's Gunn's fusion of *imitatio* and derivation—his simultaneous neoclassical and Romantic impulses—that puts Bloom off the scent.
158. *SL*, 131.
159. Ibid., 142.
160. Winters, *Forms of Discovery*, 345.
161. Ibid., 350.
162. *SL*, 207.
163. Ibid., 210.
164. Michael Davidson, *Ghostlier Demarcations: Modern Poetry and the Material World* (Berkeley: University of California Press, 1997), 181.

165. Ibid.
166. Robert Duncan, *Poems from the Margins of Thom Gunn's "Moly"* (San Francisco: Author, 1972).
167. Ibid.
168. Gunn, *Moly,* and *My Sad Captains,* 5. *CP,* 185.
169. A time evoked by the archetypal conflict of Gunn's "Rite of Passage" quoted above, and echoed more autobiographically by Duncan's preface to the series, in which he conjures up "Ghosts and lovers of my sixteenth year."
170. Duncan, *Poems from the Margins of Thom Gunn's "Moly."*
171. Ibid.
172. This is the project that would become both the chapbook "At the Barriers" and Gunn's final full-length collection *Boss Cupid,* and it's important to note that while the former is dedicated to the memory of Duncan, the latter begins with an elegy bearing his name, a tribute to the time out of which the book arose and to the figure whose energies paradoxically—fittingly—inspired the groundwork for what would be Gunn's most epigrammatic and Jonsonian project.
173. BL, 1950 prose notebook, 85.
174. Jules Cashford, trans., *The Homeric Hymns* (New York: Penguin Books, 2003), 55.
175. Thom Gunn, "Odysseus on Homer," *Sagetrieb* 4, nos. 2–3 (Fall and Winter 1985): 35.
176. *SL,* 132.
177. Ibid., 35.
178. Ibid.
179. *SL,* 206.
180. *CP,* 418.

THOM GUNN'S NEW JERUSALEM

1. *CP,* 211.
2. *OP,* 194–95.
3. *CP,* 337.
4. *OP,* 195.
5. Ibid., 194.
6. *CP,* 374.
7. *BC,* 44.
8. *CP,* 407.
9. Edward Guthmann, "A Poet's Life," *San Francisco Chronicle,* April 26, 2005.
10. *BC,* 43.
11. Ibid., 42.
12. Ibid., 44.
13. *CP,* 456.
14. Ibid., 245–46.
15. W. H. Auden, introduction to *The Poet's Tongue: An Anthology,* ed. W. H. Auden and John Garrett (London: Bell, 1935), x.
16. W. B. Yeats, "A General Introduction for My Work," in *Essays and Introductions* (1961; New York: Macmillan, 1968), 509.
17. *BC,* 43.
18. Ellen Willis in *Village Voice,* January 24, 1989; quoted in SL, 215.
19. Ibid.

DOMAINS OF ECSTASY

1. William Wordsworth, *Prelude*, ed. Jonathan Wordsworth et al. (New York: Norton, 1979 [1805]), 10.222ff.
2. *CP*, 73.
3. Ibid., 3.
4. Ibid., 54.
5. Ibid., 55.
6. Ibid., 58.
7. Ibid., 165.
8. Ibid., 73.
9. Ibid., 138.
10. Ibid., 139.
11. Ibid., 178.
12. *OP*, 191.
13. Ibid., 191–92.
14. Ibid., 192.
15. *CP*, 200.
16. Ibid., 201.
17. Ibid., 202.
18. Ibid., 209–10.
19. Ibid., 221 ("At the Centre").
20. Ibid., 205.
21. *OP*, 195.
22. *CP*, 245.
23. Ibid., 207.
24. Ibid., 223 ("Sunlight").
25. Ibid., 289.
26. Ibid., 185.
27. Ibid., 290.
28. *OP*, 196.
29. *CP*, 291.
30. *OP*, 195.
31. *CP*, 291.
32. Ibid., 222.
33. Ibid., 461.
34. Ibid.
35. Ibid., 463.
36. Ibid., 461.
37. Ibid., 470 ("Still Life").
38. Ibid., 479.
39. Ibid., 471.
40. Ibid., 465.
41. Ibid., 466.
42. Ibid., 467.
43. Ibid., 468.
44. Wordsworth, *Prelude*, 10.232, 234–35.
45. Of his teacher Yvor Winters, Gunn wrote, "My relationship with him since his death has developed and changed" (*OP*, 211). As Gunn's former student, I do not

carry on such a legacy. However, I did once press upon him this interpretation of "Lament"—hoping, I suppose, to hear my teacher answer, "You're right. I never quite thought of it that way." Gunn didn't disagree with me but never gave his intentions for "Lament." In fact, he never discussed his own poems, except at readings. Nor even, at school, would he talk of being a poet—so that a student, near the end of an Introduction to Poetry course, once asked, "Mr. Gunn, there's a poet in the *Norton Anthology* called 'Thom Gunn': is that you?"

CONSIDERING "CONSIDERING THE SNAIL"

1. *CP*, 117.
2. *Oxford English Dictionary*, s.v. "consider" (hereafter cited in this essay as *OED*).
3. Italics in this quote and others added by the author.
4. John Milton, *Complete Poems and Major Prose*, ed. Merritt Y. Hughes (New York: Odyssey Press, 1957), 168.
5. *OED*, s.v. "lodg'd."
6. Geoffrey Hill, *For the Unfallen: Poems 1952–1958* (London: Andre Deutsch, 1959), 20.
7. HL, series 1, box 1.
8. *OED*, s.v. "considering."
9. *OED*, s.v. "consideration."
10. *OED*, s.v. "consider."
11. *CP*, 118.
12. Ibid.
13. *CP*, 106.
14. Earle Birney, "Slug in the Woods," in *The New Oxford Book of Canadian Verse in English*, ed. Margaret Atwood (Toronto: Oxford University Press, 1982), 114.
15. *OED*, s.v. "byrnie."
16. *CP*, 117.
17. HL, series 1, box 1.
18. *CP*, 125.
19. Ibid., 357.
20. HL, series 1, box 1.
21. *CP*, 384.
22. Ibid., 100.
23. Ibid., 357.

THOM GUNN'S "DUNCAN"

1. *BC*, 4.
2. Ibid., 3.
3. *SL*, 196.
4. *BC*, 4.
5. Ibid., 3.

CODA: THOM GUNN, INSIDE AND OUTSIDE

1. *CP*, 185.
2. Ibid., 265.
3. Ibid., 437.

CONTRIBUTORS

Born in Dublin, Ireland, and educated in London, New York, and Dublin, EAVAN BOLAND is the Mabury Knapp Professor in Humanities at Stanford University and the Lane Professor for Director of the Creative Writing Program. She has also taught at Trinity College, University College Dublin, and Bowdoin College, and was a member of the International Writing Program at the University of Iowa, as well as the Hurst Professor at Washington University in St. Louis. Boland is the author of eight books of poetry, including *Against Love Poetry* (2001), which was a *New York Times* "notable book" of 2001. In addition to her books of poems, Boland is the author of a volume of prose entitled *Object Lessons: The Life of the Woman and the Poet in Our Time* (1995) and coeditor (with Mark Strand) of *The Making of a Poem: A Norton Anthology of Poetic Forms* (2000). She published a volume of translations in 2004 entitled *After Every War,* and her latest volume of poetry—*Domestic Violence*—was published simultaneously in the United States and United Kingdom in 2006.

ALFRED CORN is the author of nine books of poems, most recently of *Stake: Selected Poems, 1972–1992* (1999) and *Contradictions* (2002). He has also published a novel, *Part of His Story,* and a collection of critical essays entitled *The Metamorphoses of Metaphor.* He has received Guggenheim and NEA fellowships, an Award in Literature from the Academy and Institute of Arts and Letters, a fellowship from the Academy of American Poets, and the Levinson Prize from *Poetry* magazine. For many years he taught in the Graduate Writing Program of the School of the Arts at Columbia University, and has held visiting posts at UCLA, the University of Cincinnati, Yale University, and the University of Tulsa. In 2001, Abrams published *Aaron Rose Photographs,* for which he supplied the introduction. In October 2003, he was a fellow of the Rockefeller Study and Conference Center at Bellagio, and in 2004–5, he held the Amy Clampitt residency in Lenox, Massachusetts. In 2005–6, he taught for the Poetry School in London, where he is spending 2008–9.

DAVID GEWANTER'S poetry books are *In the Belly* (1997) and *The Sleep of Reason* (2003). He is also the coeditor (with Frank Bidart) of *Robert Lowell: Collected Poems.* Gewanter's awards include a Hopwood prize, a Zacharis First Book Prize, a Whiting Writer's Fellowship, an Ambassador Book Award (English-Speaking Union), a Witter Bynner Fellowship, and a finalist designation for the James Laughlin Prize. His new book of poems, *War Bird,* is forthcoming from the University of Chicago Press in 2009. He teaches at Georgetown University.

AUGUST KLEINZAHLER is the author of eleven books of poetry, most recently *Sleeping It Off in Rapid City: Poems New and Selected* (2008). Among his honors and awards are the Griffin Award (Canada), fellowships from the Guggenheim Foundation, a Lila Acheson Wallace / Reader's Digest Award for Poetry, and an Award in Literature from the Academy of American Poets. He has taught writing at Brown University, at the University of California, Berkeley, and at the Iowa Writers' Workshop, as well as to homeless veterans in the Bay Area. *Cutty, One Rock,* a collection of autobiographical essays, was published in 2004. He is also the editor of Gunn's selected poems, published in 2008.

WENDY LESSER is the editor of *The Threepenny Review,* which she founded in 1980. She is the author of seven books of nonfiction and a novel. Her latest book of nonfiction, *Room for Doubt,* was published in 2007. A graduate of Harvard, Cambridge, and the University of California, Berkeley, she has won fellowships and awards from the Guggenheim Foundation, the National Endowment for the Humanities, the American Academy in Berlin, and elsewhere. She knew Thom Gunn from the late 1970s until his death in 2004. Gunn was both a close associate at *Threepenny* (where he published over forty items in twenty-four years) and a much-valued friend.

PAUL MULDOON was born in 1951 in County Armagh, Northern Ireland, and educated in Armagh and at the Queen's University of Belfast. From 1973 to 1986 he worked in Belfast as a radio and television producer for the British Broadcasting Corporation. Since 1987 he has lived in the United States, where he is now Howard G. B. Clark '21 Professor in the Humanities at Princeton University and Chair of the Lewis Center for the Arts. Between 1999 and 2004, he was professor of poetry at the University of Oxford. Muldoon is the author of ten books of poems, most recently of *Horse Latitudes* (2006), and including *Moy Sand and Gravel* (2002), for which he won the 2003 Pulitzer Prize.

JOHN PECK was born in Pittsburgh, Pennsylvania, in 1941. He has published eight books of poems, most recently *Red Strawberry Leaf: Selected Poems, 1994–2001* (2005). His degrees come from Allegheny College, Stanford University, and the C. G. Jung Institute, Zurich; he has taught literature and writing at Princeton University, Mount Holyoke College, the University of Zurich, MIT, and at Skidmore College, and has practiced as a Jungian analyst since 1993 in Vermont, Massachusetts, and Connecticut. His awards include the Prix de Rome and fellowships from the Guggenheim, Ingram-Merrill, and Bogliasco foundations.

ROBERT PINSKY'S most recent books of poetry are *Gulf Music* (2007) and *Jersey Rain* (2000). His prose works include *Democracy, Culture, and the Voice of Poetry* (2002) and *The Life of David* (2005). He is also translator of *The Inferno of Dante* (1995) and coeditor of the anthology *An Invitation to Poetry* (2004). Among his honors are the William Carlos Williams Award, the Los Angeles Times Book Prize, the Shelley Memorial Award, the PEN-Voelcker Award, and the Lenore Marshall Prize. As U.S. poet laureate from 1997 to 2000, he founded the Favorite Poem Project. He teaches in the Creative Writing Program at Boston University and is poetry editor of the online magazine *Slate*.

NEIL POWELL was born in London in 1948 and was educated at Sevenoaks School and the University of Warwick. He has taught English, owned a bookshop, and, since 1990, been a full-time author and editor. His books include six collections of poetry—*At the Edge* (1977), *A Season of Calm Weather* (1982), *True Colours* (1990), *The Stones on Thorpeness Beach* (1994), *Selected Poems* (1998), and *A Halfway House* (2004)—as well as *Carpenters of Light* (1979), *Roy Fuller: Writer and Society* (1995), *The Language of Jazz* (1997), and *George Crabbe: An English Life* (2004). His most recent book, *Amis & Son: Two Literary Generations*, was published in 2008. He reviews for the Sunday *Telegraph* and the *Times Literary Supplement* and is coordinating editor of *PN Review*. He lives in Suffolk.

TOM SLEIGH'S books include *After One, Waking, The Chain, The Dreamhouse, Far Side of the Earth, Bula Matari/Smasher of Rocks*, and a translation of Euripides' *Herakles*. His book of essays *Interview with a Ghost* was published in spring 2006 by Graywolf Press. His most recent book of poems, *Space Walk*, was published by Houghton Mifflin in spring 2007. Among his many awards are the Kingsley Tufts Award, the Shelley Prize from the Poetry Society of America, an Academy of Arts and Letters Award in Literature, an Individual Writer's Award from the Lila Wallace/Reader's Digest Fund, and grants from the Guggenheim Foundation and the National Endowment for the Arts. He teaches in the MFA program at Hunter College and lives in Brooklyn.

BRIAN TEARE is the recipient of fellowships from the National Endowment for the Arts and MacDowell Colony. He was also a Stegner Fellow in poetry at Stanford University. He has published poetry and criticism in *American Poetry Review, Boston Review, Ploughshares, Provincetown Arts, St. Mark's Poetry Project Newsletter, Seneca Review, Verse*, and *VOLT*, among many others. His first book, *The Room Where I Was Born*, was winner of the 2003 Brittingham Prize and the 2004 Thom Gunn Award for Gay Poetry. Two new books are forthcoming: *Sight Map* (University of California, 2009) and *Pleasure* (Ahsahta, 2010). He lives, teaches, and makes books by hand in San Francisco.

KEITH TUMA is the author of various essays on American, British, and Irish poetry and *Fishing by Obstinate Isles: Modern and Postmodern British Poetry and American*

Readers (1998). He is the editor of *Anthology of Twentieth-Century British and Irish Poetry* (2001) and other books on Mina Loy, poetry and performance, and African American poetry. His creative work includes film-text collaborations, two chapbooks of poetry, and the multimedia prose and poetry travelogue *Critical Path: Into the Bush* (2003, with cris cheek and William Howe as Three Little Heretics). He is completing work on a book of anecdotes and a book of poems. He teaches at Miami University.

JOSHUA WEINER is the author of two books of poems, *The World's Room* (2001) and *From the Book of Giants* (2006), both published in the Phoenix Poets series by the University of Chicago Press. His awards and honors include the Joseph Brodsky Rome Prize in Literature from the American Academy of Arts and Letters, a Whiting Foundation Writers Award, a Witter Bynner Fellowship of the Library of Congress, and a Discovery/*The Nation* award. Weiner is associate professor of English at the University of Maryland at College Park. He lives in Washington, DC.

CLIVE WILMER lives and teaches in Cambridge, where he is a Fellow of Sidney Sussex College, a Bye-Fellow of Fitzwilliam College, and an Honorary Fellow of Anglia Ruskin University. His published work includes seven volumes of his own poetry, the most recent of which is *The Mystery of Things* (2006). He edited Thom Gunn's first volume of essays, *The Occasions of Poetry*, and is currently preparing an annotated *Selected Poems* of Thom Gunn for Faber and Faber.

INDEX OF NAMES